W9-CPP-114

THE HAPPY WARRIOR

THE HAPPY WARRIOR

Political Memoirs

Donald C. MacDonald

with a foreword by
Desmond Morton

Fitzhenry & Whiteside

Published with the assistance of
The Ontario Heritage Foundation
Ontario Ministry of Culture and Communications

Fitzhenry & Whiteside
195 Allstate Parkway
Markham, Ontario L3R 4T8

Canadian Cataloguing in Publication Data

MacDonald, Donald C., 1913-
  The happy warrior

Includes index.
ISBN 0-88902-833-8 (bound) ISBN 0-88902-758-7 (pbk.)

1. MacDonald, Donald C., 1913-   . 2. Ontario –
Politics and government – 1943-1985.* 3. New
Democratic Party of Ontario – History. 4. New
Democratic Party of Ontario – Biography.
5. Politicians – Ontario – Biography. I. Title.

FC3076.1.M23A3 1988   971.3'04'0924   C88-094978-3
F1058.M23A3 1988

Printed and bound in Canada by
T. H. Best Printing Company Limited

To my wife and our children, who not only shared in campaigns, but coped with all the intrusion of politics into family life, as I was pursuing legislative and party obligations all over Ontario;

and

to the thousands of working people who shared the vision of the Co-operative Commonwealth Federation and the New Democratic Party. They have transformed a dream into a reality. Their labours and sacrifice were an inspiration for those to whom they entrusted the responsibilities of leadership. I shall always treasure the memories of their comradeship.

Table of Contents

PART III: REFLECTIONS

Foreword

In at least one respect, Ontario is an underdeveloped province. Compared to Quebec and the West, Canada's biggest province has attracted scant attention from historians and political scientists. A handful of worthy texts, a few personal memoirs and biographies, and an occasional journalist's attempt to wring a book from a dreary assignment at Queen's Park, amount to a record of secondary sources that an agile reader could absorb in under three days.

When knowledge is absent, theory abounds. Why would anyone study Ontario? Happy times have no historian. Surely the province is too rich, too contented and too well-governed to merit examination. Those of a conspiratorial turn of mind may suspect that making Ontario boring was part of the secret of Tory longevity during forty-two years of power. So long as voters believed that nothing much happened inside their ugly red toad of a legislative building, they could turn to the drama of national politics. The same flighty voters who switched allegiance in successive federal elections trooped with stolid predictability to provincial contests.

Readers of Donald MacDonald's book will be able to test those theories with knowledge. Was Ontario well-governed, when a one-sided majority and an amoral premier could bury the evidence of scandal? Were voters contented when most of them steadily supported the opposition parties? Was Ontario even rich, at least for those millions of its people who shared little of the postwar prosperity? Those who want to preserve comforting illusions about Ontario's recent past will close this book immediately and put it away. You have been warned.

1

As a politician, it now seems easy to understand why MacDonald never became Ontario's first socialist premier. Charisma was never part of his stock in trade. As a speaker, he was no match for Stephen Lewis, the golden-tongued orator who ultimately displaced him on the eve of possible triumph in 1970. Instead of the oleaginous guile that people both despise and demand in a politician, Don MacDonald brought an uncompromising honesty, evident in those passages of this book where his indignation still burns at scandals suppressed and malefactors protected.

It was no part of MacDonald's concept of a leader that followers needed to be stroked or cajoled. He treated them, instead, as equals in a common cause. His telephone calls typified his style: the briefest of pleasantries, a thorough discussion of the issue at hand — with plenty of listening on his part — and finally an abrupt conclusion, on the assumption that both parties had much else to do. To some, MacDonald's style was an inspiration; to others in his party and caucus, it was disconcerting and ultimately disillusioning. Not everyone over eighteen wants to be an adult or an equal.

Until 1953, Donald MacDonald had had very little to do with Ontario politics. After its brief triumph in 1943, the provincial CCF was on its way to oblivion. Even insiders had no great faith that a former teacher and journalist could save the organization from the normal dismal fate of Ontario third parties. Perhaps one of MacDonald's leadership rivals, Andrew Brewin or Fred Young, could have managed the feat. The fact remains that one man turned certainty around.

The significance of that feat and its historic consequences deserve mention. Without a CCF-NDP revival, Ontario Conservatives would have faced a Liberal party which, as MacDonald says, was unmistakably rural and reactionary. It is arguable that the more powerful party, which MacDonald created, was the real reason that Conservatives could hold power so long in Ontario; but it was also the reason why provincial Tories (and perhaps even federal Liberals) had to consider major social reforms in the 1960s. Without MacDonald's political building, medicare might have remained a Saskatchewan aberration, and the Canada Pension Plan would have been still-born.

Part of the job of building a home-grown party of the democratic left in Ontario was to become embedded in that complex reality called the Ontario political culture. As leader of a tiny caucus at Queen's Park, MacDonald had to master each department of government with no more than a lone assistant, the amazing Ellen Adams. Between sessions, he ranged over the province, with some indifference to speed limits and an utter indifference to what restaurant food might do to his stomach. Political instinct and personal inclination drew Donald MacDonald to the remotest of rural and northern communities. Any media entourage shared his car, and he hammered out the releases on his ancient Underwood portable.

It is almost impossible now to think of anyone who is better informed about the people, politics and government of Ontario. In 1970, when the NDP foolishly let him resign, the late Harry Crowe of York University wisely persuaded Donald MacDonald to share his knowledge with the students of Atkinson College. The onetime teacher could, as he confesses, practise one profession in daylight and another at night. Readers of this book will have some idea of the rich experience of having Donald MacDonald teach Ontario.

Frankly, that is the purpose of this book. Critics may complain that it is too much about Ontario and not enough about MacDonald. Perhaps they should know that he is a skilled angler, an enthusiastic gardener and a devotee of rice pudding. Part of his life is based on the simple pleasures of home, family and the outdoors. Like many enduring couples, Don and Simone made a marriage of opposites, bonded by a common idealism, courage and self-reliance. Yet, to anyone who knows Donald MacDonald well, the very essence of his character is reflected in this book. Here is the uncompromising honesty, the hint of earnestness, the equal absence of vanity or false modesty and, glinting like the light on his glasses, the wit of a serious man who takes almost everyone seriously but himself.

If there is a single outstanding quality in Donald MacDonald, it is an unquenchable optimism. He brought no magic to the tasks of reviving a moribund party. Most of his political career was lived in the shadows of defeat and frustration. In this book, he records only a small fraction of the abuse and hostility which he received from the acolytes of an entrenched Toryism. For over a decade as CCF-NDP leader, MacDonald had to find comfort in virtually imperceptible political progress. He was a party leader because who else would have wanted the job. Only when he had made it worth having did others crowd in to demand their turn.

Throughout his political life, Donald MacDonald has made no room for bitterness or despair. Bad news, he insists, never cost him a good night's sleep. However disastrous the polls or the vote might be, MacDonald could transform the dismal statistics into a portent of forthcoming victory. Even as supporters mocked and parodied their leader's optimism, they took heart. There were several reasons why democratic socialism in Ontario survived its years of utter failure; the most palpable was Donald C. MacDonald.

Some people write the history of their times; others make it. Donald MacDonald has done both.

Desmond Morton
Mississauga, 18 June 1988

Preface

Two cars were in collision at an intersection. There were four witnesses, one on each corner. When called to testify as to what they had seen, the accounts were so varied that the court was left to wonder whether they had witnessed the same accident. So it is with history. The facts may be undisputed, but how they are perceived is legitimately conditioned by the position of the beholder.

These memoirs are an account of Ontario's postwar politics as viewed "from one corner." They don't cover the whole story, even from the NDP point of view; that would require volumes. And certainly they don't cover everything in Ontario politics, only those issues and events in which I was involved.

The personal memoirs are covered only in so far as they indicate how the early years shaped my political beliefs and affiliation. The emphasis is on Ontario postwar politics, concerning which relatively little has been written, either by those personally involved, or by observers in the academic and the media worlds. Indeed, so sparse has been historical and political writing in Ontario that, in the concluding years of his premiership, John Robarts established the Ontario Historical Studies Series, which has commissioned works to fill the gap.

This dearth of writing on Ontario affairs, as compared with other provinces and regions of Canada, is underscored by a rather astounding fact. Whereas federal politics provides a regular flow of memoirs, mine are just the second by an Ontario politician in the one hundred and twenty years since Confederation — the first being those of E.C. Drury in *Farmer*

Premier. (The only possible exceptions to this claim are Kelso Roberts's unpublished reminiscences, available in mimeographed form in the legislative library; Morton Shulman's snapshots of events and personalities in *Member of the Legislature*, following his four years as an MPP; and Sheila Copps's account of some of her provincial experiences in *Nobody's Baby*.)[1]

The usual excuse for this small body of writing is that Ontario politics are so dull as to be unworthy of consideration. Not so. As I hope these memoirs indicate convincingly, there is much in the political life of Canada's biggest province that is fascinating and merits analysis and interpretation. Indeed, my hope is that these memoirs might encourage, perhaps even provoke, others to record their perception of events. This would help to rescue Ontario from being a "have-not" province, in terms of popular and scholarly publications.

During the writing, friends have often asked me if I was handling the subject chronologically. The answer is yes, with an important exception, which I would ask readers to bear in mind. Part I is a chronological overview, providing a political framework from which there are two thematic digressions, one covering the scandals in my first years in the legislature, and the second focusing on the development of the New Democratic Party. To have included in this chronology the details of my involvement in major issues would have been so confusing as to be incomprehensible; therefore, they are only mentioned in passing.

In Part II, however, six of these major issues — intergovernmental affairs, health, education, agriculture, energy, resources and the North — are isolated in separate chapters for fuller consideration. These issues profoundly affect the lives of Ontarians. In dealing with them separately, there is an opportunity to portray the relentless battle for change, and the impact of political infighting on the evolution of policy. At the same time, these issues provide continuity through my seventeen years as leader, twelve more as private member, as well as three years as chairman of the caucus. Seen in this perspective, the record indicates that the opposition can often have a greater impact on government policy than is apparent at the time.

Politics, for me, has been a constant fascination and enjoyment. I have often said that a person either is temperamentally suited for political life or he will die a thousand deaths a week. My temperament must have been suitable, for even the setbacks and disappointments were quickly forgotten in pursuit of the tasks that lay ahead.

At a testimonial dinner on the occasion of my tenth anniversary as an MPP — for fund raising purposes, as always, in the NDP! — Tommy Douglas dubbed me "The Happy Warrior." I am content with the description. In fond memory of that most lovable of New Democrats, I accept it, with belated acknowledgment.

Having finished reliving my political years in these memoirs, I have a major regret: there is a host of persons who are very much part of this story, and deserve mention. But to have done so at all meaningfully would have taken the volume to even greater lengths (and publishers, I found, have something to say about that), or it would have been mere name dropping. To all of these unnamed members of the team, to be found in every constituency across the province, these memoirs are dedicated in grateful appreciation.

There are many friends and colleagues to whom I must express thanks for assistance in gathering the material and preparing an acceptable manuscript. First, Kevin Quinn, who, while president of the Kingston Historical Society, assisted in searching through my papers in the Queen's Archives for some of the raw material. Second, in the typing of a succession of drafts, Marcia McVea, Mary Todorow and Betty Bib. Third, in commenting on first drafts of policy chapters, Donald Stevenson, on intergovernmental affairs; Robert Macaulay, Alan Schwartz and Jim Fisher, on energy; Walter Pitman, on education; Peter Oliver, on reform institutions; John Phillips and Glen Agnew, on agriculture; Floyd Laughren and Terry Hilborn, on the North and resource development; Gordon Wilson on labour; and Jack Stokes and Ross McClellan, on the Legislature. Fourth, the staff of the legislative library, for their unfailing courtesy and help in tracking down factual detail. Fifth, for checking one or other of the drafts for errors or questionable judgments: Terry Grier, Robin Sears, Lorne Ingle, Fred Young, Jo Surich, Alan Whitehorn, D.

McCormack Smyth, Marianne Holder, Gerry Caplan, Rosemary Speirs, George Samis, Gordon Brigden, Laurel MacDowell and Ken Bryden. Finally, when I had to cut back on excessively long first drafts on the issue chapters, Peter Mosher did a masterful job of capturing the substance, while reducing the verbiage.

The achievements of these years were probably only because an unfair share of the burden of maintaining a home and raising a family was shouldered by my wife, Simone. During my many absences and often my preoccupation with unfinished business even when at home, the normal responsibilities of family life fell to her. She made the impossible demands of the job seem more manageable all through the years, but the public image of "a happy warrior" was, at home, too often that of an otherwise preoccupied father. During the preparation of these memoirs, Simone provided in-house judgment of my recollection of events, in many of which she had an active part, and caught many a grammatical error or awkward syntax in my hastily typewritten copy.

A heartfelt thanks to Diane Mew, editorial consultant, with whom it has been my pleasure to work on previous publications, who patiently advised on cuts and additions on the first draft, and did the final editing for publication.

Special thanks, also, to the Social Sciences and Humanities Council for a grant which covered the expenditure involved in research assistance, interviews, typing and editing; to the Ontario Heritage Foundation for making available the services of Roger Hall, former editor of *Ontario History*, the quarterly journal of the Ontario Historical Society, to make suggestions for deletions and additions to improve the historical record, and for a grant-in-aid of publication; and to Robert Fitzhenry, president of Fitzhenry & Whiteside Limited, and William R. Booth, head of the firm's college division, for their enthusiastic acceptance of work in the relatively neglected field of Ontario history and politics.

For the writing throughout, and any remaining errors, I accept full responsibility.

Donald C. MacDonald
Toronto, June, 1988

Part One
Overview

My father — Charles P. MacDonald.

My mother — Florence (Jennings) MacDonald.

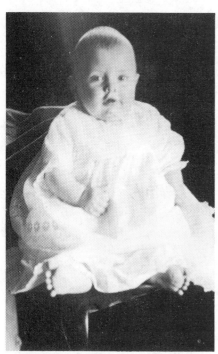

Age of 6 months — politics was not yet under consideration.

Queen's graduation — BA(1938) and MA(1939).

1

Early Years

From my high school years, I was never uncertain as to what I wanted to do, only how to go about doing it. I always intended to go into politics.

Why politics? I have been asked that question hundreds of times and I don't know the precise answer. It must lie buried in ancestral genes, for neither of my parents came from immediate families with a tradition of public life. But from high school years it was my firm resolution to go into politics. I can recall vividly an occasion in grade ten, when each member of the class had to deliver a speech on what they intended to do upon graduation. Some were uncertain, but not me: school teaching was to be the stepping stone, while doing undergraduate work, to weekly journalism, in pursuit of the goal of politics.

My father, Charles Pirie MacDonald, was the grandson of a Scottish immigrant who came to Canada in 1840, and carved a farm out of the forest in southern Quebec. The original homestead was on the English River, a small tributary of the Chateauguay, famed for the battle in the war of 1812-14. In 1857 his family moved to the site of a farm on Tullochgorum Road, lying between the villages of Ormstown and Howick, some thirty-five miles south of Montreal, just a mile or two from the national monument commemorating the repulse by the British forces of the American invaders in the 1813 battle. The family home was built three years after Confederation, and my father was born there in 1887, the second of a family of eight. He has now passed his hundredth birthday, living at the Centre d'Acceuil, an elderly persons' residence in Ormstown.

In his ninety-fifth year Dad completed the MacDonald family history. With the incredible recall of some older people for times, places and persons of years gone by, he has recaptured the past, portions of which are worthy of inclusion in any anthology of pioneering days. It's a story from which I extract a few highlights.[1]

In 1907 the harvesting had finished on the Tullochgorum farm. Dad was now twenty and felt that "a trip to the west would be a worthwhile experience." He purchased a ten dollar ticket for the harvesters' excursion and, with twelve dollars in his pocket, supplemented as he left by his mother with an additional ten dollars and a basket of roast chicken and home baking, he was off. His sister Grace drove him to the station in the milk wagon and, as they passed their father cutting weeds along the lane with a scythe, there were best wishes for a good journey. In stoical Scottish fashion, there was no emotional parting. In fact, Dad would not see home again for five years.

His three-day trip from Montreal to Winnipeg was a rollicking adventure with a train-load of farm boys from Eastern Canada. At Winnipeg the excursion ended, and each went his own way. Dad took a passenger train to Moose Jaw, met a lad from Melbourne, Quebec, and together they worked "without any loss of time for about two months," at stooking and threshing grain on farms south of the town.

At the beginning of December they parted. Dad spent a couple of days in Moose Jaw where, after two months of harvesting, he luxuriated in a Turkish bath — "I felt like a new man." He then headed for Calgary, where, it was rumoured, homestead land was available. But he found that "you couldn't buy a job. Every night homeless men crowded into a furnace room of the hotel, where they were allowed to sit or lie on the floor. . . ."

He moved on to High River, forty miles south of Calgary, spent his first Christmas away from home with three other guests at a hotel, and the next morning signed up for work at the Lineham Lumber Company's camp. Within two weeks he was "an experienced sawyer," who was teamed up with a young Scottish Highlander: "We worked together all winter and turned out a daily count of two hundred logs."

In camp he met Arthur Ashurst, who had filed the previous fall for a homestead in the Stettler area. He said there was an adjoining quarter section open, so on 17 March 1908 he paid ten dollars, and became the proud owner of one hundred and sixty acres of land. Throughout that summer he began the work of "proving up" his homestead.

In the early fall one of his neighbours was visited by a son, Arthur Smith, who was foreman of the CPR freight sheds in Fernie, British Columbia, the town which had been totally burned out in late August. Smith told Dad there was a job for him as quickly as he could get there, so he left the harvesting to Arthur Ashurst, with whom he had a working partnership, and spent the remainder of the fall and winter handling freight in the hectic rebuilding of Fernie. Shortly after his arrival, he received word that a prairie fire had swept from the south and burned Ashurst's shack and barn, along with his building, wagon and stacks of grain.

For the next two years the summers were spent breaking new land and improving the homestead, with winters back in Fernie. At Christmas, 1910, however, he returned for a final winter on the homestead to fulfil the residential requirements for claiming title.

During these years, Dad's interests slowly changed. On his first visit to British Columbia, he did not succumb to the awesome spectacle of the Rockies. The lure of the prairies remained strong: "The snow peaks of the Rocky Mountains outlined against the blue sky and white clouds have a beauty and a fascination all their own, but it is the beauty of barren desolation and majesty, while the prairies give promise of food for untold millions . . . the rise and fall of its grassy slopes are like the sweep of a frozen sea, relieved at intervals by a thin wisp of smoke rising from some homesteader's cabin. Many times I have sat on my hilltop watching the light fade from the sky. In the hush of the evening, with the first star burning in the cloudless sky, the mystery and solitude of the Great Plains wound around me like a spell. When the moon came up and the coyotes commenced their evening song, it was really something to remember. . ."

Obviously the prairies had a strong fascination for this farm boy from the east, but his interests focused more and more on the Fernie area. When he got title to his quarter-section, on 17 March 1911, he immediately sold it to Arthur Ashurst and returned to British Columbia. The reason became clear when he travelled back at Christmas for that final winter on the homestead. As he passed through Calgary he bought a ring and "mailed it back to Flo Jennings. As an engagement ring, it wasn't much," he wrote, "but on sixty-five dollars a month, you cannot go in for platinum and diamonds."

My mother's family, from Staffordshire, England, had a traumatic introduction into life in Canada. Her father, James Jennings, emigrated in 1906 and worked for the coal company in Fernie. He was in charge of the fans which withdrew dangerous gases from the mines and blew fresh air into the shafts. Within a few months, the family joined him. Mother, the eldest daughter, was eleven years old. Grandpa Jennings was plagued with chronic rheumatism, which affected his heart, and was not helped by Fernie's high altitude. He died suddenly in 1907, and the family doctor was so shocked by the turn of events that he gave Grandma Jennings two hundred dollars to cover the funeral expenses. She rented a large house, kept boarders, and took in washing to provide a family income. A diminutive woman, scarcely five feet tall, she was typical of the gritty Brit who sustained wartime bombing with equanimity.

More disaster was in the offing. In August 1908, a fire had been burning for weeks high up on the mountain. Many times Mother and Grandma Jennings had watched its harmless progress from their living room window. But one day, a gale force wind drove the fire down the mountain side. The tin roofs were torn off the homes and rolled down the streets. The mill yard, with millions of feet of lumber, and a hundred carloads of coal which had been brought into town by the mine, created an inferno that left rail lines twisted like pretzels. The boilers at the mill exploded with a roar that shook the burning town. Both the railroad and the high bridges were cindered, cutting the town off from the outside world. The top side of logs, held by a boom in the river, were aflame. The sawdust roads burned the shoes off the fleeing townsfolk.

The whole of Fernie lay in ruins. All the Jennings family's treasured pictures and mementoes were gone. The next morning, trains came in through the smoke from the west to the outskirts of the smouldering ruins. Women and children were ferried across the river and taken to Cranbrook, where they were fed and housed in the curling rink for several weeks.

But the spirit of these western pioneers was unbreakable. A new town quickly sprang up. The business section was rebuilt with more fire-resistant materials. A sewer and water system, which had not existed before, was installed. Lumber was made available for building new homes. Carpenters, plumbers, bricklayers and plasterers poured in from as far away as the Maritimes. It was into this feverish activity of rebuilding that Dad came on his first trip from the prairies.

Meanwhile, the Jennings family was living in a tent. All the neighbours were preoccupied with their own problems and Grandma Jennings, with her young family, was left to fend for herself. As winter closed in, a few men came to their rescue and threw up a two-roomed shack with no foundations. (In later years, when the sons, Bert and Jim, started to work, they moved the shack across the street to another lot and added two more rooms.) The difficulties were compounded by many unforeseen developments, including a typhoid epidemic, arising from the open cesspools. Uncle Bert came close to dying.

Dad was bunking with Bill Ramsay, a Scottish engineer. Ramsay got to know the Jennings family well because Grandma Jennings was doing his washing. Both he and the family were in the Salvation Army. Ramsay invited Dad to the Army meetings where he first saw Mother, a tall young woman, singing in the choir. When he returned to the prairies, they began corresponding.

By the winter of 1909-10, the pace of freight-yard activity had died down. Work was no longer available there, and Dad got a job as clerk in the warehouse of the Western Canada Wholesale Company, which supplied south-eastern British Columbia with dry-goods and groceries. When he returned the next winter, he found that the manager was moving to Cranbrook to set up another wholesale business, Cranbrook

Jobbers Limited. Dad asked for, and got, a job with him, as shipping and receiving clerk in the new warehouse.

In January of 1912, he made a short visit back to the family in Quebec, the first since he had left on the harvesters' excursion five years earlier. When he returned to Cranbrook Mother followed him from Fernie; they had been engaged at Christmas. She got employment with local merchants, Little and Atchison, who had opened up an ice-cream parlour which shifted to the skating rink, with the addition of hot drinks, in the winter. Dad contracted for the building of a bungalow — $1,050 for the carpentry work; beyond that was the plumbing, painting, sidewalking and fencing. Together they bought the furnishings for their new home, and on 12 July 1912, they were married.

I was born on a wintry night, 7 December 1913, when, as Dad is fond of needling me, the temperature was forty below and dropping even further with my arrival.

My first ten years were spent in the Cranbrook and Fernie areas, where five of my brothers and sisters were born. From clerking in the warehouse, Dad had gone out on the road as a salesman for the wholesaling company. There are many tales of his travelling by Model-T Ford, calling regularly on customers, in Creston to the west; Fernie, Natal and Michel to the east; north through Kimberley, and down the Columbia Valley to Golden. It was all to become familiar stomping ground for me when I ran federally in the 1953 election in this, my native constituency.

Memories of these boyhood days are vivid: fishing in the creek that ran back of town; being reported, with a number of buddies, for smoking in the quarry one Saturday, for which my teacher — in a gross violation of her jurisdiction — gave me a sound strapping on Monday morning; the weekly salvaging of stray bottles for delivery to the local soft drink works to finance my ticket to the Saturday movies; regular entry into pie-eating contests at the matinees, not so much to win, as to get the pie; to say nothing of a host of other boyhood escapades which are best left unrecorded.

After travelling for some years for Cranbrook Jobbers, Dad opened a grocery store in Cranbrook of which I have fond recollections. For a growing boy, there were many goodies, authorized by Dad, or slyly devoured when nobody was watching. My boundless energy was the source of endless mischief, and when I was at home, Mother wisely kept me busy at many tasks, including the ironing of all the flat washing — handkerchiefs, sheets and pillow-cases.

However, this interlude, including vague memories of the flu epidemic in 1918-19, came to an end in 1923. The store had not proven very prosperous, and Grandpa MacDonald was pleading with Dad to come east and take over the family farm. Mother was unenthusiastic about such a move, but eventually the decision was made, and the family moved back to Tullochgorum.

I became a farm boy at age ten. The next seven years were relatively uneventful. The family income was never more than $1,800 a year, chiefly from milk shipped to Montreal. My parents were burdened constantly with mortgage payments that fell behind. Another brother and sister arrived, and for me, the eldest of eight, it was a regular round of farm work — up at five o'clock all year round, milking cows and delivering cans of milk to Bryson Station, and in the summer, haying, harvesting and threshing.

Of course, school was my preoccupation, first in a little one-room country schoolhouse, and then high school in Ormstown bicycling in the spring and fall, and driving with a horse and cutter in the winter. I enjoyed school, and winter storms were merely an added challenge. I didn't miss a day during all the four years of high school.

My public awareness was slowly aroused during those years by a couple of developments in which Dad and Mother were involved. First was the move to church union, which brought Methodists, and most of the Presbyterians, into the United Church. Coincidentally, in 1926, the community was torn apart over the issue of school consolidation. Some, including Dad, were ardent proponents of forsaking the little red schoolhouse in favour of bussing children to a central school with greater facilities. Others were adamantly opposed, and it was interesting that the same families which opposed the location of Macdonald College in the Ormstown area in 1905 (because it was financed by tobacco money!) were those who opposed local school consolidation a generation later. Every community has its progressives and its conservatives; Dad and Mother were among the former, and played a role in the campaign leading up to a vote. Subsequently, they continued their commitment, with Dad winning the election to the new school board.

Notwithstanding the limitations imposed by farm work and a small family income, these were satisfying years. Despite our lack of money, I never felt deprived. There was good food in abundance — poultry, pork, beef and garden vegetables — and plenty of warm clothes. Presents on birthdays and Christmas were always basic needs — a sweater, or a new pair of shoes or gloves — never luxuries. Skates and a sleigh were the only things that came close to toys that I can recall from my childhood. Later, it was the prize luxury, a bicycle, which was really a necessity, providing my transportation for five miles into high school during most of the year; only in the depths of winter did it give way to a horse and cutter. At twelve or thirteen, I was doing a man's job along with Dad in the haying and harvesting. Work close to the soil gave me a life-long affinity for farm life and agricultural problems, and work habits developed in those early years have always remained.

At seventeen I finished high school, resisted Dad's suggestion to get a job at the local bank, borrowed money from a second cousin who lived on a neighbouring farm, and went off to the School for Teachers at Macdonald College. Some of the neighbours thought this was a kind of "sissy" pursuit for a strapping farm boy, but I viewed it, not only as enjoyable in itself, but as the means of pursuing a university degree.

The year at teachers' college was a mixed blessing. I enjoyed it, but for reasons that have always mystified me, I fell into disfavour with one of the college staff, one Dr. Brunt, who taught English. As a result of his influence, I received only a probationary diploma, subject to approval from inspectors' reports. The first visit from the inspector that fall wiped out the restriction, so that it was an inconsequential setback. More important, however, another of the college staff, Dorothy J. Seiveright, who taught history and geography, vigorously championed my cause, and out of it grew a deep friendship which was to last until her death.

Dorothy Seiveright was one of those remarkable teachers who influenced profoundly the lives of the young people who came within her orbit. She never married. Her fiancé had been killed in the first world war, but with years of teaching school throughout Quebec, and then at the School for Teachers, she built up a "family" with whom she maintained close contact. She wrote geography books which were standard texts for years in Quebec and Ontario schools. Her own retirement was spent with her sister at Preston Spring Gardens, in what is now Cambridge, Ontario. During my years of teaching, and other activities, we maintained a lively correspondence in which I poured out my hopes and problems, always receiving her wise counsel.[2] She became a beloved "Auntie Dorothy" to our children.

With widespread unemployment, the bottom fell out of the teaching profession in my year (1931-32) at Macdonald College, so that most of my classmates were scrambling for a job after graduation. I spent the summer of 1932 working on a construction gang building a new school in Ormstown for a wage of thirty-five cents an hour, ultimately increased to forty cents. I recall one day wheel-barrowing two hundred and fifty-six loads of cement from the mixer, down a gang plank for the floor of the basement. The next morning, my legs were so stiff that I dropped to my knees when I got out of bed.

September neared, and I still had no teaching contract for the coming year. But luck was with me. From the daughter of a neighbour who was teaching in the Ottawa Valley, I learned of a vacancy at Bristol Ridge, back of Shawville, in Pontiac County. I rushed off an application, and in ten days it was accepted.

Still eighteen, I began a five-year teaching career. From a little country school house at Bristol Ridge, with the first seven grades, I went on to continuation schools in Shawville and Bedford, where lower grade teaching was supplemented with history in the upper grades, and finally, to high school teaching in Sherbrooke. There were extracurricular activities, coaching hockey, football or basketball, and during these years I pursued my bachelor degree extramurally from Queen's University: two courses each winter, and another two each summer, combined with three summer schools in Kingston, which were working holidays. Those five years netted an annual salary of $740, which didn't allow for luxuries. Yet, while a dollar was hard to come by, it went a long way, and I have constantly marvelled in recalling that the total expenditure of my undergraduate work (1932-38) at Queen's — books, examination fees, three summer schools, and my senior year in attendance to qualify for an honours degree — amounted to some $1,875!

As politics remained my ultimate goal, I seized upon every opportunity for public speaking during those teaching years — in churches, service clubs and other community organizations. In small towns, and even in a city like Sherbrooke, such occasions were plentiful, so I gained valuable experience.

My senior year at Queen's brought an honours degree in history, politics and economics, but equally fruitful was a range of campus activities which, as events proved, were to open the door to future opportunities. I wrote a regular column, *Current Comment*, for the student paper. I was a member of the executive for the debating union and involved in intercollegiate debating. George Grant, now a renowned philosopher-historian, was ill and had to drop out as Queen's delegate to a conference of international relations clubs at St. Lawrence University, in Canton, New York. Replacing him, I was elected to the executive of the next year's conference, scheduled for Swarthmore College, near Philadelphia. Over the Christmas holidays I was one of the Queen's delegation to the founding convention of the Canadian Student Union in Winnipeg. The year concluded with a fellowship, which allowed me to go on to graduate work. Teaching had been satisfying, but I had no intention of making a career of it. With no other opportunities immediately at hand, I decided to complete a master's degree.

That year, 1938, produced a real stroke of fortune. In November I was on the Queen's team which debated with visiting Australians. They had swept the boards in their cross-Canada tour. We were opposing the resolution "That the British Empire Must Disintegrate." My partner, D.W.H. Henry, and I, didn't match the eloquence and light-hearted humour of our opponents, but we presented solid arguments which they failed to refute. The judges concluded that we had won — as might have been expected on that topic, at that time, in Kingston.

Unknown to me, in the audience for the debate was Arthur Newell, lecturer for the Associates for Anglo-American Understanding. This was an organization which had been set up by a Gloucester-born Englishman, who had had a successful business career in the United States. Upon visiting his homeland, he was appalled at the ignorance of the average Englishman concerning the United States. He organized a committee to exchange lecturers between the two countries, in a modest effort to create better understanding. The organization had grown to include a Canadian committee, chaired by V.C. Wansbrough, then principal of Lower Canada College, and involving such distinguished Canadians as Brooke Claxton, a Liberal cabinet minister from Montreal, and James Richardson, of the well-known Winnipeg business family.

It was widely believed in those days that Canada was the logical interpreter of Britain to the United States, and vice versa, so the Canadian committee of the Associates was looking for a Canadian lecturer to add to the team. Well-known Canadians had been sought, but since the salary offered was only $2,000 a year, not surprisingly, none had responded. Arthur Newell had come to Queen's to inquire of Principal R.C. Wallace whether there was any suitable prospect on campus. Dr. Wallace told him of the debate with the visiting Australians, scheduled for that evening, and suggested he stay over.

At the reception held in Principal Wallace's home after the debate, Newell sought me out. I was emotionally drained from the tensions of the evening and the euphoria of victory, so when he asked me whether I'd be interested in becoming a travelling lecturer in the United Kingdom and United States, I said yes, without realizing the significance of the situation.

As I walked that night to my boarding house, the reality slowly began to dawn.

Principal Wallace, and Dr. R.G. Trotter, head of the History Department, backed me in an urgent request that my departure be delayed so that I could finish my master's thesis. I did that by the end of March, and was off on a cross-country trip to get up up-to-date picture of Canada. It involved interviews with leading public figures, including Premier Aberhart of Alberta. I stopped off at Kingston to write final exams, then at home to bid my parents farewell, and headed for Saint John to catch a boat for Britain. It was an exciting career opening.

I had vaguely contemplated doctoral work, if nothing else emerged, but all those plans were forsaken. The travelling lectureship was an experience more in line with my political aspirations. In speaking to audiences of many kinds, it gave me a wealth of experience in getting to know the English, Welsh and Scottish peoples, in communities from southern England and Wales to the Scottish Highlands. It was followed by a month's visit to the continent — Holland, Germany and Danzig — from which I returned through France just two weeks before the war broke out. My most vivid recollection of Europe at that time was the expressions of surprise by Germans at what they perceived as "war fever" in Britain. They had been on a war footing for so long that it was normal, whereas Britain was feverishly preparing in the post-Munich awakening.

The outbreak of war wrecked plans for a scheduled tour in the United States, but the remainder of the first year's commitment was filled with a Canadian Club tour which the Canadian Committee of the Associates for Anglo-American Understanding was able to arrange. For a person born in British Columbia, raised in Quebec and educated in Ontario, this was a rare experience, deepening contacts all across the country. Besides, the $2,000 salary for the year, with all expenses paid, wiped out my university debts.

The one-year travelling lectureship contract was fulfilled. The war in Europe was stalled. Where now? My university studies, and all my activities, had been involved with national and particularly international affairs. I was approached to consider becoming secretary of the Canadian Institute of International Affairs which, in one sense, would have been a logical step. However, I had long been attracted to combining a career of journalism and politics, in the British tradition, so I got a job with the Montreal *Gazette*. It was the most influential newspaper of the day in Canadian politics, read assiduously every morning by Members of Parliament in Ottawa. I started on the proofreading desk, a useful spot for an overview of the whole paper, and then, for nearly two years, I was assigned to the education and consular "beats."

Education was a lively issue at the time, because the Quebec government under Adelard Godbout was contemplating the belated introduction of compulsory education. I became involved in the public build-up for this development through a series of twenty articles, exploring every aspect of the question. It was said that they played a part in developing public support for the government move, in the face of long-standing Catholic Church opposition. I would like to believe that to be true.

The consular beat in Montreal was replete with exiled governments and shipping agencies, which had been driven from their homelands by the Nazi sweep over Europe. With information gleaned from them, I compiled a regular weekly column, entitled *Under Gestapo Rule*. Otto Strasser, originally an aide to Hitler before breaking away in 1933, had taken refuge in Montreal. He had detailed personal knowledge of all the leading personalities in the Nazi party from the early years, so he was able to comment significantly on many events. I helped him write a regular series of articles for the *Gazette* — my first and only effort at ghost writing.

It was all very engaging, but the "sitzkrieg" phase of the war had ended and Europe was aflame. In February of 1942, I decided to join the navy. "Chief" Carpenter, managing editor, expressed his regrets at my decision, informing me that my salary was about to be raised, from $28 dollars a week to $35. It didn't dissuade me.

I was turned down by the officer's selection board, for reasons that I never learned, so I enlisted as an ordinary seaman, in the wireless branch, the only opening available because I wore glasses. In the month of February 1942, I left the *Gazette*, joined the navy, and on a weekend pass, married Simone Bourcheix. Together, we had a hundred dollars in the bank at the time.

Simone was the daughter of an old country French family which had emigrated to Montreal, lived for some time in the United States, and returned to Canada. We had met as delegates to the student conference in Winnipeg in 1938, but she had gone off for postgraduate work at Columbia University, in New York City, and my wanderings had covered two continents. By a quirk of fate, I was assigned by the *Gazette* editorial desk one evening to cover Sir Wilfred Bovey's speech to the Montreal Translators' Society. Simone had been persuaded by a friend to come and hear Dr. Bovey and we were seated at adjoining tables — a wholly fortuitous set of circumstances. My working hours prevented our getting together again for six weeks or more, but get together we did. Six months later we were engaged. Simone accepted, with tears, my decision to join the navy, and with the imminent prospect of my going to sea, we decided on a weekend wedding and a two-day honeymoon out to the family farm, all in a blinding snowstorm. That's the precipitous way such milestone events in life were handled during the war.

After eight weeks of basic training in Montreal, I was off to Ste. Hyacinthe for a wireless course. For me, this introduction to service life was something of a holiday routine. I had been accustomed to the long hours on a morning newspaper, beginning with a luncheon meeting and running until after midnight, when the last edition was put to bed. To be subjected to a nine-to-five routine, with regular meals, and all evenings free, was a little difficult to take. I had been reviewing books while with the *Gazette*, and I cleared it with the station authorities to continue, so that the free hours were filled with one or two books a week. Also, of course, I was absorbing the technical details of wireless telegraphy, becoming efficient in Morse code, and involved in the inevitable lower deck drill. Meanwhile, Simone was teaching in Montreal. She came out to Ste. Hyacinthe every second weekend and we got together in my off-duty hours.

Once again, fate intervened. During a coffee break at one of the morning classes, I noticed a copy of the *Queen's Review* on the window sill, and discovered that the instructor was a fellow alumnus.

"When were you at Queen's?" he asked.

"Oh, I got my BA in '38 and my MA in '39," I replied.

"Well, what the hell are you doing here?" he exclaimed. Most of the men in the class had not finished high school.

I smiled, saying it was all a mystery of the personnel branch: "My application for a commission had been turned down, but my decision to join the navy wasn't an idle one, so here I am."

In any case, my class instructor happened to lunch at the captain's table that day, and he recounted this exchange. That afternoon, by remarkable coincidence, the captain received a signal from headquarters in Ottawa asking if he could recommend anybody "aboard ship" who might be qualified to become secretary of an interservice intelligence committee. The qualifications required at least a general knowledge of wireless (which, of course, I had just acquired), so as to be able to understand the language of the activity, along with an educational background and experience for a full-time administrator for the committee work.

The captain called me in to ask if I was interested. My overwhelming desire in joining the navy was to get to sea, a yearning which had always been with me. The prospect of being posted to headquarters as a "sailor on Dow's Lake" in Ottawa, was not exactly what I had in mind. But, I replied, if it were felt that I could contribute on this job, then, yes, I'd be interested. So, instead of completing my wireless training and going to sea, I packed my bags for Ottawa. Once again I went before an officer selection board, and in view of my new posting, it was a foregone conclusion: I became a sub-lieutenant.

For the next eighteen months I was secretary of the so-called "Y" committee, another experience for which one would be

willing to pay good money. The committee brought together
the directors of signals for the army, navy and air force, along
with representatives from the departments of Transport and
External Affairs. Its work was top secret, because it coordinated a vast network of signal receptions from enemy sub-
marines in the Atlantic and the Gulf of St. Lawrence, and
transmitted them to centres where the location of the sub was
plotted, so that information could be transmitted to the air
force — all in a matter of minutes, enabling planes to be
dispatched for bombing the sub.

The committee worked with its counterparts in both the
United States and the United Kingdom. It was an interesting
challenge, setting up a new organization and establishing its
procedures. It provided an inside picture of both service and
civilian departments of government at work in wartime.

However, after eighteen months, the "Y" committee work
had become a routine and another opening came my way. The
Information to the Armed Forces Section of the Wartime Information Board was headed by Dr. Gregory Vlastos, an air
force officer, whom I had known as a professor at Queen's.
He invited me to seek a seconding from the navy to help with
an expansion of their activities. The directors of intelligence
in the three armed services were my boss, and they did not
object, so I moved on.

For some time the Information to the Armed Forces Section had been producing a pamphlet, entitled *Current Affairs*,
dealing with a range of topics which would help the service
personnel prepare themselves for a return to civilian life. The
authorities were mindful of serious disturbances which arose
among men and women waiting for months to get home, after
the end of the first world war, and the difficulties they had
in fitting back into civilian life after years overseas. It was
felt that *Current Affairs*, a group discussion pamphlet, might
lessen the dangers of these difficulties being repeated when
hostilities ended.

A companion proposal was also under consideration. By
late 1943, some Canadians had been overseas for four years.
They were now more familiar with life in Britain, and increasingly out of touch with events and developments back home.

My father, in his room at the Centre d'Acceuil, Ormstown, Quebec, following his 100th birthday.

Simone in college years *(above)* and a few years earlier *(right)*, with her parents.

As chairman, CBC's Serviceman's Forum, 1945.

Our wedding — two weeks after I joined the navy in February, 1942.

Asleep *(above)* and awake *(right)* while in the Navy as an ordinary Seaman.

It was proposed that a Readers Digest-styled monthly publication should be published, including a range of topics which had appeared in Canada. Thus *Canada Digest* emerged and I became its first editor. It was a joy to plan, edit and publish a new magazine. There was no difficulty in getting reprinting rights from Canadian sources, and within a month or two, *Canada Digest* began circulating among personnel overseas, supplementing the group discussion pamphlet, *Current Affairs*.

After a year with *Canada Digest*, its production had become a routine, and another project was under consideration. During the 1940s an outstanding feature of adult education in Canada was the CBC's Citizen Forum, Farm Forum and Labour Forum. They had become social and educational means for bringing friends and neighbours together to discuss current topics. Why not a servicemen's forum, to open up discussion among service personnel on the topics for which *Current Affairs* provided background reading? The three armed forces approved the project, but the CBC reacted to the proposal with caution, if not trepidation. It was one thing to bring "responsible" experts together on a broadcast panel, but quite another thing to bring together ordinary "Joes" and "Janes," who might sound off in an "irresponsible" manner, to the embarrassment of all concerned. However, the CBC agreed to experiment with the project. Thus emerged *Servicemen's Forum*, to which I was seconded as chairman, with Robert G. Allen as producer. Together we turned up each week at an army, navy, or air force base, first in Canada, then in Britain after VE-Day, and later in Europe, at sites ranging from Paris to Copenhagen. The procedure was straightforward. With the assistance of the educational officer on base we brought together a group of twenty-five to thirty for a free-wheeling discussion. From them, a panel of three to five was chosen. They discussed a topic — such as jobs after the war, completing an interrupted education, or housing — and Bob Allen and I scripted their views. The actual panel discussion was then held, usually before an audience of service personnel, and transmitted directly to the CBC for broadcast in Canada, or recorded and airmailed back from points in Britain and Europe. The overseas programs were also broadcast over the Armed Forces Network in the United Kingdom and on the continent.

Far from amateurs having a problem, experience proved that, since they had no reputation to maintain, they were less inhibited than professionals. Consequently, they often created a livelier broadcast, which admirably served the purpose of opening up group discussion.

Bob Allen and I were provided with transportation and a driver, and given a letter of introduction from London headquarters to the commanding officers at navy, army and air force bases requesting full cooperation in our work. This was, without exception, obligingly provided: lodging, meals and gasoline were readily available. Moreover, the week's broadcast was usually recorded on Thursday, not later than Friday, so that we had the weekend, in Europe's short distances, to get to the next base. That provided opportunities for viewing conditions in war-torn cities. Two such occasions stand out: one weekend when we went to Berlin, and inspected both sections of the occupied city, and the rubble heap of the former Reich Chancellery; and another when we visited Celle, in central Germany, for a first-hand view of the trial of the infamous Irma Grese, the concentration camp official reputed to have made lampshades out of human scalps, and the exhuming from mass graves which had been found in the forests on the outskirts of the city.

These were experiences whose memory will never fade. They were at once impressive, depressing and chilling. Visual reminders of the holocaust, and of the awesome destruction of bombing, had to be seen to be fully believed. I don't normally keep a diary, but every day or so I recorded impressions from our travels in a letter back home to Simone. For anyone patient enough to decipher my writing, they provide fleeting snapshots of postwar Europe.[3]

All this was another rewarding experience of inestimable benefit for my chosen pursuit of journalism and public life. But with the end of 1945, Bob Allen and I were on our way home, along with the thousands of service personnel, to go through the procedure of demobilization and a return to "civvy street."

2

Finding My Political Home

The political thinking and possible party association of my youth underwent an evolution which, in retrospect, seemed a very natural development. I have already indicated that, from high school years, I had always intended to go into politics. That was my constant goal, but how, and where, and with what party, were open questions.

To follow the evolutionary process, it is necessary to understand the surroundings in which I grew up and first became politically aware. My home constituency was Chateauguay-Huntingdon. Its politics were highly traditional, having escaped most of the social and economic farm revolt during and after the first world war. It had returned Liberals in every election since Confederation with (in my youth) just two exceptions — early in the century, and again with the Conservative sweep under R.B. Bennett in 1930. In all the years of the CCF (1933-61), there was not even a token candidate.

My initial reaction, as a teenager, was that such a one-party monopoly was not healthy, and something should be done to break the Liberal stranglehold. Therefore, in the federal election of 1930, the first in which I felt personally involved, I was a supporter of the Conservative party — at least in all the political arguments. In the years since, there have been periodic allegations in newspaper articles and cross-fire in the Legislature that I was originally a Conservative. At best that's a half-truth, more accurately, a quarter-truth.

As I delivered the cans of milk to Bryson Station each morning, for shipment to Montreal, it is true that I used to get into arguments with farmers of Liberal persuasion. They

must have considered me — not without some justification
— as a brash young whipper-snapper. The Bennett victory em-
boldened my political stance in a way which might be expected
for a sixteen-year-old. Because of these vigorous political arguments, it's possible that our neighbours were persuaded that
I had had associations with the Conservative party from birth.
Not so. My parents were never members of any party. My
interest in the Conservative party was not as much for what
it was as for what it might become as a vehicle for the changes
which the depression obviously required.

In 1935, the first federal election in which I was entitled
to vote, I was effectively disenfranchised. I had just moved
to a new teaching position at Sherbrooke High School, but
arrived in the city too late to be enumerated. I found it particularly galling because, as I learned later, I was on the voters'
list at Bedford, where I had taught the year before, and at
home, near Ormstown, where my parents had had me
enumerated. It is not every election when one has two votes,
hundreds of miles away, and none where one is actually
residing.

I was at Queen's summer school in 1935 and remember the
kickoff for the Liberal campaign, when Mackenzie King was
the leading speaker at a rally in the local armoury for a new
candidate, Norman McLeod Rogers, who became minister of
labour, and later defence, until his death in a plane crash early
in the war.

At the time of the 1937 provincial campaign I had my first
introduction to Ontario provincial politics. I was at home in
Quebec, just across the river from Ontario radio stations, completing two reading courses, plus a voluntary enrolment in
German A for exposure to a foreign language. I remember
following the Ontario campaign, as radio background to my
reading, because Earl Rowe, the new Tory leader, was
challenging Mitch Hepburn's Liberals, and George Drew was
breaking ranks with his party because Rowe was critical of
Hepburn's brutal tactics against the CIO's organization of the
autoworkers in Oshawa.

With the defeat of the federal Conservatives in 1935 and
the return of Chateauguay-Huntingdon to the Liberal fold,

I became even more interested in how an effective alternative to the Liberal party might be built. These were the days when the Roosevelt New Deal dominated political thinking. One of the old parties in the United States had been modernized from within. Was it possible that the same could be achieved with the Conservative party in Canada? Bennett had appeared to seek that with his series of radio broadcasts, toward the conclusion of the 1935 election campaign — the so-called Bennett New Deal. But it had all the earmarks of a death-bed repentance, which I did not find convincing.

In the next few years there were three occasions which helped to clear my political thinking. The first was at the time of an intercollegiate debate in the fall of 1937 when I was on the Queen's team that travelled to Osgoode Hall in Toronto. It had been suggested to me that I should have a chat with J.M. Macdonnell, then head of National Trust Company, and later MP for Toronto Beaches-Greenwood. He was chairman of the board at Queen's and an uncle of George Grant whom I knew.

The chat was very disillusioning. Regarding my interest in politics, Macdonnell said, in effect, "Young man, if you're interested in politics, first establish your financial independence, and then go for it." As far as I was concerned, the discussion ended there. I was interested in politics as a career. In my youthful view, it had been the hobby of older men for too long.

The second event was two years later. During my travelling lectureship, I wrote to R.B. Bennett, who had retired to Britain, asking if it might be possible to meet him. I received a warm affirmative reply, and spent a couple of hours with him at his hotel residence in London. I used the occasion to ask a number of questions. Would he advise that a person considering a political career seek legal training? To my surprise, he replied that he didn't feel it was a prerequisite. My key question was: Is it possible to remake the Conservative party from within, in the fashion that Roosevelt had done with the Democratic party in the United States?

I shall never forget his reply. He shook his head, firmly asserting that it couldn't be done. For me, it was a profoundly eloquent response. Coming from the man who had attempted it, perhaps as little more than a gesture in face of impending election defeat, it went far to dispel any illusion I had about reshaping the Tory party to my satisfaction.

The clincher came with my work at the Montreal *Gazette*, a leading voice for Canadian conservatives. Robert Manion was the Conservative leader at the time and, while the paper supported him editorially, there was much internal criticism, in part because he was a Catholic. I found this narrow-minded and offensive. When, added to that, there were often blatant anti-semitic comments from the managing editor, it was too much: If this was typical of the Tory party, as far as I was concerned it was rotten at the core.

On one occasion I was summoned to the office of the publisher, John Bassett (father of John Bassett Sr. of Toronto's media/sports family). The publisher of the Huntingdon *Gleaner*, Adam Sellar, had written to inform him that he had a local boy on his staff. It was a kindly gesture on Sellar's part, but I shall never forget that meeting. Bassett's advice was to forget about politics, because "you can be more effective in journalism."

"You can lash the politicians," he said with a sweep of his hand. In the midst of our discussion, his secretary stepped into the office to clarify details with regard to train reservations; he impatiently barked at her to get out and use her own judgment. It was a chilling experience, which deepened my doubts and concerns about those in command of this bastion of conservatism.

In later years, when I used to drop in during Montreal visits for a chat with Charlie Peters, who succeeded Bassett as publisher, I once told him that it was the *Gazette* which made me a socialist. He blanched.

When I was posted to Ottawa by the navy in June 1942, my daytime activities were with the inter-service intelligence committee, but my evenings were free. Simone had a teaching contract in Montreal, so being footloose, I spent virtually every evening around the Parliament Buildings, seeking out contacts in every party.

One of those visits was unforgettable. The Conservative MP for Kootenay East, representing Cranbrook, where I was born, was George MacKinnon, the doctor who had brought me into the world. He was an attractive old gentleman who had been persuaded to run as the Tory candidate in the 1940 election. To his obvious regret, he had been elected, for he was completely lost in the House of Commons. Being a very conscientious person, he faithfully sat in his seat, but never felt at home in the place. Given his disillusionment, he must have found it strange that a young man whom he had ushered into the world, should be so enthusiastic about politics.

The members who attracted me were those in the CCF caucus. I had briefly met J.S. Woodsworth in Winnipeg, at the 1937 conference which launched the National Student Union, but he had since died, and Stanley Knowles had succeeded him as MP for Winnipeg North Centre. There was an impressive group of party pioneers: M.J. Coldwell, Tommy Douglas, Angus and Grace MacInnis, Clarie Gillis, and Joe Noseworthy, the newly-elected member for York South. At the start, I had fewer personal contacts with them that with the old parties, but they were easy to met, and it wasn't long until I was on a first-name basis with them all. Very quickly, I found CCFers to be political soul-mates.

Those few weeks — from June to August 1942 — were an exciting political awakening. The circumstances of my upbringing and early career had isolated me, not from the ferment of ideas that characterized the 1930s, but from their impact on the political parties, notably the emergence of the CCF.

The struggle on the limited family income while growing up, and later while teaching and pursuing university work, had left no bitterness, but it did create a sense of basic injustice toward a system where sixteen hours of hard labour every day was rewarded with such inadequate returns. During the depression there were constant reminders of poverty and hunger, nowhere more so than in teaching, where the consequences for deprived children were evident every day in the classroom. My conviction grew that such conditions need not be, or at least, that people could, and should, be sheltered from their disastrous impact. Therefore, economic and social considerations, not religion, should be the stuff of politics. I reacted negatively to the traditional religious cleavage between the old parties, in Ontario as well as Quebec. To be voting Conservative because you were a Protestant, or Liberal because you were a Catholic, struck me as being irrelevant in the face of the conditions of the 1930s.

These political beliefs were strengthened by a succession of events which indicated that the old order was in drastic need of reshaping: the general failure of the Liberals under King, and the Conservatives under Bennett, to respond adequately to human needs during the depression; the consumer price exploitation documented in the report of the 1935 Price Spreads Inquiry, headed by H.H. Stevens; the corruption of politics by big corporations in receipt of government contracts, as revealed by the $750,000 contribution to the Liberals by the construction firm building the Beauharnois Canal; the RCMP crackdown on the cross-country trek of the unemployed in the Regina riots; the brutal repression of industrial workers as they sought to organize in face of Hepburn's Hussars.

Internationally, there was the fateful emergence of fascism in Europe and Japanese military expansion in Asia. Hitler's overrunning of Austria, Mussolini's invasion of Ethiopia, the Japanese march into Manchuria, the Spanish Civil War — these events were foreboding.

I had always followed these domestic and international developments closely. I dealt with them in my daily teaching, in my public speaking with church and community groups, in my "lessons," which were the weekly commitment of extramural studies, in debates and my *Current Comment* column in the student newspaper at Queen's. Later, my travelling lectureship in Britain and Canada, and experience as a working journalist, broadened my knowledge and deepened my convictions. Without realizing it, my political philosophy had become that of a democratic socialist long before I met members of the CCF caucus. That is evident now, in reviewing what I said and wrote during those years. All that remained was to recognize which party offered the best prospect of fulfilling my ideas.

On 25 August 1942, I visited Lloyd Shaw in the CCF national office. Lloyd was executive secretary to M.J. Coldwell and had been engaged in party research for some years. I asked him how one could join the party. He accepted my application for a sustaining membership for $25. It was the beginning of a continuing friendship, now strengthened by the fact that his daughter, Alexa McDonough, is leader of the NDP in Nova Scotia. From that point on, I was increasingly involved in CCF activities. I joined the editorial board of *News Comment*, the research publication of the national office, and did research for MPs on such subjects as the future prospects of civil aviation in Canada, working with Stanley Knowles, who was championing this issue in the Commons. In fact, I recall doing an article for *Canadian Business* magazine on "Little Planes Can Be Big Business." Because of my position in the navy, however, I did not get involved publicly in constituency work.

When the Ontario provincial election took place on 5 August 1943, opening the forty-two-year regime of the Tories, Simone and I were on a nine-hundred-mile bicycle trip during my two-week furlough. We had booked into a Prescott hotel the night of the election, and had a first-hand picture of the mixed reaction of the local burghers, who were elated at the election of thirty-eight Tories, but dumbfounded by the near victory of that new party, the CCF. Obviously I was very excited by the results: they seemed to confirm that with the CCF I had made not only the correct, but also the winning, choice.

With demobilization after my return from Europe in 1946, I was faced with a critical decision. For the previous eight years or so, I had kept contact with Adam Sellar, publisher of the Huntingdon *Gleaner*, and written a regular column for it, my hometown weekly. Adam was a brother of Watson Sellar, who in his later years was auditor general of Canada. They were sons of John Sellar, who had been picked by George Brown in the 1860s to establish a voice of Liberalism among those of predominantly British stock in the upper reaches of the Chateauguay Valley. He had become one of those rugged weekly newspapermen who was quoted continent-wide. Adam had remained with the weekly paper and, being without heirs, was anxious for me to join the *Gleaner* and ultimately take it over. I was attracted to the idea of weekly journalism in combination with politics, so the proposition had been in my mind for years. While at Queen's I had written a regular column for the student newspaper — just to gain experience.

In fact, as far back as 1940, Sellar had urged me to consider the Liberal candidacy. He was a key man in the local organization and was not enamoured of Donald Black, the incumbent, so he might have been able to engineer a change; and since the seat had been "safe" for the Liberals, candidacy was tantamount to election. However, I was not ready for elected office at that time and, more important, it was the wrong party. At the end of the war the invitation to join the *Gleaner* was still open.

Sellar had built a big printing establishment, overshadowing the weekly paper that was my primary interest. When I contemplated the half-million dollar price tag, and the years of job printing needed to finance the purchase, I forsook my dream of combining weekly journalism with running for Parliament. Besides, there were competing prospects. In my overseas travels with *Servicemen's Forum*, I had worked closely with Robert McKenzie of the Army Education Branch. Bob had been with the adult education department of the University of British Columbia before joining the service, but was planning to go on to postgraduate work at the London School of Economics. He did so, remaining in Britain where he became a noted political scientist and BBC commentator.

Bob had mentioned my name to Dr. Gordon Shrum, of the University of British Columbia, for an adult education position when the war was over. Dr. Shrum discussed the matter with me on one of his eastern visits early in 1946. Much of my work had been ideal experience for proceeding to adult education, within a university context. For an alumnus of the extramural department at Queen's it had added attractions, but it would have been a serious digression from my primary interest of politics. My decision was made easier by David Lewis, then federal secretary of the CCF. David was administrator, strategist, organizer and policy-maker all rolled into one. His tough practical implementation of socialist theory, in the Canadian context, gave the party a sense of purpose and direction.[1] As a volunteer I had had the opportunity of working closely with him. The prospect of becoming a full-time colleague was not only attractive but exciting; so when he invited me to join the expanding national office staff of the party as publicity and education director, I enthusiastically accepted. This was adult education in my chosen field of politics. Moreover, the experience in journalism, editing, broadcasting and public speaking — communication of many kinds — had been ideal preparation. It looked like a perfect fit of experience and future hopes.

Simone found the prospect attractive. Though essentially an apolitical person, in marrying me she knew that politics would be our preoccupation. Moreover, as a city girl, she was not enamoured of the thought of moving to a small town; so settling in Ottawa, with which we were both familiar, was inviting. In addition, the thought of moving from an apartment to a house of our own was a welcome change from all the unsettled conditions of the war years.

While the decision was under consideration, one evening while coming home from a meeting on nursery school developments in which she was involved, Simone encountered David and Sophie Lewis on the streetcar. David expressed the hope that I would join the staff. That helped to dismiss any lingering doubts. In May 1946, I joined the team at the CCF national office, then operating out of crowded office space at 56 Sparks Street.

It was the most important decision of my political life, a culmination of all that had gone on before, and the gateway to what was to follow. I had determined that henceforth I would devote my efforts to building an alternative to the old parties.

3
Building the Party

David Lewis's memoirs, *The Good Fight*, provide a graphic description of the mood of the party in 1946. Hopes had been riding high in the latter years of the war, and not without reason. In 1941 the CCF had become the largest single party in British Columbia, forcing the Liberals and Conservatives into a ten-year coalition. From no representation in the Ontario Legislature, in 1943 the CCF elected thirty-four members, as compared to the Conservatives thirty-eight and were thus within four seats of a claim to minority government. And of course, Tommy Douglas had swept to power in Saskatchewan in 1944.

Most people — and not least, CCFers — believed that the CCF was destined for a national breakthrough. Mackenzie King's diaries document the extent to which he felt the Liberals must respond to the threat from the left. Unemployment insurance had been legislated in 1941; his government added family allowances and renewed glowing promises of a health insurance program. But in 1945 the CCF bubble burst, particularly in Ontario. Provincially the party was cut back from official opposition to eight seats; and a week later Joe Noseworthy, the only Ontario MP, lost in York South.

David Lewis read the election results of 1945 correctly, and recognized that the party was in for a long haul. A major concern was the financial position of the national office. It had traditionally relied on a quota payment from each of the provincial sections, but they faced the same shortage of revenue and often (with the exception of Saskatchewan) were unable to meet their commitment. David proposed a national membership plan, whereby one dollar would be added to each membership at the provincial level, with the added revenue to be passed on to the national office. It provided a modest, but more secure, financial base; but even before the plan became operative, the expansion of the staff took place. Lorne Ingle, an Albertan party activist, recently demobilized from the army, succeeded Stuart Jamieson as director of research. In addition, David was determined that "at least one more senior functionary would be added to deal with educational activities within the party and publicity outside."[1] In his view, this would be the vital long-term need. Lorne and I started at a salary of $3,000 a year, a figure which had increased to $4,200 when I left seven years later.

The official date for assuming my new duties was 1 June 1946. David was off to the west on one of his innumerable trips across the country. It was obvious that we couldn't continue to operate with expanded staff in the limited office quarters at 56 Sparks Street, so he asked me if I would look around for a suitable property to become the party's national home.

My chief preoccupation during the month of May, between demobilization and taking up my new job, had been getting the family settled. Our first daughter was two years old, and a second, Joy, was on the way. Having found a comfortable, and with my wartime savings, financially manageable house, I returned to the same real estate agent and told him of the party's needs. By good fortune, he came up with 301 Metcalfe Street, at a price of $12,500. When David returned, we proceeded to buy it, and named the building Woodsworth House. A campaign launched among members and friends across the country netted $25,000, so that the building and the necessary renovations were covered by the contributors. Their names were listed in a "bible" proudly displayed for years in a glass case in Woodsworth House, which remained the national office of the New Democratic Party until 1987. "Woodsworth House was a defiant symbol of survival and permanence," David Lewis has written. After the reversal of party fortunes in the elections of 1945, it certainly became one.

I had no illusions that the main responsiblity for publicity, as far as the national office was concerned, would remain with David Lewis. He had been a leading spokesman for the party since the mid-thirties, but with the contacts which I had built up in the media world, I was able to assist and relieve him of much of the routine work involved. At the start, education work within the party was my chief concern. Faced with an electorate which generally was not sympathetic, this was a prime need among the membership. Initial efforts were directed to building more effective committees in each province, for there were obvious limits to what one person could do from Ottawa. Moreover, there were not copious funds for travel, so I concentrated on central Canada.

My first visit to the Quebec provincial office revealed the proportions of the task. I was curious as to what memberships there were in my original home riding of Chateauguay-Huntingdon. I discovered there were six, all United Church ministers, who had banded together in a monthly study group. Ontario, however, was more fruitful, and there were many visits to Toronto and other points in the province, to help launch more provincial and constituency educational activities.

Among the interesting ventures I developed was a number of correspondence courses for isolated members who were eager, in the absence of any local activity, to do something for themselves. I persuaded a number of people to draw up course material, with accompanying reading lists, on party organization between and during elections; on the trade union movement; on farm movements and their role in the party; and on various current policy topics. Members, who were registered for these courses, turned in regular essays which I commented on and returned. This was a direct steal from my own experience in extramural work at Queen's during my undergraduate years. For persons eager to further their political education, particularly those living in rural or northern communities, it proved to be a modest success.

As it turned out, I had created a Frankenstein monster for myself. Reading and commenting on all the essays was too great a burden. Nevertheless, from the experiment flowed a useful series of publications. The course material was reproduced in booklet form, and widely distributed throughout the party, helping to encourage individual and group education activities.

These publications spawned Woodsworth House Publishers. While overseas in 1945 I had been struck by the extensive display of publications available in every United Kingdom bookstand. Included among them was the regular material from the Fabian Society, and an astounding flow of books from Gollancz, a left-wing publishing house in Britain. Why not a Gollancz in Canada? I soon discovered that none of the traditional distribution agencies which kept the bookstands filled with papers and magazines was interested; one-shot publications did not fit into their operations. Furthermore, the Canadian market for serious pamphlet material was incredibly small.

On one occasion, when I was pressing the chief officer of one of these periodical distribution agencies to consider handling publications from Woodsworth House Publishers, he turned the tables on me by saying, "How much will you pay me?" That is, in addition to the usual discount on the retail price. He ended the argument by telling me that during the war they had handled a series of small pamphlets published, as I recall, by Oxford University Press. The sales for each pamphlet, throughout all Canada, amounted to about eight hundred.

Obviously, there was no possibility of distribution through the existing commercial channels, so I determined to build a distribution system within the party and trade union organizations. Those involved in educational work were always eager to get new material, so there was a ready response. It simply meant establishing a myriad of contacts, and keeping a regular flow of promotional material to the provincial and local groups. This was not difficult, but required a mountain of work.

One of the titles released by Woodsworth House Publishers was a roaring success. In the mid-thirties Louis Rosenberg, a western party activist, under the pseudonym of Watt Hugh McCollum, had written a little booklet entitled *Who Owns Canada?*, detailing the interlocking directorates of Canada's fifty largest corporations. It got wide circulation among progressives in the west, and, ironically, was extensively used by "Bible Bill" Aberhart in the broadcasts through which he built the Social Credit party. I sought out Rosenberg, who produced an up-to-date version. The original run of twenty-five thousand disappeared within three months, and twenty-five thousand more were printed. That would qualify as a bestseller even today. These publication efforts produced a modest revenue for the national office, which helped to finance other educational activities.

As president of the Ottawa East Riding Association I was gaining experience in local party activities by the fall of 1946. When I attended my first provincial convention, as a relative unknown in the party, I managed to win the last spot among those elected to the provincial council. As a full-time staff member living in eastern Ontario, I was given the challenging task of digging up candidates in the dozen or more ridings within the triangle of Kingston, Cornwall and Pembroke. This was my first experience, though not my last, of travelling those eastern counties; eventually they became as familiar as my own backyard. In 1948, when the provincial party enjoyed a resurgence which restored it to the official opposition, it was a more rewarding experience than expected. In many ridings, the CCF candidate polled a few thousand, rather than the customary few hundred, votes.

Events were soon to take me into organizational work full time. A.M. (Sandy) Nicholson was defeated in his Saskatchewan riding of Mackenzie in the 1949 election; and at the subsequent federal convention he was elected national treasurer. Sandy raised money at meetings in far greater amounts than virtually anybody else, but after a year of this exhausting activity he indicated that he would not stand for a second term. He was completing his annual coast-to-coast efforts in the spring of 1950 with visits to all the ridings in Ontario. David asked me if I would like to try my hand at helping Sandy cover the province.

The one thing I had always found distasteful was asking people for money, even for a worthy cause. Now I came to enjoy it, particularly when it was tied to building a basic organization, which is, of course, the way it should always be done in a political party of democratic socialist persuasion. The result was that at the next national convention I was elected national treasurer and organizer, with all Canada as my stomping ground.

It was crucial that we put fund-raising in each province on a more systematic basis, riding by riding, with enough money flowing into the provincial office to get full-time organizers in the field. Each fall I would leave home in Ottawa to cover the four western provinces. Those were tough years for Simone and the children, who had grown to three in number — Brian was born in 1948. There is one poignant family story of how Sandi, our elder daughter, looked at my photo on the dresser and said to her mother: "It's a good thing we have a picture of Daddy, or we'd forget what he looks like."

The winters of 1950 to 1953 were spent in the Maritimes, covering the three provinces; Newfoundland had just come into Confederation and was not included in my itinerary. I worked for the first time — but not for the last — with Fred Young. He was an ordained United Church minister who had switched to YWCA work as Halifax teemed with service personnel. From voluntary efforts with the emerging CCF, he soon moved into full-time organizing work in all three provinces. During the spring, my travels were confined to Ontario, where at least there was something of an ongoing local organization with which to work.

During the second year of this attempt to cover the country, coast to coast, it became clear that more full-time organizers were needed to coordinate the work of the volunteers. Since we knew it was beyond the financial capacity of the provinces to field such a staff I proposed to the federal executive that a national organization fund be established to hire five organizers, one for each of Manitoba, British Columbia and the Maritimes, and two for Ontario. Each would be paid $6,000 with the province covering the expenses. We asked the Steelworkers and Autoworkers unions for $12,000 each and the smaller Packinghouse workers union for $6,000.

The Packinghouse workers were never able to respond but

the Autoworkers provided the $12,000. There were difficulties with the Steelworkers: the international office at Pittsburgh was not amenable to allocating money. However, Charlie Millard, the Canadian director, solved that problem. Charlie had played a key role in the Autoworkers original confrontation with Mitch Hepburn in Oshawa in 1937, and subsequently rose to become Canadian director of the Steelworkers. He was strongly committed to political action, having been elected to the Legislature for York West in 1948. The post of international president of the Steelworkers was up for election, and Charlie exacted a commitment from David MacDonald, ultimately the victorious candidate, that if the Canadian delegates supported him he would agree to the appointment of two "political action reps," to be placed on staff in Canada and made available to the CCF for organizational work.

The result was a real lift for the struggling CCF in Ontario. Fred Young needed a change from the frustrating work in the Maritimes, where local organizations had to be rebuilt every year, because of emigration to central Canada or the New England states. He was taken on staff by the Steelworkers and made available to the CCF to cover southern Ontario. For the second Ontario organizer I had the great pleasure of luring C.C. ("Doc") Ames from behind his pharmacy counter in Kirkland Lake to take on the vast expanse of northern Ontario. As a first-aid worker in the mines, Doc had gone out with the workers in the famous 1941 Kirkland Lake strike. That heroic action, combined with his association with the local hockey team when they won the Allan Cup, had made him a legendary figure throughout the north. He quickly established a rapport with all the northern ridings which continued through his retirement in 1973 until his death in 1982.

That left the Autoworkers' contribution available to field an organizer to replace Fred Young in the Maritimes, and to have another in British Columbia. Something had been achieved in putting fund-raising in the party on a more systematic basis, and a start had been made at getting full-time organizers on staff, to assist in building the volunteer work. But it was not enough to counter the decline in the party. The ferment of wartime and immediate postwar years had

Landscaping Woodsworth House in Ottawa after it became federal party headquarters in 1946.

A longtime colleague with David Lewis, first at the federal office, later as provincial and federal representatives in York South, and still later as president and leader of the party.

The family in our Ottawa home before becoming Ontario leader.

The CCF leadership contestants in 1953 — Fred Young *(left)* and Andrew Brown *(right)*.

given way to a public yearning for "normalcy." Election setbacks had been experienced, notably in central Canada. Only British Columbia provided a tantalizing exception. The ten-year coalition of old parties had disintegrated and in 1952, with W.A.C. Bennett, a dissenter from Conservative ranks as leader, Social Credit had narrowly edged out the CCF. In 1953 a run-off election was called and I was dispatched to British Columbia to help.

In the course of my earlier visits I had covered all the southern part of the province each year, including my native Kootenay East, where the CCF member had been defeated by a handful of votes in the 1949 election. The local riding association was looking for a candidate, since its previous member was a clergyman who had moved down to the coast. Since elected office had long been my ultimate goal, this looked like a promising prospect. The national executive approved, so I was acclaimed as candidate — a native son returning home.

In the campaign I worked in the five or six ridings lying within, or neighbouring, Kootenay East. In two months I canvassed two-thirds of the homes in the southern stretch of the Kootenays from Fernie, through Cranbrook to Creston, and northwards, through Kimberley, and the picturesque towns and villages of the Columbia Valley, to Golden and Field. There were widespread expectations that I would win, but the election results confirmed Bennett firmly in power. When the votes in my riding were counted, a little-known Social Credit candidate rode the popularity of "Wacky" Bennett's crusade, and got unexpected support. Many of the opposition votes which I expected were siphoned off. The Liberal plurality was cut to two hundred, but they held the seat. It was my first, and only, election defeat.

Simone had come out for the final weeks of the campaign, and we had covered the riding with Susie, a 1939 Plymouth, my first car, which I had purchased for $200 for the campaign. I remember picking up M.J. Coldwell, then the CCF national leader, from the train in Cranbrook, and driving to a rally in Kimberley. In his gentlemanly way, M.J. commented after his ride that he hadn't experienced such a vehicle since the "Bennett buggies" of the depression thirties. Appropriately,

Susie gave up the ghost on election day. We dispatched her to the junk heap, and headed home for Ottawa by train.

At that point, I had been away for five months. My desk had been kept clear during my absence. There was only one "private and confidential" letter awaiting me. It was from Dudley Bristow, a member of the Ontario provincial council, who noted that Ted Jolliffe had resigned a few weeks before. Ted had been CCF leader since 1942, but following his personal defeat in York South in the 1951 election, he found it impossible to fulfil the responsibilities of the office, in combination with law practice. There would be a leadership convention that fall to elect his successor. Dudley suggested that I should throw my hat in the ring. Never in my wildest moments had I considered going into provincial politics. My interests had been in national and international affairs. But one thing had become clear in my work across the country: until the CCF could become established in at least one of the central provinces, it would never be a truly national party. Obviously Quebec was not an immediate prospect. That left Ontario.

Preoccupied with this critical decision, I went off to spend the weekend with my family after five months' absence. Simone had had a taste of politics as the candidate's wife, and had enjoyed her first experience in the Rockies. Now there was the prospect of continued involvement, this time as the leader's wife. At least it held the possibility of being confined to Ontario, without lonely stretches of two or three months when I'd be away from home. The opportunity for party leadership was not a challenge to be casually dismissed. All of these considerations swirled through our minds. Within a week, the decision was made: if the Ontario party chose me, fine. If not, I'd be glad to continue at the national office. A leadership convention was called for late November of 1953. In September, Andrew Brewin and I indicated our intention to stand. Andy had been active in the party for years — on the provincial council and executive, and as candidate in both provincial and federal elections. He had established a national reputation as a lawyer, notably in defence of the Japanese

Canadians when they were so ruthlessly deprived of their civil rights by the federal government during the war. By comparison, I was a relative newcomer.

The campaign was extremely civil. It did not receive a great deal of publicity, because the party fortunes were at such a low ebb. Each of us had committees, which raised a few thousand dollars and built a network of supporters across the province. Whenever the troops got into vigorous infighting, Andy and I cooled them down. We were personal friends and had no desire to build animosities, which would create greater difficulties for the party. The approach was relatively straightforward: "Here we are. The choice is yours. May the better man win."

However, in the final weeks the campaign took on greater excitement when Fred Young was finally persuaded to enter the race. Fred had been the only full-time organizer in southern Ontario following the 1951 debacle, and for two years had built up favourable personal relations with riding leadership. In addition, he had the support of a formidable pair of organizers, Marj Pinney and Joan MacIntosh, two of the most dedicated party activists.

The convention drew some three hundred and fifty delegates to the old Legion hall (now renovated as the Superior Acceptance Building at 22 College Street). It was a one-day affair, devoted exclusively to the leadership contest. The delegates and observers filled the hall floor and balcony to overflowing but as conventions go, it wasn't a big crowd. There was some placard-waving, but none of the bands and hoopla of today's leadership conventions. Each of us made his speech and the first ballot took place. Fred Young led with 154, I placed second with 125 and Andy Brewin was third with 76.

A fateful half-hour intervened between ballots. There were no walkie-talkies to corral floating votes; no television cameras, for they had not yet come into general use. A small knot of print and radio reporters were off to one side of the stage but they did not engage in the now familiar feverish chase for comments from the candidates and their organizers. For the most part Andy Brewin's supporters made their second choice without arm-twisting. When the ballots were counted, Brewin's support had split two to one in my favour and I edged Fred Young by six.

I made a few remarks in acceptance and the delegates adjourned for a banquet in the old Prince George Hotel on King Street, now replaced by one of the bank towers. I delivered my first speech as leader, in sober but upbeat terms. Little did the assembled audience, or I, realize the long road that lay ahead.

4

A Leader Without a Seat
1953 to 1955

In the grey dawn of the morning after, when the euphoria of the convention had faded, the magnitude of the job slowly became more evident. Fortunately, there was no lingering bitterness from the leadership contest; both Andy Brewin and Fred Young swung in behind me with no ill feelings. Otherwise, the general situation was challenging.

Party morale had dropped to rock bottom after the 1951 election, when the caucus had been reduced from official opposition to two members — Bill Grummett from Timmins and Tommy Thomas from Oshawa. The party had been virtually leaderless for two years. There had been staff cutbacks, leaving only three senior people: Ken Bryden, who moved from research director of the now-decimated caucus to become provincial secretary, and two organizers, Doc Ames in the north and Fred Young in the south.

However, this is a retrospective assessment, reflecting the long struggle for recovery, rather than my mood at the time. I should have been overwhelmed, but fortunately, I wasn't. I am by nature an optimist, an "incorrigible optimist," according to my friends. Moreover, at the outset realism dictated that, if morale were to be lifted and the basic organization rebuilt, the job had to be tackled in a positive way, stressing assets rather than liabilities, possibilities rather than problems. I have always had a profound conviction that there is a place in Ontario for a party of the democratic left, and further, that Ontario is the key to building a truly national party. For me, to paraphrase that familiar office slogan, the task was not impossible; it would just take a little more time.

On the personal level, there was the immediate question of the changes the family would have to make. Following my election as leader, Simone and I returned to Ottawa to shuffle the deck for the new game. It was decided that she and the children would remain there for a few months in order to avoid, as much as possible, disruption of their school year. Meanwhile, she would sell the house in Ottawa while I hunted for another in Toronto. By mid-week, I was back in Toronto to start that process — but there were many other demands.

Since I had no seat in the Legislature, I had neither staff nor office. A desk was made available for me at the provincial office of the party. Having no staff was not a worry, because I had operated alone while travelling on two continents, with only my trusty 1938 Underwood portable as companion. Hotel accommodation was beyond the limited expense account, so the hospitality of friends was gratefully accepted: from Bill and Dorothy Dennison, both of whom had pioneered in the days of the United Farmers of Ontario (Bill later was elected an MPP and then mayor of Toronto); Ken and Marion Bryden, both of whom subsequently became MPPs; and Morden and Margaret Lazarus, two stalwarts in party and trade union activities.

The political challenge was formidable. Meetings were held with the party executive and committees, and within days a new agenda was set. On 1 December I stated that the objective of the Ontario CCF was to carry the message into every community throughout the length and breadth of the province, providing the kind of constructive opposition that the Conservative government of Leslie Frost urgently needed. Within another week, plans for the months ahead had been made. The revitalization of the party had begun in the fall during the build-up to the leadership convention. A research committee had been set up under Andy Brewin's chairmanship, with subcommittees covering the important phases of provincial life. On 9 December I announced that a draft statement of policy would be considered by the provincial council meeting over the weekend of 16 January. Beyond it, a series of regional conferences was scheduled for February and

March, in Port Arthur, North Bay, Hamilton, London, Owen Sound, Ottawa, Peterborough and Toronto and district.

Meanwhile, I tackled the leader's ongoing task of keeping the party before the public on current issues by a series of press releases: on 17 December deploring the lockout and layoff of fifteen hundred workers in the Hollinger Consolidated Gold Mines; on 18 December welcoming the government's announced consideration of distributing natural gas through a commission along the lines of Ontario Hydro; and on the following day criticizing Premier Frost's plea that the federal government should provide grants to cover hospital deficits amounting to $20 million. In that last case, I argued that the provincial government was the victim of its own neglect in not organizing soundly financed hospital services. It was the opening gun in the long battle for health insurance.

Not surprisingly, my pronouncements did not get headline coverage, but from the outset I personally delivered my press releases to each of the three Toronto dailies and the major news agencies. I relied on the Canadian Press wire service to reach the radio and TV stations. On the road, by using onion-skin paper, I was able to produce six copies on my typewriter, which enabled me to make personal contact with editors in the weekly papers and broadcast outlets wherever I happened to be.

This practice evoked some puzzlement. Political leaders usually had staff to deliver their press releases; no doubt it was viewed as evidence of the CCF's rudimentary operations. But gradually the practice became more asset than liability. I established personal contacts which, as a former newspaperman, I enjoyed, and they often resulted in impromptu interviews. At least I was assured that what I had to say reached the news desk even if it got no further.

The search for a new home in Toronto had proven tedious: house after house was either inadequate for a party leader, or beyond our financial means. Finally, I found a suitable residence, at 138 Raglan Avenue, in the southeast corner of York South, where I intended to seek nomination. Friends lent me $1,500 for a down-payment. Simone came down from

Ottawa to see if it met her expectations, and I left her to close the deal because I was scheduled for a northern tour.

While I was away the provincial council had worked its way through the preliminary draft of a CCF program prepared by the research committees — an eight-thousand-word document entitled "Looking to the Future." Over the next two months, the local membership added their revisions at the regional conferences, and a final draft was debated and adopted at the regular CCF convention, held at the King Edward Hotel in Toronto, from 21 to 23 May 1954. The party was pulling itself together after years of drift.

Having covered the north in my first leadership tour, I attempted to establish personal contact with the ridings lying south of the French River. Most of them were within one hundred and fifty or so kilometres of Toronto, and after a meeting, I would usually wind down in the two-hour drive home. The more distant areas, in southwestern and eastern Ontario, were covered in periodic sorties of two or three days.

In fact, I concentrated on eastern ridings during the summer months, when our family would spend time at Breezehill, the summer home of Simone's parents — a delightful five acres atop the hill overlooking the Ottawa River at Cumberland, just east of Ottawa. Simone's father had turned this poor farmland into a veritable garden of Eden, with fresh vegetables and berries, along with an orchard of thirty-five fruit trees of many kinds.

Alternatively, we spent some weeks at a co-op camp which a group of Ottawa CCFers, including me, had built in the late 1940s on Otty Lake, near Perth. While the family enjoyed these summer locations, I would fan out to meet with riding executives, attend picnics or visit individual farm leaders, until the back concessions of the eastern counties became familiar territory. This was renewing earlier experiences when, on the national office staff, I had been assigned the task of seeking out candidates in every election.

For the greater part of the year I remained close to Toronto. While the Legislature was sitting, it was important that I follow proceedings, albeit from a seat under the gallery, off the floor restricted to elected members. Government reaction to the escalation of CCF activities emerged periodically, reaching its most ludicrous instance on 22 March 1955. It was common practice for ministers to leave their seats and consult with officials sitting under the gallery, but when Bill Grummett, the CCF House leader, did the same with me, he was strongly criticized by Premier Frost. I seized upon the incident in a public statement that evening asserting that ''it was unworthy of the Premier to have stooped to criticizing such a respected member of the Legislature as Bill Grummett because he left his seat to discuss with me matters of public concern.'' It was indicative of the government intolerance of any opposition.

There was another reason why I stuck close to Toronto. I dared not neglect my own riding. There are few events more upsetting for a political party than to have its leader defeated in his own riding. This spectre haunted CCFers in York South, for it had happened twice to Ted Jolliffe. He had won handily in 1943 and 1948, but lost marginally in 1945 and 1951. There is no such thing as a safe seat in politics, but York South was winnable if the organizational work was done.[1] It was up to me, as a newcomer, and the corps of volunteers, to make certain that the work was done. The task of winning was all the more formidable because the Tory incumbent, Bill Beech, was a former reeve, had run a travel agency for years in the heart of the riding, and was on the Dominion Command of the Royal Canadian Legion. The six veterans' branches represented one of the most influential grass-roots organizations in the community. I joined the Silverthorn Branch.

There were, of course, many other community organizations — ratepayers and service clubs, the social planning council, as well as the municipal council and its committees. Local government in the Township of York was dominated by a coalition of old party supporters, so the process of breaking into the existing networks took time and effort. For the first few months I concentrated on getting to know the CCF members. They had won victories, federally and provincially, more often than not, since the federal by-election of 1942 which was the CCF's breakthrough in Ontario politics. My first objective was to win the nomination, and for that, the CCF members were the only voters.

By the end of the school year, Simone and the family had moved down to our new house. As a resident and a taxpayer in the municipality, my credentials were improved. At a nomination convention in the fall of 1954, I was acclaimed as candidate. Now there was the challenge of winning support from the electorate at large.

In the general effort to establish a stronger presence for the party, the inevitable jockeying began between the opposition parties. Feeble as the CCF position was, that of the Liberals wasn't much better. With the personal defeat of its leader, Walter Thomson, in 1951, Farquhar Oliver had resumed the leadership. The caucus had been reduced to eight, and did not provide vigorous opposition to the overwhelming Tory ranks of seventy-nine members.

By the session of 1955 I was taking solid aim at the Liberals because they claimed to be an opposition while providing none. I deplored the fact that, in his ninety-minute contribution to the throne debate, Farquhar Oliver had not even mentioned the rising tide of unemployment, while decrying those who claimed business profits were too high. After corporations have paid their taxes, he said, "the supposed profits are lowered to a very small figure indeed." "All this," I pointed out at a meeting in Vermillion Bay, on 9 March, "when 1954 saw the highest dividend payments in Canadian history."

In the strong plea to get back to free enterprise, Oliver urged that price-fixing in the sale of beer and wine should be abolished. Taken in conjunction with the call a year earlier by Albert Wren, Liberal MPP for Kenora, that permission should be granted for the sale of beer in grocery stores, it was a preview of the Liberal stance in the 1980s. My reaction then was that "it all adds up to an unashamed bid by the Liberals for financial support from the liquor and hotel interests. The Liberal Party is now in the process of selling its soul anew in a desperate bid for election funds." The only difference between the Liberals and Conservatives, I added, was "that, provincially, the Conservatives are at least an effective champion of Big Business interests, while the Liberals are pathetically ineffective. . . . We've had enough of the puppetry of old party politics, with both parties financed, and therefore

Ted Jolliffe, my predecessor as provincial leader and MPP in York South.

Joe Noseworthy, my federal partner in York South until his death in 1957.

My first nominating convention in York South, 1954.

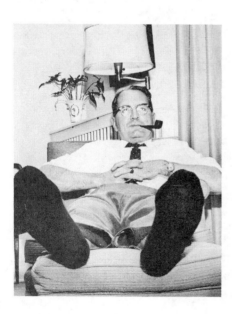

The campaign was over and the feet were sore — after my first campaign in 1955.

effectively controlled, from behind the scenes, by Big Business."

This theme became the general outcry, not just for the CCFers for whom it was standard fare, but for many others. On 5 April 1953, Blair Fraser, Ottawa editor of *Maclean's* magazine, had written an article entitled "Our Illegal Elections," subtitled "Most of our lawmakers become law-breakers in the very act of getting elected" because the major contributors to their election funds were contractors who did business with the government. Not only were such contributions a violation of the Criminal Code, but they posed a moral dilemma for thoughtful members of Parliament: "Voters may well share their concern," Fraser concluded, "because, directly or indirectly, we voters pay for the political funds in the end."

Twenty years later the validity of this contention was acknowledged. With the support of all parties, the 1975 Election Finances Reform Act opened all campaign contributions and expenditures to public scrutiny. But at this time it was part of the "underworld" of politics, and leaders disclaimed any knowledge of how money was raised or spent in elections.

In 1954 the election funds issue became the dominant theme of Ontario politics. Questions had arisen regarding the role of road contractors in financing the Conservative party. The resulting investigation revealed what came to be known as the Highway Scandal. In the lead-up to the 1955 election, public interest, if not concern, was heightened by the revelation that James Dempsey, the Tory member for Renfrew South, had received a contribution of $8,500 from a local timber operator. Premier Frost disowned Dempsey; it was a classic example of being penalized, not for being guilty, but for being caught.

At a CCF nominating convention in Lindsay I dealt with the Highway Scandal and Dempsey's revelation of the campaign contribution from a timber operator. The incident provided "another glimpse of how the financing of the old parties is a constant source of corruption of our public life." A week later, at his own nominating convention, Frost accused me of slandering the Conservative party. I seized the occasion, in a CBC election broadcast on 19 May, to review what had happened:

There is a particularly dangerous feature of all these developments. It has now become a well developed habit of the Conservative Party to use the Premier's reputation to hide from public view the whole underworld of activity carried on by the rotten Tory machine. The time has come for the people of this province to view the Premier apart, to pay tribute to him because tribute is due, but to face up to the fact that behind this front of unimpeachable integrity, there has grown up a situation of shocking and dangerous proportions. The Tory machine is using and abusing more and more of the government departments and administration for its own political purposes. . . . In the highway situation, instead of digging to the bottom of it, the government has moved heaven and earth to cover it up. . . . Four minor officials were charged and brought to trial immediately in an effort to calm the public furor. Even though they pleaded guilty and made full restitution, they all had to serve prison terms. Contrast that with the treatment of construction firms and their officials. The firms pleaded guilty, made restitution and got off with fines — because you can't put a construction firm in jail. . . . But the government dropped its charges against top officials for the fatuous reason, given in one case by the Crown Attorney, that the manager of the firm was "merely an employee."

For whatever reasons, Frost did not pursue the exchange but, as we shall see, he returned to it after the election. Meanwhile, the campaign drifted on uneventfully. The CCF had painstakingly produced its program, "Looking to the Future." There were many current problems that were in need of attention: renewed depression in agriculture, growing unemployment, disturbing conditions in the reform institutions, persistent deficits in the delivery of health services and educational problems, which had been shelved in the wake of the six-year-old Hope report.[2] The list was long, but it was overshadowed by the sensational issue of campaign funds. Inevitably, I became involved in the public debate, because it was perceived to be the only area where the Frost government was vulnerable.

I travelled the province, mostly in my own car, with two or three representatives of the Toronto dailies and Canadian Press. There was the usual series of local rallies to assist candidates. The campaign was a relatively modest one, backed by a budget that never reached five figures. Most formidable of all, public lethargy prevailed. If, as the familiar campaign dictum goes, the purpose of an election is to "scratch the voters where they itch," the simple fact was that the Ontario electorate wasn't itching anywhere. The result was a massive endorsement of the status quo.

Redistribution had enlarged the Legislature from ninety to ninety-eight seats. The Conservatives won eighty-four, up five; the Liberals eleven, up three; and the CCF, three, up one. The last remaining Communist member, Joe Salsberg, was defeated.

Fortunately, the one CCF gain was my own victory in York South. The home campaign had been difficult because most of the work had to be left to volunteers, while I travelled the province. But apparently I had established enough personal presence during the previous eighteen months, and they completed the job. When the votes were counted, I had won by 1,426. Notwithstanding pluralities as high as 8,000 in later years, in retrospect I suspect it was my greatest victory. Provincially, York South had returned to the CCF fold.

Even this minor progress — which I chose to present optimistically as a 50 per cent increase in seats — contained a setback. Bill Grummett, the veteran MPP from Timmins, who had held that seat since 1943, went down to defeat before a coalition of old party votes, because the Liberals did not field a candidate. The only northern representative was gone. Replacing him was a newcomer, Reg Gisborn, from Hamilton. Tommy Thomas retained the Oshawa seat. We were the lonesome trio, who, it was quipped around the Legislature, held their caucus meetings in a telephone booth.

5

Baptism of Fire: The Legislature, 1955 to 1958

On 9 June 1955 I became a member of the Ontario Legislature. Now it would be possible to participate in the debates, not simply follow them from a seat under the gallery. But there was no euphoric atmosphere. Understandably so. Legislative sittings were still months off, because the House was not scheduled to meet until the new year. Besides, the election results left no doubt that rebuilding the party remained the top priority.

The Legislature represented a gross distortion of the popular will. The Tories had polled less than half (48.5 per cent) of the popular vote, yet held 85 per cent of the seats; while the CCF, with 16.5 per cent of the vote held only 3 per cent of the seats. For the next four years, the reality was starkly apparent: nothing had changed; the opposition faced overwhelming numbers on the government benches. The CCF caucus of three was assigned an office which was quite pleasant, as compared with the rooms into which the larger caucuses were herded. One of its oak panelled walls had a mantelpiece and large mirror over an inoperative fireplace, which created a comfortable atmosphere.

While the Legislature did not meet in regular session until January, a special session was called for September 1955. Its purpose was to re-establish two select committees dealing with air pollution and a central registry for car liens which, appointed in the spring, had been wiped out with the calling of the election, and to establish a third one to examine the feasibility of toll roads. Apart from investigating these issues, the objective was to provide some activity for the swollen ranks of Tory backbenchers.

I raised privately with the premier whether the Legislature might sit for at least a few days, to consider important problems facing the province. Frost's initial response was negative, but a week later he called to offer a compromise: a brief debate, in which only the three party leaders would participate. It was better than nothing and the special session ran for two hours and twenty-three minutes. After electing A.W. (Wally) Downer as Speaker, the Legislature held a short debate. Liberal leader Farquhar Oliver contented himself with seeking clarification of government policy: first, on assistance to municipalities in coping with the growing unemployed, and second, on assurance of construction of the northern Ontario link of the gas pipeline (since the private developers had backed out of their trans-Canada commitment).

I picked up on both of these topics because jobs and economic development had always been major concerns of the party. My intervention drew fire from the cabinet. I argued that the absence of policy to deal with assistance to the unemployed stemmed from the Drew/Duplessis walkout from the 1945 tax conference, which left the issue unresolved. Premier Frost objected to that contention. I spoke critically of Provincial Treasurer Dana Porter's "amazing statement" that it would be unfair to bring natural gas into Ontario at a price sharply competitive with existing fuels. Notwithstanding the government's commitment to the free market, Porter defended their stand.

I then raised a third issue, health insurance, which was on the agenda for a forthcoming federal-provincial conference. Government spokesmen were needling the federal Liberals about their 1919 promise on this question. "I think it is time," I suggested, "to remember that in 1943 this government was elected on the promise of providing 'health coverage for all of us.' They are just as guilty of procrastination." It was my maiden speech, but the government had difficulty giving the traditional tolerant hearing. It was a rather quiet curtain-raiser on controversial issues which were to reverberate for years to come.

The brief session saw the curtain fall on the issue of Tory campaign funds. The government had been thrown on the defensive by the Highway Scandal — allegations of a linkage between the awarding of highway contracts and contributions to Tory campaign coffers. The former chief engineer in the department had been suspended for failure to cooperate with the provincial auditor in the investigation,[1] but before charges could be laid, he died under somewhat mysterious circumstances in a boating accident, and the chief witness was gone.

The issue of campaign funds had been revived during the election because of contributions from forest operators who had been granted timber limits in the riding of Renfrew South. The sitting Liberal MP, Dr. James D. McCann, accused the provincial Tory incumbent, Jim Dempsey, of receiving $8,000 from a forest operator. Dempsey frankly admitted it, to the embarrassment of Premier Frost, who repudiated him as the official Tory candidate. But Dempsey ran as an independent Conservative and won.

The special session of the Legislature produced a bizarre footnote to the whole affair. Dempsey rose to say that when the regular session convened in the new year he would make a full statement, giving his side of the story. But fate intervened: before the end of the year, he was dead. Thus a second witness to campaign funds was removed. The Tory party was luckier than it deserved.

Throughout the fall period, legislative work was confined to the select committees. With three committees there was one for each of us in the CCF caucus, mine being the investigation of toll roads — more accurately, highway financing. It was an interesting subject, which involved visits to the United States, as well as parts of Ontario where tolls were under consideration for bridges (Burlington) and causeways (Fort Frances). But for me, the committee was important for quite another reason: its chairman was John Robarts. He had languished on the back benches during his first term in the Legislature (1951-55), and only now was emerging from their obscurity. Frost had noted Robarts's abilities, but, concerned about his reputation for a free-wheeling lifestyle, put off for years his appointment to the cabinet. During the committee hearings and travels there was an opportunity to get to know Robarts personally. As chairman, he had a characteristically no-nonsense approach, not colourful, but practical. As a personality, particularly in off-duty hours, he was a warm and convivial character. I learned early in my legislative years that his public image as premier — a phlegmatic, even stuffy personality — was not the real John Robarts. He was a warm, companionable person, tolerant of others' views, capable of switching with ease from serious discussion of public issues to fun-loving, idle chatter. In the company of certain cabinet colleagues, he was a real "swinger."

Despite the relatively limited possibility of grappling with problems when the Legislature was not in session, the more active presence of the CCF did not escape attention. In a CBC provincial affairs broadcast on 28 November 1955 I quoted the observations of Don O'Hearn, a veteran newspaperman at Queen's Park, whose column was syndicated in dailies across the province:

> Unless the Liberal Party wakes up provincially, it is going to die a slow death in the wake of the CCF. . . . It is now nearly five months since the election, and there are no signs the shock of further defeat did anything substantial to awaken the party. For the last half dozen years the Liberals have been in a comatose state from which they have made some show of coming alive only at election times and other very rare intervals. In between these very occasional signs of life they probably have been as dead a group as politics in this province has ever seen. . . . The CCF, in contrast, is a very lively party from the viewpoint one gets of its operations here.

After reviewing the problems faced by the province, I concluded, "This range of problems merely points up the fact that Ontario has never been so desperately in need of a hard-hitting opposition . . . day in and day out. To the limit of our ability and resources, the CCF will provide that kind of opposition.''

Events soon conspired to provide a chance to do just that. The CCF had a tradition of championing the rehabilitation of offenders: it had been one of Agnes MacPhail's concerns while a member of the House of Commons and later in the Ontario Legislature. With everything else demanding attention, it had not been one of my top priorities, but that quickly changed.

The whole question had been simmering on the legislative back-burners for some years — so much so that a select committee had been appointed in the previous Legislature, and reported in 1954. The committee's assessment was unequivocal:

> Programs in institutions are generally inadequate. The Committee has examined them very carefully and the inescapable conclusion is that, with a few notable exceptions, Ontario reform institutions are not living up to their name . . . the majority of persons sentenced to Ontario institutions receive while incarcerated no effective stimulus to reform.

That report was produced by a committee the majority of whose membership was Tory.

With this documentation now in the public domain, it was not surprising that during the fall of 1955 I was approached by professionals in the field who were anxious for some legislative response. The issue came to a head over the Christmas holiday period.

A crisis had developed in the juvenile training school at Cobourg. There had been charges of brutality on the part of certain staff members, resulting in their dismissal. However, political intervention had secured their reappointment, and this created morale and discipline problems among the staff and the boys. For this the department sought to make Superintendent Bill Little the scapegoat. It was going to move Little out, but when this became known, a strong protest developed in the Cobourg community and forced the authorities to cover up with a "routine" four-way switch of superintendents within the system.

I was approached by responsible persons within the institutions, and provided with inside information regarding what was going on behind the scenes. I first commented publicly on 3 January 1956 in a speech to a CCF study group in Thistletown. I made the accurate, but inflammatory, assertion that "The military-minded approach of top officials of Ontario's Department of Reform Institutions has resulted in policies which are destroying, rather than creating, the possibility of reclaiming offenders. Restoration of corporal punishment for juveniles is a case in point."

Most countries of the western world had banned the use of corporal punishment for juveniles. During hearings of the select committee, the John Howard Society noted that from January 1948 the provincial training schools for boys had operated without corporal punishment. To cope with the developments at Cobourg, corporal punishment had been restored. It was an act "of desperation, defeatism and bankruptcy of policy," confirming that the policy-makers were living in the nineteenth century. "Cobourg is shocking proof of this," I concluded. "The situation went from bad to worse, with staff members slugging boys. It reached a point of crisis when one lad at Cobourg hanged himself a year ago last spring. Difficulties were compounded when dismissed staff members were reappointed over the superintendent's head because they were political favourites. Here was the rotten patronage system at its worst."

On 6 January I broadened the attack with revelations regarding another juvenile institution — the Girl's Training School at Galt. In the eighteen months she had been superintendent, Phyllis Bentley had destroyed one of Ontario's most promising experiments in reform institutions. Hers was a "spit and polish" disciplinary approach which conformed to the views of the core administration of the ministry. Seventeen staff members had left Galt in the previous year, many of them professionally trained personnel who had dedicated their lives to this kind of work. They left because they were "sickened

and saddened by what was happening until they could stand
it no longer.''

The *cause célèbre* at Galt was one twelve-year-old girl. Admittedly, she was a difficult case — a high-spirited native, an
undisciplined "child of the forest" from northern Ontario.
Under the regime at the Galt Training School she became a
lost cause. Attempts to subject her to rigid rules provoked a
rebellious spirit, which was met by Superintendent Bentley's
vengeful effort to crush her. This girl was placed in solitary
confinement for ninety-two days, permitted to leave only for
visits to the washroom, with meals often eaten from a tray
on the floor. Sometimes meals were even withheld as added
punishment.

When the confinement had gone on for two months, and
the child was growing more and more pallid, a rising sense
of indignation on the part of the staff, combined with the
urging of a medical doctor, persuaded the superintendent to
permit her occasionally to join in painting work parties. Eventually she was sent off to the Toronto Psychiatric Hospital
for observation. When she returned to Galt she was still a
problem, for which the superintendent had no other solution
than to impose another lengthy period in isolation. Not surprisingly, the child came to the conclusion that life was not
worth living, and attempted suicide. At this point the Galt
Training School gave up, and she was transferred to the Mercer
Reformatory in Toronto, where she appeared to fit in without
too much difficulty. During a visit to the institution on the
afternoon of my public statement, the superintendent informed
me that "this girl offers no more trouble than other girls in
her group.''

"No words are strong enough to condemn this kind of treatment of juveniles," I said. "A crime had been committed here,
a crime against humanity. Unless the conscience of the people of Ontario is aroused sufficiently to stir the government,
our reform institutions will continue to create criminals, rather
than correct them.''

On 16 January I took the issue to the people of Ontario
in a provincial affairs broadcast. Noting that the minister had
dismissed my statements as "mudslinging," and "based on

meagre and imaginary grievances from disgruntled ex-inmates and ex-employees," I countered that all my information had come from professionally trained, highly qualified people who had left our reform institutions because they were "sickened and saddened" by what was happening. I cast the whole issue in a broader context, pointing out that in the previous year there had been forty thousand people committed to one or another of our institutions, some for a short term, others for longer. That figure compared with only twenty-three thousand in Great Britain, with a population eight times that of Ontario.

The issue of reform institutions took off like a prairie fire. During January I released no fewer than ten public statements, and had countless interviews, commenting on the government's defence of the situation, and periodically pointing out where the minister's replies were "simply at variance with the facts." The controversy received such national coverage that CBC invited me to assume the "hot seat" on one of its meet-the-press radio programs.

If I was seeking a higher public presence for the CCF, I was certainly getting it. This baptism of fire was not only exciting, but reassuring. I was confident of my facts, though hard put to keep up with information from my informants, as new developments broke almost daily.

Needless to say, when the Legislature convened on 31 January 1956, my first regular session, the battle lines were drawn. It had not been my intention to storm into legislative politics, but I had no alternative. The official record of my three-hour reply to the throne speech reads like a dialogue, with relentless harassing from the government side of the House, including the premier and many of his cabinet. Simone witnessed the whole affair from a seat in the gallery, having resorted, so she confessed afterwards, to tranquillizers.

I discovered that in Parliament, when you've got the floor, you're in control. If you can cope with the barracking, you have the satisfaction that you are hitting the mark. The time for concern is when there's no reaction. After eighteen months of criticizing the government from afar on the hustings, there was now the opportunity of confronting it at a distance of only twenty feet, across the red carpet of the legislative chamber.

That was the atmosphere, but what of the substance of the debate? In my reply to the throne speech, I dealt almost exclusively with two topics. Premier Frost had raised once again the Renfrew South campaign funds issue, arguing that "the highest jury in the land" had rendered a verdict in the election, completely exonerating the government. That line of argument was too preposterous to ignore, so the whole episode was reviewed once again. The remainder of my speech picked up on the raging controversy over reform institutions. For the moment, it had preempted the political agenda. The government's reaction had been an uncompromising defence of the department, with no indication of a change in attitude, so it was necessary to review the past month's revelations in order to establish the case against their outmoded policies. That I attempted to do amid nearly two hours of interruptions, such as the Ontario Legislature had not witnessed in years.[2]

That debate was no sooner over than a further development escalated the controversy. In one of my earlier public statements I had contended that the basic problem in our reform institutions was that the department was at war with itself:

> The old and the new approaches to penal reform live side by side, unresolved, unintegrated, in open conflict with each other. The Minister gives voice to the modern approach, and that provides the window-dressing for public view. But the dominant personality in the department, shaping its day-to-day policies, is a relentlessly consistent exponent of the old punitive, almost purely custodial, approach to penal reform. In fact, the problem with our Department of Reform Institutions is that it has a bad case of schizophrenia. It is unable to do the job for which it is maintained.

My reference to "the dominant personality" in the department had been to Deputy Minister Colonel J. Hedley Basher. As had been quipped so often, he was well named for the job.

But Dr. F.B. van Nostrand, Director of Psychiatry and Neurology, assumed, because of my reference to schizophrenia, that I was referring to him. He wrote a long letter to the *Globe and Mail*, in which he purported to provide a psychiatric appraisal of me: that I was schizophrenic, the victim of "obsessive compulsive" behaviour, arising from guilt and self-condemnation because of a failure to do my duty during the war.

The *Globe and Mail*, understandably, returned the letter for revisions. Ostensibly in an effort to get my assistance, Dr. van Nostrand sent a copy to me. I received it just before going into the House for my throne speech debate, but did not have time to consider how it should be handled. However, by the next day, I had decided to raise it as a matter of privilege.[3] When I did, the record of the wrangling went on for six pages in Hansard. Government members, with the premier leading the pack, alternated between contending that I had no real question of privilege and demanding that I read the letter. Eventually I did — to a somewhat quietened House.

The premier gave me some fatherly advice about being willing to take this kind of attack with a sense of humour, combined with his familiar tactic of saying that if I had raised the matter with him privately, all would have been well. But he eventually got to the point: "I would think it is a matter for the honourable Minister of Reform Institutions. I question the advisability — even under stress or aggravation — of a civil servant writing such a letter. I agree with the honourable member's point of view in that regard. . . . I will discuss this with the honourable Minister of Reform Institutions, and perhaps with the gentleman in question, to direct that he exercise more discretion in the future."

Opposition leader Farquhar Oliver added to the fatherly advice — "the honourable member will learn as time goes on that you must expect these verbal blasts" — but then he added, "I would think, as the honourable Prime Minister has suggested, he should certainly talk this matter over with the honourable Minister in charge, because the civil servant in this instance, in my judgment, went far afield, and almost completely out of the field in which he was engaged."

Three days later the minister rose to make something of a government apology.[4] He defended his department, from Deputy Minister Colonel Basher down, assured every member of the fullest cooperation in connection with any problem they might have with his department, and then read a letter which he had written and van Nostrand's reply. Dr. van Nostrand apologized for offending "against the usual order of things," emphasized that he felt my attack on his division was "unfair and without any basis in fact," and "withdrew his remarks" about my war service.

The irony of the whole episode was that my attack had not been directed at him or his division — he was correct in acknowledging a certain paranoia — but rather toward Deputy Minister Basher, who had not been mentioned at all in the debate, but whom the minister had gone out of his way to defend.

The personal implications of the matter ended there. Years later I attended a farm meeting north of Toronto. In the audience was a gentleman farmer who came up afterwards and introduced himself. We had a friendly chat about current farm problems, with nothing but a fleeting reference to the past. It was Dr. van Nostrand.

Once the Pandora's box had been opened, revelation of deplorable conditions in the Ontario institutions continued for months. I had no difficulty in presenting case after case of mistreatment to undermine the government's defence. My efforts were greatly assisted as professionals entered the controversy.

On 16 February the Toronto branch of the Canadian Association of Social Workers wrote to Premier Frost, restating the basic problem: "The Ontario reformatories do not reform. . . . One third of them [offenders in the Guelph reformatory], have been there more than three times. This is failure, not reform. Why? There is no effective rehabilitation system for paroled or discharged inmates. . . . From the events of the past year it is clear that there is a strong conflict within the department between the punitive and reformative philosophies and practices. . . ." The association called for an authoritative independent investigation.

The letter provided solid professional backing for all I had said, but there was no government response, so I continued, throughout the session, to raise specific examples of the tragic consequences of the department's policies. These juvenile case histories, along with the documented evidence of confusion and incompetence within the department, established penal reform in the mainstream of politics, creating a climate for consideration of other aspects of the subject. In my public statements I had often contrasted Canada's practices with those in Britain, where the overwhelming majority of first offenders were not incarcerated, but put on probation, thereby permitting them and their families to continue life normally, at little cost to the state.

Probation came under the jurisdiction of Attorney General Kelso Roberts, but here, too, the government's attitude was backward. When I pressed him for an expansion of the probation services, he pleaded lack of funds: "We cannot do everything at once."[5] The folly of this stance was evident from the most cursory review of the statistics, which revealed that probation was not only less costly but more effective in rehabilitating offenders: three out of every four committed to Ontario institutions became repeaters, while almost three out of every four placed on probation stayed clear of the law from then on. Furthermore, while offenders were in penal institutions, the cost to society was reported to be $1,500 a year, but if they were on probation, with the current case load of probation officers, the cost was only $50. "In short," I pointed out, "the government refused to spend one dollar in order to save thirty."[6] The issue graphically symbolized Tory indifference.

If I have created the impression that penal reform was the only string to my bow, let me hasten to dispel it. It was the issue which had launched me into legislative politics, but it was rapidly accompanied by many others.

As the federal Liberals and provincial Tories jockeyed themselves into adopting hospital coverage, health insurance became a major item on the political agenda, where it remains to this day. As gas pipelines toppled the government in Ottawa, and forced resignations from the provincial cabinet (of which more later), energy became a political preoccupation, which it remains through to the 1980s. As Ontario expanded its secondary schools and university system, and moved slowly to establish greater equality between the public and separate school systems, educational questions were a topic of persistent debate. As agriculture slipped into a chronic depression, with recurring confrontations with the government, its problems were always before the Legislature. As a satisfactory resolution of federal-provincial relations seemed to be elusive, and gradually evolved into the constitutional crisis of the 1970s and 1980s, these issues commanded more and more legislative attention. And northern Ontario's sense of alienation and exclusion from a fair share of the province's prosperity was unrelieved.

Throughout my first years in the Legislature, I was involved in these major issues, which touched the lives of more Ontarians than did reform institutions. Rarely did a week pass during sessions without some, or all, of them hitting the floor of the Legislature, during question period, general debates or consideration of departmental estimates. It was through these issues that the party appealed to the people of Ontario, and sought to strengthen its position. Each one of them became a continuing theme in Ontario's postwar politics, illustrating the struggle for change in face of a government with overwhelming majorities, intolerant of opposition, and often insensitive to urgent needs of the people.[7]

I operated on the assumption that the CCF was the only real opposition and that the government had to be attacked on all fronts. My speeches in the throne debate or in response to the budget invariably ran up to three hours. With a caucus of three, it was a formidable task to cover the full range of government affairs. But my two colleagues brought a wealth of experience. Tommy Thomas was an experienced legislative member, and had sat on the Oshawa city council, so he covered municipal affairs as well as highways and public welfare. Reg Gisborn was elected while holding the presidency of Hamilton Steelworkers Local 1005, and was thoroughly familiar with labour and related matters. Through his connections with the steelworkers, he had both an interest in, and a knowledge of, the mining industry, so he was a natural for the departments of labour and mines. But there were twenty-two departments in all, and that left some eighteen falling to me — something which inspired Duncan MacPherson's cartoon in the Toronto *Star*, captioned "MacDonald's One-Man Band."

We had no staff for either public relations or research. To begin with, even clerical assistance was limited to calling for a stenographer from the Speaker's secretarial pool. But early in 1956 we were assigned a full-time secretary. Fortunately, there was a fourth corner in our office, so she could be fitted in with desk, typewriter and phone.

Actually, Ellen (Camnitzer) Adams was more of a fourth member of caucus than a secretary. She and her sister had escaped Nazi Germany during the war, joined the British women's army corps, and later emigrated to Canada, where I first knew her in a number of capacities at the CCF national office. Ellen was an extremely resourceful person. As caucus secretary, she became an indispensable member of the team. An indefatigable scrounger, she accumulated enough office supplies during that brief session to last us the rest of the year. More important, she established a working relationship with the press, the party, the trade union movement and members of the public who sought out caucus members. Gradually, she built a network of contacts in the civil service and the community at large which took her into an influential role in the municipal reform movement in Toronto. She ran unsuccessfully in a provincial by-election in St. George riding in 1973. When Arthur Maloney, Ontario's first ombudsman, staffed his agency, Ellen was appointed one of its divisional heads. She worked there until her untimely death in 1983.

The key to operations, during the heat of the session, was my filing system. It was quite simple: a file for each department. Into it went clippings gathered throughout the year, copies of any of my press releases dealing with relevant topics, along with background research papers, publicly available, or prepared by party members or persons in community organizations eager to have their interests raised in the Legislature. Ellen kept all this accumulation of material in working order, and the evening before a departmental estimate was scheduled, I took it home and absorbed its contents. Usually there was real policy substance; certainly there was plenty of ammunition for mounting an attack on the inadequacies of the administration.

A perusal of Hansard for those years indicates that rarely did my colleagues or I fail to present constructive policy alternatives, though they seldom received media coverage. By definition, news is normally considered to be something that is sensational, or at least exceptional. Political programs, albeit constructive ones, don't qualify, especially when being advanced by a third party. On the other hand, if there was even passing mention in an hour-long speech of some government maladministration or scandal, that was news which overshadowed everything positive that was said.

As a result, during these years the caucus, and I in particular, were perceived as being negative and muck-raking. That was the dominant image, though there were exceptions. On 15 February 1956, only two weeks into the first session, the Oshawa *Times Gazette* commented: "At least there is something like an opposition. . . . There had been some question how CCF Leader MacDonald would make out in the House. Last Thursday he gave the answer. He'll be OK."

It was not an assessment with which the government would have agreed. As my first year drew to a close, the St. Catharines *Standard*, another traditional Tory supporter, editorialized on 25 October 1956:

Incidentally, a good word on behalf of Mr. MacDonald. No matter how sour one may be about some of his thinking you have to agree he is doing a job. . . . He is at present the only effective political opposition in the province. He by himself undoubtedly has been more effective than the entire Liberal bench of 11 members. He works . . . and he does offer alternatives.

These exceptional observations revealed a recognition, usually not articulated, of the government's difficulty in coping with any real opposition, but there was no change in the official attitude. Any challenge to its position was deemed to be out of order. Those who feel they rule by divine right regard criticism as heresy.

Moreover, the legislative battles were enlivened by some in the Tory ranks who assumed the role of self-appointed defenders — of the party and the province — from a threat to their "values and traditions." Prominent among them was Robert Macaulay. Unlike others, whose interjections during debates were nothing more than juvenile political harassment, Macaulay mounted a formidable attack, which reflected the strong ideological antipathy of his colleagues. In later years we developed a mutual respect, but at the outset the gloves were off.

Macaulay sought to undermine the credibility of the CCF by attacks on the policies of the Saskatchewan government, the only CCF administration which, at that time, had been elected in Canada. In the legislative session of 1958, he launched a ten-point attack on the Saskatchewan educational system. When the news hit the prairies, an authoritative observer, the secretary of the Saskatchewan Teachers' Federation, commented that "Mr. Macaulay had achieved a perfect score. He was wrong on every count."

In speaking to the Young Progressive Conservatives, gathered at a leadership conference at Atherley, Ontario, Macaulay described Saskatchewan as "the bloated cow of human betterment." Breathing the heady air of Lake Couchiching, he went on to declare that "socialism" was destroying our capacity to save.

"That's strange," I countered, "because for the past month, in watching our economy fight off a depression with its 'buy now' efforts, I'd come to the conclusion that capitalism was doing its best to destroy the urge to save." And I added that when Mr. Macaulay got around to the question of unions, he wasn't content with being inaccurate; he became positively fatuous. He warned that socialism means an end to trade unions; that unions can't survive under "such a system. . . Of course, this is precisely the point which is worrying Mr. Macaulay. Canadian labour has just decided to help build a genuine people's party. For that reason, Mr. Macaulay knows the CCF is a real threat in Ontario. He recognized the real alternative to the Tories in power.''

Full as the agenda of Ontario's twenty-fifth legislative session must now appear, there was another feature which overshadowed everything else — a succession of scandals for which the Highway Scandal had been just a curtain-raiser.

It was certainly never my intention, or expectation, that my legislative activity would be dominated by consideration of scandals. Politics interested me chiefly as a means of improving the lot of ordinary people. Although standards of public morality, conflicts between private interests and public responsibilities, breaches of parliamentary procedure and the use (or abuse) of public institutions for partisan political purposes, are noteworthy, they are actually part of the overall process and don't deal directly with the basic objective of meeting people's needs. However, the situation left me with no alternative but to become involved. Having determined to fulfil the role of an opposition, I was faced frequently with circumstances which an opposition party could not ignore. To have done so would have been a shirking of responsibility.

These events, more than anything else, were indicative of the political mores of the day, and certainly had an impact on the political fortunes of the parties involved. I pause, therefore, in my chronological account of these years, to review what was perceived at the time as scandal-mongering.

My two colleagues during the Legislature — 1955 - 59 — Reg Gisborn *(left)* and Tommy Thomas *(right)*.

Duncan Macpherson's depiction of my "one-man" role in the Legislature.

Quite frankly, I wasn't as puzzled, nor Premier Frost as self-satisfied, during the NONG scandal as Macpherson suggested.

Three leaders — Leslie Frost, John Wintermeyer and myself — about 1959.

6
Scandals

The Northern Ontario Natural Gas (NONG) scandal was a small cloud on the horizon in the 1955 election. In the next four years it became a political tornado, toppling three cabinet ministers and dealing a devastating blow to the integrity of public administration.

These were the days when pipelines dominated the headlines and provoked storms of unprecedented intensity in the House of Commons. The groundwork had been laid: in May 1954 Trans-Canada Pipelines Limited had obtained a federal permit to remove 4.35 trillion cubic feet of natural gas from Alberta over a twenty-seven-year period. Later that year the company received leave from the Board of Transport Commissioners to build a pipeline to Montreal, with a spur over the border at Emerson, Manitoba. Early in 1955 Trans-Canada applied to the government for aid, having been unsuccessful in arranging the finances for the relatively easy first section across the prairies. C.D. Howe responded with a loan of $80 million.

However, Trans-Canada felt that the northern Ontario section would not be profitable, because of construction costs through a difficult terrain and a limited market because of a small population and scattered industry. They pleaded inability to build this link, and C.D. Howe obliged again by agreeing that the northern Ontario section would be built by a crown corporation. At this point Ontario was drawn in by its acceptance of one-third of the cost. In 1955 the Legislature formally authorized this commitment. However questionable the financing, and however acrimonious the debates at the federal level, the stage was set for an equally stormy succession of events in Ontario.

On 6 May 1954, a group of promoter-investors with a shrewd sense of the potential for future profits had incorporated the Northern Ontario Natural Gas Company (NONG), with a capitalization of $40,000, for which the initial promoters put up only a few hundred dollars. In addition, very generous rights were offered to shareholders. The potential for pyramiding of profits was nothing short of dazzling, particularly when the value of NONG stock rose from an original five cents to a high of $26 in 1957.

In a masterpiece of understatement, Kelso Roberts, who was attorney general at the time, commented years later in his reminiscences, "some of those associated with the Trans-Canada project made sizeable fortunes and when the Borden Commission on Energy reported to the government, it condemned such practices in public financing of government projects."[1]

Gordon McLean, nephew of Mines Minister Philip Kelly, received a 40 per cent share of the original venture, although he contributed nothing but the idea which, he told his associates, had come from his uncle. Kelly received 50 per cent of his nephew's holdings, although his name never appeared as stockholder or in any trading transaction.

The NONG promoters lobbied vigorously with the federal Board of Transport Commissioners to make sure that the chosen route went through their territory — eastward from the Lakehead by way of Kapuskasing, instead of down the Lake Superior shoreline. When that had been achieved, they negotiated a contract with Trans-Canada for natural gas delivery from the west. With both contracts in their pocket, they had a valuable asset for seeking local franchise rights with industries and municipalities along the route. To achieve their ends, they arranged a vast network of people at the legislative, party and municipal levels, kept together through free-wheeling distribution of NONG stock, at prices enabling quick profits.

With a fuller account now available in Kelso Roberts's autobiography, we know that he was concerned about the irregular financial dealings of the NONG promoters.[2] While campaigning throughout northern Ontario in the federal election of 1957, he learned that candidates were critical of NONG transactions. On his way home, he was shown a Bracebridge newspaper, carrying a paid announcement of a public offering of the stocks and bonds of NONG. He immediately phoned the chairman of the Securities Commission, and subsequently wrote Premier Frost on 12 June 1957, expressing his concerns. They centred primarily on the technical, but important, point of permitting non par value (NPV) shares (which he subsequently banned through an amendment to the statute), and on the fact that, in their prospectus, the promoters had not revealed their contract with Trans-Canada, which was a powerful advantage in seeking local distributing franchises. In short, the NONG directors had not maintained a proper distinction between their roles as directors and promoters.

Roberts's concerns went further. "I was at a loss to understand why the provincial secretary's office would have allowed such splits (amounting to 500 for one) without clear-cut and justifiable reasons." In his letter to the premier he stressed "the peculiar situation as to the past . . . with possible serious political repercussions for the future."

The attorney general was more prophetic than he knew. After the bill authorizing Ontario's participation in the northern Ontario section of the Trans-Canada line, Premier Frost contended under my questioning that he raised the potential conflict of interest with each member of his cabinet.[3] His instructions were that, "under no circumstances, either by themselves or by their agents or by any other way, were they to have anything to do with pipeline stock." That instruction was repeated later by the premier, and on another occasion by Malcolm McIntyre, secretary to the cabinet.

In July 1957 Philip Kelly resigned as minister of mines. From a number of sources I had picked up information indicating that his resignation had been brought about because of involvement in the pipeline development. On 10 March 1958, I first raised the issue in the House. Frost's reaction was one of righteous indignation. He accused me of being a "master of insinuation and innuendo." He called me ungentlemanly for suggesting that pipeline profiteering was "close to home" at Queen's Park. In the seductive manner which was his hallmark, he said that if I had just asked him about Kelly's resignation, or whether any cabinet member was implicated, he would have told me. (His stance should be considered in light of a *Globe and Mail* report four months later that Kelly's resignation was "a cut and dried affair. . . . The Premier had Mr. Kelly's resignation typed out when the minister arrived in Mr. Frost's office. It was simply a case of Mr. Kelly reading the letter and signing it."[4])

James Maloney, the member for South Renfrew, then entered the fray, daring me to repeat my comments outside the House, and offering his legal services to Kelly for launching a libel suit. I repeated the statements outside, and nothing happened — for a very good reason. Two days later, Kelly publicly confirmed that "one of the main reasons for his resignation was his family connections with the pipeline deals."

Throughout the unfolding of events, Frost made a virtue of necessity by admitting only what had been revealed by someone else. But in April 1958, the government's case was badly shaken. A Toronto *Star* reporter had bought a NONG share and exercised his rights to examine the list of stockholders. On the list he found Colonel William Griesinger, the minister of public works, who held stock in defiance of the premier's repeated instructions. With that revelation, Griesinger resigned.

There was a second name in the *Star*'s sensational revelation: Liberal leader John Wintermeyer. When the *Star* called Wintermeyer, informing him that the news of his holdings was out, and asking his comment, he replied, "Oh my God, I'll have to think about that. . . . I'll call you back when I've thought about it." When he called back, he stated that he had bought the shares in his own name, and through his bank.

From the time I first raised the NONG affair in March 1957, I had repeatedly called for a judicial inquiry. In order to keep the situation under control, the premier decided on a piecemeal approach — on the one hand an investigation by himself, and on the other a tribunal of three appointed by the attorney general.

Although Kelso Roberts had been extremely concerned about the highly questionable practices of the NONG promoters, to the point of alerting the premier, he did not proceed with this inquiry until a year later, long after Kelly's resignation and after the storm broke, following the *Star*'s revelation of another minister's involvement. Even stranger, though he had been critical of the inadequate prospectus accepted by the Securities Commission, two of the three people appointed to conduct the inquiry were previous officials of that commission.

In July 1958 two other developments kept the controversy alive. Kelso Roberts made a statement concerning the report prepared by his three appointees. However, neither the report itself, nor the transcript of the private hearings, was made available. Moreover, the attorney general said that the report documented Wintermeyer's involvement as one of stockholders. Obviously, the government tactic was to involve the Liberals in the whole affair in order to inhibit their criticisms.

Wintermeyer assisted them in their strategy by changing his explanation with every revelation, just as the government had done. In his initial statement, in May, Wintermeyer said he "didn't buy his stock on any tip he had picked up at Queen's Park." Now he admitted "that Kelly had mentioned the project to me and I had ordered some shares." Kelly subsequently explained that he had included Wintermeyer to compensate him for losses on an earlier bad tip he had given him on the stock market!

Further, Wintermeyer stated that, "After I became leader of the party and *before the pipeline scandal* broke I made immediate arrangements to dispose of my holdings" (my emphasis). But he became leader in April, and declared he was disposing of his holdings only after the *Star*'s revelations in May, months after the NONG scandal broke.

Also in July, another development added further fuel to the fire when the Toronto *Star* reported that Clare Mapledoram, minister of lands and forests, had also received a block of promotional stock, purchased through George Durica, his brother-in-law. So he resigned — the third cabinet minister to go.

For the rest of the year, the scandal remained unresolved. Then, in an interview carried in the Toronto papers on 6 and 7 February 1958, Kelly stated that if the record of shareholders were examined, "you might come up with some very interesting stuff." Further, that "if I stood in the House today, I could back a few of them off their chairs."

Kelso Roberts had insisted that the investigation of the stock transactions was an internal inquiry by his department, and its report would not be made public. But the government bowed to the growing public criticisms, by releasing both the report and the 1,540-page transcript of the hearings. This was done by tabling them in the Legislature on 12 February 1959, at which time Roberts reviewed the situation in a two-hour address.

Typical of the news coverage was Harold Greer's front-page story in the *Globe and Mail*, which presented the background of the company and the stock transactions under a heavy black headline: "Seven Made $2,500,000 Profit." Those seven insiders were Ralph K. Farris, president of NONG, who made a profit of $300,000 on his original seventy-five charter shares, and at the time of public issuance on 4 June 1957 held 15,000 of the 500-for-one split shares, as well as a controlling interest in Charter Oil Limited of Calgary, which held 37,000 shares; Spencer Clark of Seattle, a NONG director, who made a profit of $317,965 and still held 6,584 shares; A.D. McKenzie, president of the Progressive Conservative Association of Ontario, who sold blocks of shares at a market value which netted $87,000 and still retained 4,300 shares; Beverley Matthews, financial organizer for the national Progressive Conservative Party who sold some shares for a profit of $69,036 and still retained 5,000; as well as Gordon McLean, who received a 40 per cent interest in the venture before the 500-for-one split, half of which he held for his uncle, Philip Kelly.

The overall conclusion in the *Globe and Mail* account was: "While raising their eyebrows at the ethics of many of the things done, the investigators found no legal wrong-doing beyond those charges which had already been laid and processed in the courts. In particular, they found no evidence of bribery or corruption at any level of government, municipal or provincial." As subsequent developments proved, it was not a valid conclusion.

In tabling the report, the attorney general stated "there can be no shadow of doubt that it is complete. . . . I know of no stone left unturned *if one can believe* the sworn evidence of those who know the story" (my emphasis). In retrospect, it was a significant qualification. However, it was the government's fervent hope that the episode would now be closed: "I think now this House should get on with constructive and useful business," Roberts declared.

It was a vain hope. Top Conservatives, in both the party and the cabinet, were involved. Details of the stock transactions raised as many questions as they answered. The investigation had been limited to the promotional stage, prior to the public listing of NONG on 4 June 1957. It had no power to subpoena key persons in Vancouver in connection with the critical account of the Convesto Company, where 14,000 shares had been deposited at favourable prices. And, other than Twin-City Gas at the Lakehead, examination of NONG's relationship with other local gas distribution companies had been excluded from the terms of reference.

The debate on the report was called for 18 March 1959. It proved to be the most memorable of all my years in the Legislature. I had carefully read not only the report itself, but the transcript upon which it was based. Travelling through the North, I had picked up bits of information, some of it gossip, some of it solidly documented. The transcript proved to be a veritable gold mine of detail, which confirmed the rumours and gave a much clearer picture of what had gone on behind the scenes in the promotion of the company. I prepared a lengthy analysis.

The debate opened with a brief statement from Attorney General Roberts. He noted that the investigators had been instructed to consider any possible infraction of the Securities Act, the Criminal Code or the Corporations Act. Certain charges had been laid, and they had resulted in fines of $150 for the company and $500 each for Ralph Farris and Spencer Clark, top officers of the company, for selling stock to the public before qualifying before the Securities Commission. But, Roberts emphasized, there had been no evidence of bribery or corruption at any level of government, municipal or provincial. He added: "I do not believe that there is anything further or material . . . in relation to this troublesome matter other than these things which have already been dealt with, I think, in a very thorough and impartial manner. . . . I say that the time has come for us to finally dispose of this."

Liberal leader Wintermeyer spoke briefly. It was a defensive effort, indicating conclusively, as the Toronto *Star* had commented editorially, that he was "gagged" by his personal involvement. In justifying his call for a full and complete inquiry, he dealt only with the fact that testimony had not been secured from A.D. McKenzie, who had been on holiday during the initial hearings and was not subsequently called, on the excuse that some of the matters were before the courts.

Wintermeyer's point, though isolated, was very valid. Nothing was more illustrative of the government's determination to hide the truth than the handling of McKenzie's involvement. The matters before the court were breaches of the Securities Act, under which top NONG officers were charged, convicted and given inconsequential fines. But there were other matters which the inquiry was supposed to investigate, such as whether stock had been made available at favourable prices to persons in the provincial and municipal governments. Moreover, the hearings were held *in camera*, so that McKenzie's testimony could have been taken without any breach of the jurisdiction of the courts. Because of his position in the party, and his personal involvement, McKenzie would then have been able to provide key evidence, rather than have it dribble out for years to come. This was, as I had charged, another instance where the inquiry "stopped at precisely the point where it should have been most intensive."

My contribution filled twenty-two pages of Hansard,[5] and was replete with interruptions, mostly from the premier and the attorney general. I documented from the transcript that three of the key witnesses — Farris, Kelly and McLean — had given false witness under oath. That produced repeated calls

of "What are you trying to prove — that everybody's a liar?"
I argued that the hard-nosed businessmen involved — Farris,
Clark and others — had bowed to McLean's original demand
for half the charter stock (with the compromise of 40 per cent),
because they knew that his uncle, Philip Kelly, was involved.
And I added: "In any case, starting from the one unrevealed
contact with the cabinet, it is astounding to piece together the
story and see to what extent the promoters ultimately involved
others in the cabinet, the honourable finance critic of the
Liberal party, the top echelons of the Tory party, and, in one
very interesting instance a key person at the local level of the
Liberal party."

Farris had testified that McKenzie had acted as a consultant or adviser. "He had an excellent knowledge of the territory and the people in it. I personally, and Mr. Clark, were
very ignorant of the people and the towns, what made them
tick, the local wishes and the needs. Mr. McKenzie was able
to provide us with a lot of guidance."

I commented:

How admirably equipped he was to do the job! For he
is, as honourable members of this House well know, top
man in the Tory machine, the man who controls the slush
funds of the party, the man who is so powerful that it
has been suggested that new cabinet appointments have
to pass the acid test of his approval before the honourable
Prime Minister can act. . . .

This picture now becomes clear. The services of top
men in the Tory party were available to Northern Ontario
Natural Gas — Mr. Kelly from within the cabinet and
Mr. McKenzie from the top echelons of the Tory party.
The shocking thing is that those services were available
for a return which made each a much richer man.

The key person at the local level of the Liberal party was
Cy Young. He was the man who had engineered a coalition
between the Liberals and Conservatives in 1955 in the ridings
of Cochrane South and Temiskaming, as a result of which the
Liberals did not run candidates, leading to the defeat of CCF

House leader Bill Grummett. Farris had testified: "Mr. Cyril Young was sort of an old man of the north. . . . We put him on the payroll at, I think, $10,000 a year to continue as an employee of the company to keep that liaison and friendly relationship between the northern communities and our company. He was effective at it in a quiet and old man's sort of way."

In his testimony, Clark indicated that Young had been a director of the company at one time, but had been asked to resign at the annual meeting in February 1957. Why? "Well, we found, quite frankly, Mr. Young somewhat embarrassing. He had gone out and made statements to the press . . . without first clearing them with us. . . . He is an elderly gentleman and, in my opinion, somewhat senile, who, to paraphrase it, mounts his horse and rides off in all directions at once without thinking very clearly about the course. . . . His unfortunate qualities overrode his good ones."

Among the significant points in the testimony, I pointed out, was that the Royal York Hotel was abuzz among politicians with gossip about NONG stock and its availability from Kelly. Cabinet ministers Griesenger and Mapledoram, Liberal leader Wintermeyer, PC Association president A.D. McKenzie all knew of Kelly's involvement in NONG during the promotional years. "Every one of those people asked for the stock," Kelly testified.

In spite of this, when I first accused the premier on 10 March 1958 of having forced Kelly's resignation from the cabinet because of his involvement in the pipeline development, he flatly denied that this was the case. He said he knew nothing of Kelly's role in NONG. If that were true, there were two cabinet ministers who could have spoken up privately, if not publicly. Besides, the leader of the opposition could have risen and enlightened the premier. The silence of these three men persisted when the premier rose a second time on 11 March, and a third time the next day, to repeat that Kelly was not involved. Ironically, the man who publicly informed the premier a few days later was Kelly himself.

But in view of all of the evidence available from the inquiry transcript, I stressed that it was inconceivable that the premier did not know, given the further factor of his relationship with A.D. McKenzie. As president of the Progressive Conservative Association McKenzie ran the political machine. He and Frost were intimate colleagues who had breakfast together in the Royal York Hotel most mornings each week, when the premier was kept abreast of the situation within the party and, no doubt, vice versa.

Kelso Roberts defended the government, without reservation, during the debate. But ten years later in his memoirs he wrote, "Previous to the authorization of the investigation, it was common knowledge that Mr. Kelly had an interest through his nephew, Gordon McLean, in a substantial quantity of shares in NONG. These shares had been held in nominee accounts and some of them had been sold by Kelly in personal deals between himself and the persons concerned."

Since McKenzie himself had been the recipient of a block of shares, it is inconceivable that he would not have alerted the premier of the situation, particularly after Frost's repeated contention to the contrary. The premier, as well as others involved in this sorry affair, simply did not level with the Legislature or the public.

The evidence was equally conclusive in relation to another key issue under investigation: whether stock had been used to "sweeten up" officials of northern communities with whom NONG was negotiating for local distribution franchises. Quite apart from the possibility of a NONG promoter making his own, or company, shares available as a "sweetener," or making available the rights to shares which had accompanied all the stock splits, the major concern was the 14,000 shares which had gone to the Convesto account in Vancouver at the preferred price of $2.50 per share, far below the then current market value. The inquiry did receive evidence that these shares were "on behalf of clients," but it did not pursue the matter to find out who the clients were.

Once again, Kelso Roberts clarifies this aspect of the hearings in his memoirs.[6] John McGraw, a former president of the Vancouver Stock Exchange and head of the Convesto Company, was not a witness who could be subpoenaed, and he was not willing to come voluntarily. However, he did say that if the commissioners wanted to question him, they could do so through the British Columbia Superintendent of Brokers. Incredibly, Roberts stated that, in the view of the commissioners, because of their "exhaustive inquiry . . . the evidence of McGraw was not necessary for the purposes of the investigation." Yet the inquiry reported that there was no evidence of bribery and corruption through stock distribution to municipal officials along the northern Ontario route. There was no evidence because they didn't seek it. Once again, the inquiry had given up at precisely the point where it was on a hot trail.

If more evidence were needed for anybody who cared to read the inquiry transcript, it was contained in testimony in relation to Twin City, a Thunder Bay local distribution company. The inquiry's terms of reference excluded any investigation into local distribution franchises, but some of it crept in with regard to Twin City because of that local company's relationship as a subsidiary of NONG.

In the early stages of the battle for local franchises, Twin City, covering the area of the former twin cities of the Lakehead, was in a gloves-off battle with NONG. Throughout the rest of northwestern Ontario, NONG finally won out, but there was strong sentiment at the Lakehead for a locally owned company. Twin City, notably through its president, F.E. Shaw, catered to this sentiment and appeared to triumph in getting public support, except that it was finally revealed that NONG actually held a controlling interest in Twin City. Before the commission, Shaw's performance was one of evasion, aided and abetted by his lawyer, Gavin Young, who was a director of Twin City. His testimony revealed, however, that Twin City's posture as a locally owned company had been one of deliberate deception of the Lakehead public.

Sudbury was another example. The Sudbury area was of paramount importance, because it was the prospective consumer of 50 per cent of NONG's distribution, due to its heavy industrial usage. There was considerable support for a locally owned company, although it was opposed by Mayor Leo Landreville. NONG's president Farris devoted a great deal of personal attention to securing the Sudbury franchise. His efforts, combined with the cooperation of Landreville, resulted in passage of an enabling by-law on 16 August 1956. Three members of council were in bitter opposition, including Joe Fabbro, who later became mayor when Landreville was appointed a judge.

I visited Sudbury in 1959, examined the city records and interviewed Mayor Fabbro. He was surprised by my detailed knowledge of all that had gone on. I explained that it was readily available in the transcript and report of the hearings. In the course of our discussion, he mentioned that on one occasion Landreville had complained that he had sold his NONG stock too early, and missed a great deal of potential profit. That, of course, was precisely what I wanted to confirm.

While not mentioning Landreville in the debate, I said: "I have personally been told by many reputable persons in Sudbury that Northern Ontario Natural Gas stock was distributed in the area. Furthermore, at least one of those involved in the franchise battle boasted that he had made a great deal of money. . . . It is time that the facts were sifted from rumour in this situation." Interestingly, in his reply, Attorney General Roberts named Landreville: "I have found no evidence at all that indicates to me that the honourable Mr. Justice Landreville had, in any way, any improper connection with this company at any stage of the proceedings."

The remainder of the debate took off in an orgy of sustained verbal violence. Roberts contended that I "had made attacks of the most vicious and unwarranted nature on the former leader of the opposition (Farquhar Oliver), on Mr. Cyril Young, on the Prime Minister. . . ." He succeeded in bringing the Liberals on side, for they accused me of character assassination, despite the fact that all of the evidence I had presented was quoted from the transcript of the inquiry hearings.

Roberts climaxed with the reassertion that "I do not think that I would in any way be doing my duty by attempting to investigate any single person, further than what has happened now on the evidence. . . . What is more, I would not be worthy of this office if I were to fail my duty, and I stake my reputation on that statement."

As for Premier Frost, I am certain he had never read the transcript, so that much of the evidence was new to him. When caught in an embarrassing situation, habitually he threw a political tantrum which, inevitably, received the news coverage, rather than the substance of the case against him.

But what a tantrum! It rambles on for pages in Hansard. The premier became increasingly unparliamentary in his language, inveighing at me with "shut your mouth," "close your trap," "get up and don't sit chittering like a pig in trough." Or, at another point, "let him yammer away, and get down in the sewer and get himself covered with it. . . . All he does is run around this province making cowardly insinuations and half truths and using twisted evidence and things of that sort. . . ."

"I, for one," concluded the premier, "feel that this matter has been thoroughly, fairly and impartially investigated and the full facts have been given to the people."

Interestingly, the premier rose before the orders of the day at the next sitting to say that when he got home that night, the "leader of the opposition" (his wife) told him he had gone too far. It was in the nature of an apology, implied, if not explicitly stated.

The NONG scandal is a long and complicated one. It covered five years, from 1954 to 1959, with subsequent revelations, as we shall see, extended into the 1960s. "The whole affair, including the government's handling of it," I stated during the debate, "represents a most disturbing revelation of the moral depths to which public and business life have sunk."

Paralleling the NONG scandal for a brief period during the 1957 session was another of a totally different kind — revealing the willingness of the government to breach traditional parliamentary principles in order to have its own way.

At issue was Bill 25, An Act Representing the Township of Scarborough. The background can be briefly put. While the Township of Scarborough was expanding rapidly, a number of developers had contracted to install oversize watermains. If the capital outlay were to be debentured, rather than applied against the mill rate for the year, the law required that the projects be approved by the Ontario Municipal Board *before the work began*. Otherwise, payment could not be legally made.

The Scarborough bill covered projects as far back as 1952, on which developers had proceeded, often with oral approval of municipal officers, in order to capitalize on the booming markets. There was no doubt, as irate citizens pointed out, that the cost of the watermains had been included in the price of the land paid by subdividers, and, in turn, passed on to the builders, and ultimately to the homeowners. There was no evidence that the developers had sought payment a second time, yet that is precisely what Bill 25 was designed to provide.

Questionable as the whole purpose of the bill was, even more questionable was what happened once it reached the Legislature. Scarborough Township had been advised to pursue this route for further payment by its solicitor, H.E. Beckett, the Tory member for York East. Secondly, the bill was introduced by R.E. Sutton, Tory member for Scarborough East, who held a mortgage for $375,000 on a property, previously his farm, which he had sold to Green Cedars Development Corporation, which would share in the $400,000 authorized by the bill. Further, Harold Fishleigh, Tory member for Woodbine, was president and part owner of Keystone Realties, another company that would share in payments authorized by the bill for which he voted.

My contention in the Legislature was simply that one member, Beckett, in his capacity as solicitor, had advised Scarborough council to seek this private legislation authorizing a second payment, for which there was no moral claim; and even more objectionable, that two other members of the Legislature, Sutton and Fishleigh, had sponsored and/or voted for a bill, from which they would privately gain financially. Such a conflict of interest was in clear violation of long-standing parliamentary practice. My position drew support from the Toronto *Telegram* on 29 March 1957: "The allegation that three members are interested, however indirectly, in the passage of the bill on which they have voted, is not to be ignored . . . this is a matter that should not be dropped in silence."

The *Telegram* need not have feared. On a motion made by Beckett, and seconded by Sutton, the allegation was referred to the Committee on Elections and Privileges. With dispatch, the committee met on 2 April. The accused members were defended by distinguished counsel, such as Joseph Sedgwick, Q.C. None of the charges regarding the financial interests of the members was disputed; indeed, they were all acknowledged. Yet the committee, eleven of whose fifteen members were Conservatives, brought in a report which stated in defiance of the acknowledged facts, that "Mr. MacDonald failed to substantiate the charges made by him."

When the report was made to the House, I reasserted that "my allegation is proved to the hilt, that these two members acted with impropriety, contravening Standing Rule 16 by voting for a bill, which will benefit companies in which they have a pecuniary interest." I noted the Toronto *Star* had editorialized that the situation merited a judicial probe, and I quoted Conservative leader George Drew, in dealing with a comparable situation in the House of Commons, that "the whole subject has now become a simple but fundamentally important question of principle." Further, it was "not only our right but our duty to act as custodian of the established principles."

Premier Frost characterized my statement as "scandalous." In fact, it was the government's conduct which was scandalous, for it revealed a striking contrast. In the Scarborough scandal the government moved with alacrity — it was all dealt with within two weeks — by securing a whitewash report from the Committee on Elections and Privileges. But later, in the NONG scandal, when Kelly cast a shadow over every member of the Legislature with his statement that if the record of shareholders was examined "you might come up with interesting stuff," and that if he "stood in the House today [he] could back a few of them off their chairs," the government chose to ignore his statements. Indeed, on my motion to bring Kelly before the bar of the House (he had already resigned his seat), no action was taken. If charges were made by someone in the opposition, they were pursued with vigour, but if they were made by somebody on the government side, adding to its embarrassment, they were studiously ignored.

Scandals came in all shapes and forms. The Niagara Parks Commission (NPC) provided ample proof of that. In 1958 trouble erupted when Chairman Charles Daley, who was also minister of labour, ousted George Inglis, eight times mayor of Niagara Falls, from membership in the commission. In the resulting charges and counter-charges, Inglis contended that the commission's operations were patronage-ridden. I viewed the whole matter as a local tempest-in-a-teapot, until contacted by Walter Haufschild, former deputy chief of the NPC police force, who provided me with documentary proof of a cover-up of criminal offences.

When I investigated the situation, I found a dazzling array of questionable business practices. There was, for example, frequent non-tendering of contracts to firms in which the commissioners had an interest. Chairman Daley had been "most annoyed" with a financial statement of expenditures exceeding income, and demanded a new statement showing a favourable balance. The luxurious refectory, ostensibly available to entertain distinguished guests, had become, with its free meals and well-stocked liquor cabinet, a private club for commissioners, their families and friends.

When the Legislature opened on 1 February 1959, I documented an added charge: that Chairman Daley was in serious conflict of interest, having purchased land that had been NPC property; having sold produce from his farm to the commission; and having had work done by NPC personnel on his private property during working hours.

Once again, the public outcry forced the government to respond, but it did so in such a manner as to keep the situation well contained. Details of the NPC operations were referred to the Public Accounts Committee, but Premier Frost chose to construe the charges against Daley as a reflection on the chairman's integrity, and referred them to the Committee of Elections and Privileges.

Subsequent developments were nothing short of a travesty. The Conservative majority on the Public Accounts Committee refused to call key witnesses, either George Inglis or Walter Haufschild, who had evidence on the cover-up of criminal actions. Daley confessed that he had learned for the first time in 1955 (more than a decade after he entered the cabinet) that it was improper for parks commissioners to be doing business with firms in which they had a private interest. Five years later, however, when Commissioner Fred Cairns was queried by a Toronto *Star* reporter, he responded, "I might have been connected with Niagara Trading when it did business with the commission. What's wrong with that?"[7]

On the question of tendering, Daley claimed that "if a job was cheaper by calling tenders, then tenders would be called; if cheaper without tenders . . . firms considered best capable would be called in"[8] — a frank admission of an open door to patronage.

On the cover-up of criminal actions, the committee simply refused to hear evidence, so I had to present it in the Legislature — the case of a man who stood "completely nude before several small girls." When the officer in charge permitted the man to go, Haufschild protested, and subsequently reported the incident in a letter to Daley, who testified that he was so disgusted he wouldn't even have it in his files. He destroyed it.

Having refused to hear key witnesses, the committee's report, as planned from the outset, exonerated the commission. Not a single opposition amendment of the report was accepted by the Conservative majority. "This is not a report of the Public Accounts Committee," I asserted, "It is a whitewash report of the government majority on the committee. Therefore, I recommend that, as long as the tyranny of the government is going to be used to thwart full investigation of alleged maladministration and malfeasance, this legislature should adopt the practice of referring such matters to an independent inquiry."

But worse was still to come from the committee. The pertinent details under review were that, while Daley was NPC chairman, certain lands were sold in breach of commission policy not to sell parks property, but to add it to the system; that the original sale was to one Arthur Schmon, a long-time business friend of Daley who, three years later, sold them to the chairman. The transaction was not at arm's length, so much so that Daley had no lawyer to protect his interests, but relied completely on the vendor's agent, who even paid the land transfer tax on Daley's behalf. Altogether, a very cosy deal. Notwithstanding this undisputed evidence, the committee concluded that there had been no collusion. However, the Liberal and CCF members insisted that Daley had been highly indiscreet and their view was included in the report. This was totally unacceptable to Premier Frost who stated that he "would not be prepared in any way to accept anything less than practical unanimity."[8]

The result was a striking example of unilateral action, in total disregard of normal procedures. In effect, the premier rejected the report and the House was given no opportunity to consider the conclusions of its committee. Within a matter of hours, the premier informed the Legislature that he had redirected the whole matter to a royal commission headed by Judge Ian M. Macdonnell. Having failed to get complete exoneration from the appropriate legislative committee, he sought it from an inquiry, ostensibly independent and beyond reproach, because it was headed by a judge.

The most incredible aspect of this irregular procedure was that the premier got the complete exoneration he sought. Judge Macdonnell's report was an unashamed endorsation of virtually everything that had happened. He concluded that, despite the evidence, there was not even the appearance of a conflict of interest in Daley's acquisition of the park land. His report contained contradictions, such as (on page 13), "on the evidence before me, I cannot escape the conclusion that the sale was an advantageous one, that a fair price was obtained, and that the law had been complied with." Yet, three pages later, he summarized, "I find this transaction was also a desirable and advantageous one for the commission, although no independent appraisals were obtained. It was, however, illegal, or at least irregular, at the time it was carried out, as it was not approved by order-in-council." After conceding the irregularity of the original sale to Schmon, the judge then rationalized: "but in view of the validating order-in-council [seven years later!], this aspect would now appear to be academic."

Judge Macdonnell went further. "I do not think, however, that any serious blame could be attached to any member of the commission, and in particular to the chairman, a layman, for overlooking the technicality. . . ." The report was a classic in sophistry. I commented in the Legislature, "This kind of reasoning is alarming. . . . Ignorance of the law is no excuse on the part of even the layman. . . . Since when is failure to live up to the law a 'mere technicality?' This is the kind of observation we have come to expect from public officials caught in breach of the law, rather than from a royal commissioner investigating an alleged breach. . . ."

Having called for an independent judicial inquiry to deal with such matters as the only escape from "the tyranny of a government majority" on legislative committees, I was left somewhat defenceless in responding to such a report. But, fortuitously, I was assisted by two distinguished Torontonians. In the CBC's *Let's Find Out* series on 28 February there was a panel discussion on the issue of public morality. John Saywell, distinguished professor of Canadian history, observed: "Royal commissions very seldom seem to find out anything that is in sharp contradiction to what the people who have appointed the commission have already decided ought to be found out." Malcolm Robb, a well-known Conservative lawyer, was even more forthright: "When a judge becomes a judge, for all practical purposes he ceases to be a politician . . . but you will never get him appointed on the matter in which the government appointing him is genuinely concerned that something will be brought out in its disfavour."

There is frequent evidence in later years that this assessment of the role of royal commissions was unduly harsh. But at the time, it was entirely accurate. Judge Ian M. Macdonnell had served his political masters admirably. Ironically, Charles Daley put it well. By way of testimony in his own defence before the inquiry, he testified that, after the 1943 election, Premier George Drew had appointed him chairman and told him to go ahead and pick his commission. He picked a circle of friends who used public property as a private club. Unwittingly, Premier Frost was even more descriptive. In professing not to be disturbed by the loose business practices of the Niagara Parks Commission, he likened it to a family business which is often run in a relaxed way. It certainly was a family business — a Tory family business.

The scandals, and subsequent inquiries, reveal dramatically the depths to which public morality had sunk in Ontario politics. During these years the integrity of even judicial inquiries was publicly questioned by responsible persons. Standard practices of public administration and time-honoured parliamentary procedures were openly breached. Power corrupts, and certainly the big Tory majorities of the 1950s came close to corrupting absolutely. Any challenge to the exercise of that power justified misrepresentation, if not open prevarication, and a massive ranging of the forces of the establishment to silence the critic. It may well be that public morality had hit an all-time low in the province's history.

7

The End of an Era: The Legislature, 1958 to 1961

The year 1958 focused increasingly on the coming provincial election. Inevitably, Ontario politics were heavily influenced by the cataclysmic events in Ottawa. Mike Pearson had succeeded Louis St. Laurent as leader of the federal Liberal party, and the twenty-two-year-old regime had gone down to defeat. John Diefenbaker had succeeded George Drew as leader of the Conservative party, and went on to form a minority government, and a year later, to win an unprecedented majority.

Leslie Frost's relationships with George Drew had always been publicly cordial, but politically cool. The provincial party had never gone all out for Drew in federal campaigns, but with Diefenbaker, that changed. With his familiar arm-around-the-shoulder pose, Frost declared Diefenbaker to be "my man" at a Massey Hall rally during the 1958 campaign.

In those days, my favourite Tory was Gratton O'Leary, publisher of the Ottawa *Journal* and keynote speaker at many Conservative conventions. He had the gift of cutting through the public image to the reality. No man was as familiar with the workings of both old parties. He was on a CBC panel following both the Pearson and Diefenbaker leadership conventions. When asked about the resolutions passed at the two conventions, he dismissed them as irrelevant: "In the Liberal and the Conservative parties, it is the prerogative of the leader to lay down policy." When queried about the difference between the two old parties, he bluntly asserted that it was a "difference of mood and bias" — one is in, the other is out; otherwise, the differences are negligible.

On the provincial scene, the big question since 1943 had been which opposition party would emerge as the alternative to the Tories. In 1943 the CCF had been the official opposition, in 1945 the Liberals. In 1948 a resurgent CCF regained the position, in 1951 the Liberals again. Though the Liberals outnumbered the CCF after the 1955 election, they had virtually abdicated the role of opposition. In 1957 the Toronto *Star* stated that the CCF "has been the real, if unofficial opposition. On the whole, the Liberals have not found too much fault with the government." After the Legislature adjourned in 1958, the *Globe and Mail* reported in a front-page news story, that the "official opposition was outdone" by the CCF[1]

Moreover, the Liberal party's position to the right of the Conservatives had been consolidated by the choice of John Wintermeyer as leader. For three years he had been financial critic, so that his basic views were well known. He was a genuine conservative, a man of principle with a well-knit political philosophy, from which his views on policy flowed naturally and logically. He was a persistent advocate of the sales tax, generally regarded as highly regressive because it falls as heavily on the necessities of the poor as on the luxuries of the rich. Both he and his party had supported the proposal of toll roads and bridges. He had expressed grave concern about compulsory farm marketing, even when a majority of producers had voted for its establishment. Most significant of all, the Liberal leader had repeatedly called for lower corporation taxes and revealed his basic social views by deploring "our mad dash for the welfare state."

This ideological stance provoked increased public speculation on the possibility of political realignment, and it was interesting to observe the reaction of the media. While the Toronto *Star*, traditionally a Liberal party supporter, was rapping Wintermeyer for being "more Tory than the Tories," the *Globe and Mail* was an enthusiastic supporter. The *Globe* went one step further, pleading with the business world not to short-change the Liberal party in its financial support, as had become the case in the long tenure of Tory power.

"The basic affinity between the Liberals and the Conservatives is always recognized by the financial interests who back both," I observed. "When the public tires of one, they can switch to the other. Such is the puppetry of the old party politics: the principals on the stage may change, but the control behind the scenes remains the same. In light of this, there is a logic, and reason, and purpose, in the efforts of the *Globe* to rebuild the Liberal party — even to assist in providing it with new sources of money."[2]

Before the election, a fascinating new chapter was added to the reform institution story. In one sense it was reassuring, for it indicated a fundamental change in the attitude of the department — at least, at the minister's level. On 22 December 1958, George Wardrope, member for Port Arthur, succeeded John Foote as minister. (Ray Connell had held the portfolio briefly in 1958.) In the legislative battles Foote had provided the progressive rhetoric. He was a kindly man who had been padre during the Dieppe raid, where he won the Victoria Cross. Certainly he had some appreciation of modern penology, but the department was in the firm control of the "top brass" who ran the institutions as though they were army detention camps. As the minister, Foote had little option but to defend the conduct of his staff, even when he was concerned about it. As a Tory, he was loyal to a government whose attitude, particularly in the case of the premier, was locked into the nineteenth century.

George Wardrope was quite a different character. In retrospect, I have often wondered what led Frost to his choice, but perhaps it was the Old Fox at his intuitive best. The government had been hammered long enough that he knew there had to be changes, even though, philosophically, he disagreed with them. The new minister must at least counter the public image of the department's rigid administration. Wardrope was a freewheeling, warm-hearted man of the north. Totally without pretensions, he was not in any way captive of the establishment, political or social. He had roughed it in the woods industry and was fully aware of the foibles of men in camp. What is more, he was forgiving. I had the impression that,

on dealing with many who had run afoul of the law, his attitude was, "There, but for the grace of God, might be me."
That approach represented a fundamental change, and the first
step toward progress.

The stories were legion. How true they were I cannot vouch,
but they accurately reflected the change. On one occasion,
when visiting the Guelph Reformatory, so the story goes,
George Wardrope asked that all the inmates from his riding
of Port Arthur be gathered in the superintendent's office. With
the reformatory staff excluded, he met with his constituents.
"Tell me," I can hear George Wardrope saying, "what the
hell is wrong around here?"

Even more dramatic was the occasion of another riot at
Guelph. The troublemakers had all been herded into the compound and kept there overnight. Wardrope visited the institution for a first-hand impression. To the consternation of the
staff, and with a mixture of indiscretion and bravery, the
minister walked out into the compound, talked to the men,
asking once again, "What the hell is wrong?"

As minister, he declared that "he was going to put reform
back in reform institutions." He gave instructions to abolish
the use of the strap. With a great flourish, he stated, "If an
official can't handle a prisoner without beating him into in-
sensibility, he's not good enough to be on the staff of my
reform institutions" — an unwitting admission of what had
often gone on in Ontario. But institutions don't change overnight, particularly those which are given low priority on the
government's agenda. So, beyond the symbolism of a less
repressive regime, I was never sure what impact Wardrope had
on the overall destiny of the department. But he did open a
new era, which continued under the more progressive ministry
of Allan Grossman in the 1960s.

The provincial election was called in May 1959. Organizationally, the party was in somewhat better shape than in my
first campaign four years earlier. Planning for the new party
was under way (see next chapter), but it was too soon for riding
associations and affiliated unions to be caught up in the

enthusiasm which was ultimately generated. Financially, provincial campaigns were still being run on a few hundred thousand dollars.

As for program, the party was definitely in better shape: not only had committees of the provincial council done the usual work on policy, but in the Legislature the CCF had carved out distinctive positions. We had successfully resisted the old parties' inclination to copy the American pay-as-you-go toll road option for highway financing. A select committee review (in which I participated) of the Labour Relations Act had revealed many statutory restrictions on trade union organization and collective bargaining, on which the CCF alone sought change. The farmers' efforts to establish effective marketing of their products were being frustrated by the Tories and questioned by the Liberals; the CCF gave unstinting support. While hospital insurance had finally been achieved, the CCF immediately opened the battle for full health coverage. The CCF alone maintained a campaign for providing natural gas, the promising new energy source, to consumers at cost, through a publicly owned distribution system paralleling that of Hydro. The Tories considered it briefly, then backed off; the Liberals opposed it, even though Liberals in a number of local utilities were strong advocates. In short, there was plenty of grist for the election mills.

The campaign got under way with a first venture on my leader's tour, which is delightful in recollection, but revealing of the limitations on CCF prospects. I had been booked for some time to attend a nominating convention, to field a candidate in Premier Frost's home riding of Victoria. It was to take place in the little hamlet of Wilberforce, where a small motel operator, an ardent CCFer, formerly a resident of Brantford, had agreed to stand.

When the election was announced, this commitment and others were simply re-booked as the initial stops on my tour. In the mid-afternoon of 12 May 1959, I left Toronto, driving my own car, but accompanied by three or four newspapermen — such was the leader's tour in those days. The reporters were quite intrigued: Where was Wilberforce? Had a party leader ever visited it, let alone kicked off his election campaign in this idyllic spot? We arrived in time for a bite to eat at a local restaurant, and then located the community hall where some eight to ten people, plus the janitor, were gathered. With all of the gusto which the situation demanded, I launched the campaign, welcomed a candidate in the premier's seat, and the newsmen wrote it up straight — as though it was a great rally. And so it was!

My press release for the occasion noted that, with the possible exception of pipelines, no topic had produced more violent storms of controversy in the Legislature than the question of how offenders were treated. "One of the major achievements during the 26th Ontario Legislature was to force a fundamental change in the penal reform policy of the Frost government. The big question remaining, however, is whether this change is so much verbal window-dressing."

The CCF had been influential but I was cautious. "It is all very well," I said, "for the Minister to announce the abolition of the strap, and to say that too often it has merely been used 'as a crutch', but if the Minister has taken the crutch away, what has he done to replace it with a real treatment and rehabilitation program as positive constructive alternative. . . ."

It was a pleasant start to a campaign during which I visited all parts of the province — travelling with my own car in the south, and by commercial airlines to the northern centres. But not all occasions were as pleasant. I arrived in Fort Frances — as far away from home base as possible while still being in Ontario — only to be told that there had been an urgent call from Toronto. It was from my committee room in York South, with the shattering information that my nomination papers had to be filed the next day, and I had not signed them before leaving. Suddenly I was faced with the spectacle of being a party leader out of the election.

Frantic telephone calls produced a possible solution. If I could get a notarized statement indicating my willingness to stand, and have it delivered to Toronto, it would be acceptable. But how? The notarized statement was secured without much difficulty, but the problem of getting it to Toronto remained. One of the local CCFers was a licensed pilot and agreed to fly the document to Winnipeg. Then he placed it in the hands of an Air Canada steward. When the flight reached Toronto, late that evening, my campaign manager was on hand to receive the precious document, and next morning, when the returning officer opened for business, it was delivered to him.

It's not the kind of experience that invites repetition. In subsequent elections, signing my nomination papers became the first order of the day, when the writ was issued.

My emphasis in the campaign was on the basic issues which touched the lives of all Ontarians, but they tended to become overshadowed with the newsy aspect of the persistent scandals. In fact, the explosive debate on NONG had taken place in March, just a few weeks before the election call. Handling the issue became even more difficult, because of the premier's reaction.

Frost had a double moral standard. While no one questioned his personal integrity, what he was willing to tolerate, or even encourage, on behalf of the party, was a totally different matter. Like John A. Macdonald in the Pacific Scandal, or Mackenzie King in the Beauharnois Scandal, violation of the law, amounting to corruption, was an acceptable moral standard when committed for the party — particularly if it remained secret. It was Frost who dismissed cabinet ministers Griesinger and Mapledoram for having breached his directive by not disposing of their pipeline stock; yet, when I pressed the issue during the campaign, he described their action as a "minor indiscretion" and chastised me for adding to the embarrassment and humiliation of their families. Even more incredible, Frost campaigned on behalf of both Griesinger and Mapledoram, asserting that they were honourable men.

"It becomes more obvious every day," I stated, "that the greatest obstacle to clearing up conditions which have produced recurring scandals in the Frost government is the attitude of the Premier himself."[3] My only consolation was that the voters in the home constituencies of the ex-cabinet ministers didn't respond to the premier's plea. Both Griesinger and Mapledoram were defeated.

As the campaign drew to a close, it appeared as though the CCF had built, and was sustaining, greater momentum, whereas the Liberals were tailing off. Early in June they announced that their advertising funds were exhausted. James Scott, executive director of the Ontario Liberal Association, stated that "he could only guess why there had been a drop in donations from the larger contributors." Liberal leader Wintermeyer was more frank: "When you're in government it's easy to raise funds. It's easy to make levies on contractors with government contracts."

I commented, "The Liberal party is whimpering into the homestretch of the campaign, making excuses for its defeat before the votes are counted. . . . They now frankly admit that they have lost the support of corporations at the top and the economic grass-roots at the bottom. Obviously, the Liberal Party is just withering away, forsaken by both Big Business and the people."[4]

When the votes were counted on 11 June, however, it was a different story. The Tories dropped thirteen seats, while the Liberals picked up eleven, and the CCF only two. Undoubtedly, the reasons were that with all the scandal-mongering, the CCF was perceived as being negative and its policy alternatives did not register with the electorate. The Ontario electorate accepted the old adage that "you can't sling mud without losing ground." In face of Frost's towering stature, there was a tendency for voters to feel sorry for "good old Les," rather than to blame him. Thus, while the CCF had done an effective job of exposing the weakness of the government, the switch in seats, for the most part, went to the Liberals as the traditional alternative.

There was some consolation. In York South, my plurality had almost quadrupled to 5,303, though it rose not so much from an increase in my vote as from a drop in that of my Tory opponent. The volunteer workers had done a magnificent job as I criss-crossed the province, dropping in briefly once a week or so to keep in touch and attend all-candidate meetings. More important, the caucus had increased to five — enough to call a recorded vote. Strategically, that was an important achievement, for we were able to force members to stand up and be counted after they had fudged matters during debate. Norm Davison's election in Hamilton Centre had doubled our representation in Hamilton and the addition of Ken Bryden from Toronto-Woodbine significantly increased the effectiveness of the legislative team. Ken was a formidable debater. In addition to being an economist, his experience as a federal civil servant, as a deputy minister in the first CCF government in Saskatchewan, as research director for the Ontario caucus during 1948-51, and later as party organizer and provincial secretary, equipped him to speak on almost any subject. He became the leading financial critic in the opposition for the next decade.

Electoral setbacks were not something over which I brooded for long and they never deprived me of a good night's sleep. So it was simply a case of reforming the ranks and forging ahead.

As we moved into the 1960s, the CCF was caught up more and more in planning for the new party. There was an added sense of purpose in the routine activities of membership expansion, riding organization and general outreach to the community at large. For me, in meetings and seminars all across the province, it was particularly satisfying to see new life emerging where it had languished, or perhaps never existed.

At the legislative level, the established pattern of provincial politics continued. Leslie Frost was still firmly in the saddle: the government majority had been reduced, but it still outnumbered the combined opposition by seventy-one to twenty-seven. The "highest jury in the land" had reaffirmed the Tory mandate, so there was no compulsion to change. Moreover, there was no change in the general position of the Liberals. Their right-wing stance, more often than not in support of the government, not only continued, but the confusion in party policy reached comic proportions in 1961 over the sales tax issue.

As I had repeatedly pointed out, the sales tax in Ontario was "fathered" by Wintermeyer, "mothered" by the Frost government, and as of 1 September 1961, the people of

Ontario were stuck with their offspring. But the final debate involved an overnight switch. Three days before the debate opened, Wintermeyer was still talking in favour of a sales tax, as he had for the previous four years. He had begun to hedge his position, however, saying that the Liberals would not support a sales tax unless it was earmarked for education. Two days later the Liberal caucus pulled the rug out from under their leader; Farquhar Oliver announced that the party would not support the sales tax, whether earmarked for education or not. And that night, Wintermeyer went on a CBC provincial TV network, where he fell into line with the party switch.

At the government level, there was no change. With the same administration in control, the atmosphere of perpetual scandals continued, though it was now concentrated at the municipal level. The problem arose from the government's ambivalent attitude toward local government. On the one hand, municipalities are creatures of the province and their operations are subject to detailed regulations, spelled out in the Municipal Act and related statutes. On the other hand, the government professed to respect local autonomy, and therefore would wink at maladministration, or even malfeasance, arguing that responsibility for coping with it rested with the local electorate. This posture was often maintained even when its own laws and regulations were being broken.

The most flagrant case was that of the Town of Eastview (now Vanier) where the difficulties were compounded by the fact that the mayor, Gordon Lavergne, was also the Tory MPP for the riding of Russell. Under Lavergne's direction, as mayor for twelve years, the town's debt had grown enormously. A bill was introduced to authorize the debenturing of the floating debt, but following its review, the Municipal Board recommended that the bill not be passed. The reason cited was gross mismanagement. The board stated that the mounting deficit was due to a failure of the council to prepare and adopt realistic estimates of revenue and expenditure; a failure to levy taxes sufficient to cover estimated expenditures, including principal and interest payments on the debt; and a failure to limit expenditures authorized in the annual budget.

This mismanagement was coupled with the council's violation of its own by-laws and breaches of municipal statutes and regulations.[5] The report went on to recommend that if the Legislature decided that the bill should be passed, at least it should be amended to place the financial affairs of Eastview under the supervision of the Department of Municipal Affairs, as long as the debenture debt was outstanding.

This recommendation wasn't frivolous; it should not, therefore, have been dismissed. But for reasons which were, at least in part, to protect the political fortunes of one of its own members, the government chose to ignore both the Municipal Board recommendations. The situation went from bad to worse. Just how much worse was revealed two years later, when the Department of Municipal Affairs, having neglected to exercise its supervisory powers, was obliged to conduct an audit in response to a petition from Eastview ratepayers.

But if the government's refusal to act up to this point had been puzzling, its continued refusal to act in face of the new audit added up to gross negligence. On almost every one of the seventy-four pages of the Eastview report there was a record of irregularities and illegalities. As I stated at the time; "It reveals that the town's affairs were dominated by a tight little family compact who were advancing their own interests at the expense of the public welfare."

Despite periodic protests from the municipal auditor, the mayor kept the treasurer, Adrienne Laroche, on staff. The members of council increased their own remuneration, through the device of payments from a fund of $3,200 for receiving distinguished guests. The mayor received half of the fund, and he actually drew his cheque the day before the council passed the motion authorizing it. From this litany of maladministration, the report moved to malfeasance: the charge by one Mrs. Pharand that she had been obliged to pay a $100 bribe to a member of the 1959 council before she could get a building permit. And finally, the testimony of William Bolton, auditor of the Department of Municipal Affairs, that the mayor and the treasurer on more than one occasion urged him not to report a shortage of funds if the missing money were replaced — something which in itself was a criminal offence.

(To skip ahead in this story, Treasurer Laroche was not only fired subsequently, but she was the only one against whom charges were preferred. All the other charges were ignored by the local crown attorney and the attorney general's department.)

During the legislative debates, Lavergne ignored the listing of irregularities, and gave a glowing account of the town's progress. "The people wanted the work done, and we got it done," he boasted, with this innocent caveat: "Perhaps, sir, I was politically indiscreet in not having the sanction of the Municipal Board before doing the work."

Premier Frost weighed in with his familiar admonition. "Both batches of the opposition, the right and the left, might just remember that the jury of the people will be tapping them on their shoulders shortly [municipal elections were pending] in the form of the people of Eastview, who might consider that it would be a great deal better if the honourable members would leave the matter to them, without making political speeches in the Assembly." The good people of Eastview did speak. They elected a new council, and Lavergne was defeated as mayor.

Faced with that new reality, Municipal Affairs Minister William Warrender casually dismissed the whole affair. "We tried to help in Eastview, but for certain reasons, as the honourable member for Russell (Lavergne) said, they wished to carry on as they were doing. So far as Eastview was concerned, there is now a new council."

On another occasion, Warrender was more explicit on his concept of the government's responsibility. He said that his department had no intention of forcing itself on unwilling communities. A roving corps of inspectors, he said, would be "a gestapo." This government attitude did nothing to discourage conditions in municipal administration, which were achieving crisis proportions. "Within little more than a year," I pointed out in a CBC provincial TV network broadcast on the eve of local elections, "we've had Belleville, then York Township, and now Arnprior and Eastview — with public investigations that captured the headlines and official reports that revealed most disturbing conditions."

In the case of Arnprior, a development company, in establishing a new subdivision, had agreed in 1957 to pay for water and sewer services, as called for by the by-law, but the next year the company lawyers drafted another agreement, transferring the cost of the sewers to the taxpayers. Then as councilmen, the two lawyers voted for it. The lawyers were J.J. Greene, later a federal cabinet minister and, candidate for the provincial leadership of the Liberal party, and Conlin Mulvihill, president of the local Conservative Association.

Finally, there was the case of the Township of York, sad to relate, my home municipality. There had been rumours of council decisions being influenced by developers in questionable ways. Citizens' groups were frustrated in their efforts to get answers to their questions, let alone any corrective action — so much so that the government was persuaded to appoint Judge Joseph A. Sweet to conduct an inquiry. I had not been involved in the public outcry, and knew nothing of the government decision to establish an inquiry until it was publicly announced.[6]

The Sweet report was devastating. The judge documented "flagrant and continued infractions of the by-laws," and commented that "the disregard by a law-making body for its own laws could only be expected ultimately to result in a general disrespect for the laws . . . illegality is an evil thing . . . it spreads and it contaminates. Where there is the evil of illegality in the administration of a municipality the public welfare is indeed imperilled."

In York, as in other municipalities, there was a growing tendency, not only to wink at the law, but in some instances to engage in a calculated effort to violate it. Judge Sweet was extremely critical of the council's handling of land sales, among them the sale of public land, through a nominee, to the reeve, Chris Tonks. His Lordship said, "Whether or not the township received an adequate price for the land is not of the greatest importance in this matter. Whether or not there was financial loss to the municipality is not the factor which is of the greatest significance in the situation. What is of greatest significance and importance, and what is most deplorable, is that there appears to have been an attempt to avoid the law. That attempt seems to have been studied and planned.''

Although it is alleged that this kind of questionable conduct has always existed in varying degrees in municipal politics, the reasons for its epidemic proportions during these years stemmed in part from a widespread tolerance by the general public, and more particularly, from the government's attitude.

When the Ontario Association of Mayors and Reeves met in 1961 in the wake of all these revelations, there was no indication of regret or shame. The audience applauded when one mayor proclaimed that he was known as "the man who breaks the by-laws." J.W.P. Carter, assistant to the deputy minister of municipal affairs, told the gathering that "sixty percent of councils in Ontario seem to think they have individual discretion to keep or break their own by-laws." When his minister, William Warrender, was asked about Carter's remarks, he said he wouldn't criticize his deputy because he knew of a municipality which had been violating statutes for two generations, but "no one," he said, "is being harmed."

Here was the root of the problem, and it was all dressed up in the noble garb of democracy by none other than Premier Frost himself. Speaking to the Ontario Association of Mayors and Reeves, the premier dealt with the vexing problem of the extent to which the provincial government should intervene in municipal affairs, particularly when an inquiry had provided solid evidence that all is not well in the administration. He summed up his case by saying; "We are all living under a democratic system. Basically that means government according to the wishes of those governed. Can this be achieved if local government is subject to interference of another government above? I think not." It was the kind of statement calculated to ingratiate himself with municipal leaders; the premier used the local autonomy argument whenever it served his purpose.

In discussing the problem with my own riding association, I pointed out:

While it can be agreed that the greatest possible degree of local autonomy is desirable, Premier Frost's case was based on an exaggerated concept of the degree of local autonomy now held by municipalities, and therefore, his implied conclusion that intervention is not warranted even under extraordinary circumstances, such as have been revealed in York Township, is open to serious question. . . .

Municipalities are the creatures of the province. They operate with powers that are granted by the province. These powers can be, and are, added to and subtracted from, by the decision of the provincial government whenever it sees fit. Municipal budgets are subject to extensive supervision and intervention by the provincial government.

Under these circumstances it was idle for the provincial government to hide behind the cloak of municipal autonomy and fail to take action when one of its creatures was found guilty of violating its own by-laws as well as provincial statutes and regulations.

On 22 February 1961, the Toronto *Star* again asked the pertinent question, "Is Premier Frost content to appear as a respectable front for lawlessness and corruption? If he is not content with the apparent role, he will act on the record of blatant illegalities in the Ottawa suburb of Eastview, under the administration of ex-mayor Gordon Lavergne, who now sits on the government side of the Legislature."

The record would indicate that Premier Frost was indeed content, and by his inaction condoned and encouraged corruption. But he was too astute a politician not to realize that this stance was increasingly unacceptable.

Leslie Frost left politics in 1961, except for behind-the-scenes counselling to his successor in times of political crisis. Apart from attending his funeral, my last recollection was of a friendly chat I had with him in the hallway at Queen's Park toward the mid-1960s. He had been assigned an office to tidy up his political affairs, and periodically he came back. "You know, Donald," he said, "this place has so changed that it is like foreign territory to me now."

History has passed by the Laird of Lindsay, the Silver Fox, the Great Tranquillizer, and Old Man Ontario — the epithet he cherished most. It was the end of an era. The year 1961 was also the end of an era for me in a very personal way. In the same month that Frost gave way to John Parmenter Robarts, the CCF evolved into the New Democratic Party.

8

The New Democratic Party

The three-year build-up to the launching of the New Democratic Party in August 1961 has been described as the greatest exercise in participatory democracy in Canadian political history. The general perception is that the initiative for the development came with the resolution passed at the Canadian Labour Congress (CLC) Convention in Winnipeg, in April 1958:

> The time has come for a fundamental re-alignment of political forces in Canada. There is a need for a broadly based people's political movement, which embraces the CCF, the labour movement, farm organizations, professional people and other liberal-minded persons interested in basic social reform and reconstruction through our parliamentary system of government.

But that resolution was the product of at least three years of planning, virtually all of which occurred in Ontario. When the provincial setback in 1951 was followed with no breakthrough, particularly in Ontario, during the 1953 federal election, it was obvious that some new strategy was required. Informal discussions emerged among party and trade union leaders. I was not intimately involved, as was David Lewis, federal president of the party and its leading strategist. David was practising law in Toronto, mostly in the labour field, and from our long working relationship, I was kept in general touch with the behind-the-scenes developments.

The idea of the new party had pretty well jelled by 1955,

but it had to be put on hold because the trade union preoccupation was with uniting the house of labour through a merger convention which took place in Toronto in 1956. Another key figure in the continuing discussions was Claude Jodoin, who had been elected president of the Trades and Labour Congress (TLC) in 1954. Although a former Liberal member of the Quebec Legislative Assembly, he was first and foremost a trade unionist, and receptive to whatever was in labour's interests. The new party was considered along with plans for the merger convention, but political action was not on the formal agenda. At that time internal trade union considerations were paramount to bring together the Canadian Congress of Labour (CCL) which had been endorsing the CCF at every convention since 1942, and the Trades and Labour Congress which had always forsworn affiliation with any party, in the old Gompers tradition.

However, party leaders continued to work closely with the leadership of the new Canadian Labour Congress (CLC). and particularly with Claude Jodoin, who became its first president. Two years later when the CLC met in convention in Winnipeg, the historic step was taken. As Stanley Knowles has pointed out in his book on *The New Party*, the 1958 decision was "not a sudden idea, it was a culmination"[1]

The CLC call to build a new party was taken less than a month after the massive sweep of the Diefenbaker Conservatives in March 1958, in which veterans of the CCF such as M.J. Coldwell and Stanley Knowles went down to defeat, and the caucus was reduced to a mere rump. It was surely not the most propitious time for reforming the ranks of democratic socialists in Canada. But the decision had been taken before the election and the disastrous results didn't weaken the resolve.

In fact, Ken Bryden relates that he, as CCF provincial secretary, got a call after the election from David Lewis, then federal president, and it was agreed that they should meet with Claude Jodoin and other labour leaders to review the decision. When Lewis suggested that labour might want to reconsider its commitment in light of the new circumstances, it was

Jodoin who reacted most vigorously, contending that they weren't going to change their minds just because of one defeat. The new CLC leadership, drawn from the old CCL and TLC, fell behind Jodoin's enthusiastic lead and the resolution calling for the building of a new party received almost unanimous approval at the Winnipeg convention.

While I had not played an active part in the early development, my role changed with the Ontario CCF annual convention in 1958 when the following resolution was adopted:

> Be it resolved that this convention wholeheartedly endorses the recent move of the CLC and the CCF National Convention to move hand in hand with like-minded progressive organizations towards the formation of a broadly based Canadian people's party.

I became a member of the National Committee for the New Party (NCNP) which directed organizational and educational activities during the next three years. And, of course, I was deeply involved in the work of the Ontario Committee for the New Party (OCNP). That meant an intensive effort to reach out to new adherents while not neglecting the task of strengthening the CCF base. The report of the 1958 convention clearly set the course: "The only political organizational facilities which will be available to the New Party when it comes into being will be those provided by the CCF. An active and flourishing CCF organization will therefore be of great importance to it."

While an enthusiastic supporter of these developments, I had concerns. The fortunes of the CCF had faded; the trade union movement was not the most popular organization. I felt strongly that the concept of the New Party had to be broadened beyond these two organizations to include those in the general public who were not happy with either of the old parties. Repeatedly, in the meetings of the committees for the New Party, both federal and provincial, I urged the creation of some mechanism through which others — those not belonging to the CCF or the unions — might become involved in the New Party movement.

Initially the idea was viewed with some skepticism, if not opposition, but in November 1959, the National Committee approved of the formation of New Party clubs to provide the mechanism for involving newcomers. A full-time staff position was created and R.D. "Des" Sparham was hired by the NCNP to head up the program. While theoretically the New Party club option was available nationally, activity in promoting it was concentrated in Ontario. Des had been working in the mental health field, and in my association with the York Mental Health Council, and its membership in the Metro Council, I had become familiar with his community work. He was an irrepressible enthusiast for everything he undertook; that served the New Party movement well as he tackled the amorphous task of reaching out to anyone who might be interested. In Ontario, Lyal Tait, a prominent Elgin County farmer, was appointed to work with Fred Young as full-time New Party club organizers in the rural areas of southern Ontario. Lyal had been the CCF candidate in a 1958 by-election in Elgin. As a respected leader in local farm organizations, he brought greater credibility to the New Party.

However, progress in rural areas was limited. Farm organizations felt that they had been "burned" through their venture into politics after the First World War, and were generally committed to a non-partisan approach. Though the organizations were not sympathetic, a growing number of individual farmers did respond to the prospect of an alternative to the old parties. Gradually, organizational activities for New Party clubs emerged throughout the north and in the cities and mixed ridings of the south. In fact, the strategy was to build New Party clubs in those ridings where the CCF was weak, so as to encourage newcomers who had not been attracted to the CCF. In those areas, lapsed CCF members were far more responsive to joining a club identified with the New Party, than attempting to revive the moribund CCF organization.

The challenge of the New Party produced a significant increase in local activity. Within the CCF, membership recruitment was intensified. Within trade union locals, there was debate over the appropriate role for organized labour in the New Party. Within the clubs, newcomers to the political movement provided their ideas for policy and helped to reach out to those who had never been interested in, or had become disillusioned with, party politics.

There was a growing range of organizational and policy gatherings at the local or regional level. For those of us in the leadership, that involved an endless series of engagements across the province. Within the Ontario Federation of Labour, these activities were headed by Morden Lazarus, a long-time CCF activist, and Henry Weisbach, a respected trade union official. Within the CCF, Peg Stewart, provincial secretary, and others like Ken Bryden, devoted countless hours beyond their normal party obligations. Within the New Party clubs, new figures appeared with every passing month.

If the CCF had become "a protest movement becalmed," as Leo Zakuta has written, the New Party movement had set the sails anew. There were problems to be solved, and tensions to be relieved, but that was inevitable in such a massive effort, and they tended to become lost in the rising political spirits.

Nothing in the whole build-up for the New Party provided a greater lift than the "Peterborough miracle." In 1960 the Tory member for Peterborough died. In the previous election he had polled nineteen thousand votes while the CCF had received only nineteen hundred. Discouraged by the prospect of a by-election, the riding executive had announced that the CCF would not field a candidate. Logical as that decision appeared from the local point of view, it aroused concern among those leading the New Party development. How could the public be persuaded of the seriousness of our efforts if we were not willing, or able, to contest elections? I was assigned the task of persuading the local executive to reverse its decision. In late July I drove to Peterborough where we met in a rather dingy office of the old labour centre. There were five or six of the local riding executive in attendance.

I presented the situation, as seen by the national and Ontario committees for the New Party, and after an hour or so, there was a tentative agreement to field a candidate. But who was to be the sacrificial lamb?

Before arriving in town that afternoon, I had heard of a local school teacher who had recently joined the CCF — one Walter Pitman. A telephone call to his home brought no response. Inquiries in a number of quarters finally resulted in information from the editor of the Peterborough *Examiner* that Walter was at his cottage, south of Highway 7, some eighty-five miles east of Peterborough. I added Walter's name to the list of persons whom the group should approach for candidacy. When the meeting broke up at about 9:30, I accepted the responsibility of seeking him out.

I took off immediately, and toward eleven o'clock attempted in vain to find the Pitman cottage in the dark. Nothing could be done but to seek overnight accommodation at a motel back on Highway 7, and the next morning I left at seven o'clock, only to find that Walter had departed earlier for Kingston, where he was teaching summer school at the teacher's college.

So it was off to Kingston, in the hope of catching him briefly during the mid-morning coffee break. The situation could hardly have been less promising for raising the proposition of political candidacy. In fact, the circumstances were even worse than expected: Walter had wrenched his back the day before in carrying a canoe, and was in excruciating pain. (In fact, an hour or so after our meeting, he actually collapsed and was transported in a van, from which he had to crawl on his hands and knees into the cottage.) But there was nothing to do but grasp the nettle: in the brief coffee break, I told him of the previous night's meeting. His only query was whether the party intended to put on a serious campaign, to which I replied with a vigorous affirmative. It is a measure of the quality of the man that under those conditions, he said he would consider it.

Two weeks later, the answer came. "Yes, if the campaign could be conducted under the banner of the New Party." Where this idea came from is a matter of conjecture: my recollection is that it was from Walter; his recollection is that

it was part and parcel of my proposal. It may well be that
it was an idea whose time was emerging, in part as the result
of a stunning experience. On 18 June, less than two months
before, a by-election had been held in the provincial riding
of Temiskaming. The CCF candidate was Cal Taylor, a
popular railroader who had held the seat from 1943 to 1951.
But there was widespread antipathy among local CCFers to
the whole idea of the New Party, engendered in a good part
by the federal CCF member, Arnold Peters. Taylor ran a poor
third, and certain obvious lessons were drawn: first, opposition to the New Party, in combination with such a determination to stick with the old CCF, failed to capitalize on the enthusiasm for the new movement which was slowly building;
and secondly, as Doc Ames, the party's organizer, emphasized, the election was lost because of "a lack of poll and community activity by our own local CCF . . . there is an urgent
need for active newcomers."

In any case, wherever the idea to run under the New Party
banner came from, it was a stroke of genius. The anomaly
of running a candidate for a party that did not yet exist proved
to be advantageous: looking to a brighter future rather than
to a none-too-successful past. Dispirited CCFers were revi-
talized. Trade unionists were captivated by the idea of fighting
for a party which they were engaged in creating. Potential supporters responded to an attractive candidate like Walter. At
the outset, I didn't really feel that a victory was possible, but
when I returned to speak to the nominating convention in early
September, the campaign had picked up great momentum. I
told the assembled nominating convention that a miracle was
in the making.

Under the experienced direction of Fred Young as campaign
manager, and with Walter campaigning tirelessly before and
after school hours, the miracle was wrought. By-elections can
often be very unexciting because the fates of governments do
not hang on their results, but this one was a rousing exception. Walter was an extremely popular teacher. A combination of his popularity and the possibility of helping to usher
a new party into being through the election of its first member

of Parliament resulted in a spontaneous wave of support. The campaign headquarters didn't have to create the excitement; it simply had to channel it.

When the votes were counted, appropriately on Hallowe'en night, the Tories had dropped from nineteen thousand to ten thousand and the New Party had polled thirteen thousand votes. That evening, when I got a call from Peterborough with the unbelievable news, the caller asked, "How did you know seven weeks ago that a miracle was possible?" I confessed I didn't know. It was the normal hype in which a political leader had to indulge.

Understandably, the results electrified the whole New Party movement. In a by-election the same day in Niagara Falls (in which Judy LaMarsh, later a Liberal cabinet minister, entered politics), the CCF candidate came in a good second. In fact, the CCF/New Party polled more votes in the two by-elections than either of the old parties.

As the founding convention neared, the momentum picked up. Behind the scenes there were difficult negotiations on critical constitutional questions. David Archer, president of the Ontario Federation of Labour and a member of the CCF, had been assigned the task of producing a constitution. Included in his first draft was a key clause that read: "Affiliated organizations shall participate in the activities of the constituency association on a basis to be decided by the constituency association and the affiliated organizations."

This proposal masked intense pressure to have affiliated members granted equal status with individual members at nominating conventions, and the recommendation of Archer's constitution committee was to leave this controversial issue for decision by the constituency association in consultation with local affiliated organizations. When the draft was considered by the OCNP in July 1961 it decided that members of affiliated organizations should be given *full* voting rights at constituency nominating conventions, on an equal basis with individual members. I was certain that decision opened the door to the appearance, perhaps the reality, of trade union domination of the party, something which union leaders themselves had repeatedly stated was neither their desire nor their intention.

In my own riding of York South, for example, the individual memberships ranged from five hundred to one thousand, but there were literally thousands of affiliated members. Under the proposal they would all be entitled to turn up at a nominating convention, even though they had not been involved in the on-going activities of the riding. I took the lead among the CCF members of the OCNP in voicing misgivings. I wrote to Archer on 16 July 1961, arguing that "this is a reversal of what has generally been understood in the whole promotion of the New Party . . . it had never been understood that every affiliate member would have full voting rights in the choice of candidate. . . . In short, the decision which we accepted at the OCNP is not only a very fundamental one, but at variance with the accepted view of a great many key persons in the whole New Party development."

I was not opposed to affiliated organization involvement in nominating conventions, but I felt it should be a *delegate* basis. Equal status for affiliated members would

take all the steam out of any campaign to persuade affiliate members to become full individual members, and assume all their rights and obligations in the party . . . not just in choice of candidate, but in the day-to-day organizational work, policy resolutions, choice of riding delegates to conventions, etc. . . . The granting of full voting rights to every affiliate member will destroy the image of a broadly-based party, involving all sectors of the community. . . . I shudder to think of how completely that kind of situation would be made to order for our opponents. In fact, my fear would be that the granting of full voting rights for every affiliate member at nominating conventions would within a few years become as much of a bug-a-boo in the New Party as the block vote in the British Labour Party.

These arguments were heeded, at least partially. The OCNP

At the 1958 Convention when the CCF accepted the move to the New Democratic Party. From left to right, Stanley Knowles, Claude Jodoin, Thérèse Casgrain, David Lewis and M.J. Coldwell.

Walter Pitman *(right)* elected as a New Party MP before the party was founded. Fred Young *(left)* was his campaign manager.

Chatting with Tommy Douglas at the Founding Convention, August 1961.

My first election as NDP leader at the Niagara Falls Founding Convention, October, 1961.

stated that the voting eligibility of affiliated members at nominating conventions should be left to constituency associations. The constitution committee presented a resolution giving affiliated members the right to participate fully at nominating conventions, with the stipulation that they must register with the convention secretary at least thirty days in advance. The resolution passed by a narrow majority.

The passage of this controversial resolution was indicative on the one hand of the desire to keep the party open to wider participation; and on the other, of the continuing emphasis on the importance of membership. Interestingly, the emphasis on membership finally won out: in subsequent years the party gradually moved, with the full support of the trade union movement, to restricting voting rights at conventions to full members.

In the field, these behind-the-scenes conflicts had little or no impact. At the national and Ontario committees for the New Party, the New Party clubs had been given full status, so that now the trilogy of founding groups was officially completed. Within the unions, the CCF and the New Party clubs there was a drive to maximize the delegate attendance at the founding convention. But nowhere was the momentum more evident than among the New Party clubs.

They had emerged among teachers, doctors, professors, insurance agents, engineers, ethnic groups, women and farmers. Two or three of these groups held their first meeting at my Toronto home. In the weaker CCF ridings they had often filled the gap where organization was moribund. Originally, the stipulation had been that clubs could not be organized within a local trade union, but that was eased to permit trade unionists to become members of a community club, as long as they did not dominate it in their numbers. And as the convention neared there was a further easing of guidelines to permit a club to be organized within a trade union local, particularly if it faced a constitutional barrier to political action. The result was a remarkable burgeoning of New Party clubs. In February 1961 there were forty-nine; by September there were one hundred and fifty-four. In fact, the growth was so rapid that as the founding convention neared, Azoulay states that the OCNP was sometimes not even aware where they had sprung up.[3]

However, there were severe growing pains and significant blocs of opposition, within and outside the party. On the whole, the media were cool to the New Party development and headlined every difficulty or evidence of dissent within the party. The media reaction was not unexpected, even if regretted, but the dissent within the party was more troublesome because its leading protagonist was Douglas Fisher, the CCF federal member for Port Arthur. He had the support of other northern delegates at the CCF annual convention in October 1959, in good part because they opposed the close association with the trade union movement which the New Party envisaged. In addition, Fisher was critical of the "party brass," especially David Lewis. Writing in the *Canadian Forum*, September 1960, he argued that Lewis, along with "his henchman, Stanley Knowles," had masterminded the whole New Party idea from its inception and had succeeded in brainwashing the CCF membership into supporting it. Fisher staked his cause on a challenge for the presidency of the party, and was soundly defeated. In July 1961 he came out in full support of the candidacy of Hazen Argue, against Tommy Douglas, for the federal leadership.

Despite the negative reactions of the press and the continuing, if dwindling, dissent within the movement, by the convention week of 31 July to 4 August 1961, there were twenty-two hundred delegates in attendance at the Exhibition Coliseum in Ottawa. For those in attendance, it was an unforgettable event, not matched in the party until the convention in Montreal in 1987. Media coverage captured the mood of spontaneity and celebration, and conveyed it to all Canadians.

No CCF or NDP convention escapes extended consideration of policy, but in this instance policy issues had been worked over in countless meetings during the three years of preparation. For understandable reasons, they were overshadowed by preoccupation with all the basic requirements of setting up a new party. The constitution was adopted with relative ease, because of all the advance consideration it had received.

Controversy centred on the role of trade union delegates: need they be full members of the party? For the moment, the decision was no, on the assumption that no trade unionist was likely to attend a convention without being persuaded to take out full membership. In later years, it became a prior requirement.

Throughout the convention, Walter Pitman was greeted as the symbolic hero of the whole development. After all, he had been the first member to be elected on the New Party ticket. But now that the party had formally come into being, what should it be named? There was quite heated debate on this topic. Some preferred a name that acknowledged the basic socialist philosophy: the Socialist or Social Democratic Party of Canada. Interestingly, nobody, even among the trade union delegates, argued strongly for a name suggesting exclusive identification with labour, as in Great Britain. Eventually, the majority opted simply for New Democratic Party.

The high point of the convention came with the choice of the leader. Hazen Argue had been elected leader at the previous convention, following the resignation of M.J. Coldwell. But once Tommy Douglas was persuaded to leave the premiership of Saskatchewan, it was no contest. Having successfully led the first socialist government in Canada for seventeen years, through five elections, to a resounding mandate for implementing full health insurance, Tommy embodied all the high hopes of Canadian social democrats. Weary delegates returned to their homes inspired by what had been the largest and liveliest political convention in Canadian history.

The party had been launched nationally, but the same task remained at the provincial level. That founding convention was scheduled for Niagara Falls, 7-8 October 1961. Preparations had been under way for a year, but there was one element of the preparations to which I gave particular attention. Efforts to recruit members in the farm community had had limited success, partly because of its basically conservative outlook, and partly because all farm organizations had constitutional barriers to partisan activity. I was determined to circumvent these hurdles.

Throughout the summer and early fall, I travelled the back concessions of rural Ontario from Ottawa to Windsor. As leader and agricultural critic in the Legislature, my name had become known, and I was delighted to discover many individual farmers, sometimes with antecedents reaching back to Progressive and United Farmers of Ontario days, who were sympathetic. The result was the formation of a farm committee, numbering from forty to fifty representatives of top officials in both the Federation of Agriculture and the Farmers Union, past presidents of the United Co-operatives of Ontario, leaders in many of the commodity groups, as well as rank and file farmers from all areas of the provinces. Thirty-five of them were registered delegates at the founding convention. The committee was chaired by Robert Good, son of W.C. Good, former MP and pioneer in the cooperative and farm movements. Their presence produced one of the inspirational moments of the convention. The delegates, and the public, felt that a few farmers would be in attendance as token representation. But when the debate on farm issues came up, they proved to be not only vocal, but obviously top-flight people. The convention realized, with surprise and delight, that farmers were on the team.

Their presence also helped to achieve the broadly based goal which the New Party movement had sought from the outset. In the original plans, the OCNP had arranged to have only Tommy Douglas, newly elected leader of the national party, as the guest speaker. At its 16 August meeting I suggested that the tripartite nature of the party should be emphasized by having speakers from all three sections. The agenda was revised to include speeches by OFL president David Archer, CCF president Carrol Coburn, and New Party club director Des Sparham.

The tripartite nature of the convention was also evident in the election of the new executive. The three top positions went to former CCFers: I was acclaimed as leader, and George Cadbury and Peg Stewart were elected as president and secretary, respectively. The rest of the executive comprised farmers, professors, teachers, doctors and union representatives, among them a goodly number of the newcomers.

Although the Ontario convention was intended to be a no-nonsense, working gathering, it was a very lively affair. The *New Democrat* for November 1961 quoted one observer:

The meeting had none of the suspense or drama of the Ottawa Convention. There was no leadership race to quicken the pulse. There were few surprises and floor revolts. There was little of the colour and song that won the national convention superlatives in the press. And yet, by God, it was never dull.

When I was acclaimed as leader, I returned to my constant theme of building a stronger membership base:

Let us go forth as political missionaries. Seek out friends and neighbours — yes, even strangers, and talk to them about the new party . . . Only if each one of us, including myself, does his part, will this broadly-based movement be built in the limited time at our disposal [i.e. before the federal election].

Premier Frost's announcement of his resignation bolstered convention enthusiasm. "We have launched," I declared with some rhetorical flourish, "a political force that will sweep the province like a mighty Niagara." Certainly one historic chapter had closed. I had eight years of CCF leadership behind me. A new chapter had opened.

9

Progress Delayed, 1961 to 1964

In October 1961 John Robarts succeeded Leslie Frost as leader of the Progressive Conservative party. Four years earlier Farquhar Oliver had relinquished the leadership of the Liberal party for a second time, and John Wintermeyer took over. These two developments made me dean of the leaders. With only six years in the Legislature, I had the greatest seniority.

The atmosphere in the Ontario Legislature changed significantly with John Robarts at the helm. Instead of being a first minister like Frost, who dominated the House, Robarts was more laid-back, giving cabinet members freer rein. The change was perhaps more difficult for the government backbenchers than for the opposition because, particularly at the start, Robarts didn't rally the troops with tub-thumping speeches, a tactic at which Frost was a past master.

The atmosphere also changed in another way. Although echoes of old scandals haunted Ontario politics, and a significant new one emerged in the government's handling of organized crime, there was growing consideration of issues which touched the lives of Ontarians more intimately. The educational system was virtually revolutionized, and the financing of the two branches of the province's publicly funded schools was put on a fairer basis. Medical insurance crowded onto the centre of the political stage. While the public furore over gas pipelines subsided, the political debate over farm marketing escalated. Pension issues became a running federal-provincial battle, with the Liberal federal health and welfare minister, Judy LaMarsh, baiting Robarts over Ontario's reluctance to support a national plan. And, as usual, the elusive goal of assuring the north of a fair share of the province's prosperity was a contant preoccupation.[1]

Throughout 1962 Robarts enjoyed the usual honeymoon respite for new leaders, during which he gradually asserted his style of control over the party. There was also by-election sampling of the political waters in Brant, Renfrew South and Eglinton ridings, none of which provided the prospect of a significant boost for the NDP.

In Brant, Harry C. Nixon died in October 1961. He had been, without interruption, a member of the Legislature since 1919; a cabinet minister in the Drury and Hepburn governments, and premier for a few months before the Liberals were swept from office in 1943. Three months later Robert Nixon succeeded his father, thereby perpetuating the most impregnable political fiefdom in Ontario. Robert Good was the NDP candidate in the by-election, another reminder of the continuity of Ontario's political traditions.

On the same day there was a by-election in Renfrew South which was more eventful. The seat had been held by James Maloney, a member of the Frost cabinet, and one of my regular adversaries in the Legislature. Upon his death, the Tories nominated Conlin Mulvihill, a lawyer and member of the town council of Arnprior. The NDP candidate was Len Laventure, a member of the executive of the Ontario Federation of Agriculture, who had been a farm representative on the national committee for the New Party. The NDP put on a stirring campaign, in which I was very much involved. In spite of running a disappointing third, the party tripled the previous CCF vote, cutting into the Tory support in the eastern end of the riding, with the result that a traditional Tory seat was won by the Liberals. However, the Liberals held it for only a year before it returned to the Tory fold in the 1963 election.

An explosive political situation was in the making from the time that Robarts assumed the premiership: crime was becoming a preoccupation of the public and governments. Some of this activity — payola, kickbacks, and bribes — resulted in the establishment of the Ontario Provincial Police rackets squad. But the business aspect of crime was overshadowed by the growing public concern with organized crime and its corruption of society in general, and governments in particular.

On the American side of the border investigations had been launched by Senator Estes Kefauver and the new attorney general, Robert Kennedy. Indeed, as far back as 1958, a commission of investigation had been established in neighbouring New York state, and, reporting in 1961, it documented the existence of illegal gambling in the border city of Buffalo which reached into many Ontario cities. In Ontario the anti-gambling branch of the OPP uncovered a case of bribery of a police officer by gambling club operators.

When confronted with the recurrent evidence, Attorney General Roberts's reaction had been one of complacent dismissal. He simply didn't believe that a dangerous situation existed in Ontario. He had confidence in the police, which turned out to be somewhat misplaced. In ten of Ontario's thirty cities, he stated that there was no evidence of organized crime, but he didn't report on the remaining twenty.

"The fact of the matter," I warned, "is that organized crime is established in the province — how widely, nobody knows exactly, including the government. That's why this complacency is so inexcusable." I cited three different aspects of the situation which merited careful investigation:

First, the leaders of organized crime have operated, sometimes with the tacit, sometimes with the active, co-operation of persons in high places. Secondly, government departments and agencies have wittingly, or unwittingly on occasion, assisted the leaders of organized crime in extending their activities. Thirdly, organized crime has become established because it has built a place in legitimate businesses, bought or established with its millions of tax-free profits. This is how gangland became an integral part of many big American cities.[3]

I documented government involvement, through the chartering of so-called social clubs by the provincial secretary's department. These clubs carried on gambling behind barred double doors, which frustrated police when they raided. I noted that the press had cited the Town Tavern, in Toronto, as a favourite hang-out of the leaders of organized crime; that it was on those premises that Max Bluestein, a well-known bookmaker, was beaten up in full public view; that, in spite of this evidence, when the owners of Town Tavern bought a nearby restaurant, they were granted a transfer of liquor licence with the approval of the Liquor Licensing Board.

Despite the acknowledgement that illegal bookmaking was the source of much of the profits of organized crime, there was no concerted effort to check it. Not only did the government lose revenue, but there were persistent rumours of payoffs to avoid police raids. Further, when the provincially chartered social clubs were established, they invariably had banks of telephones which ran up thousands of dollars in long-distance telephone bills to well-known American race tracks. When Bell Telephone was asked to install a half-dozen telephones in the back section of pool rooms, no questions were asked, and the police imposed no obligation to inform them.

In short, authorities in general winked at a wide range of activities which were obviously tied to organized crime. Furthermore, there were startling revelations of the threat to the integrity of law enforcement and the judiciary, which would be worthy of TV dramatization. Constable Douglas Wright had been on the OPP gambling squad for years and, without explanation, he was demoted to detachment duty in Belleville. A few weeks later, Wright approached Constable George Scott on the gambling squad, indicating that $200 a month was available if he would tip off Vincent F. Feeley and Joseph McDermott, two well-known gamblers, when raids were to be made on the Ramsay Club in Niagara Falls and the Vets Club on Centre Road in Cooksville. Scott reported this to his seniors and was instructed to act as an undercover agent, as a result of which charges of keeping a common gambling house were laid against Feeley and McDermott. In preparing the case, evidence of conspiracy was gathered, and a charge of conspiracy to bribe was laid against Feeley, McDermott and Wright.

To the consternation of those responsible for the prosecution, and the public, all three accused were acquitted when the case came to trial in March 1961. The special crown attorney described the findings of the jury as "perverse." To make matters worse, there were press rumours of jury tampering, forcing the attorney general to order a police investigation of alleged attempts to corrupt the judicial process. Charges were laid, though they were eventually dismissed because of a lack of conclusive evidence.

Not surprisingly, these developments heightened concern among those responsible for law enforcement. Following a meeting of the Ontario Chief Constables Association in June 1961, Chief George Kerr of Brantford, the newly elected president, warned that "Every pressure will be exerted on Attorney General Roberts to meet the problem of crime. Our directors will insist on his complete co-operation." It was significant that the police felt it necessary to make such a comment about the chief law officer of the province.

The pressure had reached a point where the attorney general had to forsake his ostrich posture. In July 1961 he appointed Professor J.D. Morton, of Osgoode Hall Law School, to survey the gambling problem and recommend legislation to cope with it more effectively. When the session opened in November the Morton report was tabled. It warned: "There is grave danger, if the present illegal gambling operation is permitted to continue, that either domestic or foreign criminal elements will prosper to such an extent as to undermine the very nature of our society."

The session was no more than two weeks old when the organized crime issue exploded, with repercussions that were to reverberate for months, even years. Liberal spokesmen had been pursuing the question for some time without particular emphasis, but that all changed in a dramatic fashion. The *Globe and Mail* had assigned Harold Greer, a veteran reporter, as head of an investigative team to track down rumours of crime in Ontario. On the advice of their lawyers, the paper decided not to print Greer's findings which, they felt, did not have enough hard evidence.

According to A.K. McDougall, Robarts's biographer, Greer took his story to W.M. McIntyre, secretary to the cabinet, who also rejected it as being based largely on gossip. Suspecting a cover-up, Greer took his story to Wintermeyer, and convinced him he should challenge the government in its handling of the whole issue.[4]

The result was a two-and-one-half hour speech by Wintermeyer in the Legislature, written by Greer, who left the *Globe* to join the staff of the Liberal leader. The familiar evidence was reviewed and documented from the notebooks of an OPP constable, who had been associated with criminals in the course of gathering evidence of the bribery charges a year earlier. Wintermeyer called for a royal commission.

A week later the issue took on even more sensational proportions. John White, Tory MPP for London South, dismissed Wintermeyer's call for a royal commission, argued that the proposed police commission was the appropriate body to investigate, described Wintermeyer's "hollow offer" to waive parliamentary immunity as hypocritical, and challenged Wintermeyer "to step out into the corridor and read the speech again." Wintermeyer did that. Standing in the hallway outside the Assembly, he read the entire litany of accusations to members of the press gallery.

A controversy developed in cabinet over how to respond. Attorney General Roberts and some other members advised the premier to ignore Wintermeyer's call for a royal commission and refer the whole matter to the new police commission. On the other hand, Robert Macaulay urged Roberts to establish an independent inquiry, arguing that the proposed police commission would not be perceived as adequate. Macaulay felt so strongly about the issue that he threatened resignation if Roberts did not establish an independent inquiry.

The premier informed the House that the government would make its position on the administration of justice clear the following Monday. The cabinet crisis continued throughout the weekend, but a compromise was worked out: the government would proceed with a bill establishing a police commission with the initial responsibility for investigating the state of crime in the province, but Wintermeyer's allegations would be referred to a royal commission headed by Mr. Justice Wilfrid Roach.

Attorney General Roberts had no alternative but to live with the cabinet decision, but he was very much opposed. The result was a bizarre sequence of events over the next few months, in which he both criticized, and intruded upon, the royal commission. On 25 January 1962 he went so far as to express doubts about the effectiveness of crime investigations, and alleged that certain persons, including well-known Liberals, were involved in organized crime. I described his statement as "the first stage in a campaign whose ultimate objective was to implicate the Liberals in order to absolve the Tories." In another public statement I noted that the attorney general, in a speech in Welland, had said that he believed the normal judicial procedure to be superior "to any repressive system which permits punishment on suspicion or belief, rather than on proper proof of guilt." It was a thinly veiled attack on the commission, in the midst of its hearings.

"That a Minister of the Crown, without resigning his seat in the cabinet, should repeatedly attack a royal commission set up to investigate his own department, is surely without precedent in Canadian history." In my public statement on 14 May 1962 I went on to describe the conduct of departmental officials, and concluded: "The commissioner is being asked to cope with unsolicited and unwarranted intervention of the attorney general's department and its senior officials while seeking to investigate [their] conduct. . . . Only one man can bring a halt to this intolerable situation. That is Premier Roberts."[5]

Robarts did nothing publicly, though he may have intervened privately because the attorney general's public criticism ceased. When Robarts shuffled his cabinet in October 1962, Roberts was transferred to Lands and Forests.

The Roach report was made public the following March (1963). Its 383 pages were replete with evidence of administrative laxity and a general lack of vigour in coping with the growing threat of organized crime, whose existence was acknowledged and documented. With regard to the chartering of social clubs, the commissioner stated, "In some instances, there was strong evidence of illegal gambling on club premises but the [provincial secretary's] department did not avail itself of the fact as a basis of cancellation until 1960," and, "in some instances the department was put on notice that there had been false returns made but did nothing about it." With reference to the courts, "too much leniency has been shown to book-makers in the matter of punishment." But most disturbing of all was an array of evidence that a group of gamblers successfully carried on extensive operations, despite previous criminal records, because of their corruption of the OPP.

The report revealed that Deputy Commissioner James Bartlett of the OPP, and Inspector J.S. Stringer, in charge of the Peterborough division, had acted as pawns for the gamblers. The commissioner stated flatly that their usefulness to the force had ended. Further, that former Staff Sergeant John F. Cronin, who had been in charge of the anti-gambling squad until his retirement, had enriched himself by providing information to Feeley and McDermott. Lesser lights in the OPP had also accepted bribes.

Even more alarming was the success with which the criminals, of whom the commission spoke in terms of the greatest contempt, were able to secure political influence to assist their plans. While the report exonerated officials within the attorney general's department, it named others, including the late James Maloney, minister of mines. The evidence documented his close associations with the criminals and large-scale gamblers, and his improper intervention on behalf of Feeley and McDermott in their application for a licence to operate small loans companies.

The report went on and on, voluminously documenting general charges that I had been making for three years or more. Mr. Justice Roach added a point, worthy of "urgent attention." He made it clear that he believed the evidence sworn before him, not only by gamblers, but by a number of police officers, was perjured testimony. I commented, "If the administration of justice and the efficacy of public inquiries is to be maintained, it will be necessary for the attorney general to take prompt and vigorous action to follow up this matter."

But there was no follow-up. The news coverage emphasized the exoneration of the attorney general's department and that most of Wintermeyer's specific charges were unfounded. Incredible as it may seem, the incriminating elements of the Roach report didn't register with the public, and the media virtually dropped the matter. There was one day's heated debate in the Legislature, after which the issue seemed to die.

As the 1963 election drew nearer, two ghosts of the scandal-ridden past emerged to haunt the government, even if fleetingly. On 14 September 1962, just a few weeks before he was transferred from the portfolio of attorney general, Robarts informed a gathering of securities administrators in Toronto that the investigation into the NONG affair had been re-opened. The casual nature of the revelation masked the extent to which events had trapped him.

During a British Columbia investigation into the transactions of a former securities commissioner, the RCMP uncovered evidence of the distribution of stock from the Convesto account. It will be recalled that the Ontario inquiry had learned that a block of NONG stock had been deposited there at favourable prices "on behalf of clients," but the investigators did not pursue the matter to find out who the clients were. For that reason, I had argued the government could deny that stocks had been used to "sweeten up" municipal officials along the pipeline route throughout northern Ontario, including former mayor Leo Landreville of Sudbury.

Both Premier Frost and Attorney General Roberts had argued, back in 1959, that further information was not sought because the inquiry had been "exhaustive." Roberts went so far as to say that he "would not be worthy of [his] office" if he had attempted to investigate any other persons, and "I stake my reputation on that statement." Now the RCMP had confronted the attorney general with the very evidence which he had not sought, and he had no alternative but to reappoint Messrs. Bray and Chisholm to complete their investigation. The final report was never made public. "Perhaps it was thought unnecessary," Roberts confided in his memoirs years later, "in view of the prosecutions which took place."

And what were the prosecutions? Precisely the ones which I had designated as necessary three years earlier in the raucous debate of 18 March 1959. The Ontario inquiry had ceased at the very point where the trail became hot. The evidence had always been available on the distribution from the Convesto account; the RCMP revealed what the Ontario inquiry concealed, by their failure to seek it. As a result, charges were laid against municipal officials along the route in Ontario, and convictions secured. Leo Landreville was found to be one of the recipients of the stock, as a result of which a subsequent parliamentary inquiry in Ottawa led to his resigning his judgeship. And Farris, president of NONG, was charged, convicted of perjury, and sentenced to Kingston Penitentiary.

"The long period of suspense and uncertainty had been replaced with finality," Kelso Roberts observed in his memoirs, adding that "As it subsequently turned out, there were key people, some in very responsible positions who, if they [had followed] the procedures in the Legislature as published in the press . . . could not help but be aware of the suspicions of undisclosed interests which were raised, particularly by the leader of the NDP party, and who would have saved everybody a lot of trouble and themselves a great deal of subsequent worry and concern if they had come forward voluntarily and given information within their knowledge. They did not do so."

It was a feeble lament, belatedly acknowledged. There were many in the government, including Roberts, who had been determined to cover up the scandal. Ultimately events conspired to frustrate their efforts. However, for political purposes, they had succeeded. One wonders what effect, if any, the full story might have had in the 1959 election. Certainly, its revelation three years later was low key and piecemeal and it was treated as yesterday's news. Kelso Roberts's braggadocio about staking his reputation on the completeness of the original Ontario inquiry remains mercifully buried in the pages of Hansard.

There were also postscripts to the rash of municipal scandals. The case of Chris Tonks had complications for me in York South. As a general practice I had not intervened in municipal politics, but in the wake of the Sweet report on procedures in the Township of York, there was a widespread reform movement which cut across party lines and involved the NDP. For the first time a party member, Fred Taylor, was elected as reeve, and he had the support of some members of council. Chris Tonks never forgave my involvement and, while himself a Liberal, thereafter he was active in support of Tory and Liberal candidates who ran against me. The case of his conflict of interest in the purchase of land from the municipality through a nominee was appealed up to the Supreme Court of Canada where judgment deprived him of the home which he had built on the land. Columnists Ron Haggart and Pierre Berton, of the Toronto *Star*, gave York affairs extensive coverage, and Chris Tonks never again won an election on a municipal-wide, as opposed to a ward, basis. But the loss of his home aroused sympathy among voters in his own ward which he has continued to represent, and his son Allan was mayor of the City of York for two terms and ran as Liberal candidate against Bob Rae in the 1987 election.

If I had to cope with fall-out from municipal politics in York South, the Conservatives, and particularly Premier Robarts, had even more in the riding of Russell, as the Eastview scandal reverberated throughout the provincial campagin. In 1959 Gordon Lavergne had successfully gained re-election in the midst of the Eastview irregularities, because he had the support of the government, and particularly of Premier Frost. By the time the 1963 election came the Russell riding association was deeply divided, with one faction supporting Lavergne, and another championing a young lawyer, A.B.R. (Bert) Lawrence, who won the nomination. The Lavergne faction refused to accept defeat and appealed to Elmer Bell, president of the Ontario Progressive Conservative Association. He reviewed the situation, and confirmed Lawrence's nomination. The Lavergne faction promptly held their own convention and nominated their "hero" as Conservative candidate. This time an appeal for support went directly to Robarts, who not only dismissed it, but when Lavergne ran as an independent, visited the riding twice to campaign for Lawrence. It was perhaps the most striking example of the difference between Frost and Robarts, in coping with misdemeanors among their colleagues. Lavergne was defeated and drifted into political oblivion.

With the 1963 election in prospect, the political situation had altered somewhat. The Liberal party was much more aggressive, particularly on the crime issue. The Roach report had said that Liberal leader Wintermeyer's specific charges were unfounded. Understandably, the Liberal party, with Harold Greer quarterbacking the effort, was determined to fight back. But on key issues, such as health insurance, the party had vacillated and was generally viewed as espousing right-wing positions, so much so that it lost the traditional endorsement of the Toronto *Star*.

The Tories had gotten off to a slow start under Robarts's leadership, but throughout 1962 and 1963, they had developed a range of issues underpinned by Robert Macaulay's twenty-point program on economic development. On paper, and in political promises, Robarts simply said: "Done!" In a rousing speech in the Legislature, for the first time reminiscent of Frost's rallying efforts, he had ticked off all the government's accomplishments, to the resounding applause of rejuvenated backbenchers. All of these claims overshadowed the issue of crime when the Roach report concluded that, while there was organized crime, there were no links with the Mafia, and no corruption or cover-ups in the attorney general's department.

As for the NDP, the party approached the election with moderately higher hopes. The founding convention of 1961 had been preoccupied with constitutional and other matters, as the CCF evolved into the new political structure. But in 1962 the first regular policy convention adopted a wide-ranging platform. On all the major issues — notably education, health insurance and farm marketing — the party had established a position different from that of the Liberals, and in vigorous opposition to the Tories. While there had not been time to consolidate the wider public support which the new party had evoked, it was hoped that the popular vote would increase, and produce a few more seats. Redistribution was under way, but not completed: as an interim measure ten new seats were added in the swollen suburban areas of Metro Toronto, Ottawa and Kitchener-Waterloo, enlarging the Legislature from ninety-eight to one hundred and eight seats.

The NDP campaign remained on a relatively modest scale. The leader's tour was still limited to my car and such representatives of the media as chose to travel with me. When the votes were counted, the NDP gains were minimal — up from five to seven seats. The Tories had six more seats, up to seventy-seven, and the Liberals two more, up to twenty-four. The popular vote accurately reflected these shifts, with the Tories increased marginally to 48.9 per cent while the Liberals and NDP dropped marginally to 35.5 per cent and 15.5 per cent respectively. Thus the Tory domination of the House remained, with a better than two-to-one majority over the combined opposition. This majority not only gave Robarts a personal mandate, but consolidated his leadership. Memories of Leslie Frost had faded, though Old Man Ontario was a behind-the-scenes adviser whenever the government got into trouble.

In retrospect, the NDP's limited gains were the result of the third party being overshadowed in a knock-down battle between the Conservatives and the Liberals. Wintermeyer fought "a scandal-a-day campaign" which didn't add to his party's credibility. It has always been my view that he was Robarts's greatest asset: the longer the shrill attack went on, the more attractive became the solid, chairman-of-the-board image of Robarts. Wintermeyer lost his own seat in Kitchener. The polarized situation postponed any electoral reflection of growing public support for the NDP.

I drew consolation from the fact that I had held my seat with over 47 per cent of the vote, fractionally increased over 1959. More important, Fred Young (Yorkview), with his long experience in the party and in municipal affairs, and Stephen Lewis (Scarborough West), widely acknowledged for his organizational and debating skills, were added to caucus. I was struck by the number of political opponents who confided that they had expected the NDP to do better. I couldn't help but agree with them.

On 19 March 1964, well into the first session of the new Legislature, Attorney General Fred Cass introduced Bill 99. If the government had any illusions that the Roach report, and Wintermeyer's defeat in the election, had disposed of the organized crime issue, they were in for a thundering disillusionment. Ironically, their own mishandling of the issue raised it once again.

Ostensibly, Bill 99, immediately dubbed the Police State Bill, sought to strengthen the powers of the police to cope with organized crime, but it was perceived to be a serious threat to basic civil rights. The results were politically more explosive than any single event at Queen's Park in the postwar years. To understand what happened, the personality of the attorney general, and the administrative problems which he faced, must be considered. In his previous portfolios, Fred Cass had proven to be an able administrator, but he was a prickly individual who tended to respond to people rather arbitrarily. Therefore he had difficulty reconciling the differences in relationships among his department, the OPP and the Ontario Police Commission. It was, as A.K. McDougall, Robarts's biographer, has commented, "a major department of government headed by a minister with a confused and conflicting set of responsibilities."[5]

As chief law officer of the Crown, the attorney general must sit in judgment over his cabinet colleagues, and yet at the same time respect the convention of cabinet solidarity. This isolation had been strengthened during Kelso Roberts's long tenure as attorney general, because he was, as I have noted, an outsider and a loner in the Frost and Robarts cabinets.

Added to these basic conflicts were new ones arising from the establishment of the Ontario Police Commission which had broad, but vague, authority over the Ontario police forces, as well as responsibility for keeping on top of organized crime. Kelso Roberts had appointed Judge B.J.S. Macdonald as the first chairman of the Ontario Police Commission. In response to the crime problem, Eric H. Silk, a man who was "blunt, forceful and experienced at administrative reform," had been appointed commissioner of the Ontario Provincial Police. Thus, there were three powerful men charged with responsibilities to improve policing and law enforcement — Cass as attorney general, Macdonald at the Police Commission, and Silk, head of the OPP, with lines of jurisdiction and coordination between them ill-defined. The stage was set for a clash, particularly between Cass and Macdonald.

The Roach commission inflamed, rather than solved, the problem, for while it documented the existence of crime, it contended that it had not reached the stage of being syndicated in Ontario. It was a fine distinction with which police authorities, notably RCMP Commissioner Harvison, publicly disagreed. Judge Macdonald assumed that it was the responsibility of the new Police Commission to pursue the investigations and resolve these different assessments, but he was uncertain of the commission's power to gather evidence. So he asked the attorney general for authority to hold hearings in private, to give assurance of secrecy to witnesses and to compel attendance at private hearings.

Bill 99 was the government's response to this request. The explanatory note inoffensively read, "This new section provides for the machinery necessary for the commission to investigate matters relating to the extent, investigation and control of crime in Ontario." In processing the bill, an incredible series of events, adding up to neglect, eventually compounded by bad judgment on the part of the attorney general, created a situation which burst upon the political scene.

The premier was greatly preoccupied with a surfeit of legislative business and outside commitments, to which was added the death and funeral of his father. Understandably, he was emotionally drained, and not on top of developments. When the draft bill passed cabinet, many members were absent, including Kelso Roberts, which left him free to play the role of critic. Before presentation in the House it had been considered at a Conservative caucus, when only ten of the seventy-five members were present. When the Legislature convened an hour later, Cass introduced the bill with comments on first reading that were disarmingly innocuous.

Later, however, at a press conference, he lit a short fuse to a political time bomb. He expressed fears that section 14 of the bill might constitute a threat to individual rights. When queried by Peter Reilly of CBC TV, he replied: "Yes, that's what bothers me." But when Reilly asked him to repeat his observations on camera, he went on to say, "It is drastic, it is dangerous and it is new and it is terrible legislation in an English common law country." When asked the obvious question as to why, then, he had introduced the bill, Cass retorted, "Don't ask me, ask Judge Macdonald." True, the request for the amendments had come from Judge Macdonald, but now it was Cass's bill, and the revelation of tension between the two men added fuel to the media fire. It was a classic case of sloppy government preparation of legislation.

Oblivious to the fast-developing storm, Robarts and many of his colleagues were entertaining members of the press at the Royal York Hotel, when the "bull-dog" edition of the *Globe and Mail* hit the street with screaming headlines. Drastic, dangerous, terrible, Star Chamber legislation, Bill of Wrong: the media led Ontarians into a veritable "hurricane of outraged protest."

Reflective of the outcry was the crisis that developed in cabinet, and more broadly in the Conservative party. Kelso Roberts led the way, but others rapidly followed. Allan Lawrence threatened to cross the floor if the bill were passed. Len Reilly, MPP for Eglinton, said he would leave the party if such dangerous legislation were enacted. The phones were ringing off the wall.

Robarts spent the weekend closeted with close aides, including Leslie Frost, who helped draft a counter offensive. When the House convened on Monday, the atmosphere was electric and the galleries were full for the debate — a rare occurrence at Queen's Park.

Robarts gave his assurance, "If there is a conflict between the rights of the individual and the necessity for powers to deal with the criminal elements in our society, then the rights of the individual must be supreme, even if it means that in so doing we gave the criminal elements in our society an advantage which we would rather they did not have." The government could have withdrawn the bill altogether. But Robarts had decided to save face by fighting the issue out in committee, and he moved that Bill 99 be sent for review by the Legal

Bills Committee. That left the door open for Farquhar Oliver, acting Liberal leader, to amend Robarts's motion, calling for withdrawal of the bill.

My contribution to the debate at this stage was repetition of the now-familiar dangers of the proposed legislation, emphasizing that in addition to all the confusion and conflict within the government ranks, they were unrepentant in their contention that individual rights were not endangered by section 14. The debate raged on throughout the afternoon, and continued well into the evening.[6] At the normal adjournment hour, the Liberal amendment calling for withdrawal of the bill was defeated. I immediately rose and stated that I wished to speak to the main motion for which a further amendment was in order. I moved simply that the bill be sent to committee with instructions that the offensive section 14 be deleted.

Robarts accepted my amendment, but attempted to maintain the government's contention that the dangers in the bill were exaggerated. His dilemma was that advisers steadfastly contended that section 14 did not abrogate the traditional protection of individual rights. Obviously, there were sharp differences of opinion on this point, but the premier suggested they could be threshed out in committee. My amendment was adopted ninety-six to zero — a very rare occurrence, indeed, in my legislative career.

The following week I had an exchange with Robarts during a chance encounter in the legislative hallways, and his comments revealed another reason for the government's reluctance to back off. Having been badgered mercilessly on the crime issue by the opposition, particularly by the Liberals, from the time of Wintermeyer's speech leading to the appointment of the Roach commission, he was angered by the Liberals' readiness to exploit Bill 99, which was the government's way of strengthening police capacity to deal with organized crime. Overnight, in Robarts's view, they had forsaken their concern in favour of a sensational exploiting of the civil liberties issue. "I was willing to support your motion," he confided, "but not the amendment of those goddamn Liberals."

However, the New Democratic Party caucus was not content to leave the issue of individual rights at that point. On

14 April I gave notice of a motion calling for the appointment of a select committee to explore the need for safeguarding the fundamental rights of citizens from infringement, either by statute or various regulations and procedures. I pointed out that, even if the federal Bill of Rights were strengthened through entrenchment in our constitution, it would not apply to offending provincial statutes. There was need for a provincial Bill of Rights. The CCF government in Saskatchewan had passed one twenty years earlier. Now was the appropriate time for a comprehensive study and report to the Legislature on all these areas in which basic rights of our people should be more effectively safeguarded.

Having been burned badly in the whole Bill 99 affair, Robarts was anxious to repair the image of the administration as being insensitive to the protection of these rights, and he went one better. He announced the appointment of former Chief Justice James C. McRuer to head an inquiry into civil rights. In the next five years McRuer combed the statutes and regulations of the province of Ontario and revealed an astounding array of unwitting violations of basic rights. His monumental study, released in 1968 and thereafter, became a guide to governments, not only in Canada, but throughout the free world.

The aftermath of the 1963 election clarified the relationship between political parties in Ontario and, strangely, set the stage for the next exciting chapter in NDP history. While the opposition parties had received more than half the popular vote, they won only thirty-one of the one hundred and eight seats. How long were the Tories to dominate Ontario politics, while supported by only a minority of the electorate? Frustration grew in both NDP and the Liberal ranks.

On 23 December 1963 a front-page story by Mark Gayn in the Toronto *Star* revealed that private meetings had been held:

Highly secret conversations have been in progress between Liberal and New Democratic Party leaders on both the federal and Ontario provincial levels. Involved in these contacts — described variously as "shadowy," "exploratory," and "tentative" — have been a number of federal cabinet ministers [including] Finance Minister Walter Gordon and Labour Minister Allan MacEachen. Also participating was Keith Davey, the Liberal Party's national organizer. Federal NDP leaders taking part in these tenuous conversations included T.C. Douglas, party leader; Douglas Fisher, its whip in the House of Commons, and David Lewis, the party's vice-chairman.

The purpose of the federal contacts had been to explore whether, sometime in the future, the two parties might find a common meeting ground. All the participants approached the talks with skepticism; on each side they were acting as individuals rather than party representatives. However, the *Star* reported, "The secret and almost reluctant dialogue in Ottawa seems to have been suspended after the discovery that members of the two parties in Ontario were engaged in a somewhat similar enterprise." But whereas the meetings in Ottawa were said to be in search of points of policy and philosophy on which the two parties might agree, it was alleged that the Ontario talks "have been specific and far more advanced."

The most prominent Liberals engaged in the Ontario discussions included John Wintermeyer, who had resigned as leader the previous September following his personal defeat in the general election; Arthur Reaume, MPP for Essex North; Andrew Thompson, MPP for Dovercourt, one of the rising party stars; Vernon Singer, MPP for York Centre; and Mark MacGuigan, then professor of law at the University of Toronto.

As far as the Ontario NDP was concerned, there had been no authorized participation. Initially I was unaware of the meetings. Those who took part in the talks were Eamon Park, a Steelworker official and NDP national treasurer; Murray Cotterill, public relations director of the Steelworkers; and Desmond Sparham, who had been director of the New Party clubs and had since headed up a group known as "Exchange of Political Ideas in Canada."

Wintermeyer had taken the lead in the whole effort. Typical

of the meetings was one at his home on Sherbourne Street, when "most of those invited seem not to have been told in advance why they had been invited." At that particular meeting, in attendance were Dr. Boyd Upper, who had been executive secretary of the Ontario Liberal party while Wintermeyer was leader, and Harold Greer, who had been the leading Liberal party strategist during the 1963 campaign.

The *Star*'s description of the meeting (held in late fall of 1963) and its purpose was that "the group discussed the feasibility of an anti-Conservative grouping. . . . The gathering appears to have been sensitive to its own limitations. One reason for this was clearly the fact that the host's influence in the party had declined sharply after his defeat and resignation in September."

These meetings took on potentially great political significance but their initiative had stemmed from a legitimate trade union concern. In a recent speech in Niagara Falls, Wintermeyer had promised major labour reform, including a minimum wage of $1.25 an hour, industrial self-government and restrictions on strike-breaking. The Steelworker leaders were seeking to clarify this apparently new direction in Liberal policy.

When the *Star* broke the news of the meetings, William Mahoney, Canadian director of the Steelworkers, issued a statement that the meetings had been neither secret nor official; that no one had proposed a merger of the parties; that there was a substantial number of Liberals in Ontario who were concerned with the party's program, financing and basically undemocratic structure, who had approached people they knew in the NDP, inquiring about the possibility of a new left alignment in Ontario. The Steelworkers' position was set forth unequivocally by Murray Cotterill in *Steel Labour*, the union's house organ, and received wide coverage in the daily press:

There is a black spot to the surface of this rosy picture of opposition unanimity. The big black spot is, while there isn't any doubt, due to the structure and financing of the NDP, MacDonald would have the support of the party in enacting legislation if he can win enough seats to form

a government, Wintermeyer and his followers can
guarantee no such support from the Liberal party. It is
this same structural deficiency which makes any talk of
the NDP/Liberal merger an impossibility.

Outside the party, the press was very much in the game.
Both the *Globe and Mail* and the Toronto *Star* had periodically
suggested editorially that the NDP should get together with the
Liberals. I had dealt with these proposals in a CBC TV network broadcast a few weeks earlier:

> You will forgive us, I am sure, if we consider all this
> advice with something more than normal care. After all,
> the *Globe*, though traditionally Conservative, supported
> the federal Liberals last April; and in September, the *Star*,
> traditionally Liberal, supported the Conservatives in the
> provincial election. There is obviously no serious difficulty
> for Liberals and Conservatives to support each other
> when the common interests for which they speak need
> to be protected. Furthermore, you must find it as dif-
> ficult as I have to follow the editorial logic, particularly
> when the line of reasoning keeps changing.

The time had come for a frank statement of a basic reality
in Canadian politics, namely, that a new party, with a fundamentally different philosophy, was needed; but that decision had been made in 1932-33, when the CCF was founded,
and again in 1961 when the New Democratic Party was
launched. I issued a statement which had been endorsed by
the provincial executive:

> The New Democratic Party represents in the 1960s the
> culmination of many attempts to give expression to the
> progressive tradition in Canadian politics.
>   Down through the years farmer and labour parties,
> farmer-labour parties, socialist parties, the Progressives
> and the CCF have all represented a continuing protest of
> the people and their economic organizations — a protest
> based on the conviction that the Old Parties have failed

to represent their interests. Countless thousands have sacrificed their time and energy, their limited resources, and even their careers, in pursuit of this goal. . . .

This realignment of political forces in Canada is in keeping with developments throughout most of the democratic world, but it has only just begun. There are progressives among the Conservatives and Liberals whose political hopes are constantly frustrated by the dominant group from the business world which finances and controls both the Liberal and Conservative Parties. These genuine progressives and liberals belong on the democratic left — within a party such as the New Democratic Party seeks to be. . . .

We in the New Democratic Party freely acknowledge that we have not yet united all the progressive forces on the Canadian political scene. We agree that Canada needs a strong party on the democratic left which only these forces can build — a party which will represent, among others, the legitimate interests of the business community while free of the domination of Big Business. We have every intention of continuing to work for the achievement of this vital need in Canadian politics.

To do otherwise would be to betray the sacrifices of those who have struggled down through the years to build an alternative to the democratic right which has governed Canada since Confederation. If the New Democratic Party were to forsake this historical goal, then as surely as night follows day, another new party would spring up to carry on, and a significant proportion of New Democratic vote would go to it. The result would not be to unite the progressive forces in Canadian politics, but to divide them further; not to move closer to the day of a rational realignment of parties in this country, but to its indefinite postponement.

In stating this, the New Democratic Party takes no doctrinaire stand. We are not close-minded to those, either inside or outside our ranks, who are critical and seek to adapt our basic philosophy of social democracy to modern needs and conditions.[7]

That remains as a basic statement of the NDP's philosophy and position in Canadian politics. But lest it be perceived as being unduly rigid and uncooperative in the normal operation of the parliamentary system, I emphasized that "We will cooperate with any party, whether it be the Conservatives in power or the Liberals in opposition, when we are convinced that cooperation is in the best interests of the people of Ontario."

A generation later, the potential of that cooperation emerged in the NDP-Liberal Accord, bringing an end to forty-two years of Tory rule. In 1963 my proposal was made in specific policy terms. The government had determined to proceed with health insurance on a private basis, in cooperation with the medical profession and the insurance companies. The Liberals had vacillated from one policy to another. The Hall commission, appointed by the Diefenbaker government, was soon to bring in a report vigorously asserting that the public model, developed in Saskatchewan, was unquestionably the best. If the Liberals could see their way clear to end their vacillation and come out solidly for public health insurance, the NDP would welcome joint efforts to persuade the government to forsake its mistaken ways.

I went a step further. Car insurance was a lively issue. The CCF/NDP government in Saskatchewan had pioneered public car insurance, which proved to be so superior that Manitoba and British Columbia copied the model and, significantly, no subsequent government in all three provinces, notwithstanding its free enterprise philosophy, has dared to return to private car insurance. I invited the Liberals to join forces with the NDP in support of public car insurance in Ontario.

Regrettably, no such cooperation developed. Though both opposition parties were in support of comprehensive public health insurance, they were ineffective in face of the government's overwhelming majority. As for public car insurance, those Liberals who supported it were silenced by the dominant right wing.

It provoked me to a caustic comment: "The Liberal party is like Toronto's new city hall. It has a big right wing and a smaller left wing, and a centre that goes round and round."

A Toronto campaign rally in 1963.

Relaxing — off the campaign trail, with Debbie, the pet that ran the family.

Sweet victory — after one of the York South campaigns — Simone *(left)* and Joy *(right)*.

10

Breakthrough, 1964 to 1977

Political trends often defy rational assessment. For ten years, the CCF/NDP had fought titanic battles, with virtually no progress in terms of popular vote, which fluctuated in the range of 15 per cent through three elections, and limited electoral success in terms of seats. For reasons that were not readily apparent, the tide began to turn in 1964. It may be, as I have suggested earlier, that greater electoral support, as a result of the impetus of the New Party, was delayed in the 1963 election because of the knock-down battle between the old parties.

In any case, added support began to emerge in 1964. The first evidence of it was in the Riverdale by-election which was brought about by the resignation of Robert Macaulay, who had provided much of the dynamic in the government during the earlier Robarts years. A fall by-election was called and the campaign attracted province-wide attention. The Liberal candidate was Charles Templeton, a former evangelist and broadcaster, who was currently running for the Liberal leadership. The NDP candidate was James Renwick, a respected corporation lawyer with a Liberal firm. Renwick had attended the federal Liberal think-tank in Kingston in 1960, and came away unimpressed. He then attended the first regular convention of the provincial NDP in 1962 and was sufficiently impressed that he joined the party. He ran federally in York East in 1963, but was not successful. There was some overlap in the boundaries of the then York East federal riding and the Riverdale provincial riding, and he was nominated for the provincial by-election.

That campaign became a classic in the NDP strategy of

door-to-door canvassing. It became known as the NDP's secret weapon. Stephen Lewis master-minded the campaign, with the assistance of Marj (Pinney) Wells, who helped to perfect the technique. It influenced the style of campaigning in Ontario politics because it was so successful as to force other parties to emulate it.

I always found by-elections to be a satisfying experience. Not only was there the advantage of lending the prestige of the leader to the campaign, but it provided an opportunity to join with the volunteer canvassers in genuine grass-roots politicking. I was assigned a poll in the heart of the riding, lying south of Queen Street, covering Logan and Booth avenues. The campaign managers were intrigued: in a riding that had been strongly Tory, this poll had been Liberal. On my first canvass, I discovered one of the reasons: a significant proportion of the voters were French Canadians with the traditional Liberal voting preference. So Simone came in to canvass them in their own language. By the time the campaign was over, I had become so well known in every home and local variety store that when I appeared on the street, the kids flocked around like old friends. When the votes were counted, the Liberals had held their support, but the NDP had catapulted from a poor third to winner of the poll.

What happened in this poll was typical of the overall results. The intense communication with the voters through three or four canvasses increased the turnout from just over 50 per cent to the mid-sixties, and most of these new voters went for the NDP. Jim Renwick won handily, and Charles Templeton came in third.

A few weeks later, this triumph was repeated in the federal riding of Waterloo South. The NDP candidate was Max Saltsman, a respected local businessman. Keith Davey, later familiarly known as the "Rainmaker," had persuaded the previous NDP candidate to switch to the Liberals, so there was an added edge to the campaign.

For me, it was perhaps the most memorable in my many years of campaigning. Fired up with the Riverdale victory, I turned up to seek a poll for canvassing. The first offer was one in the urban area of Hespeler. I objected. If the NDP couldn't get canvassers for the urban polls, we were in a bad way. Was there not somewhere else, where I might be more useful? To which the reply was, "What about Wilmot Township?" Quite frankly, I had never heard of Wilmot Township. It lay south of the cities of Kitchener and Waterloo, and comprised some fifteen polls. There was only a handful — precisely five, as I remember — of NDP members. But it was a rural area, and offered the chance to get a first-hand picture of farm problems, always one of my major legislative interests.

I soon discovered that, like all rural areas lying within the shadow of a city, its population was heavily urbanized. So, starting in Kitchener-Waterloo, I sought out people who worked in the city, but lived in the country. By combing the personnel lists of unions and the two universities, I quickly came up with some forty to fifty people resident in Wilmot Township. One of them was the registrar at Waterloo University; another was the president of the NDP club on campus, who happened to be the son of the mayor of New Dundee, one of the towns in Wilmot. Before long, I had acquired twelve to fifteen canvassers, who were willing to work their local polls. At campaign headquarters, I was dubbed the "Baron of Wilmot," a title which stuck to me on every visit in subsequent years.

We didn't win Wilmot, but we cut the usual plurality of fifteen hundred against the NDP to three hundred. Max Saltsman won the election to begin a distinguished career in the House of Commons. And in later elections, he always got a good vote in Wilmot Township.

Two by-election wins, within a matter of weeks, provided a great fillip for the party. Federally, animosity between Pearson and Diefenbaker was alienating the electorate and the NDP's support was starting to rise.

In the Legislature the NDP was having a greater impact, in part because the Liberal opposition was floundering. Andy Thompson had beaten Charles Templeton for the leadership. While he had represented the Toronto riding of Dovercourt since 1959, he had not played a major legislative role; his efforts had been devoted primarily to organizing Walter Gordon's federal candidacy following years of work for the federal Liberal party among new Canadians in Toronto's west end. However, Thompson had burst upon the political scene with a speech in the debate on the infamous Bill 99. Because of it, overnight he became a leadership hope of the Liberal party. But his leadership years were undistinguished, and ended in a physical breakdown in 1966, paving the way for Robert Nixon to become the Liberal leader a few months before the 1967 election.

However, the growing impact of the NDP was not so much because of the vacuum left by the Liberals as because of the more effective efforts of a small, but greatly strengthened team. Ken Bryden continued as an authoritative spokesman on many issues, notably in the budgetary field. Stephen Lewis was increasingly effective in driving home social issues. Jim Renwick, as a corporation lawyer, commanded attention in policy areas, which the NDP normally was not able to capture. And Fred Young, as an experienced municipal politician, became an authoritative spokesman on local government, as well as on an ever-widening range of issues. My contribution was viewed less and less as scandal-mongering. During these years, the NDP was recognized more and more as the champion of the major concerns of the people of Ontario.[1]

Equally important was the gradual strengthening of the party organization. George Cadbury was president during the first six years of the NDP. His background was in the English confectionery manufacturing family. He had come to Canada on a five-year contract, as chairman of the planning board of the first CCF government in Saskatchewan, but he never returned to England. George provided a wealth of administrative and policy experience. His proudest achievement was that he left the presidency with the party clear of debt — a not inconsiderable achievement.

Peg Stewart had carried on as provincial secretary during the transition from CCF to NDP. Along with her husband Miller, who was president in the latter CCF years, she had made an important contribution to the party, including her co-authorship, with Doris French, of *Ask No Quarter*, a biography of Agnes Macphail. Her communication skills continue with her sons Walter and Sandy, well-known figures in the Canadian media world.

Jim Bury took over from Peg Stewart as provincial secretary in 1962, bringing long experience as organizer with the Packinghouse Workers. In later years, Jim went on to work with trade unionists in the emerging nations of Africa, and eventually, as labour attaché with the Canadian High Commission in London. With him on the provincial office staff was Gordon Brigden, who had first taken on part-time organizational work to consolidate my home base in York South, but then went on to become provincial organizer, provincial secretary and national treasurer. Gordon brought a solid grass-roots appreciation of the basic need for organization, and how it can be achieved — so much so that he is now much sought after as a trouble-shooter in election campaigns across the country.

This increasingly effective team was further strengthened in 1964, with the appointment of Desmond Morton as assistant provincial secretary. Today, Des is known as one of Canada's ablest — certainly most prolific — historians and political commentators. He is the son of an army brigadier. As an undergraduate at Royal Military College, he won a Rhodes Scholarship in 1959. While in Britain, he joined the New Party club in London, which included such illustrious names as Donald Gordon, Jr. (son of CNR president Donald Gordon) and Charles Taylor (son of financier E.P. Taylor) and now an established journalist. I first met Des when he was stationed at Camp Borden, and turned up at a house meeting (of six persons) in Alliston, which I attended in an effort to breathe life into the virtually non-existent CCF riding association of Dufferin-Simcoe. A year or so later, he worked in my 1963 York South campaign, where his organizational skills captured attention. As a result, in 1964 he was "bought out" of the army by the NDP at a cost of some $8,000, which Des insisted should be returned to the party by taking a reduced salary. For four years he was officially on staff as assistant provincial secretary, during which time the party benefited from his phenomenal energy and imaginative approach to all activities.

In 1965 Des left the payroll, but continued with volunteer work tantamount to a full-time staffer, in order to free up money for another expansion. Two candidates were being advocated for provincial secretary: John Harney, who had been federal candidate in Guelph while teaching at the Ontario Agricultural College, and Wally Ross, a top organizer with the Steelworkers. These two men resolved the contest in advance of the convention. They met one evening and found that they enjoyed the prospect of working together and decided that Harney would run for secretary and Ross for director of organization. The convention confirmed their decision. Shortly afterward, Ken Goldstein was hired as public relations director. Although only recently graduated from Ryerson Polytechnical Institute, Ken was fast establishing himself as a "whiz kid" of the communication world.

The party now had a staff which was small, but experienced and sophisticated. Person for person, they were a match for the personnel of the old parties. But in the NDP, while full-time staff is important, it is the membership and voluntary leadership which ultimately makes the overall effort effective. For years the membership had stalled in the ten to twelve thousand range. In the mid-sixties, with an increasingly favourable political climate, it had doubled to twenty-five thousand. For the first time the NDP had enough troops on the ground to do a more effective job.

Challenging them from the level of the organizing committee of the provincial council was Val Scott. He had been the candidate in the big federal riding of York Centre where he always ran second, but with larger votes than any other elected MP. Val set the party sights high, with the slogan of "67 in '67" for the next provincial campaign. The whole campaign was presented in a more sophisticated way, through the volunteer assistance of Keith Woollard, chairman of the NDP communications committee, who added the expertise of his regular work as director of communications at the headquarters of the United Church of Canada.

Paralleling the staff expansion at the party level was a similar development at the caucus. During the 1960s John Robarts brought the Ontario Legislature into the twentieth century.

He acknowledged the important role which the opposition plays in the parliamentary system, and gradually allocated financial resources for staff, to provide some balance with those available to the governing party. For ten years the CCF/NDP caucus staff had been the indefatigable Ellen Adams, nominally secretary, but in fact a "Jill of all trades," handling anything and everything that had to be done.

Of the hundreds of press releases that went out from my office, all (with the exception of five) had been written by me on my ancient Underwood. There was no research staff and no press relations personnel. In 1966 Terry Grier left the post of federal NDP secretary to become my executive assistant. No political leader could ask for an *alter ego* more completely compatible. For the first time I had assistance in preparing speeches and public statements. From my office Terry and Ellen developed working relationships with the media, which were thirsting for news of more effective opposition to the government, given the lowly fortunes of the Liberal party at that time.

The expansion didn't end there. In 1965, Jurgen Hesse was appointed to assist with research, but he returned to Vancouver in less than a year and Marion Bryden became director of research. She had nobody to direct, other than such volunteer effort as we were able to encourage. Tax reform was a dominant issue of those days, with the Carter Commission federally, and the Smith Committee provincially, investigating the regressive tax system. While on the staff of the Canadian Tax Foundation, Marion had acquired a reputation which was acknowledged in legislative debates by the government front benchers.

As the 1967 election drew near, the rising fortunes of the party were attracting a growing range of persons, who were perceived as champions of disadvantaged groups in society. First was John Brown, who had built a network of camps and rehabilitation facilities for emotionally disturbed children. In spite of criticism (and subsequent legal difficulties), Brown Camps were providing a desperately needed service, and at a per capita cost to the government that was lower than that of provincial institutions such as Thistletown.

Even more sensational was the decision of Dr. Morton Shulman. Morty had a running battle with the Tory establishment while a Metro coroner, and decided that action could be achieved only through the political process. He scouted the field, found the Liberals unconvincing on the issues which he was championing, and eventually threw in his lot with the NDP. The announcement of this decision, and his introduction to the 1966 convention, sent party spirits soaring.

Less sensational, though nevertheless significant, were developments in that section of the Ministry of Welfare dealing with native peoples. There had long been rumblings of concern about the inadequacies of public policy, and John Yaremko, the minister of the day, had made glowing statements about change. Those responsible for implementing the policy felt that the gap between policy and performance had so widened that a group of them resigned in protest. Leading the group was Ross McClellan, a social worker, who pursued his profession in other areas, until winning election to the Legislature in Toronto Bellwoods in 1975.

The experience of Mac Makarchuk in Brantford was indicative of problems the party faced, and the breaks which were coming our way. Mac won the NDP nomination, and, as a result, was fired from his position as farm reporter for the *Expositor*. He proceeded to win the election.

Events such as these created the impression that the NDP was a constructive and growing opposition at Queen's Park. The NDP contended, and the evidence became more convincing, that it was generating the political action. In his syndicated column in newspapers across Canada, Peter C. Newman observed, "The remarkable upsurge of the NDP — both federally and provincially — has suddenly become the dominant fact of Canadian politics."

For the first time, the NDP had all the ingredients for fighting an effective election campaign. At the staff level, both in the party and at the caucus, a highly professional campaign was planned and ready for launching with the issue of the election writ. The resources were still pathetically inadequate, as compared with the old parties, particularly the Tories, but with

Simone on the campaign trail, 1967.

Tommy Douglas with David Lewis and George Cadbury, at another fund raising event in the Canadian Room at the Royal York Hotel on the occasion of my 10th anniversary as an MPP.

Simone after the campaign, 1967.

David Lewis, Woodrow Lloyd and George Cadbury in a convention pose.

the NDP, after years of drought, a little went a long way.

Marion Bryden turned out documented policy material. Keith Wollard and Ken Goldstein packaged the program attractively. Wally Ross, assisted by John Harney, Gordon Brigden and Des Morton, along with the reserves of elections organizers, beefed up local campaigns in a fashion that had never before been accomplished. Most important of all, the campaign had a direction and strategy, known to all, which were consistently followed.

The Liberals had just come through a difficult leadership period, resolved by the acclamation of Bob Nixon as leader, on the eve of the election. John Robarts was building a personal reputation as a leading Father of Re-Confederation, climaxed by his calling of the Confederation of Tomorrow Conference in Toronto in 1967. But the Tory party organization had been neglected, and the premier's personal relations with the media were, as always, somewhat cool. This left an opening of which Terry Grier and Ellen Adams took advantage. Under the circumstances, the NDP campaign slogan "67 in '67," though preposterously optimistic, appeared more credible. I constantly reminded audiences that the Farmer-Labour government had been elected in 1919 with nothing other than two earlier by-election victories, that the Socreds in Alberta had gone from no seats to a government in 1935. Canadian experience indicated, so I argued, that it was not inconceivable that a party could jump from eight seats to at least minority government in Ontario.

Symbolic of the new-found strength and resources of the party was the emergence of a leadership tour worthy of the name. We had a bus, emblazoned with banners, and all the familiar trappings of major party campaigning. On the bus was Terry Grier, who was not only thoroughly familiar with all phases of the election preparation, but a first-rate strategist. Joining him, for an experience in grass-roots politics, was George Rawlyk, a historian from Queen's University, who contributed his time and effort to the preparation of speeches, interviews and broadcasts. Everything seemed to come together.

For the first time, too, Simone joined the campaign trail.

She had worked in every election — enumerating, canvassing and doing myriad tasks at campaign headquarters in York South, particularly on election day. As our children grew older, they pitched in to assure their father's elections, while I was travelling all over the province. They became experienced campaigners at an early age. Brian augmented the sign crew with school pals who got caught up in the excitement of electioneering. But in addition to this work at the riding level, Simone now became the "first lady" on the leader's tour. Every year she had hosted the annual press party at our home and got to know the reporters and broadcasters personally. On the touring bus she helped to provide a generally congenial atmosphere. In addition, her command of French supplemented my inadequate grasp of the language, so that in the francophone communities she was much in demand for interviews.

In the early stages of the campaign the Tories attempted to coast on Robarts's reputation as a leading Canadian statesman. It was an obvious strategy for them, but it was not enough to counter the NDP's relentless pounding of the basic issues which touched people's lives: cost of living, taxes and housing. Whatever new item I might introduce at every meeting, to freshen the appeal, at some point I would revert to a listing of the "three gut issues." It became such a familiar routine that the reporters, usually seated at a table beneath, or to the side of, the speaker's podium, would feign a frantic scribbling of this familiar ritual. But the issues slowly registered with the electorate; in the final week the government sensed a slippage, and began to respond. The NDP had effectively set the agenda for the campaign.

When the votes were counted, the NDP had achieved a breakthrough to major party status, something which had been lost since the heady days of the CCF in the 1940s. Our popular vote had jumped from 15 per cent to 26 per cent, with an increase in seats from eight to twenty. The Tories had slipped from 49 per cent to 42 per cent, with a loss of eight seats, while the Liberals dropped from 35 per cent to 31 per cent, though gaining four seats. The redistribution of riding boundaries had been completed, raising the number of seats from one hundred and eight to one hundred and seventeen, and the NDP had benefited most from the larger House.

Most important of all, the NDP caucus was now more representative of the province: in the north, we had bolstered our presence with four new members: Elie Martel (Sudbury East), Jack Stokes (Thunder Bay), Donald Jackson (Temiskaming) and Bill Ferrier (Cochrane South); in Windsor, Fred Burr (Windsor-Riverside) and Hugh Peacock (Windsor West) had emerged; in Brantford, Mac Makarchuk; in Oshawa, Cliff Pilkey; in Peterborough, Walter Pitman; in Hamilton, Ian Deans (Wentworth) joined Reg Gisborn (Hamilton East) and Norm Davison (Hamilton Centre). In Metropolitan Toronto, our numbers had doubled: added to the "old gang" of Fred Young (Yorkview), Stephen Lewis (Scarborough West), James Renwick (Riverdale) and me in York South, were Pat Lawlor (Lakeshore), Margaret Renwick (Scarborough Centre), John Brown (Beaches-Woodbine) and Morton Shulman (High Park).

It had been a long road back from near oblivion in 1951, but the NDP was on the march again. For the first time I came out of an election where the results spoke for themselves, and I didn't have to make any excuses.

11
Last of the Leadership Years, 1967 to 1970

The 1967 breakthrough created a new situation. Overnight the NDP was transformed into a potential winner. This set up a new dynamic, within both the Legislature and the party.

In the Legislature the focus was more sharply on issues. With constitutional questions high on the political agenda, federal-provincial relations were prominent. After years of wrangling, health insurance was about to be implemented. The income crisis on the farm front reached unprecedented proportions, and farmers demonstrated their discontent at Queen's Park. The public was coming to feel that the benefits of the phenomenal expansion in our secondary and post-secondary educational facilities carried an excessive financial burden. The reports on tax reform of the federal Carter Commission and the provincial Smith Committee generated public debates which the government could no longer ignore. Stephen Lewis and John Brown raised social issues, notably child care in schools, and other provincial institutions, to a level of public awareness that had not existed hitherto. Morton Shulman and Pat Lawlor, with regular unannounced visits to correctional institutions, revived the question of penal reform; and Morty, in his inimitable fashion, had the government on the defensive on a wide array of situations. The four new northern members became dogged champions of the neglected northern communities[1] With our strengthened ranks in the caucus, we could vigorously pursue the issues which we had highlighted during the election campaign. The Legislature became a forum for genuine debate, to a degree that had not existed during a generation of the Tory dominance.

The resurgence of the NDP created a livelier atmosphere. Speaking to the Oxford County Insurance Underwriters in the fall of 1967, shortly after the election, the financial and commercial affairs minister, Leslie H. Rowntree, declared "the great mistake that the voters made" had nothing to do with defeating the Tories and electing a Liberal (as they had in Oxford), rather it had to do with the support they had given the NDP. He called upon his audience to forget their differences as Liberals and Conservatives, "not to divide the forces of decency," and to make sure that "subversive elements" do not upset the Ontario economy.

Provincial Treasurer Charles MacNaughton pursued this theme, both in and out of the Legislature. To a picnic gathering in Huron County, he said, "It is my opinion that the forces of socialism — and I may be charitable when I continue to call it socialism — are actively at work in their own particular destructive manner." In the House he repeated these accusations, on one occasion lashing across the floor, "I hate your bloody guts."

It was an old and familiar Tory tactic which was pursued in the Legislature where I took up the challenge. I noted that there was general agreement that the budget debate had been the best in years. It was, I suggested, "just that — a debate, instead of a succession of speeches which ignored what had gone on before. Not only issues, but their underlying political philosophy, were dealt with, and out of it all emerged something of a consensus."

I then proceeded to make a basic point:

A consensus doesn't necessarily mean agreement in all instances. A consensus within a democratic society also involves the clarification and acceptance of areas of disagreement with which we are willing to live. Indeed, those areas of disagreement, stemming from different political philosophies, represent the strength and vitality of democracy. Areas of disagreement provide the choice which is offered to the electorate so that, when and if the voters so desire, they have an opportunity to make a change in government and not just a change in administration.

In threshing out these areas of disagreement, it is inevitable that personalities should become involved, though I would agree that the issues, rather than the personalities which embody them, should remain paramount. It is also inevitable that sharp exchanges, even bitter words, should enter the debate. Within the limits, this is not to be deplored. It is part of the cut and thrust which elevates parliamentary debate from the routine to the memorable. Some of the greatest debates down through the centuries in the Mother of Parliament contain passages that have scorched their place in the pages of history. Let us not reduce the tone of debate in this House to a milk-toast, panty-waist level whose outstanding characteristic happens to be banality.

The differences, I submit, should be expressed within a framework which we all accept. That is the framework of a democratic society, and agreement that those differences will be worked out through the democratic process.

I then dealt with the ideological confrontation:

Let me make my point another way. There are some members of the governing party . . . who are very conservative in their views. This is their right and their privilege. Theirs is a legitimate position within the spectrum of a democratic society. I disagree with those conservative, often extreme right-wing views. That is why I am in the New Democratic Party. But if I were to dismiss those views, or to characterize them, as fascist, I would be unfair. . . . By the same token, those who hold those views have no right to characterize my views, or those of my colleagues, as being "insidious forces" which threaten our way of life; as representing an attack on "the forces of decency," or as being Marxist — that is, that we are less fervent upholders of the democratic process than themselves.

I concluded:

The position of the democratic right and the democratic left has been put forward with vigour. . . . All this is good. There has been no hesitancy on either side to relate issues to basic political philosophy. That is not only good; that is progress. It means that the clash of opinion, honestly and sincerely held, has deepened and broadened, and in such a confrontation the people of Ontario can only stand to benefit. If honourable members opposite, and to my right [the Liberals], when they sometimes join in this type of argument, persist in imputing sinister motives to us, that is up to them. For our part, we prefer that the confrontation in this Legislature should take place on the genuine issues of our time. On our approach to these issues, the solutions and views that we put forward, we are prepared to have the people judge us.[2]

Twenty years later, I have no revisions to make on that statement on the role of political parties in a democratic society. But if the basic argument is now more widely accepted by political parties themselves, it is interesting to note that it is right-wing forces, such as the National Citizens Coalition, rather than organizations of the left, that have emerged today. Ironically, their attack is often directed as much at the Tories as the New Democrats!

If there was confrontation in the Legislature, it also emerged in the party. For some members, the 1967 breakthrough was regarded not so much as progress but as a missed opportunity. It was argued that with a younger leader, presenting a fresh image, and in keeping with the militancy of the sixties and the Kennedy youth mystique which had captured the popular imagination of the North American continent, we could have won at least the official opposition. This had an understandable appeal among young people and the many newcomers who had doubled the party membership in the build-up to the election. After all, I had been leader for over fifteen years, and those were the days when a generation gap opened up after six months.

One of those who held this view was Jim Renwick. In the summer of 1968, less than a year after the election, he dropped into my office in advance of the party convention, and handed me a "Dear Don . . ." letter, indicating that he was going to challenge me for the leadership.[3] Having gone through twelve conventions without any contest, from the CCF through into the NDP, this was something new for me. I was momentarily taken aback, but an immediate check with a few of my caucus colleagues confirmed my assessment: they did not feel a leadership change at that time would be in the interests of the party. I got on the phone, and within a few days had a network of supporters all across the province. I soon made it clear that I had no intention of stepping down.

Jim's campaign got off to a bad start. He had no organizational back-up and even poorer public relations. Most of the caucus sided with me. I had widespread support among the local leadership in the party, with whom I had worked in the long struggle back from near oblivion. Jim had attacked the trade union leadership for their support of me, and his campaign became mired in charges and counter-charges.

Stephen Lewis's role in the campaign gradually clarified. He and Renwick were close; he had successfully promoted Jim for the party's federal presidency in 1967 against J.H. Brockelbank, a Saskatchewan veteran. He had been in Africa when Jim declared, and his organizational skills were sorely lacking during the first weeks. It was a classic challenge of the younger generation against what was perceived to be the old guard. There is no doubt that Stephen was active in the background of Jim's leadership bid, and by the end he was perceived by the media as being his campaign manager.

At the Kitchener convention, when delegates demonstrated support for their chosen candidate with all the cheering and familiar hoopla, one of those in the Renwick parade, vigorously waving a placard, was Michele Landsberg, Stephen's wife. For a person who normally avoided political involvement, her presence represented a family commitment.

I retained the leadership with a 70 per cent vote, but in the process, a latent coalition of forces took shape, reflective of the bullish feeling in the party. Within the caucus, it took the form of a much greater emphasis on extra-parliamentary activities. This had been a major theme in Renwick's leadership challenge. For some time after the convention, caucus members bussed out to join the picket lines as far away as Proctor-Silex in Prince Edward County. But this enthusiasm dwindled, not because the MPPs disapproved, but in their heavy work load, they had other priorities.

The more bullish feeling both within caucus and throughout the party centred around Stephen and he built the coalition with consummate skill. There was dissatisfaction in the caucus with parliamentary pay, particularly among northern members with young families. Premier Robarts was dragging his feet on the issue, but I was confident that the raise would come by fall, and would be retroactive to the beginning of the fiscal year, so I cautioned patience rather than publicly demanding the increase. Stephen sided with the complainers and, as one Queen's Park correspondent put it, "the quarrel became a festering sore with more and more backbenchers looking to Lewis as their champion."[4]

Meanwhile, Stephen was sounding out the grass roots, not only as to whether there should be a leadership contest at the 1970 convention, but whether they would support a challenge. This survey was conducted right up to the announcement of his candidacy. On one occasion when I discussed his intentions, he feigned indecision until he had a more definitive sampling.

Finally, Stephen did a masterly job of marshalling support among trade union affiliates. As caucus chairman, Walter Pitman had urged a shuffling of portfolio critics in advance of the 1968 session, in order to deepen the knowledge and experience of the team. Stephen sought labour, and I concurred because I had tended to take organized labour support for granted, and had not maintained as close contact with the leadership as was desirable. It was in the party's interest that these ties should be strengthened. Stephen built warm personal relationships which did strengthen the ties, and in the process, laid the groundwork for support in a leadership challenge.

As with the local constituency leaders, Stephen inquired of

the trade union heads whether there was a consensus in support of a leadership change. Twenty-five major Ontario union leaders caucused secretly at the Edmonton CLC convention, and concluded that there should be no challenge for three reasons: that my mandate had been renewed in 1968; that the party's election prospects looked good with the existing team; and that a leadership contest would divert time and effort from election preparations. This decision was reported by David Archer, president of the Ontario Federation of Labour, to Stephen and five other members of caucus, including Walter Pitman and NDP president Gordon Vichert. With Archer were four other union leaders, including UAW Canadian director Dennis McDermott, who had not been at the Edmonton meeting, because he was attending Walter Reuther's funeral. McDermott disavowed UAW support for the Edmonton decision, arguing that the trade union movement should remain neutral. It was known, however, that he had been supporting a challenge by Stephen for some time.

The secret meeting in Edmonton was reported in the Toronto *Telegram* by Marc Zwelling, who attended the convention with a press and delegate badge; he was also active in Stephen's campaign. It provoked the usual protests about labour trying to dictate what the NDP should do, and in the process, strengthened the McDermott option for neutrality. Thus the consensus arrived at in Edmonton collapsed. Stephen was able to argue that the trade union leaders were not really opposed to a leadership contest. In reality, the argument for neutrality was a front behind which intensive campaigning went on. The UAW led by McDermott, was marshalling the trade union forces for Stephen. The Steelworkers, notably Larry Sefton and his colleagues at the District Six office, headed the forces seeking to maintain my leadership.

On one occasion — in early 1970, as I recall — I had a telephone call from David Lewis, in the course of which he expressed his concerns about a pre-election leadership contest. By coincidence, I had had a call a few hours before from Sefton asking, "What the hell's going on?" He had been talking with David on matters of mutual concern, during which

David cautiously solicited the Steelworkers' support for Stephen.

I have no doubt that, experienced politician that he was, David shared the concerns about a leadership change at that time. He had always been an enthusiastic supporter of my leadership. But the ties between father and son in that remarkable Lewis family were strong, despite frequent differences, publicly expressed, on policy. David's doubts were superseded by family loyalty. That telephone call was the only occasion, in forty years of a close working relationship with David, in which there was a stand-off. Once I informed him that I had just learned from Sefton of his bid for Steelworker support of Stephen, the conversation quickly ended.

The developing situation created a real dilemma for me. In the fall of 1969 our party fortunes were steadily rising. The Robarts government had refused to accept the federal Liberal medical insurance plan, proclaiming it to be an unwarranted intervention into provincial jurisdiction. As a result, Ontario had foregone nearly $200 million in transfer payments. It was a high price to pay for stonewalling a popular social issue. The NDP highlighted the question in the Middlesex South by-election, and Archdeacon Kenneth Bolton won a sensational victory for us right in Robarts's own London area.

Robarts himself couldn't help but acknowledge what was happening. Winding up the budget speech in December 1969, he suddenly turned from a contemptuous dismissal of the Liberals, pointed across the floor in the House, and thundered, "We know where the enemy is, and we shall fight."

I remember being rather surprised by this. Even if the premier had become persuaded that the NDP was the enemy, why would he publicly admit it? After all, to concede that we were the challenger was to lend further credibility to our claims to be an alternative government. But it was no mere political thrust, made in an unguarded moment. It became a running theme in public statements of leading Tory spokesmen.

In May 1970 the Tories held a campaign school in Barrie. The Toronto *Star* reported that "top (Tory) party organizers have results in a recent survey by private consultants showing a major drop in support for their twenty-seven-year-old government. . . . The NDP is the third party in the Legislature, but, say the Conservatives, it is the one that concerns them the most." A week or so later, Arthur Harnett, PC executive director, in addressing a nominating convention in the riding of Nipissing, was reported in the North Bay *Nugget* as saying that "the battle in the next provincial election is with the New Democratic Party because the 'Liberals have nowhere to go'." Finally, in a news article in the *Globe and Mail*, Frances Russell reported how the three parties saw the next election shaping up. She wrote: "The Conservatives make no secret of the fact that they believe the NDP is their most significant challenge. They have taken polls that show the NDP could more than double its seats to around forty-eight."[5]

All this was very encouraging, but I could not close my eyes to developments in the party. By the time of a provincial council meeting in Niagara Falls, in April 1970, I was persuaded by close colleagues that the evidence of a systematic leadership challenge was building and should no longer be ignored. It was decided that executive and council members should be canvassed, to ascertain what the consensus was on the desirability of a leadership change and where their support would be if a challenge were made. The survey revealed that a majority of the leadership felt that the interests of the party would not be served by a leadership challenge at a pre-election convention. That majority included most of the provincial executive and council, the Young New Democrats, and some among the affiliated unions.

But a more significant fact emerged with the passing weeks. The majority feeling among the party leadership remained immobilized. The same situation existed among union affiliates where, as I have noted, the consensus among Ontario leaders at the Edmonton CLC convention, crumbled in face of the specious plea of remaining neutral.

If there was a contest, I was convinced that I could win, but the battle would be tough, perhaps bitter. And even if I won, it would be a phyrric victory, for, as victor, I would go into an election with opponents contending that I did not have

The NDP caucus, 1967-71, after recapturing major party status.

Archdeacon Kenneth Bolton — the Middlesex by-election victor in 1969.

I've forgotten what pertinent advice Premier John Robarts was giving Bob Nixon and me on this occasion, all presided over by Lieutenant Govenor Ross Macdonald.

Party leaders pictured with George Drew, during a visit to Queen's Park in 1971. Lieutenant Governor Ross Macdonald is centre.

In a friendly chat with M.J. Coldwell and Stephen Lewis. Stephen had left his pipe at home!

the wholehearted support of my own party. In short, the edge would be taken off the rising party fortunes. The prospect of a personal win, which added up to a party loss, gave me no satisfaction.

Therefore, in what was publicly perceived as a surprise announcement, I called a press conference at Queen's Park on 25 June 1970 to indicate that I would not be seeking re-election as leader at our October convention. I stated:

> I am convinced from my assessment that, as in 1968, I could retain the leadership. But the campaign would only be at the cost of serious diversion of time and energy from the top priority of election preparation, and inevitably, the contest would have the appearance of a long-time leader trying to hang on beyond his day. I have always promised myself that I would never do that; that I would prefer to hand on the responsibility of leadership too early, rather than too late. Indeed, a leadership contest at this time without the inhibiting presence of an incumbent leader could be very beneficial to the party. It would unleash added vigour and involvement.

I was not able to resist a few asides, such as: "Over that time [my seventeen leadership years] I have outlasted every political leader in Canada with but two exceptions: Joey Smallwood, who is obviously living on borrowed time, and 'Wacky' Bennett who, after all, is 'plugged into God.' I have been the dean of the Ontario party leaders since 1961. I have seen three Liberal leaders come and go. A historian friend of mine has suggested — and I haven't gone to the records to confirm it — that my tenure as leader has been longer than that of any other opposition party leader in Canadian history." However, I stressed that I had every intention of remaining an active member of the NDP team in Ontario, and that I intended to seek re-election in York South. Further, that I had no regrets, and certainly no bitterness.

While a decision of such complexity cannot be made without second thoughts, even doubts, as to its advisability, those doubts quickly faded. I had always relished political battles with opponents, but my resilience to cope with internal battles with colleagues had diminished.

In any case, those battles were now behind me. The leadership race quickly took form. With my withdrawal, the majority of trade union affiliates coalesced in support of Stephen. But there was a minority in their ranks, combined with a majority in the party leadership at the provincial and local level, which supported Walter Pitman. Much earlier, I had urged Walter to consider seeking the leadership. I had done so, partly out of a conviction that a good contest would be healthy, but also because I was convinced that he was more in tune with the Ontario electorate. The papers soon revealed, not inaccurately, that while officially neutral, I was supporting Walter.

I have always felt that there is an obligation on leaders not to resign under circumstances which leave the party in disarray, with no obvious successor on the scene. Any party which had a choice between two persons of the experience and proven ability of Stephen and Walter was fortunate. Rosemary Speirs expressed my feelings accurately in a Toronto *Star* front page article on 24 August 1970, "It may be that MacDonald feels Pitman is more in the MacDonald tradition of stressing practical answers over socialist theory and of presenting a reassuring 'reasonable man' image to the electorate."

Down through the years, I had constantly reminded New Democrats of the basic nature of Ontario politics — its pragmatic, small 'c' conservatism — which must always be borne in mind in presenting our more radical alternative. In fact, at the provincial council meeting in Niagara Falls on 11 April 1970, three months before my decision not to seek re-election, I had stated, "What we must do as a party is continue to espouse the more radical consensus which we, as political activists, can reach, but we must espouse those principles in the language and style which will attract the people of this province. . . . To maintain the balance between radicalism and this Canadian conservatism will not be easy, but it must be done, and with discipline, it can be done." I added a fundamental of my basic credo:

For every one of those voters to our 'left', there were hundreds, indeed thousands, who believe that they are in the centre. . . . We must continue to give voice to radical groups in our province; to do otherwise would be to fail both ourselves and society as a whole. But we must do so within the context of a balanced, broader appeal to the countless thousands whose disillusionment with the old parties grows greater day by day. Only in that way will our voice be truly effective.

Eric Dowd captured this approach accurately in the Toronto *Telegram* on 18 August 1970 when he said:

There is a considerable feeling in the party that the electorate needs to be wooed, not jolted. Some of those now supporting Mr. Pitman feel, probably with justification that Mr. Lewis would bring a more radical and flamboyant style of attack and they fear it might shock people into voting the other way. They feel that Mr. Lewis' impeccable articulation may be less appealing to the Ontario electorate than Mr. Pitman's comparatively homespun style. They feel that Mr. Lewis will be just a little long on bringing challenges for the future and short on stimulating confidence in himself and the party.

In fact, the contrast in the style of the two candidates was well illustrated in an exchange which took place between two professors working in the rival camps. University of Waterloo political scientist John Wilson declared in a campaign document that Pitman had the better chance to lead the party to victory because he portrayed "the progressive change and cautious common sense that was the current mood of the electorate." To which Gerald Caplan, Lewis's campaign manager and history professor at the Ontario Institute for Studies in Education, replied that Pitman's stand would simply make NDPers "into a fresher bank of Progressive Conservatives." Caplan contended that the electorate was in a more radical mood than Wilson realized, and therefore the party shouldn't blur its image, but instead sell itself forcefully with an "exciting leader."

While there was no fundamental difference in the ideological position of the two candidates, the public perception of a polarization between the left and right grew. That being the case, most of the Waffle, a radical group which had emerged in the party, supported Lewis, particularly when Jim Laxer, a Waffle leader, then a lecturer at Queen's University, eventually decided not to throw his hat into the ring.

Whatever the balance of all these opposing forces, when the votes were counted at the October convention, Stephen won with a comfortable majority.

Stephen Lewis's election fitted conveniently into the Tory plans. In *The Power and the Tories*, Jonathan Manthorpe recorded their reaction:

The Conservatives received the news of Lewis' victory with glee. His strident tones, hawkish appearance, and apparently uncompromising social philosophy would allow them to fight the next election on their favorite theme: the real threat of a socialist government in Ontario.

Before the NDP convention the Robarts cabinet had conducted a little poll, and the results were quietly leaked afterwards. The Ministers, it was reported, regarded Pitman as the greatest menace to the Tories, because his 'moderate' style could win seats from them in their rural power base. Any gains that Lewis made would be at the expense of the Liberals in the urban areas. . . .

After Lewis' victory this piece of bravado was leaked in order to convey to the public that the Tories were not rattled. To the business community their message was different and simple: 'It's either us or them. Which would you rather have?' The industrialists and businessmen didn't have to ponder long over that one, and dollars started pouring into the Conservatives' war chest.[6]

The Liberals, too, were please with the leadership change. Robert Nixon was quoted as saying that "the resignation of Donald MacDonald will help the Liberals in the election expected next year."[7]

What impact the change in leadership would have on the party fortunes, time alone would tell. The next two or three elections told the story.

12

Private Member, 1970 to 1982

The 1970 session was a novel experience for me. For the first time, after fifteen years in the Legislature, I was a private member, albeit a front-bencher. The change was not as difficult as might be imagined, because I was assigned the responsibility of financial critic and therefore had the task of presenting the party's overall position in the budget debate. Yet an ex-leader has a delicate balance to maintain, in contributing from his experience while not appearing to compete with his successor.

In any case, a new era had opened in Ontario politics. John Robarts, true to his assertion when he became leader that he did not intend to spend a lifetime in politics, had stepped down as leader. William Davis was perceived as being the heir apparent but, in a tense leadership race, came within forty-four votes of losing. An election was imminent, and the Tory campaign theme had been firmly established: it was free enterprise versus socialism.

Once the writ had been issued in 1971, Walter Pitman and I were launched on mini-tours to back up Stephen. It was a logical move, though it proved to be relatively ineffective. In a modern election campaign the focus is almost entirely on the leader, particularly with a new and charismatic figure like Stephen. We drew small meetings, and no doubt Walter's absence from Peterborough for much of the campaign contributed to his defeat. My position in York South was well enough established that, in spite of a formidable Tory candidate in Doug Saunders, a controller on the municipal council, I won with a plurality of 2,877.

The Tories were returned with an overall majority of thirty-nine, and the NDP trailed the Liberals by only one seat. Ironically, Walter's defeat alone denied the party a tie with the Liberals, and he has always attributed it to the difficulty in countering the more radical image of the party in a swing riding like Peterborough.

Gerry Caplan had been a key figure in Stephen's leadership campaign and a major strategist in the election. He became Stephen's executive assistant. A couple of years later I wrote a mildly critical review of the basic pessimism, if not defeatism, in *The Dilemma of Canadian Socialism*, his history of the Ontario CCF until the late 1940s. He responded in a letter to the *New Democrat*. Noting my emphasis that our socialism must be "an evolutionary growth from the mainstream of Ontario political and economic history," he stated: "I entirely agree."[1]

Unfortunately, that is precisely what Stephen's first campaign did not project. It was perceived as an effort to "jolt" rather than "woo" the Ontario electorate. It played into the Tory strategy, which was intent on a right-left polarization. Stephen and Gerry, both shrewd political strategists, read the situation, even if belatedly, and together they made an effective effort to change the image of the party and its leader.

Stephen adapted to the realities of the Ontario political culture. His strident tones were moderated. His extraordinary political skills and electrifying eloquence with audiences, both within and outside the party, created an increasingly attractive and comfortable relationship with the public. So much so that, in the 1975 election, the Tories were reduced to a minority government with the NDP regaining the official opposition which had eluded it for twenty years. It was an achievement which some in the party thought we should have attained in 1967, and which, in my view, we would have achieved in 1971, had we not had a leadership change.

Overlapping the later years of my leadership and the early years of Stephen's, the NDP experienced the throes of the Waffle movement. This was a classic example of the left-wing factionalism which punctuates the history of democratic socialist parties. My own reaction, from start to finish, was ambivalent. From years as leader, I had become positioned in the centre of the socialist political spectrum, in a constant effort to maintain unity between the left and the right. Some perceived my position as right of centre, whereas I felt myself to be slightly to the left because of my conviction that a vigorous left wing is legitimate in any social democratic party. My credo on this point was expressed in my review of Gerry Caplan's history of the Ontario party:

> Adapting the principles of socialism so that they become part of, rather than offensive to, the political culture of any province or country, does not necessarily mean that the integrity of those principles is being prostituted in the process. I acknowledge that there is a danger that can happen; but it can be guarded against, and in no better way than by a strong left wing within the party.

My views were tested by the Waffle movement. While it had national ramifications, it was centred in Ontario under the leadership of economics professor Mel Watkins and Jim Laxer. It climaxed nationally, first, in a memorable debate at the Winnipeg convention in 1969, and again two years later, when Jim Laxer challenged David Lewis for the federal leadership. On both occasions the Waffle vote was swollen by those holding any gripe against the party establishment, thereby giving the appearance of considerable support. But the more moderate, mainstream forces prevailed.

My ambivalence stemmed from the fact that, while I considered the views of the left wing to be legitimate, I found its tactics increasingly offensive. I disliked its attitude because its leaders, notably Mel Watkins, were newcomers to the party and had had close political associations, if not membership, with the Liberal party. Watkins had achieved a national profile through a study of foreign ownership for the federal finance minister, Walter Gordon, which had not been favourably received in the Liberal party. Almost overnight, he appeared in the New Democratic Party as the most radical

It must have been funny! But when you've just been presented with a new car, life takes on a rosy hue.

When I left the leadership, a farewell gift of a car, presented in the Canadian Room at the Royal York in 1971.

Simone and I, at a celebration in York South on my 20th anniversary as MPP.

With Francie Kendal, my riding president presenting a gift on the occasion of my 20th anniversary as an MPP.

of radicals. Those who had carried the burden of the struggle for years were labelled "right-wing finks."

While all that might be dismissed as overheated rhetoric, on both sides, the role of the Waffle became intolerable because it ceased to be merely the expression of a legitimate point of view and rapidly developed into a party within a party, complete with leadership, membership, organization and separate financing, which refused to abide by normal democratic procedures. When any group lost a vote in the councils of the party, the decision was accepted in accordance with normal democratic practice. But the Waffle's regular procedure was to go out immediately, hold a press conference, and pursue the debate among members and the public. The unity of the party was seriously threatened.

As the emergence of a full-fledged party within the party became more evident, the issue was joined at a provincial council meeting held in Orillia. Stephen had been taking a firm stand on the Waffle, while negotiating privately with its leaders to arrive at a more acceptable course. I had not played any public role in the growing debate, so when the issue came up for resolution, I was asked to chair the potentially divisive debate. The almost universal portrayal of this event, particularly in academic circles, has been that the Waffle was expelled. Not so. What the resolution, with overwhelming support, stated was that the Waffle, as a separate organization within the New Democratic Party, must be disbanded. Nobody was expelled. And as a matter of record, when the Waffle organization was disbanded, while a few voluntarily left, the overwhelming majority of its membership and supporters remained with the party. In fact, by the 1975 election, Jim Laxer was a member of an informal advisory group throughout Stephen's campaign. Mel Watkins is today an active and respected member of the NDP.

The Lewis years are a subject worthy of in-depth research, not only because of the achievements of Stephen's first term, following the disappointment of the 1971 election, but also because, after two years as official opposition in the first Davis minority government (1975-77), the bloom came off the NDP rose. The party seemed to lose momentum. Whatever the reasons for the malaise, it was not just confined to the leadership. As a result, in the familiar see-saw of election results, the NDP lost the official opposition in 1977, again by only one seat, as was the case in 1971.

Within a few months, Stephen resigned the leadership and his seat for Scarborough West. New Democrats were saddened and puzzled. Ken Bryden, a long-time activist, former provincial secretary and MPP for Beaches-Woodbine, reflected the opinion of many (including myself) when he observed, "We could have won [at least the official opposition], in 1977 if Mr. Lewis hadn't lost his interest. But it was typical of him. He had no staying power. He moved in too soon as leader and left too early."[2]

Reasons for the loss of momentum in the party still elude me, but as far as Stephen was concerned, it was a case of political burn-out. He had been involved in politics, in one way or another, from his mid-teens, if not earlier. At forty years of age, he was politically an old man. The prospect of progress had slipped away, at least temporarily. He had a young family. He yearned for other pursuits. They have carried him to the important post of Canadian ambassador to the United Nations where, on the world stage, he has played a critically important role.

Freed of the responsibilities of leadership, I soon became involved in related activities. The first was an invitation from Harry Crowe, dean of Atkinson College, York University, to map out and teach a course on the government and politics of Ontario. Very little written material existed in the field, and it was assumed that I had become something of a walking encyclopedia on the subject. So for seventeen years, it has been my privilege to practise politics by day, and teach it by night to mature students at Atkinson College. I soon became aware of a common complaint among my fellow academics: while a veritable Niagara of information poured out of Queen's Park — press releases, policy statements, Hansard, task force and royal commission reports — it was all undigested. The news coverage was, at best, spotty and there was no basic text to provide a framework for these studies.

After listening to this complaint for two years, I decided to apply a little political organization to the academic world. Inviting fellow teachers from universities and colleges in southern Ontario to a meeting in my home, we took about thirty seconds to decide that something should be done, and spent the rest of the evening mapping out a table of contents and potential contributors for such a text. The result was *Government and Politics of Ontario*, a volume which was first published in 1975, with a third edition in 1985. Over twenty persons, thoroughly familiar with various aspects of Ontario's political life, contributed essays which, together, provide an overview for teachers and students. It remains the only text available, and therefore fills a yawning gap.

Within a year of my leaving the leadership in 1970, a national convention was held. Every NDP convention is a leadership convention, in that the incumbent must stand anew for the position, and any member is free to run against him. This one was a genuine leadership convention, because Tommy Douglas had indicated his intention not to run again.

Three candidates emerged: David Lewis, John Harney and Jim Laxer. Initially I gave my support to John Harney. My reasons were that Tommy had stepped down because of a growing feeling in the party that it was time to move on to a new generation of leadership. Notwithstanding his admirable qualifications, David was only five years younger than Tommy, and was certainly identified with the old guard. In retrospect, I feel that I was wrong in my assessment; and in any case, when Harney was dropped in the voting, David had my wholehearted support over Laxer, the Waffle candidate.

My attitude during the leadership race didn't affect my long working relationship with David. I was urged by many, including him, to run for the federal presidency. I held that basically administrative office for two terms, from 1971 through to 1975. It provided an opportunity to resume a deeper involvement in the federal party, which had been my original preoccupation. As a provincial leader, I had been a member of the federal council ever since relinquishing the position of national treasurer and organizer for the Ontario leadership in 1953. The presidency required visits to all the provinces and territories, always a refreshing experience for me, especially since they included Newfoundland and Labrador and the Yukon and Northwest Territories, which had not been covered in my earlier work. Among the new colleagues was Tony Penikett, who was one of my successors in the presidency and now heads the first NDP government in the Yukon.

Continuing membership on the federal council led to a key role in the next three federal conventions in a behind-the-scenes capacity. Every party experiences intense politicking among delegates in the election of its new executive and council. The idealists argue that this exercise should be left to a free and open democratic process, but due to the disparity in the number of delegates from the larger and smaller provinces, an unorganized election would almost certainly result in various regions being short-changed in representation on the decision-making bodies. Thus, the inevitable emergence of a slate to ensure capable and balanced representation.

For years, this was achieved in the NDP by a somewhat clandestine mechanism known as "Committee A." Through it, an effort was made to draw up an acceptable slate of nominees. Rarely was the slate broken in the convention vote, but invariably its behind-the-scenes operations aroused suspicion and rancorous debate. Gradually, over three conventions, a new procedure was developed, which transformed Committee A into an official nominating committee, with representation from each of the provinces and territories, as well as from labour and women. It is an open democratic process.

However, at the 1983 convention the nominating committee was presented with an added requirement: in the course of coming up with an acceptable balance of nominees from each section of the party, there would have to be gender parity among the table officers and the twenty council members elected by the convention. A study of the total council membership revealed that, despite repeated resolutions affirming the principle of gender parity, it was not being implemented. In 1983, the party constitution was amended to stipulate that, henceforth, as least half of the officers and council members elected by the convention must be women.

This challenge was accomplished with unexpected ease. All the old arguments about there not being enough capable women willing to stand for office proved fallacious. Hitherto, I had been one who felt that fixing quotas to assure gender parity was undesirable. Overnight I became a convert to their necessity, at least for a transitional period, because the voluntary process does not work in face of embedded systemic discrimination. Tedious as this nuts-and-bolts work sometimes is, it can also be rewarding in the fulfilment of highly desirable goals.

No member of the Legislature can survive without careful tending of his home constituency. In this respect I was extremely fortunate, in having a succession of assistants, first at Queen's Park, and later in my constituency office, to respond to the burden of appeals for help. As indicated earlier, Ellen Adams was, for years, caucus secretary. That entailed handling most of the case work for York South because, more often than not, as leader I was otherwise occupied. When I reverted to private member status, Ellen remained with the leader's staff, and my next assistant was Marianne Holder, who held the fort for ten years. In addition to the normal routine of legislative and constituency case work, she was active in the party, particularly in the women's movement, as chairperson of the NDP women's committee and Ontario representative on POW (Participation of Women Committee) at the federal level.

The seventies saw women's issues move increasingly into the mainstream of politics. For all of us — especially the men — this was a learning experience. The CCF and NDP had always had a significant number of women active within the party, often in decision-making positions. But overall, women were still grossly under-represented, not only in caucus but at the provincial and constituency levels. The women's committee pressed for correction of this imbalance, and with Marianne Holder in my office, I was privy to the day-to-day struggle. I gradually recognized that, while the initial focus of the women's movement was to raise the consciousness of women, there was a particular responsibility for men to respond to their goals. After all, men are still dominant in politics, business and society in general, and therefore have an obligation to assist in striving for gender equity.

Marianne's extra-curricular activities on the women's committee resulted in her appointment as women's coordinator at the caucus — a position which disappeared with the cutbacks following the 1981 election. My legislative assistant for the concluding two years as MPP was Marianne (Skinner) Gallagher. With her, as with her predecessors, the job was handled so well that I was free to play a fuller role in the party and the Legislature than would otherwise have been the case.

Following the Camp Commission recommendations on legislative reform in 1975, each MPP was provided with an office in his riding, staffed by a constituency assistant. The case load was growing every year, and it was recognized that, if members were to play their role as legislators, the burden of constituency work would have to be shared. Once again I had the good fortune of having, in succession, two constituency assistants — first, Francie Kendall, a party activist who shouldered the added load of riding association president. Francie covered all the facets of the work, far beyond the call of duty, and when she "retired" to raise a family, her work was taken over by Jacquie Chic, who carried on in the exemplary tradition. She, too, was politically active, running provincially in the neighbouring riding of Humber, as well as municipally in the Borough of York. When I left the Legislature, Jacquie worked for a time with the Parkdale Legal Aid Clinic, and is now on the staff of the Ontario ombudsman.

I must pay a resounding tribute to my assistants, first at the legislative level and later shared in the constituency: they carried the office load, including the growing burden of case work, so that I was not tied down in either office, or in endless appeals before tribunals, such as the Workers' Compensation Board. It left me free for personal visits with constituents, and community activities. In fact, my colleagues at the Legislature were often incredulous when I confessed that I never, literally never, in my twenty-seven years as MPP took an appeal to the Workers' Compensation Board. Time did not permit when I was a leader, but the practice continued

Marianne Holder (centre) was my legislative assistant throughout the 1970s, and
Jacquie Chic, my constituency assistant from 1979 to 1982.

Eileen Adams, my first (1956) secretary,
and a key person in the caucus for 15
years.

Marianne (Skinner) Gallagher, legislative
assistant during my last year as an MPP.

With Joan Milling, Executive Director of York Community Centre, at the old building now replaced, at 1651 Keele Street, Toronto.

With Francie Kendal, my riding president and campaign manager in the elections of 1975 and 1977.

as a private member. I was never burdened with the "case work syndrome," which the Camp Commission found was overwhelming some members. The credit goes to a remarkable team — Ellen Adams, Marianne Holder, Marianne Gallagher, Francie Kendall and Jacquie Chic. No member of the Ontario Legislature was ever more fortunate.

Once I was out of the leadership, it was publicly perceived — for reasons that always puzzled me — that I was less partisan and the requests for community involvement increased. Since I had more time, I was glad to respond. In 1970, for example, when the government unfroze grants for mental health facilities, I had just become chairman of the York Mental Health Council. Plans for expansion at Humber Memorial and the building of new psychiatric unit facilities at Northwestern, the two hospitals in the riding, had for some time been on hold. It was drawn to my attention from within the Ministry of Health that recent amendments to the mental health legislation required the establishment of community-based facilities in connection with new or expanded psychiatric wings of local hospitals. The Mental Health Council sponsored a seminar to bring together all who might be interested in this service, and out of that one-day gathering evolved an imaginative proposal: why mental health services in isolation? Why not in conjunction with other health and social services?

The result was plans for a multi-service centre which drew the enthusiastic support of provincial ministries and other agencies. Funds were made available by the provincial government to renovate facilities, conduct community surveys and provide a core staff. Other staff were seconded by existing agencies. The centre has operated under the policy direction of a community board. Previously, most agency services for the municipality of York had been delivered from downtown or other suburban municipalities. Now they were all drawn together under one roof, and available in a coordinated fashion, so that a person in need did not have to travel hither and yon to have problems met. A legal aid clinic was soon added. As new community needs were identified, they were met — ranging from assistance to senior citizens through home visits or snow removal, to adult protection workers to super-

vise persons returned to the community from large provincial institutions. Today, York Community Services provides
the most comprehensive and coordinated range of services of
any multi-service centre in Ontario. Being involved in its
development from the outset has been one of the most satisfying experiences of my public life. I remain active as a
member of its board of directors.

Interesting and enriching as all these activities were, the
Legislature remained the centrepiece. From 1970 to 1975, my
responsibility to lead off for the party, in response to the
budget, maintained a detailed overview of the work of caucus.
With minority government in 1975, that focus was lost to a
concentration on energy issues, because of my appointment
to the chairmanship of the Select Committee on Hydro
Affairs, which continued through to 1981.

With no farmer in our ranks, I became, once again, spokes-
person for agricultural and rural issues, a top concern from
my earliest legislative years. Details of these energy and
agriculture responsibilities are dealt with elsewhere.[3] I enjoyed
my positions on the NDP team as fully as I had the leadership years.

Periodically, a private member has the satisfaction of in-
troducing a new proposal to the Legislature, and through it
to the public. Rarely does the proposal, when presented as
a bill, proceed beyond second reading, but at least it becomes
a subject for public consideration. Such was my experience
with freedom of information. My private member's bill was
the subject of debate in 1974, 1975 and 1976, though on the
last occasion it was sponsored by Pat Lawlor, MPP for
Lakeshore. The bill received support in principle from
spokesmen of all parties, but it soon became clear that there
was a hard core of opposition in the cabinet, and no further
action would be taken. When the issue was taken up by a
"ginger group" within the Tory ranks, the government felt
obliged to respond, and took the familiar escape route of
appointing a royal commission.

The royal commission reported in 1980, and Allan Pope,
the minister charged with the responsibility for its implemen-

tation, stated that legislation would follow "before Christmas." Unfortunately, he didn't say which year. For four years, cabinet opposition persisted and Norman Sterling, the new minister in charge, stonewalled genuine freedom of information. The bill, which was finally introduced in 1984, was such a travesty of the real thing that it was roundly condemned in the Legislature and the media. It died with the Davis government and in fulfilment of the Liberal-NDP Accord, another bill was introduced in the first two weeks of the David Peterson administration.

During the late 1970s and the early 1980s, both the party and the caucus were beset by leadership changes and problems. When Stephen Lewis resigned, a leadership convention was scheduled for February 1978. I attempted to persuade a number of persons to stand, notably Jim Foulds, the member for Port Arthur. For personal reasons, Jim did not feel that he was ready for the challenge, otherwise he might well have won under the particular circumstances of that convention.

Three members of caucus became candidates: Michael Breaugh from Oshawa, Michael Cassidy from Ottawa Centre and Ian Deans from Hamilton Mountain. Breaugh was dropped on the first ballot; but he played an important role during the Tory and Liberal minority governments, as chairman of the procedural affairs committee which took the initiative in a massive reform of the rules of the Legislature, as chairman of caucus and as one of the NDP team which negotiated the NDP-Liberal Accord.

Cassidy and Deans were on the final ballot. For a time I had withheld any indication of whom I would support. Michael had proven to be a very effective private member. He had won a seat on the Ottawa City Council, running on the NDP ticket, back in the 1960s — in itself no mean feat. He served his people so well that he was elected to the Legislature in 1971, and when he later switched to federal politics, he duplicated that achievement by winning a seat in the House of Commons in 1984. As a member he was a tireless worker, covering more ground, and at greater length, than any other member of caucus. But his relationships with his colleagues, and particularly with the media, were not good. He lacked the qualities of sensitivity and team play so necessary in a leader.

Ian had proven to be an outstanding member, and was chosen by his colleagues as House leader. In that capacity, he had served the caucus well. He was a good speaker, a tough bargainer, with an intuitive political sense. The majority of caucus supported him. Ultimately I was asked, and agreed, to nominate him at the convention.

However, the campaign witnessed unexpected trends. The longer it went on, the more momentum Michael picked up. He had a good team, including Jim Laxer as policy adviser. His harsh edges appeared to soften, and at the convention he gave the better speech. Ian's campaign never took off. The sparkle, of which he is so capable, never materialized. At the convention he was clearly bested by Michael, who won handily.

Michael Cassidy's leadership years were an unhappy interlude for both him and the party. The caucus loyally got behind him, but the improvements during his campaign for the leadership did not continue. Relations with the media remained hostile, and the strains in the party grew. The 1977 election results compounded the difficulties, for inevitably the continuing slippage tended to be attributed to him. When the party dropped twelve seats and a quarter of its popular vote in the 1981 election, it was clear to all, including Michael, that another leadership change had to be made. Within a few months he resigned and a convention was called for February 1982.

Three worthy candidates presented themselves: Jim Foulds, Richard Johnston and Bob Rae. I was one of many who urged Bob to forsake the impressive niche he had carved out for himself in federal politics. It was imperative that the decline of the party, in a major province like Ontario, be halted. The favourable profile which he had established as financial critic for the federal caucus made him the choice of a majority of the provincial leadership and members. Membership increased sharply and morale picked up quickly from the shattering blow of the election losses. Bob Rae won decisively on the first ballot. Once again, the party was on the march.

Everyone at both the party and caucus levels agreed that Bob should spend the remaining winter and spring months touring the province, to get a first-hand picture of conditions. It was also agreed that Bob's entry into the Legislature should not be postponed beyond the fall, because a leader had to be in the centre of political activity, which meant the Legislature. A number of members from outside Toronto offered to make their seats available, but the preference was for a Toronto seat, if possible in the east end, where Bob had sunk his political roots in a by-election and two general elections. When it became evident that no seat was available in the preferred area, and the lead-time required for opening a seat was fast disappearing, I announced my resignation on 6 July 1982, to become effective at the end of the month.

Leaving the Legislature after twenty-seven years was not an easy decision. It had become a second home. But it was imperative that the new leader should take his place in the House. The good people of York South had elected me eight times, and they obliged by returning Bob Rae as their MPP in a by-election on 2 November 1982. There are always other positions where one can make a contribution, and I moved to them.

With Bud Gregory, PC MPP, and David Peterson, newly elected MPP for London North, above, on the road, and below in 1975-76 committee work.

13

Chairman of Caucus, 1982 to 1985

Out of the Legislature but still in politics — that was my situation as of August 1982. Any trauma that I might have experienced with sudden withdrawal from legislative politics, after so many years, was totally removed by the decision of my colleagues. Bob Rae asked me to remain as special adviser to the leader, and the caucus elected me as its chairman. That position brought me more in touch with the central direction of the legislative work than had been the case as a private member. Apart from the administrative details involved with the caucus chairmanship, my major involvement was in the two policy areas with which I had been preoccupied in the minority government years: agriculture and energy.

Mel Swart, MPP for Welland-Thorold, succeeded me as critic for the portfolio of agriculture and food. With his family connection in farming, and his leadership in the citizens' movement to protect the fruitlands of the Niagara peninsula, he was an able critic. Agriculture faced a growing crisis, with high interest rates added to the chronic problems of the industry, and Mel headed a task force that held public hearings all over the province, in order to get the latest information for a comprehensive statement of policy. I assisted with a number of the regional hearings, and out of the whole effort emerged, in 1984, a report entitled "And Now There are None . . . ," indicative of the farmers numerical drop from being a dominant group, to a mere 4 per cent of the population today. The report reflected years of work by the party on behalf of agriculture, and provided an up-to-date platform for the 1985 election.

Also, at the leader's request, I headed an internal task force on Ontario Hydro's affairs. With his regaining of a legislative majority in 1981, Premier Davis refused to reappoint the select committee which I had chaired from 1975 to 1981. In effect, I carried on with that unfinished work, but from within the party. The result was a comprehensive report, entitled *Harnessing Hydro*, released in 1984, stressing the need for greater accountability.

Leaving my seat in the Legislature strengthened the perception of less partisan identification, and a number of other opportunities emerged. I accepted one, an invitation to become a public member of the Ontario Press Council. In part, this arose because the secretary of the council was Fraser McDougall, a former head of the Toronto Bureau of Canadian Press, whom I had first met when personally delivering my press releases in the 1950s. That proved to be a most interesting experience — with its illuminating glimpse of grievances against the print media, and their adjudication by a balanced group of professionals (publishers, editors and reporters) and public representatives. Regrettably, after only two years my press council membership came to an end, because it was found that my pecuniary relationship, through freelancing, was in conflict with the council's constitution. Doris Anderson, the well-known Canadian editor and Toronto *Star* columnist, also had to leave at the same time and for the same reason.

While I was freed of legislative sittings and the growing committee work, there was, if anything, greater demand for extra-parliamentary activities. Being chairman of caucus proved to be as high profile as being an MPP and, since most of the members were swamped with requests for speaking engagements, I was able to take one or two a week. While most were NDP engagements, providing an opportunity to renew old friendships and gain new ones, there was a growing involvement in all-party activities, and an outreach to the general public.

Among the most satisfying of these activities was that of political commentator at leadership conventions, of which there were many in the 1980s: the provincial NDP and Liberals in 1982, the federal Conservatives in 1983, and the provincial

Conservatives in February and again in October 1985. A generation ago, radio and TV stations tended to rely on so-called non-partisan commentators, usually from the newspaper or academic world. In the mid-1960s I once put the case to Godfrey Hudson, then the Queen's Park correspondent for radio station CKEY, that in excluding politicians they were missing the most detailed knowledge of events and personalities — in short, that more effective commentary was possible from a balanced panel of active politicians from all parties. As a result, I was invited to share in the CKEY panel for the Liberal convention early in 1967 at which Robert Nixon was acclaimed, and again later that year on the CBC panel for the federal Conservative convention which choose Robert Stanfield. (Unfortunately, I had to pull out in the middle of that convention, because John Robarts called the provincial election.) From that day forward, however, I attended every leadership convention held in Ontario, federal as well as provincial. For an active politician, there are few more interesting events than conventions of opposing parties where one is not personally involved.

The 1980s witnessed a new development in convention broadcasting. Normally, because of regular schedule commitments, live network coverage is restricted to the highlights, supplemented with news coverage and round-ups at the end of the day. Beginning with the NDP and Liberal conventions (at which Bob Rae and David Peterson were elected), Rogers Cable TV provided gavel-to-gavel coverage, interspersed with frequent panel commentary. This coverage was picked up by other cable companies, so that a significant portion of the general public had the opportunity to "participate" even more fully than the delegates, because they had a flow of information from all over the convention floor, and from behind the scenes. This was particularly the case in the tense and colourful manoeuvring which resulted in the election of Frank Miller as Tory leader in February 1985, and the re-run later that year when Larry Grossman succeeded on his second try.

Undoubtedly, the highlight of these years was the provincial

At the gala event for Simone and me after I left the Legislature — above, an intimate pose with Stephen Lewis and Ed Broadbent.

A picture of relaxed contentment.

Strategizing with Bob Rae during the by-election, November 1981, when Bob succeeded me as MPP in York South.

At the victory podium after Bob Rae's by-election in 1982.

Our six grandchildren.

general election of 1985, which ended the forty-two-year-old Tory regime, and led to the Liberal succession to power, as the result of an accord with the NDP. Time alone will tell how significant a landmark this development is in Ontario's political history. The short-term assessment is that it may well be as important a change as that of 1905, when the nineteenth-century Liberal dominance of Ontario politics gave way to the Tories for eighty years, broken only by the brief interlude of the Farmer-Labour government of 1919-23, and the Hepburn Liberals from 1934 to 1943. However, the picture has been fundamentally changed by the presence of the CCF/NDP since 1943. Unlike any other province, Ontario now has a mature three-party system.

Following the 1981 election setback, when the NDP dropped a quarter of its popular vote and a third of its seats, the party rebounded with increased membership and organizational activity during the 1982 leadership race. Three years later, when the Tories, under Frank Miller's leadership, slipped badly and opened the way for an opposition party to take over, it was the Liberals who capitalized on the drop of the Tories, getting one per cent more popular vote, and almost as many seats, while the NDP made only marginal gains.

The reason for this remains an important area for research and assessment. This much is beyond dispute: the NDP campaign got off to a slow start and was never able to catch up to the Liberals, whose campaign clicked from the day the election was called. More important, the NDP campaign failed to adapt to a fundamental shift in the political situation: at the start, the Tories were high in the polls, seemingly as unbeatable as they had been for over forty years; but the longer the campaign went on, the more obvious it became that they were not only beatable, but a growing proportion of the electorate welcomed the prospect.

During the election, surveys reflected the persistent drop in Tory popularity, but there was one poll which, in my view, provided the most illuminating glimpse of what was happening. The CTV network, controlled by the Bassett family, well known for its Tory sympathies, commissioned a survey by

Martin Goldfarb, the traditional Liberal pollster. That sample was taken over the weekend, just five days prior to voting. It revealed that the Tories had dropped ten points to thirty-eight during the campaign; but the Liberals were still in their usual range of thirty-three, while the NDP had risen to twenty-nine. Traditionally, NDP support has always sagged between elections and then recouped during campaigns; it appeared that this was happening again. But during the last five days, if the Goldfarb snapshot of the electorate's view was accurate, five points of popular support switched from the NDP to the Liberals as the opposition party in the best position to defeat the Tories.

In retrospect, this development was not surprising: it had become increasingly unclear where the Tory party stood with Miller's personal right-wing stance seemingly contradicted by progressive campaign promises. Furthermore, the separate school extension had been so mishandled as to indicate that the Tories had lost their capacity to manage important issues. Anglican Archbishop Lewis Garnsworthy's inflammatory charges on the school issue had shaken the body politic more than any single intervention of recent years. The government was obviously in the process of defeating itself, and the electorate was turning to the opposition as an alternative.

The election resulted in fifty-two Tory seats, forty-eight Liberal and twenty-five NDP. Parliamentary convention dictated that the Tories would have first crack at forming a government. Throughout the postwar years they had never gained a majority of popular vote, but with the opposition forces divided, they had always been able to retain power. This time, the situation was different: not only were 63 per cent of the electorate opposed, but the Liberals had almost as many seats and a higher popular vote. The message from the people was clear, even if, for the moment, indecisive: they sought a change, and the NDP determined that it would be an agent for that change.

But how? With the concurrence of the caucus and party executive, Bob Rae felt strongly that the traditional operation of minority governments was unacceptable. They had always proceeded as though they were a majority, with virtually full control over what would be on, or left off, the legislative agenda, and with freedom to manipulate developments for the most advantageous time to call another election.

As chairman of caucus, I presided over almost daily meetings, formal and informal, between the election of 2 May and the signing of the NDP-Liberal Accord on 28 May. There were a few who found any kind of relationship with either of the older parties so unacceptable that they favoured living with the traditional minority government procedures. There were some who felt that the credibility of the party in having the capacity to govern would be best enhanced by sharing in a coalition government. But the majority in caucus, and an even bigger majority in the party, rejected coalition with either older party. The idea had always been considered offensive, and under the pressure of post-election developments there was no time to discuss the proposal among the rank and file membership. To have opted for coalition, without lengthy deliberation in the councils of the party, would have been very divisive.

But the proposal, unprecedented though it was, of proceeding to what emerged as the Accord, had overwhelming support. During the election, the NDP had done more than any other party to establish the issues. It had received two-thirds as much popular support as either of the old parties, and therefore had a mandate to pursue those issues. The NDP objective was to secure a commitment that they would be fulfilled; that the government would have at least two years, free of an election, to get on with the people's business; and that during those two years opposition parties would be free to play their traditional role in debating, amending and even opposing government legislation.

The result was a period in Ontario politics equivalent to the Quiet Revolution in Quebec — a period of catch-up on a wide range of issues which the Davis government had stonewalled, or even opposed. It has been accurately and succinctly stated by Rosemary Speirs, in *Out of the Blue*:

Whether he likes it or not, Peterson was the main beneficiary of the negotiations with the NDP, not only because the deal put him in power, but because it saved him from the floundering indecision he'd displayed in the past. The Accord gave his government a legislative program and a timetable of reforms to keep things humming for the first two years of Liberal administration. It put starch in spines that might have bent under the pressure of vigorous business lobbying against the promises of equal pay for work of equal value and other reforms. The Accord assured that the Liberals would be liberal.[1]

Once the election was over, it was understood that I would step down as chairman of caucus. I had established another forum for dealing with public affairs, a regular column in the *Sunday Star*. But there was such a surfeit of activities following the fall of the Miller government, the takeover by the Peterson Liberals, and the hectic two-week session in July, that the formal change did not take place until a special caucus meeting later in the summer. Mike Breaugh, MPP for Oshawa, was elected chairman.

My exit from politics was now complete. It had taken place in instalments: from the leadership in 1970; from my seat in 1982; and from the chairmanship of caucus in 1985. For the first time in forty years I held no official position in the party or the Legislature. Looking back, it was an epic thirty years from 1955 to 1985. The party had struggled back from near extinction to an established position in Ontario politics. Its credibility had been restored in the Legislature and with the media and the public. The foundations have been laid for the future, even if that future does not unfold overnight. Ontario politics would be fundamentally different today if the NDP were not a key component. My reflections on its future are more fully expanded later.

There is a footnote worthy of record. During my three years as chairman of caucus I had contended, half jocularly, that it was the first time in British parliamentary history that a non-member had held that position. Eventually I felt it would be wise to verify this ostensibly extravagant claim. What better way than to inquire of Eugene Forsey, one of Canada's leading constitutional experts, and a veritable encyclopedia of historical detail. Eugene replied with characteristic crispness: "I have never heard of another case like yours in Canada. Most interesting." And he added, "My Australian lawyer friend, Graham Eglinton, who knows his Australian constitution from stem to gudgeon, says he never heard of any such thing in Australia. So you probably bear away the palm uncontested in the whole Commonwealth."[2]

Who am I to dispute such an authority?

Part Two
Issues

14

Intergovernmental Affairs

Before the Second World War, federal and provincial governments operated in their own spheres almost entirely, and there were few areas of joint responsibility. After the war, however, this changed drastically. The financial burden of social security, for example, and the desire for equal standards across Canada, involved the federal government extensively. It became clear, as well, that provinces should have a role in shaping and implementing economic policies.

Tax sharing was the most controversial area following the great centralization of taxes with the federal government during the war. Federal-provincial conferences became almost another level of government, where first ministers often made decisions that left the House of Commons and provincial legislatures with little more than a rubber-stamping role.

From the outset of my legislative career, I fought to achieve better accountability. In a radio broadcast in April 1955, even before I was elected, I criticized Prime Minister St. Laurent and Premier Frost for blaming constitutional problems, instead of their own lack of will, in dealing with such issues as health insurance, unemployment and farm marketing. "When these excuses are gone," I said, "don't expect that these old parties will then tackle the problems with vigour or determination. They will then dream up another set of excuses, because the old parties are controlled and financed by powerful groups who are not interested in solving these problems. It will conflict with their private interests." The tortuous development of public health insurance was a classic in the interplay of federal-provincial relations.

In the l960s federal-provincial affairs moved to centre stage, in good part because of the Quiet Revolution in Quebec and the Lesage government's demands, raising the need for constitutional reform.

I was keenly interested in these developments. I'd been raised and schooled in Quebec, taught in four of that province's communities, and spent two years as a journalist when educational issues, like compulsory school attendance, were a major concern. I considered myself a Quebecois, albeit from Anglo roots. As a student of history, I was fascinated by the sweeping away of years, indeed centuries, of static, if not repressive, social and economic conditions.

My feeling for the province was given focus by one of those seemingly inconsequential events that, in retrospect, appear to be a historical turning point. In June 1963, the press galleries of the Ontario and Quebec legislatures organized a visit to Quebec City where they were joined by the premiers of both provinces. The warmth of that gathering and its mood of reconciliation were remarkable, at a time when Canadians were deeply concerned about the future, even the survival, of Confederation. The highlight for me was the speech by Premier Robarts at the final banquet when, in his matter-of-fact way, he expressed genuine appreciation of the aspirations of French Canadians. The occasion was the launching pad for Robarts's emergence as what I termed a Father of re-Confederation.

I returned from Quebec City with renewed pride in being a Canadian, but worried about Premier Lesage's demand that his own formula for a bigger tax share from Ottawa be met within ten months — or else. The obvious question was: Or else, what? The ultimatum sounded too much like Premier Duplessis of yesteryear. My worries grew when Premier Robarts replied that he thought Quebec's demands were reasonable. I spelled out my concern publicly in a speech to the Wiarton Rotary Club on 20 June 1963, pointing out that re-Confederation talks would be useless if they were approached in a confrontational manner.

My fears proved groundless. Both premiers were laying the groundwork for negotiations, and conferences followed that became workshops for constitutional reform well into the 1980s. But I would like to believe that my publicly expressed concerns were noted, perhaps even influential.

Inevitably, the public saw constitutional problems as between Quebec and Ottawa. In a speech in November 1963 I tried to counter this by pointing out that we should recognize Quebec's special place in Confederation, but we should realize as well that *all* provincial demands posed a threat to Confederation as we had known it. Quebec, I argued, should be allowed to opt out of fiscal agreements, but Ontario should then give leadership to other provinces to develop a greater measure of cooperative federalism.

Because there was no legislation associated with it, elected members were rarely given a chance to share in the debate over reshaping Confederation. They could, however, use general debates in the Legislature to express their views, as I did in the reply to the speech from the throne in 1964.[1]

A hundred years ago, I reminded the Legislature, the British American colonists were so beset with problems that their independent survival was the dominant question of the day. The armed might of the United States, occupied at that time in a civil war, might soon be free to strike northward. The domestic policies of the British colonies, notably in Canada East and Canada West, were paralysed with what Mackenzie Bowell, writing in the *Belleville Intelligence* on 14 October 1864, called the "petty strife and contentions which formed the staple product of political warfare." But leaders of the day buried their differences, led the way in the delicate negotiations which shaped Canada, and are honoured as Fathers of Confederation

"Today we are faced with the critical problems of re-Confederation. . . . [Negotiations] will be just as delicate as those a hundred years ago. They will require just as great statesmanship. If they don't succeed, our centenary in 1967 will turn out to be a wake instead of a celebration."

I noted that the *Globe and Mail* headline before the November 1963 conference read, "Pearson, Provincial

Premiers Meet Head-on in 'Last Chance' Conference.'' But the conference revealed that tensions had eased, at least temporarily, and John Robarts headed west for the Grey Cup game, that modern sports symbol of national unity, with a characteristic assertion: "Tough old Canada is going to survive.''

I commented on the Canadian tendency to downplay our accomplishments:

Too often we forget that we have achieved modern nationhood without the necessity of resorting to the violence of civil war, as did the United States, France, and even Britain in its earlier history. Oh, I know we had our rebellions — in 1837, on the Red River, and in the Northwest, but relatively speaking, they were minor skirmishes, which we have tended to exaggerate in our efforts to 'keep up with the Joneses' in writing our history. . . .

In the same way, we have tended to be obsessed with continuing frictions in the relationships between English and French Canada, failing to remember that friction is fairly normal in the pattern of human relationships. We have forgotten to review these continuing problems in the full perspective of the historic achievement which our English-French partnership represents. . . .

From the very outset, Confederation was a unique achievement. It was the first time that colonies worked out nationhood, without it being thrust upon them by the mother country. Through these achievements, we created a relationship between colony and mother country that ultimately made it possible to transform an Empire into a Commonwealth.

The idea of federating the British colonies had been raised earlier, and George Brown had broached it again at a Reform convention in 1857. In 1864 he described his vision during the Confederation debates:

One hundred years have passed away since these provinces became by conquest part of the British Empire. Here today the victors and the vanquished in the fight of 1759, with all the differences of language, religion, civil law and social habit . . . sit, seeking amicably to find a remedy for constitutional ills and injustices complained of — by the vanquished? No, sir, but complained of by the conquerors. Here sit the French population, discussing in French tongue whether we shall have it.

Just as our political forefathers had risen above "the petty strife and contentions," I said, our challenge was "to do the same, to capture that vision once again, and to reshape it to meet the needs of our day."

I asked those who decried the suggestion of a special place in Confederation for Quebec to remember their history: the Quebec Act of 1774, just fifteen years after the battle on the Plains of Abraham, granted Quebec special rights in language, religion and law:

Canada remained British because it was French. . . . Just a mile from the farm where I grew up in the Chateauguay Valley south of Montreal, stands a monument where the troops of Colonels de Salaberry and Macdonnell turned back an American force headed for Montreal. . . . A special place for Quebec in Canadian Confederation is not something new. It is part and parcel of our history.

As to the threat of Quebec separatism, I pointed out that the first separatists were the United Empire Loyalists of Upper Canada, predominantly Anglo-Saxon and Protestant, who wanted to separate from the predominantly French and Catholic population of the United Canadas. Their motives were the same as Quebec's now: the protection of the cultural, language and religious rights of the minority. "Will anyone deny that Canada is a better country today because those basic English minority rights were recognized, and not crushed by imposing the different culture, language and religion of the French majority of the day?"

Despite the integral role of Quebec in Canada's history, I lamented that "anti-French Canadian sentiment throughout much of Canada is like a virus running through the blood stream of the nation. . . . I have often felt my blood run cold as I heard fellow Canadians say to somebody who was speaking French: 'Why don't you speak white?'"

John A. Macdonald wrote, in a letter in 1856, that the British of Canada East "struggle not for equality but for ascendancy . . . Trust them [the French] as a nation and they will act as a free people do — generously. Call them a faction, and they will become fractious. . . ."

I pointed out the irony that, one hundred years later, the "two nations" concept was incomprehensible to many Canadians. "People who are living in a Commonwealth so flexible as to encompass republics within an association of nations headed by a monarch find a two-nation concept impossible!"

I quoted Sir John A.'s ringing denunciation of a bill to abolish the status of French in the Northwest Territories (which at the time included what became Alberta and Saskatchewan): "I have no accord with the desire expressed in some quarters that, by any mode whatever, there should be an attempt made to oppress the one language or to render it inferior to the other. I believe that would be impossible if it were tried, and it would be foolish and wicked if it were possible. . . . We have a constitution now under which all British subjects are in a position of absolute equality, having equal rights of every kind — of language, of religion, of property and of person. There is no paramount race in this country. There is no conquered race in this country. . . ."

There, I suggested, was "an admirable prescription for both the attitude and action of English Canadians toward their French Canadian compatriots, as they seek to recapture the dream of a bilingual and bicultural nation that has dimmed over the years."

I said I was proud of Premier Robarts's attitude at the Quebec conference in November 1963. "My hope would be that he can withstand the forces in his own party, and continue to play the role . . . [for] it is one of the supreme ironies of Canadian history that no party has forsaken the traditions of Sir John A. Macdonald, particularly his attitude toward French Canada, more than the Conservative Party which he created. . . . For the simple fact is that in this century, the Conservative Party has never understood Quebec. They have constantly flirted with the idea of writing off Quebec and openly seeking a majority outside of the province, even if it meant splitting the nation down the middle. . . ."

"Even on two occasions [R.B. Bennett in 1930, and John G. Diefenbaker in 1958] when they won a significant number of seats in French Canada, they have never developed leaders of any stature, and their strength held for just a fleeting moment of history. . . . If Premier Robarts can break with the 20th century tradition of his party, and continue to manifest an understanding of French Canada's aspirations and grievances in the manner that he has done to date, then he will do a real service, not only for Ontario, but to Canada. . . . He will have an honoured place among the Fathers of re-Confederation."

The destiny of our nation may have hung in the balance, but that didn't stop the bickering over the provinces' share of federal tax revenues. Since a growing proportion of government spending was under provincial responsibility, either the BNA Act would have to be amended to give more of the responsibility for these programs (and their cost) back to Ottawa, or Ottawa would have to share its revenues more generously with the provinces, so that they could afford to meet their responsibilities.

The November 1963 federal-provincial conference showed that the basic differences lay not between Ottawa and Quebec, but between Ottawa and all ten provinces. John Robarts and the other premiers shouted as loudly in English as Premier Lesage shouted in French.

The Ontario government set up a non-partisan advisory committee on Confederation. I didn't object to distinguished people doing some collective thinking about the province's role in reshaping Confederation, and I appreciated the need for expert committees and federal-provincial meetings. But, in contrast to the three years of public meetings and debate that preceded the final Confederation agreement in 1867, members of provincial legislatures this time were given practically no role at all.

"For the most part, the decisions which come before members of this Legislature have been made in the secrecy of federal-provincial conferences," I repeated in the throne speech debate on 29 January 1965. "Now we face the prospect of them being made by an advisory committee, with the result that our role is reduced to relatively purposeless debate."

The tragedy of this period was that Prime Minister Pearson was very weak, and his position was further undermined by scandals in high places. At the same time, Ontario was willing to "drift along in the same old rut, content with the status quo in an age so revolutionary that it demands radically new approaches."

While there was "a socialist leaven in the loaf" of Quebec social and economic policies, Ontario refused to move on a national pension plan or public health, hospital or auto insurance. In short, the Tories were playing a negative role while Quebec was dynamic and aggressive.

"It is developments such as this," I concluded, "which have shattered my sincerely expressed pride a year ago in the part that had been played until then by the first minister of Ontario in the overall problem of reshaping Confederation. I express my views more in sorrow than in anger, for this is the common ground upon which all political parties in Canada could, and should, be united."

Early in 1966 Premier Robarts called for new efforts toward an acceptable formula for amending the BNA Act, without resort to the British Parliament. The previous March, the Tories and Liberals in the Legislature had approved the Fulton-Favreau amending formula, which specified five categories in the constitution of Canada, some of which would require the consent of not only the Parliament of Canada, but of all the legislatures. We in the NDP opposed that formula, in the belief that it would put the nation in a constitutional straitjacket, and on 21 January 1966, I called for a select committee to study the matter. On 17 March the Legislature debated a resolution by A.B.R Lawrence, MPP for Russell, an Ottawa-area riding. The debate revealed that not all Tories were as sympathetic to Quebec's aspiration as Robarts.

The resolution stated that our faith in Canada as a nation "transcends the whole question of the status of independent provinces within Confederation." Those words masked the real contention that Quebec should not be accorded special status. "To suggest that the special status of an individual province is a distracting irrelevancy in our nation-building is to reveal a monumental ignorance of Canadian history," I said, listing special considerations extended to almost all provinces to entice them into Confederation. "In short, this nation has been built by a patchwork of special arrangements to meet special needs. They represent the warp and woof of our national framework."

I mentioned again the "persistent incapacity" of the Tories to appreciate the aspirations of French Canada, and said it was strange that the member who complained "in waspish overtones" about special status for Quebec represented a riding whose population was half francophone.

In May the Legislature debated my proposal for a select committee. I argued that, if the forthcoming series of federal-provincial conferences were to be a continuing "constitutional workshop," they could usefully be accompanied by a committee involving provincial members and, through them, people back home. But there was no response from the Tories.

In the throne speech of 25 January 1967 Premier Robarts promised a Confederation of Tomorrow conference. It sought to achieve a consensus among the provinces and break the constitutional impasse which had developed at the federal level, but it was viewed with considerable apprehension by many of his colleagues, and greeted coolly by federal authorities. However, it was an appropriate companion piece to Expo '67 and the euphoric events of centennial year that engendered such pride in Canadians.

Ottawa was increasingly negative toward a special status for Quebec, and in favour of treating all provinces exactly the same — to me, a historically fallacious argument. I felt that, at the Confederation for Tomorrow conference, Ontario could give leadership to the other nine provinces, and coordinate their joint approach to Quebec's status. The view from the conference site — the fifty-fourth floor of the unfinished Toronto-Dominion Bank building, at that time the highest structure in Canada — surely couldn't help but expand the horizons of the assembled leaders.

The federal government refused to attend, "partly out of a sense of pique that protocol had been breached" (because of Ontario's initiative) and "partly because the federal Liberals were openly predicting that the conference would be a failure," I recalled in the Legislature a few months later. Nevertheless, I believe the conference halted the drift toward a crisis in Confederation. The very fact that it was a provincial initiative was a significant achievement. Furthermore, the meeting revealed the possibility of a consensus among provincial leaders on the basic problems plaguing Canadian Confederation.

The momentum was building, and the positive mood continued in February 1968 at a constitutional conference in Ottawa. My most vivid recollection, as an observer of its proceedings, was that so many premiers seemed to be facing up to the reality of the crisis in English-French relations for the first time. Despite their understandable preoccupation with economic problems, rooted in regional economic disparities, the Atlantic premiers acknowledged the urgency. And despite the difficulties western premiers had in comprehending the "Quebec problem," they too were willing to deal with it, to strengthen Confederation.

In short, a consensus began to emerge — tentative and fragile, but hopeful. "There was agreement on the problems, and on the establishment of machinery to grapple with them," I concluded, "and there was above everything else a spirit of goodwill and a determination to push on with the task. Men of goodwill, who accepted a common objective, can achieve tomorrow what appears to be impossible today. For that reason, there is every reason for cautious confidence."

The conference helped create the public climate for acceptance of a practical program to remove one of the sources of tension — the recommendations of the report of the Royal Commission on Bilingualism and Biculturalism.

The first B&B report, published in December 1967, proclaimed dire warnings of the widening gulf between English and French Canada. I welcomed the guiding principle of the first volume, "that both official languages be recognized whenever the minority is numerous enough to be viable as a group." I considered the recommendations for language and cultural equality as the logical next step after the Confederation of Tomorrow conference. Failure by Robarts to act on them would mean a critical loss of momentum in the whole process of re-Confederation.

On 13 December I announced the NDP caucus's enthusiastic endorsation of the report's principles and recommendations. I quoted Premier Robarts's concluding words to the Confederation of Tomorrow conference: "Do not oppose change in one breath and appeal for national unity in the next." One positive step, we suggested, was that simultaneous translation facilities be set up in the Legislature without delay, to show leadership in according French and English equal status. And we called for "establishing French language instruction within the framework of the secondary school system."

However, Pierre Trudeau, then minister of justice, was obviously seeking a confrontation with Quebec Premier Daniel Johnson, and this threatened the working partnership built at the Confederation of Tomorrow conference and jeopardized future constitutional conferences. "It may be good politics to take on Mr. Johnson in open battle, but I have doubts that it is good nation-building," I suggested in the Legislature.[2]

The core of the problem was that the federal government had accepted Trudeau's position that "if bilingual and bicultural rights are assured all across the country, then Quebec can be treated constitutionally as 'une province comme les autres'." On the other hand, Johnson argued passionately for so many more powers for Quebec to protect its traditions and culture that they might endanger the federal government's role on behalf of the nation as a whole. My own assessment of the relative merits of the two positions was heavily influenced by developments in Quebec politics. "Whatever may be our reactions in English-speaking Canada to the position taken by Daniel Johnson today, we must not forget that his position is the most moderate put forward by any party in Quebec provincial politics at the moment."

A united separatist movement was emerging under the leadership of René Lévesque, while the Liberal official opposition caucus had adopted a constitutional document, drafted by Paul Gérin-Lajoie, which was more nationalist than that of Daniel Johnson's Union Nationale.

"There is no doubt," I stressed, "that Premier Johnson was right when he told the constitutional conference that they should not react to his position as a personal one because, if he were to go, there is every possibility that his successor would be making even more extreme demands. These are the political realities of Quebec today; whether we like them or not, is irrelevant. We must cope with them if Confederation, including Quebec, is to be saved."

Premier Robarts had made a proposal to resolve the dilemma of an acceptable redivision of powers between Ottawa and the provinces. While Johnson was arguing for a great decentralization of powers from the central government to the provinces, Robarts was suggesting that the provinces should agree on the minimum powers needed for a strong central government, advocated by all provinces except Quebec. The nine provinces could then delegate back the powers needed by Ottawa to provide direction and equality for the nation as a whole.

"As we seek to reconcile these two positions," I stated, "we will reach a point where Quebec will insist on certain powers which the other nine provinces and the federal government want vested in Ottawa. At that point, the challenge to the Fathers of re-Confederation will be to find the constitutional means of achieving that accommodation. How exactly it will be done, I venture to suggest, no one knows at this time. But if all those involved are determined that it shall be achieved

to save Canada, a way must be found. When it has been found
. . . then we will have established — dare I use the term —
a special status for Quebec within a new Confederation."

I concluded, "Speaking personally, I am profoundly
grateful for the privilege of attending the Confederation of
Tomorrow and the Constitutional Conference in Ottawa. I
would not have missed them for anything. Years hence, I shall
cherish the experience, as though it had been my privilege to
have attended the Charlottetown and Quebec Conferences."

From the time of the release of the B&B report, I had maintained that its recommendations offered a program for
immediate action in an important aspect of constitutional
developments. With this, Premier Robarts appeared to be in
agreement. At the Constitutional Conference in Ottawa he had
said, "If we choose to be hesitant and negative in our attitude
toward the linguistic and cultural question, then we shall play
into the hands of those who wish to put the future of our country in jeopardy." And further, that "more formal recognition of the two linguistic communities in Canada is a modest
— indeed, a minimum — investment which must be made in
the new Canada."

Four task forces had been set up in Ontario to look into
implementing the B&B recommendations on equality of the
French language in the administration of justice, the
Legislature and provincial statutes, municipal administration,
and the provincial public service.

The Legislature was assured that education in French within
the existing public secondary school system would be implemented shortly, and that language courses would be available
for civil servants who required French on the job. I said that
members of the Legislature should lead the way toward more
bilingualism, and, with a number of my colleagues, I enrolled
in French immersion classes one or two evenings a week. I
used French in the Legislature and on CBC network broadcasts a few times, but I am not a natural linguist, and speaking
French was always a tense experience that I thankfully forsook after I left the party leadership in 1970.

I pursued other B&B recommendations — for instance, that

New Brunswick and Ontario should declare themselves officially bilingual. New Brunswick did so, but Ontario, despite having the largest francophone population outside Quebec, refused. I argued for simultaneous translation in the Legislature, in contrast with Liberal Leader Robert Nixon, who said it was unnecessary:

> All of this can be done within the concept set forth by the B&B report, namely, that nobody is going to be forced to speak French — French is not going to be rammed down anybody's throat — but the facilities for the use of the two languages should be readily available for all those who wish to do so.

The emphasis of the B&B report on relations between the two founding nations produced a negative reaction among that growing "third" of the population — the so-called New Canadians — who had come from all over the world. Quite naturally, they wondered where they fitted in this debate over founding "nations." The Ontario NDP had suggested, at the B&B commission's public hearings, that the preamble to a new constitution should acknowledge the contribution of the growing number of newcomers. "The multinational character of Canada's population, superimposed on the original founding nations of French and English, is nowhere better exemplified than in Ontario," our brief pointed out.

Premier Robarts had stated Ontario's position bluntly during the throne speech debate in February 1968: ". . .while the government of Ontario has accepted bilingualism, we have not accepted biculturalism. It is a fact of life that Canada is a multicultural mosaic. . . . Of this we are very proud, and we think the multicultural aspects of our country are really part of the true Canadian nationality."

This "true Canadian nationality," I said, "can be achieved through building a working relationship between the original French-English partnership and the new mosaic of many national backgrounds. . . . Moreover, there is a strong bond between language and culture. Culture is to the group. . . what personality is to the individual. If, to borrow [Robarts's] phraseology once again, the 'multicultural mosaic' which is basic to the 'true Canadian nationality' is to survive and grow, then linguistic rights must be acknowledged. Without linguistic rights, cultures will wither and die."

Dr. J.B. Rudnyckyj, one of the B&B commissioners, had written a dissent to the report, calling for regional linguistic rights for any group with sufficient numbers to make it feasible. I argued that it was possible economically, administratively and politically to guarantee these languages rights.

I called on the compelling arguments put forward by another B&B commissioner, Walter Tarnopolsky, then dean of law at the University of Windsor and now a justice of the Court of Appeal for Ontario. He attributed Canada's "mosaic" development in large part to French Canadians:

Once the British conquerors recognized in the Quebec Act that one did not have to be an English-speaking Protestant to participate in the public life of the colony, their descendants could not subsequently deny similar recognition to others. Moreover, as Premier Lesage stated in western Canada a few years ago, no "ethnic" group has the same numbers, or the same concentration in one area, nor the same developed institutions of business, politics and learning as the French Canadians have in Quebec. It is a recognition of reality, not as a recognition of the two classes of Canadians — those who founded Canada and those who did not — that I recognize the validity of the promises of the B&B report. I would say to those premiers who refer to the greater numbers of other ethnic groups in their provinces that this is not a basis for denying facilities for French-language schools, wherever sufficient numbers warrant them, but as a basis for recognizing that in addition to French-language schools, all schools should introduce language instruction at an early age. In places where sufficient numbers warrant this, students in English-language schools could take a course in French, Ukrainian, or German, or Italian, or Cree or Eskimo.[3]

Dean Tarnopolsky noted that, in stressing the need for assuring the linguistic rights of French and English, the B&B report stated that "nothing in this section shall be taken to diminish or restrict the use, as established by future law or practice, or any other language in Canada."

Thus was the constitutional case for regional language rights made. "We do not feel," stated Dean Tarnopolsky, "that this contradicts our principles in any way, for in all cases English and French will retain their official status. Rather, it would be a way of showing respect for minorities using languages other than English and French, and of recognizing their contribution to the cultural enrichment of Canada."

During the 1968 federal election campaign Pierre Trudeau, then prime minister, said that the NDP was speaking with two voices regarding Quebec's place in Confederation. "People who live in glass houses shouldn't throw stones," I answered. I pointed out that Trudeau's constitutional position was opposed by none other than Jean Lesage, the Quebec Liberal leader. The position of federal Conservative leader Robert Stanfield on Quebec was defensible; Diefenbaker was lurking in the wings and no one could doubt his strong, even bitter opposition.

The irony of the situation was that "on the issue of Canadian unity, both old parties are sharply divided within their own ranks. Alone among the parties, the New Democratic Party presents a policy on which they are themselves united and which is flexible enough to unite Canada" — a statement which was true at the time, but subsequently has often been belied.

In the NDP, provincial leaders are usually involved in federal elections, and I spoke at nominating meetings in New Brunswick that year. My overall theme was that Canada must level the regional disparities in incomes and services. The per capita income for Ontario was $2,454; the average for Canada was $2,144; and in New Brunswick it was only $1,475. On 14 February 1968 the Saint John *Telegraph Journal* had asked editorially, "Is the federal government really prepared to recognize this disparity, this discrimination, this economic injustice, with more than lip service?'' I responded at a meeting in Moncton, ''National unity depends far more on bringing those figures into balance than it does on the legal niceties of the BNA Act.''

However, Trudeaumania carried the day. Viewed in English Canada as the man who could deal with Quebec, Trudeau was swept into power, and the confrontation he had begun with Premier Johnson carried on with the succeeding Liberal regime of Robert Bourassa. The fragile consensus reached at the Confederation of Tomorrow conference was disintegrating, and I became much less optimistic as we approached the 1971 provincial election.

Historically, the Liberal party had permitted, and even advocated, American economic expansion in Canada, and a report prepared by economist Mel Watkins for the Liberal finance minister, Walter Gordon, documented the growing American domination of our economy. A surge of Canadian nationalism emerged as a result. Pierre Trudeau was the villain, I argued at a Carleton nominating meeting, because he has made it perfectly clear that his classical liberalism will not permit him to interfere, either with economic takeovers, or with what Professor Charles Taylor has called ''the colonization of the mind,'' which is often a more insidious influence.

I didn't ignore the political opponent on home turf. If Ottawa was unwilling to stand up for Canada, what about Ontario, the wealthiest province and the headquarters of most foreign-controlled corporations?

''The Robarts government,'' I stated, ''not only has no plans to halt the erosion of our economy and culture, but under the guidance of that old-time carnival barker, Stan Randall [minister of economics and development], this province even gives grants of public monies — jokingly referred to as forgivable loans — to aid these American corporations in their efforts to establish here.''

Ontario was not without power to halt the drift to foreign control of the economy. It could use its general powers over property and civil rights, or set ground rules for companies seeking incorporation. It could use the regulatory powers of the Toronto Stock Exchange, which is under provincial jurisdiction. And, through an Ontario Development Corporation, it could actively participate in promoting domestically controlled industrial growth.

As the newly elected federal NDP president, I was uncharacteristically pessimistic in a speech in Welland on 15 May 1971:

> The Trudeau government was elected in the belief that it offered the best prospect of achieving a greater measure of national unity. In fact, however, there is a disturbing accumulation of evidence that Canada is drifting relentlessly toward dissolution.
>
> The whole country and its people are being subjected to greater tensions about its future and the shape of its institutions. In the west and Atlantic provinces, profound discontent with the central government is manifesting itself. The rich and powerful voice of Ontario is now adding a strident protest. On the core issue of national unity, French-English relations, and positions and attitudes between Quebec and the rest of the country are hardening.
>
> Because of this uncertainty, a sort of psychological drift has set in, which raises the grave prospect of an acceptance of the inevitability of Quebec separation. This psychological drift is to be found not only in French Canada, but in English Canada too. It is reflected in the frequent exasperation: "Well, if Quebec wants to separate, then to hell with them. Let them go!"

In this sharp descent from the euphoric atmosphere of centennial year and the capturing of its mood by the Confederation of Tomorrow conference, I began more and more to take refuge in an expression of faith in this country:

> Personally, I have the profoundest conviction that, if Quebec separates, French Canada will be no better off. As for the rest of Canada, it will become difficult, if not

impossible, to avoid future dismemberment in face of the relentless pull from the giant to the south. . . .

We New Democrats believe that the two peoples who formed the original Canadian union can only succeed in building a country which meets their full aspirations, if they remain together. Only together can we overcome poverty, inequality and the countless daily cruelties of our prevailing social order. Only together can we assert our economic independence and our hope of building a different and better society in North America. If we are to stop this drift towards break-up, dramatic action is required. We must get on with the job of renegotiations of our constitutional arrangements. . . . But this process will be possible only if there is a frank recognition of how wide is the chasm that had opened between English and French Canada.

In my speeches I often stressed the divided nature of all parties on this question. At its federal convention, the New Democratic Party frankly acknowledged these areas of differences and made no attempt to hide them: "Within the party we are going to attempt to resolve them, in the hope that our deliberations will assist in the broader national negotiations."

The Conservative party had just experienced a break within its own Quebec wing, as well as between it and the rest of the party:

Only the Liberal Party gives the appearance of effectively coping with the situation. The appearance is both deceiving and dangerous. The Liberals dominate Quebec federally, but they do so by default. No other party provides a viable alternative, and increasingly the people of Quebec are opting out federally, and seeking an expression of their identity through their provincial government.

The rigidity of the Trudeau concept of federalism, and the essentially conservative nature of both his government and that of Bourassa provincially, increasingly leaves the people of Quebec with no alternative than through the Parti Québecois.

In the previous election, the Parti Québécois had received 23 per cent of the vote, but 90 per cent of the English-speaking vote had gone Liberal. Among the 50 per cent of the francophone population which opted for the PQ, a distinct majority were under thirty-five years of age. As Claude Ryan, editor of *Le Devoir* had warned, "the younger generation is already inheriting the future."

"In fact," I said, "when moderates and such committed federalists as Claude Ryan now publicly assert that they have no alternative but to vote PQ in the next provincial election, we have a chilling reminder of how much the chasm has widened — and how urgent is the need for action rather than drift."

My growing concern was bolstered by the new tone of the Ontario government. Premier William Davis had reverted to the traditional role of Hepburn and Drew — a calculated confrontation with the central government. A belligerent parochialism, expressed in the 1971 throne speech, was carried through into the budget and in farm marketing legislation, which sharply escalated the interprovincial trade warfare.

"Not that the federal position isn't open to serious objection," I contended, in the search for a balance. "It is! That's the pity of it. But much of the validity of Ontario's case is lost in the noise and fury which it is deliberately creating. . . If it is merely political warfare that the Davis government is engaged in, as they build up for a provincial election, then it is both reprehensible and irresponsible." If the Davis government's belligerent parochialism continued at the upcoming federal-provincial conference in Victoria, "then history may well record that Ontario gave this nation the final, decisive push down the road toward dissolution of Canadian Confederation."

In retrospect, my assessment was too gloomy, but it reflects the depressing build-up of events at that juncture of our history.

When the Victoria conference was taking place I was in Quebec City as one of the Ontario delegation at a meeting of the Commonwealth Parliamentary Association. My private chats with members of the Quebec legislature showed me that the people of Quebec were becoming increasingly determined to take greater control over their own destiny. I reported on my return that any Quebec government, no matter what its political complexion, must take a position which would appear to English-speaking Canadians to be separatist in some degree. This made it difficult for us to distinguish among Jean Lesage, Daniel Johnson or Robert Bourassa, all professed federalists, and René Lévesque's avowedly separatist Parti Québécois. I modified my own views on constitutional reform because of this insight, and concluded that a united Canada required a looser kind of federation with more provincial powers.

In fact, a willingness to accept a somewhat looser arrangement emerged at Victoria. But Trudeau remained tough and inflexible on provincial demands, notably those of Quebec. According to reports of the closed meetings, provinces led by such "redneck" premiers as W.A.C. Bennett of British Columbia, went along. So did Bill Davis. My fear that he would carry his belligerent parochialism into the conference was unfounded; instead, he abdicated the decisive conciliatory role that Robarts had played.

I publicly regretted the absence of Robarts, whose stands had so often relieved the isolation of Quebec. He did so, I pointed out:

> not because he was "soft" toward Quebec, but because he recognized, first, that English-speaking Canada must go some distance to accommodate any Quebec premier who hopes to survive the nationalist forces within the province; and, secondly, that in granting Quebec the right to opt out of certain national programs, with fiscal equivalents, the interests of Ontario and her people are not being sacrificed or injured. Rather, since such an attitude makes it possible for Quebec to live more comfortably within the Canadian federation, it helps to keep the country more united, and thereby serves the interests of all Canadians. . . .

In spite of the overwhelming majority that Trudeau received in Quebec in the last election the unhappiness within the provincial Liberal ranks with his general stance on federal-provincial relations is widespread and privately vocal. . . . [Liberal backbenchers] asserted, without qualification, that in no way would they help the federal Liberal Party in the next election.

Given this strong feeling, it wasn't surprising that the Liberal majority in the Quebec Legislature rejected the Victoria Charter. What was significant was that both the Union Nationale and Parti Québécois opposition parties also rejected it.

Within a few days I had a chance to address the situation in the Legislature during the debate on the spending estimates of the Department of Treasury and Economics, whose minister, Darcy McKeough, had been an important figure in the Ontario delegation at Victoria:

It is obvious that the Quebec Liberal caucus has, in the past six or eight months, moved away from the subservience which characterized its position during the crisis which provoked the invocation of the War Measures Act. Then, its leader, Robert Bourassa, had been very much the puppet of decisions essentially made in Ottawa, but no longer. . .

The image in this country . . . has been that the Conservative Party and the New Democratic Party have had very great difficulty in achieving unanimity and a viable policy with regard to . . . the problem of the province of Quebec in federal-provincial relations, whereas the Liberal Party has achieved unanimity on the issue. Well, the myth of that unanimity has been rather disastrously shattered. The rejection of the Victoria Charter was nearly unanimous, and why?

I quoted from an article by Claude Lemelin, of *Le Devoir*, carried by the Toronto *Telegram* on June 24:

Quebeckers can easily sympathize with the shock and

disillusion that has swept across English Canada, following Premier Bourassa's rejection of the Victoria Charter.

For those among us who have been warning for years that Prime Minister Trudeau was leading the rest of the country up the garden path on the Quebec 'problem' it was of course, all too predictable. . . .

Sooner or later, Trudeau's bluff had to be called. It is perhaps fitting — and most significant — that it was finally called by a government in Quebec that has strong affinities with Mr. Trudeau's party, whose decisiveness and coherence of vision leaves much to be desired, and which was elected on precisely the sort of platform that fits the base political motivations the Prime Minister ascribes to the Quebec "masses": 100,000 new jobs, the juicy plans of profitable federalism, the end of petty squabbles with Ottawa, and so forth.

At no time since the beginning of the Quiet Revolution has the writing on the wall been clearer; and if English Canadians can be brought to read that stubborn message, hope can be rescued from the Victoria fiasco.

My remarks were directed during the debate to how we might rescue hope from the Victoria Charter fiasco. Not only was the vote in the Quebec Legislature nearly unanimous, but across the province a united front had emerged, involving the teachers and the CNTU as well as the Quebec Federation of Labour and the St. Jean Baptiste Society. If Bourassa had not rejected the Victoria Charter, there was good reason to believe that two or three, and perhaps five, of his cabinet would have resigned.

At Victoria, Prime Minister Trudeau had climaxed his tough stance with a ten-day ultimatum that, if the Victoria Charter were turned down, the process of constitutional review would be postponed for the indefinite future.

Throughout this unfortunate confrontation, "the whole thrust of the government of Ontario was to get the conference over as quickly as possible," I said. By not even mentioning Quebec's basic demands, Ontario "played a part in the subtle game of collusion with Ottawa that resulted in the isolation of Quebec.'' Rejection of the Victoria Charter left the Parti Québecois with ''a powerful argument that Victoria proved conclusively once again that Quebec's fundamental demands cannot be met constitutionally.'' I argued that Ontario must play a key role in breaking the deadlock created by Trudeau's intransigence.

I cited areas, such as provincial control over manpower retraining and communication, particularly cable TV, where Quebec's demands were precisely what Ontario wanted. ''Why were these areas of agreement not emphasized in Victoria, instead of permitting this disastrous polarization?'' I asked.

When negotiations resulted from Quebec's earlier opposition, social policy across Canada had been improved. For instance, because of the give-and-take in reconciling the Quebec Pension Plan with the Canada Pension Plan, the federal benefits were increased, and contributions to the Canada plan were for the most part going back to the provinces instead of staying in Ottawa.

Ontario now had an opportunity, I concluded, ''to return to its historic role in Confederation, that is, as an unofficial leader of the English-speaking provinces, partly because it is [politically] the largest and most powerful of the provinces, and partly because it has the very great advantage of historical and geographical associations with the province of Quebec, which makes it possible for Ontario, with enlightened, vigorous, imaginative leadership, to do something that can bring results.''

Trudeau was right in one respect: the rejection of the Victoria Charter meant a postponement of constitutional review. In part, this was because the political situation was destabilized. In 1975 Davis's Tories suffered the same fate as Trudeau's Liberals in 1972: reduction to a minority government. And a snap election call in 1977 produced another minority for the Ontario Tories. Furthermore, it was increasingly difficult for either the federal or Ontario governments to negotiate with a Quebec government, elected in 1976 on a platform of leaving the federation for some form of sovereignty-association.

Moreover, my personal situation had so changed as to exclude such an intensive pursuit of federal-provincial affairs. Not only was I out of the leadership of the party, but with minority government, there was a sharing of the chairmanships of standing and select committees, and I was assigned by the NDP caucus to chair the Select Committee on Hydro Affairs. It became a preoccupation during the minority years from 1975 to 1981.

But if the constitutional debate had dropped from the legislative agenda, it continued with undiminished vigour within the party. Throughout all the years since its founding in 1961, the NDP had sought to work out with the Quebec section of the party an acceptable constitutional statement on French-English relations.

A national constitutional committee, chaired by federal leader Ed Broadbent, worked to coordinate studies being pursued in many of the provinces. In Ontario, I chaired a caucus committee, in which fourteen of the thirty-four NDP members were active. Seven or eight prepared papers on various aspects of the constitutional question, to clarify in our own minds Ontario's position in Confederation. That position, we realized, had changed radically.

Ontario never had to fight for its regional needs, because, as the main beneficiary of Confederation, her interests had been met. Instead, Ontario had been the conciliator, resolving differences among others. I often expressed the hope that that role should continue, but in the future, Ontario would also have to be a more vigorous advocate of its own interests, countering the militant posture of the western provinces, notably Alberta. The challenge, as I saw it, was how to "shape a constitution so that it is more reflective of the reality of the day, when Ontario is an equal rather than a dominant force in Confederation."

With the return of the Trudeau Liberals in 1980, following the short-lived Clark administration, and with the crisis created by the upcoming Quebec referendum on separatism, the Ontario government belatedly provided an opportunity to debate the constitutional problem. This took place during the week of 5-9 May 1980, and was so unusual that participants were later presented with a bound copy of the proceedings.

Leading off for the NDP, I called the debate a first step, to be followed by negotiations as soon as possible after the referendum in Quebec. It would all lead, I hoped, to a new, made-in-Canada, amendable in Canada, constitution, with "new means for resolving the grievances of all the regions of Canada, and providing the prospect of fulfilling the diverse aspirations of all Canadians."

For me, the occasion was memorable, for personal reasons which I explained in the Legislature:

I come to this debate with profoundly mixed emotions. I was born in British Columbia. I was raised in Quebec and worked there for a couple of years as a journalist. I had my university education in Ontario, and I have lived and worked in this province for the past thirty-five to forty years. I have had the extreme good fortune, in all of that work in various fields, of being able to move and to have contacts with fellow-Canadians in every province, in the Northwest Territories and in the Yukon.

In addition to all that, family associations have broadened and strengthened what I would like to describe as my Canadianism. My father was the grandson of a Scotsman who came out and carved a farm out of the bush, some thirty-five to forty miles south of Montreal. He, like many other young men, went west and homesteaded on the prairies, and subsequently moved into British Columbia. My mother was the daughter of an English miner who came out to the coal mines of southeastern British Columbia.

My wife is French, born in Montreal, I have two daughters, one of whom is married to a Jew, the other to a native Indian, a member of the Six Nations Reserve.

The House will understand, then, why I love this country. I love it in all its richness and diversity. Having said that, I have to confess that Ontario is home. All parts of Canada are to me an inspiration . . . but Ontario is home. I am proud to have been a member of this Legislature for some twenty-five years.

I am fascinated with the work in my own riding, which originally was basically Anglo-Saxon, but by the process of redistribution and of the ever-moving peoples of this great metropolitan area, today has an added mix of Italians, Polish, Ukrainian, Maltese, Portuguese, Latin-American, Caribbean, East Indian, Pakistani, and now Vietnamese. It is a microcosm of the world. You will understand, therefore, Mr. Speaker, why my vision of this nation is broader than Ontario, but centred in Ontario.

I then proceeded to emphasize Ontario's changed position. The public perception was that the problems of Canada arose primarily from Quebec; or the Atlantic provinces, economically disadvantaged throughout the first hundred years of Confederation; or the western provinces, short-changed by Confederation, now with burgeoning economic strength, and determined to redress the historic imbalance. "But dare I suggest that *one* major problem, if not *the* major problem, in restructuring Confederation lies here in Ontario, and not elsewhere."

I quoted John Robarts's remark that he no longer believed Ontario could simply go along with change if other provinces wanted it, but instead must make fundamental constitutional changes "in a way that can be seen to be done." Other provinces were still wondering whether the change was "just rhetorical rather than substantive," I said. "Suspicions die slowly."

With the 180 degree turn that provincial spokesmen had taken in the last decade, I warned: "This is going to be a little painful for us in Ontario, to step down from what is perceived to be a smug pedestal, as the major beneficiary of Confederation, and face the grim realities of a rapidly changing Canada." With economic development in the west, and the prospect of it in the east, Ontario had become, in the economic slow-down of the 1970s and early 1980s, a have-not province, dropping below the national average in per capita revenue.

Moreover, Ontario was "odd man out" at federal-provincial conferences. An editorial in the London *Free Press* said it was "unrealistic to expect a country to survive and prosper when the main unifying force seems to be, as Newfoundland's Premier Brian Peckford has observed, everyone's hatred of Ontario."

The resolution, around which the debate revolved, read, "That we, the Legislative Assembly of Ontario, commit ourselves, as our highest priority, to support full negotiations of a new constitution to satisfy the diverse aspirations of all Canadians, and to replace the *status quo* which is clearly unacceptable." I summed up my position:

> For years the question has been: what does Quebec want? Now we know. . . . We also have plenty of evidence as to what the west and the Atlantic provinces want. But there is an unresolved question. . . . What does Ontario want? Now that we have forsaken our contentment with the *status quo*, now that we are committed to meaningful constitutional reform, what exactly do we want? What do we want by way of change in the constitution? How can we preserve the central benefits of Confederation while satisfying the demands of those who challenge the system? How can we reaffirm our support for the basic duality upon which this nation has been built, and yet move to acknowledge the reality of the multicultural nature of Canada? How can we rebuild our historic working relationship with Quebec, so as to provide the key to English-French relationships throughout this country? These are the questions, but we haven't got the answers.

I was occupied as chairman of the Hydro Affairs committee and couldn't serve on the Select Committee on Constitutional Reform, set up after the debate. The NDP members were James Renwick, George Samis, Richard Johnston and Odoardo Di Santo. The committee reported on 21 October 1980.

Meanwhile, Trudeau had become prime minister again, and the Quebec voters had rejected the separatist option. During the referendum campaign, Ottawa and the provinces had promised quick action on constitutional reform, and two years of feverish activity now culminated in the acceptance of the Constitution Act, 1982 — made and amendable in Canada. It was not all that was hoped for — but that is another story.

Ironically, I was not involved in the climactic finish; by that time I had resigned my seat in the Legislature. But as chairman of the NDP caucus, I made frequent representations to Hugh Segal, adviser to Premier Davis on constitutional matters — usually a plea that Ontario should intervene more vigorously to reconcile the differences between the "Gang of Eight" provinces and the federal government. It didn't happen, perhaps because Ontario, like New Brunswick, was in the federal camp.

There were intensive negotiations behind the scenes for months, particularly in the final deal. It may be that Ontario did all that could be done. Readers will come to their own conclusion.[4]

With Alexa McDonough, now NDP leader in Nova Scotia, during a visit in 1986.

With the pigeons on Trafalgar Square during a visit of all party leaders to commemorate the 100th anniversary (1969) of Ontario House in London.

Centre back row — well kimonoed during a visit to Japan in Expo year.

Chatting with young Chinese in Beijing, 1985.

Atop the Great Wall of China during a visit in 1985.

Sharing a head table with Papendreau, now Prime Minister of Greece, when he was living, in exile, in Toronto.

Leaving Moscow, after a visit in 1974.

A farewell gathering with Rumanian hosts following a visit to the USSR in 1974.

My faithful 1938 Underwood, which is almost a major character in these memoirs.

With Saskatchewan's pioneering as a model, the Ontario NDP led the fight for medicare.

15
Health

George Drew's "twenty-two points," the platform that brought the Tories to power in Ontario in 1943, included the following promise. "Health insurance will be established so that medical, dental and other health protection will be available to all." For the next ten years, nothing happened to fulfil that promise.

As for the federal Liberals, their platform had included public health insurance since 1919. But theirs was as meaningless a promise as the Tories'. In the 1945 federal election the Liberals advocated a specific plan, then gradually forsook it after their re-election. By the 1953 campaign, Prime Minister St. Laurent was saying that Ottawa would cooperate, but responsibility rested with the provinces.

In contrast, for the CCF, health insurance was a firm, long-standing commitment. Within eighteen months of its election in 1944, the Saskatchewan government of Tommy Douglas took the first step, by providing hospital coverage. This was done without federal help, by a have-not province that had pulled itself out of depression bankruptcy during the war years.

So the Ontario CCF had a ready target in the unfulfilled promises of both old parties, and a successful example to point to in Saskatchewan. Not surprisingly, health insurance was a major item on my agenda from my first weeks in provincial politics. The next fifteen years were a relentless struggle.

Early in 1954, Blue Cross, the private insurer, announced a 26 per cent rate increase. Health Minister Mackinnon Phillips was stung into words, if not action. He said there should be a form of health insurance covering everybody, within about five years. Later, recanting and reversing himself, he said the government was opposed to any form of "state insurance," which, I pointed out, simply meant any plan designed to cover everybody.

Premier Frost said the government would not move on the issue while hospitals were running at a deficit — even though better provincial grants, to cover long-term patients, were the only way they could balance their books. He also constantly resorted to the scare tactics of excessive costs, repeating the inaccurate claim that governments with public plans had to bail them out and subsidize them.

"Why can't Conservative spokesmen stop confusing the issue with propaganda attacks on 'subsidization', and face up to the fact that hospitals are now being subsidized by municipal governments and the federal government — to say nothing of the provincial government itself — to the tune of $20 million last year?" I argued at a West York CCF meeting in March 1954:

> The choice before the province is a simple one. It can continue to accept, under a Conservative government, the present hodge-podge of hospital plans, filling in bits and pieces of the picture, but still not providing overall coverage for Ontario's five million people, despite a provincial government subsidy. Or it can lend its support to a government-sponsored plan. in which individuals pay a premium within the means of an average budget, thereby providing them with complete hospital coverage, as of right, with the spectre of hospital bills banished forever.

The case for public insurance was supported strongly by Professor Malcolm Taylor, a former director of research for the Saskatchewan plan, who was now doing studies for the Frost government. He told a well-heeled audience at the Canadian Manufacturers' Association, in blunt language, that they were almost certainly all protected under some health plan, and "if health insurance is desirable for you, it is desirable for all."

The issue, he said, "has been subjected to more emotional

pleading, more outright distortion, more red herrings, more exaggerated cost estimates, more unwarranted predictions of evil consequences, than any other matter of public attention since Halley's Comet.''

He countered the insurance companies' claims that a government plan wasn't needed because voluntary insurance was spreading so rapidly by pointing out that outside British Columbia and Saskatchewan, which had government plans, only 46.3 per cent of Canadians were protected against costs of hospital care in 1954. As for the alleged high costs of public plans, Dr. Taylor pointed out that in fact they were more efficient and economical than private enterprise: they covered everybody, and more of the subscriber's premium went to pay the actual medical and hospital bills, instead of sales, advertising and profits.

I calculated that only $20 million, added to current federal and provincial spending on health care for some groups, would provide health insurance for everybody. Furthermore, the prime minister had already promised that Ottawa would share in the costs.

Despite this, the Frost government refused to move. Their dog-in-the-manger attitude was not only depriving the people of Ontario, but blocking the way toward a full-scale plan for all Canadians.

The government's other excuse, apart from cost, was that health insurance was a field of "greatest unknowns. " The fact was, of course, that the pioneering Saskatchewan and British Columbia plans had revealed most, if not all, the "unknowns," and Dr. Taylor's detailed study of all the ramifications for the Ontario government was available by the fall of 1954.[1]

The public debate raged on, but political skirmishing gave way to federal-provincial negotiations, and some prospect of action.

At the federal-provincial conference in October, 1955, the federal Liberals and Ontario Tories blamed each other for delaying government health insurance — and backed themselves into a corner, where the only escape was actually a step toward what they had been pretending to want all along.

The first step, in this case, was hospital insurance. But the Ontario government's proposals were very far from the comprehensive coverage already in effect in Saskatchewan and British Columbia. Premier Frost demanded that Ottawa agree to pay at least 50 per cent of the costs before the province would move. Coverage would then be phased in: diagnostic services, then a home care program, then extraordinary hospital costs, then maternal care. Each would take a year or two to implement, so it would be up to eight years before the government would establish coverage of full hospital services.

Speaking to the Ontario Federation of Labour convention on 2 November 1955, I called the Frost proposals "a patchwork of bits and pieces which will have the effect of postponing hospital insurance for about ten years."

While a federal-provincial Health Services Committee negotiated who would pay, and how much, a Legislature committee studied all the background material from the Malcolm Taylor reports and the ongoing negotiations. Mr. Frost and I weren't committee members, but we both attended and participated fully. Memorably, we found some common ground.

From the report of the Superintendent of Insurance, I dug out recent figures on premiums collected and benefits paid out. For the Travelers Insurance Company, the benefits were 61 per cent of premiums; for the Mutual Benefit and Accident Company, 56 per cent; for Continental Casualty Company, 42 per cent; and for the Canada Health and Accident, 39 per cent. Clearly, if we allowed private companies to carry basic province-wide coverage, we would be increasing the costs of the plan by up to 30 or 40 per cent.

In effect, Mr. Frost agreed. I vividly recall insurance industry spokesmen arguing that if the government looked after those who could not pay hospital costs, they would cover the rest. "That sounds like a good deal for you," was Frost's blunt retort. He freely told of a personal experience: after many years of paying premiums on a private policy, he made a small claim, only to be faced with a lengthy exchange of letters challenging it. He was so indignant that he cancelled the policy. So Frost had no problem disputing the companies' claim that private insurance plans would meet the needs. Officially, however, government spokesmen continued to warn that the cost might be too great. In a speech to the Halton CCF in Georgetown in May 1955, I dismissed this argument as a bogey: "With the federal contribution, it is possible for the Ontario government to establish a plan without spending a single dollar more from the provincial treasury, and at a premium cost to the people of Ontario less than they are now spending individually."

Finally, on 6 March 1957, a federal-Ontario agreement was signed. It would go into effect 1 January 1959. Monthly premiums would be $4.20 for a family, higher than in Saskatchewan, even though there was still no federal share being paid there. The CCF greeted the achievement with qualified enthusiasm. It had been an unnecessarily long struggle, to achieve only the first stage of health insurance. Hospital bills had been lifted, but doctors' bills remained a burden for many. I pointed out that the Frost government was taking credit, while spending no more on hospital care than it ever had; the premiums and the federal government share covered the cost.[2]

The major battle — for full health coverage — still lay ahead.

In the first year of operation of the hospital plan, 93 per cent of the population enrolled voluntarily, and the Department of Health's spending was only $294,000 more than the year before. But there were gaps. Out-patients weren't covered for X-rays or diagnostic examinations, unless they were admitted to hospital, and that increased the shortage of hospital beds. The Toronto *Star* called that omission "social and economic nonsense."[3]

The battle for comprehensive coverage heated up in Saskatchewan, where it was the government's major platform plank in a successful election campaign in June 1960. The Saskatchewan Medical Association launched a $100,000 propaganda campaign against what it called "state" insurance.

There were indications of a concerted, nation-wide revolt by doctors. In Kirkland Lake, where everyone had apparently been satisfied with a prepaid community medical plan for eighteen years, the doctors suddenly called it "unethical" and withdrew. I also learned from authoritative sources that the Ontario Medical Association was working out a plan with insurance underwriters to forestall government action on medical coverage.

A major hurdle, as well, was the vacillating role of the provincial Liberals. John Wintermeyer in the Legislature deplored "our mad dash toward the welfare state," and former leadership aspirant Joe Greene observed that "if we are convinced that the people of Canada want a welfare state, why don't we do the graceful thing and abandon the field to the CCF?"

"Like King Canute, who stood on the shore and tried to keep back the tides with a broom, the Liberal Party is trying to beat back the demands of the people in the twentieth century," I told an audience of Packinghouse Workers in Port Hope. "They are fighting for a concept of liberalism that is as out-of-date as the horse and buggy or Aunt Minnie's hoop skirt."[4]

In November 1959 the *Globe and Mail* reported that Liberal MPPs decided at a caucus meeting that "Ontario is not ready, nor is there a demand, for state medicine." When Parkdale Liberal MPP James Trotter introduced a resolution calling for a comprehensive prepaid medical plan, without indicating whether it should be publicly or privately sponsored, I amended it in favour of a government plan. The cat was out of the bag for the Liberals: they lined up solidly with the Tories to reject my amendment. They now supported prepaid medical insurance on a so-called free enterprise basis.

"There has emerged in Canada an unholy alliance of the doctors and insurance companies on the one hand, and a working partnership with the old parties on the other, for the purpose of fighting a government-sponsored medical plan," I told a meeting in Sault Ste Marie in May 1960. "Having lost the battle on hospital insurance, they are going to fight it out to the bitter end on medical insurance."

For a couple of years, the Ontario government drifted. It introduced a comprehensive bill for full medical coverage in 1960, then let it drop. The bill was reintroduced in the fall session, but nothing more happened. In March 1961 it turned up again but got first reading only. The new premier, John Robarts, commented that health insurance was "something we shall have to consider." Meanwhile, the government's commitment was being undermined in secret meetings between the health minister, Dr. Matthew Dymond, and the Ontario Medical Association.

In Saskatchewan, the decisive battle was fought. When the CCF government introduced an insurance program on 1 July 1962, it resulted in a twenty-three-day strike by doctors, the culmination of the Canadian Medical Association's carefully orchestrated campaign to defend doctors' "rights." In fact, the Saskatchewan plan incorporated the doctors' demands for fee-for-service pay rather than a salary, and protection of the doctor-patient relationship so that every person could choose his own doctor. The profession's adamant stand was simply open defiance of the public will.

We in the Ontario NDP decided it was time to move from general rhetoric to specific proposals. We introduced a resolution calling for a comprehensive plan to cover medical, hospital, dental and optical services. We met with executive members of OMA to discuss our proposals. I remember the meeting was unexpectedly cordial because the doctors were angered at a federal Liberal government policy position that had been announced without consultation with them. At least, we extended them the courtesy of discussion.

Following a caucus meeting in August, I proposed the province adopt a medicare plan, providing complete medical, surgical, obstetrical and psychiatric care. "The NDP deserves credit for bringing this issue to a head," the Toronto *Star* editorialized, and called for all parties to cooperate to bring in a plan.

The *Star*'s hopes were based on another switch by the Ontario Liberals who, in October, had dropped their support for a plan handled by the medical profession and the insurance companies, and now wanted a universal, government-sponsored program. But in January the Liberals repudiated that position, rejecting universal coverage in favour of "insuring immediately" all those over sixty-five, the unemployed, and those on welfare or disability pensions. For everybody else the plan would be voluntary. This was precisely the Tory approach. Even worse, the Liberals were dropping the principle of government sponsorship, and were trying to work out a plan with private insurance companies. The Liberals had proved that their policy statements were not firm commitments, but merely kite-flying pronouncements subject to change without notice, whenever it seemed expedient. Or, as one columnist put it, Liberal policies "bounced back and forth like a derelict yo-yo."

Meanwhile, the NDP had calculated the costs of its proposal. The plan could be financed by a premium of thirty cents a week for a single person and sixty cents for a family, with a levy of 3 per cent on corporation profits and a 6 per cent surcharge on personal income tax. Thus, low income families who paid no income tax would pay only the basic premium.

The pressure was now rising to the point where the government could no longer ignore it. Late in 1963 Health Minister Dr. Dymond introduced a bill that would remove some of the worst abuses in the current policies, and provide a plan to assist anyone enrolling voluntarily in non-profit or private insurance coverage. The NDP (with the Liberals joining in) vehemently attacked what we saw as complete capitulation to the insurance companies and the medical profession. As we headed into the 1963 provincial election, the government appointed a committee to conduct public hearings on its proposal, and the Tories boasted proudly during the campaign of their "health care plan."

The Conservatives did well in the election, but Liberal leader John Wintermeyer lost his own seat. His successor, Andrew Thompson, was firmly committed to comprehensive, government-sponsored health insurance, and the unpredictable policy shifts came to an end.

The Canadian Medical Association carried its campaign to

absurd limits. In October its president, William Wigle, told the Yonge-Bay-Bloor Association in Toronto that if poor families weren't receiving proper medical care, it wasn't because they couldn't afford it, but because they were "not of the calibre even to get themselves to the office to get an appointment." The Ontario Medical Association managed to keep pace in absurdity a few weeks later when, in a brief to the Ontario Committee on Taxation, it called for daily charges for patients using the hospitals under prepayment plans, to discourage "over-utilization" of the system.

"Once again, Ontario doctors have exhibited symptoms of that disease known as foot-in-mouth," the *Globe and Mail* editorialized:

> The doctors. . . . have strenuously objected to any government intrusion into what they consider their business. . . . What the doctors are really saying is that they do not care to discipline their patients and prefer to have the government do it for them, with a tax. Apparently the doctor-patient relationship can admit of government interference if it is to the convenience of the doctors.

The cost of medicare was the main topic of debate. I pointed out that the easiest way to figure the costs of the government plan — which basically covered doctor's bills alone — was to examine the incomes of the practitioners. The latest figures showed the *gross* income of all doctors in Ontario was about $130 million. The average *net* income for the 5,800 self-employed doctors was $18,000. However, Dr. Dymond was saying medicare would cost $38 per capita for Ontario's six million people — a total cost of $235 million, or an average net income per doctor of $30,000.

"This, of course, is nonsense," I pointed out at a meeting in Weston on June 5, 1963. "Doctors are the highest paid profession now. I, for one, do not begrudge them this high income status, for I know of no group in society which works harder and makes a greater contribution to our needs. But the proposition that the highest paid profession should have more than a $10,000 increase in income is, I repeat, nonsense."

Our estimate was a cost of $26.25 per capita for a total provincial cost of $160 million. This was $30 million more than people were then spending, but the cost was necessary for universal and adequate coverage, and it was a far cry from the exaggerated totals the Tories bandied about to dampen public enthusiasm for medicare. Moreover, the Robarts plan was based on the myth that 70 per cent of the people were already covered, and all that was needed was to provide an overall plan to subsidize needy families. In fact, our research showed that only 50 to 60 per cent of the people had plans, and they covered only 10 to 40 per cent of their medical bills.

The experience in the two western provinces was becoming more conclusive every day. The Saskatchewan public universal plan was running smoothly now that passions had died down. In contrast, the private plan in Alberta, handled through insurance companies and doctor-sponsored plans, had attracted only 20 per cent of the people to enroll voluntarily. It simply wasn't doing the job.

At the federal level, too, health insurance was under study. In March 1961 Prime Minister John Diefenbaker had appointed Emmett Hall, Chief Justice of Saskatchewan, to head a royal commission on health services. A long-time friend of Diefenbaker's, Justice Hall at the outset favoured private insurance coverage, but as the evidence accumulated, he became an ardent convert to the model plan in his home province. His report, released in June 1964, came down solidly for universal, compulsory insurance, financially assisted by Ottawa but administered by the provinces.

With the exception of the suggestion that some funds should be raised through lotteries, Diefenbaker enthusiastically supported the proposals. New Democrats greeted the Hall report with unrestrained glee. "For over twenty years, the CCF and NDP have led this fight in Canada. . . . Now the Hall report lends impressive vindication of our persistent advocacy of a government-sponsored plan."

The response of Health Minister Matthew Dymond was amusing. Repeating his opposition to the Hall/NDP model, he nevertheless observed, "The genius of conservatism is that it can change with the times," and Ontario would probably go along with what "seems to be the trend." In fact, I pointed out, the Tories were simply making a virtue of necessity.

The Robarts government had appointed its own committee, headed by W.G. Hagey, president of the University of Waterloo, to study the matter. As expected, when their report was released in February 1955, it supported the original, private Robarts plan. "Medicare for insurers, not for the public," the Toronto *Star* commented. "The impudence of the whole proposition is breathtaking. Perhaps never before in Canadian history has a scheme to benefit private business masqueraded so brazenly as a social welfare plan." The *Star* dubbed the plan "semi-care." Late in the 1965 session, the Tories brought in their bill, based on the Hagey committee recommendations, but the Legislature recessed before it could be debated.

On 19 July 1965, at a federal-provincial conference on health services, Prime Minister Lester Pearson said Ottawa would cover 50 per cent of provincial costs, if a provincial health plan was universal, covered all physicians' services, was administered either directly by a provincial government or a non-profit provincial agency, and had fully transferable benefits from province to province.

When the Ontario bill came up for debate early the next year, the Tories ignored the requirements of the proposed national plan. The NDP and Liberals (now on side, at least for a time) attacked the Robarts plan vigorously. I said that "Robartscare" was an indescribable potpourri. "In principle it is a monstrosity — partly private, partly public and partly a mish-mash of both. The result is high administrative costs throughout."[5]

The 55 to 60 per cent of Ontarians with group coverage were left wholly at the mercy of the private carriers. Low-income groups who were caught in group coverage were thus denied the subsidy to which they would otherwise be entitled. Administrative costs would be high to subsidize the premiums of the 27 per cent of the population who qualified. And up to 18 per cent of the people were left to individual coverage — suggesting how difficult it would be to achieve the universality required to qualify for federal funds.

After almost half a century of procrastination, provinces were forcing the federal Liberals to take action. Saskatchewan, New Brunswick and Newfoundland had accepted the federal proposals. The British Columbia and Quebec plans were close to qualifying. A national health insurance plan was within reach. Ontario's indecision was "the main roadblock to the nation being able to achieve this major piece of social legislation, which has eluded us for generations," I argued. "With a firm commitment to principle from Ontario, the overwhelming majority of the Canadian people would be in on a federal plan, and the federal government could waffle no longer."

The Liberals moved an amendment calling for further study — in my opinion, a gross miscalculation in strategy. The issue had been studied to death. It was a perfect example of how the Liberals bungled their job of official opposition. The Tories voted down all amendments and brought in the Ontario Medical Services Insurance Plan — OMSIP for short.

The insurance companies now argued that over 85 per cent of the population had some sort of coverage (almost all through voluntary programs) and there was no need for a universal government program.

In September 1966 the federal Liberals backed off again, announcing a one-year delay until 1 July 1967, for the introduction of medicare, so they could fight inflation. The Toronto *Star*'s reaction was scathing. In an editorial on 9 September 1966, headlined "Medical Delay is Outrageous Deceit," it asked: "Who, in view of the forty-seven-year record of the Liberal non-fulfillment of this promise, can have confidence that the delay will be only for one year?"

Equally alarming, was the back-sliding of the federal Conservatives. Although Diefenbaker supported the Hall proposals, his caucus apparently was not with him, and the party health spokesman introduced a resolution in favour of Ontario's plan. "It is sad to see how the issue of medicare is more and more becoming a political football," I told a news conference in January 1967. "Little wonder that people are getting increasingly cynical about politics in general and medicare in particular."

Ontario Treasurer Charles McNaughton was saying the national plan would cost $50 per capita — even though, two years before, the federal Health Department had estimated $33 per capita in Ontario, and $27 for Canada as a whole. And one year before, both governments were using $40 per capita in their calculations. Moreover, McNaughton said medicare would cost up to 12 per cent of personal income tax revenue. This was another scare figure, because $805 million of the estimated $884 million cost of the first year of medicare was already being paid for by various forms of health insurance, so only another $80 million would be needed. Finally, at his most parochial, McNaughton cavilled about how much revenue, raised in Ontario, would go to other provinces to finance medicare. I compared this attitude with Robarts's suggestion that a billion-dollar development fund be set up, so that Ontario could help have-not provinces. "Which approach really represents the view of the government?" I asked.

As the federal Liberal momentum slowed, the fragile coalition was coming unstuck. The Ontario Liberals, like the federal Tories, were backing off. The new Liberal Leader, Robert Nixon, proposed that private insurance companies consider their medicare plans as a non-profit component of their operations. He felt that would satisfy the federal requirement that the plank be operated by a public agency. I was skeptical:

Private insurance companies don't do anything that doesn't involve a profit. By making this proposal, Mr. Nixon is supporting the Conservatives in protecting the right of the insurance companies to carry on a costly and inefficient form of prepayment for medical services. . . . Moreover, Mr. Nixon assumes that the percentage of coverage is already adequate. But he should know that most existing private schemes do not cover all medical expenses. . . . He has brought his party back to the

Wintermeyer position and, in the process, is helping take the provincial government off the hook.

At this point, Premier Robarts announced formally that Ontario would not enter the national plan. He said the situation was a conflict of priorities between Ottawa and the provinces. "In truth," I commented, "it is a conflict between a conservative, right-wing regime and a progressive piece of legislation that will increase productivity, equalize opportunities and bring complete health care within the reach of everyone. . . . Under medicare, the average Ontario family would pay less for complete health coverage than it does now."

I backed up this assertion with figures. In fact, I underestimated the cost of the inefficient and incomplete Robarts plan. The provincial budget of March 1968 took deep bites out of the ordinary taxpayer (with no increase in corporation taxes), including a hike in family health and hospital premiums from $228 to $309 a year. Moreover, after 1 July 1967, when the national plan went in to effect, Ontario began to lose $450,000 a day in federal sharing, the equivalent of $22 for every man, woman and child in the province. Medical insurance premiums could be cut in half, if Ontario entered the national plan, I pointed out.

At the constitutional conference on 10 February 1969 Premier Robarts made his memorable statement on public health insurance. "Medicare is a glowing example of a Machiavellian scheme that is, in my humble opinion, one of the greatest political frauds that has been perpetrated on the people of this country. The position is this: you [the federal government] are taxing our people in Ontario to the tune of $225 millions a year, to pay for a plan for which we get nothing, because it has a low priority in our plans for Ontario."

But the pressure was on. In addition to the controversial inadequacies in the existing provincial coverage, there was growing public protest that the government had already lost nearly $200 million by refusing to qualify for federal grants.

The federal Liberals now sacrificed a principle to entice

Ontario into the national plan. They allowed private insurance companies to carry health insurance if they operated it on a non-profit basis. So the Robarts government brought in the Ontario Health Services Insurance Plan (OHSIP) to incorporate coverage under OMSIP and add just enough to qualify for federal subsidies. The Ontario Liberals supported the new plan because it would, at least, bring in federal grants. We in the NDP felt that the legislation violated so many basic principles that we moved a "reasoned amendment" designed to send the legislation back, in an effort to get comprehensive coverage and a more equitable sharing of the financial burden.

I had several reasons for opposing the bill. Despite the infusion of federal money that now covered nearly half the cost, Robarts refused to lower the premiums already in effect. Moreover, while it was required that the federal grants should be spent only on health services, there was no guarantee that a province would not use them to replace existing provincial health expenditures — a "chiselling" tactic that British Columbia had already employed. And the bill did not prohibit extra billing. Already, under OMSIP some doctors were billing to cover the 10 per cent difference between what the plan paid and what the OMA fee schedule allowed them to charge. That difference would increase, if the doctors and the government could not agree on fees in the future.

The Liberals lined up with the Tories to defeat the NDP amendment. We got revenge in the Middlesex South by-election that fall, when we campaigned with the facts on the medicare plan and the Liberal/Tory voting record on it. The NDP candidate, Archdeacon Kenneth Bolton, won a sensational victory in Premier Robarts's political backyard.

The overall battle had been won, but skirmishes continued over the basic deficiencies in the Ontario plan, and particularly over its administration. In early 1970 the media reported that OHSIP was in chaos. "There's no news in that revelation," I said. "OHSIP has been in chaos since birth, indeed, since its conception from the unholy marriage of the Robarts government and the insurance companies. . . . The time has come to recognize that there are fundamental problems which are not going to be solved without radical action.''

The basic problem was that there was no effective communication between the government and those responsible for OHSIP's operation. Indeed, one official was quoted as saying that the new minister was just never around. Moreover, the government had created "a Frankenstein monster," I said, and was now being "strangled by its own creation." The bureaucratic problems involved thirty-one private insurance companies that were allowed to carry the plan; the administrative complexities of allowing doctors to bill their patients directly (so that patients then had to bill the health plan); the three public organizations managing the plan, with their three computers that could not communicate with one another; and an old-style telephone system that wasn't replaced because the Public Works Department was on an austerity program. This was "penny-wise, pound-foolish . . . sheer lunacy," I commented.

Stephen Lewis, now the NDP leader, had a passionate interest in social programs, including health services, and continued the party's unceasing efforts to maintain an adequate social security net. But the basics of a national medicare plan had been established, and its administration proceeded in a relatively routine fashion, subject only to periodic federal-provincial controversy over Ottawa's efforts to reduce its share of the rising costs.

In 1977 the federal government, through the Established Programs Financing Arrangement for post-secondary education, hospital insurance and medicare programs, replaced conditional grants with a combination of increased tax room, plus cash payments related to the growth in the economy. This resulted in a reduction in transfer payments at precisely the time when provincial costs were rising as a result of a sluggish economy.

In the 1980s, both Liberal and Conservative federal governments further damaged the open-ended principle of cost-sharing by imposing ceilings on their contributions to the programs. While done under pressure of coping with the federal budgetary deficits, it has simply transferred the federal problem to the provinces.

In 1984, with the Canada Health Act, the Liberal federal health minister, Monique Begin, banned extra billing by doctors, and gave provinces three years to respond, otherwise they would lose, dollar for dollar, in transfer payments, what they permitted in extra billing. While David Peterson had publicly supported extra billing as a safety-valve in the system only a few months before the 1985 election, its banning was a major element in the Liberal-NDP Accord of May 1985. In office, the Peterson government introduced Bill 91 to end extra billing, resulting in a dramatic confrontation with the medical profession through a three-week strike.

By now, I was out of both a seat in the Legislature and chairmanship of the NDP caucus, so that my involvement in this chapter of the continuing struggle to make health services universally available was restricted to periodic support in my weekly column in the *Sunday Star*.

Health insurance is an issue to which New Democrats respond with fierce pride and loyalty, for reasons inherent in its history.

It was Canada's first CCF government, in Saskatchewan, that pioneered hospital insurance, in spite of being one of the poorest provinces at the time. More than a decade passed before the federal Liberal government accepted a share in hospital costs, and only then would the Ontario government, presiding over the richest province, legislate the first step in health insurance.

Once the federal government accepted a share in hospital costs, the Saskatchewan government moved, again on its own resources, to coverage of doctors' bills. The result was a massive confrontation with the Canadian Medical Association, but the government held firm. At the time, Tommy Douglas predicted that its victory assured all Canadians of health insurance within a decade. He was right, for the Diefenbaker-appointed Hall royal commission recommended the Saskatchewan model, and after three years the federal Liberals, back in power, finally established full health insurance.

Meanwhile, the Ontario Tories stubbornly resisted throughout the 1960s, and were driven only by events, and a relentless NDP pressure, to the incremental implementation of full health coverage.

Today public health insurance has overwhelming public support, but its champions must remain vigilant. Steadily rising costs create a constant threat of cut-backs and service charges. They must be resisted. Moreover, there is need to free the delivery of health services from an excessive hospital-orientation and doctor-domination. The coordinated delivery of health and other social services through community centres is widely lauded, but painfully slow in its expansion.

Beyond that lies the need for an even more profound change. So far, we have established sickness, rather than health, insurance. A redirection to preventive health care is long overdue. It can reduce both the incidence of sickness and the cost of maintaining a healthy population.

16

Education

Because I had experience as a teacher, university student, newspaper reporter, CCF education secretary and parent, I was already very familiar with education issues when I became party leader in 1953. I was acutely aware that thousands of young people couldn't attend university or find technical training, because their parents couldn't afford it. F. Cyril James, the principal of McGill University, had said that young Canadians from families of modest means had less chance of getting university education than the youth of any other country with which he was familiar.

A provincial government that had led in so many other ways had already acted: the CCF government in Saskatchewan had set up a $1 million fund that had helped nearly two thousand students in four years. But Prime Minister Louis St. Laurent refused to respond to requests to set up federal government scholarships, and the Ontario Tories had done nothing.

Pressure was growing. In March 1957 I introduced a resolution calling for an Ontario student aid fund. A year later, the Tory government set up a revolving fund, the beginning of OSAP, the Ontario Student Aid Plan. It was the only resolution of mine adopted during my twenty-seven years in the Legislature (although the Tories, not surprisingly, amended it so that an opposition member would not get credit).

The main education focus in the 1950s was the failure of the school curriculum to meet modern needs. The 1950 Hope Royal Commission on Education found that for every one hundred children entering grade one:

only ninety-seven completed Grade six
only ninety completed Grade seven
only eighty-four completed Grade eight
only fifty-eight entered secondary school
only forty-six made it to Grade ten
only thirty-one were in Grade eleven
only twenty-one were in Grade twelve
only thirteen survived to Grade thirteen
only four went on to university

I argued that the time had come to stop deluding ourselves that the school system was meeting the needs of the rising generation. My position was supported by Dr. Sidney Smith, later president of the University of Toronto, who said in a study prepared for the Canadian Youth Commission:

> The secondary education of professors, lawyers, doctors, teachers and preachers is very much cheaper than that of stenographers, mechanics, electricians, farmers and carpenters; so we continue (except in the most advanced and wealthy regions) to educate the professional few and to botch the education of the great mass of workers.

The Department of Education left curriculum planning to local committees of teachers. "We must have a director of curriculum for the province," I argued. "Instead of shelving this responsibility to the local level, where the day-to-day preoccupation with teaching is such that it cannot be handled effectively, the leadership must come primarily from the departmental level." I suggested that the director of curriculum work with an advisory committee of experts on academic, technical, commercial and trades training.

Two feeble gestures had been made toward trades training: an apprenticeship training program, languishing in the Department of Labour instead of being a part of the education system, and the Provincial Institute of Trades, which was under the education department. The story of its origins illustrates the government's neglectful approach.

As far back as 1911, the Industrial Education Act authorized industrial courses in technical schools. Yet, fifty years later, not one such school had been started. So, to meet the need, private trade schools — mostly American-owned — flourished, by charging steep tuitions in advance, while only 3 to 7 per cent of students finished the course. It was such a racket that the government had to force them to register with the Department of Education. Only thirty-three of nearly two hundred schools in operation qualified for certificates.

The situation was serious. Of about nine thousand grade thirteen honour students in 1960, only thirteen came from technical courses, and none from commercial courses. The Toronto *Star* wrote that fundamental reform was long overdue in public education, describing the department as acting like "a reluctant patron." Expecting leadership from the department was like "looking for a cough drop in a coal mine," as one school board chairman colourfully put it.

"Our crying need," I urged the Tories in the Legislature in 1957, "is for *public* trade schools, not private ones, as part of our educational system, so as to be able to meet the aptitudes of that great percentage of our students who drop out of our schools, or get little or nothing if they stay in."[1] "A very fine speech," commented W.J. Dunlop, then the minister of education. But nothing followed. My words crumbled to the ground like snowballs thrown at a brick wall.

Two years after, however, John Robarts became minister of education, at a time when Canada was experiencing a serious depression. The core of the unemployed was unskilled workers. Moreover, the western world had been shocked by the Soviets' technical success in the launching of the Sputnik satellite. The Diefenbaker government provided capital grants to build technical and vocational schools.

Pressure inside and outside the Legislature, combined with those hundreds of millions of federal dollars, resulted in the Robarts Plan. It provided three steams in the public school system: the commercial and technical streams offered a four-year course leading to employment or community college; the academic would be a five-year course leading to university.

I pointed out that there should perhaps be a fourth stream — to educate parents, teachers and others who were prejudiced against technical and commercial education. On the whole, though, I welcomed the plan exuberantly, during debate of the department's spending estimates in April 1962. "This may well be as eventful a year in the history of Ontario education as any since those early days, when Egerton Ryerson laid the foundations of our system. For better or worse, we are launched into a radical recasting of Ontario education. . ."

As a footnote, an unintended but devastating summation of the department's approach was put by an official, after he forecast the vast building program for technical and commercial courses. "The Minister felt that we'd better have a plan to provide courses, which these new schools could offer," he said. Buildings first, then what to do with them afterwards.

The expansion of the secondary school system, necessary and generally welcome as it was, raised some public concern that the province was spending too much on education. I tried to put things in perspective in speaking to the Paisley Rotary Club on 17 June 1963:

> Some indication of our priorities can be seen from the fact that, for every man, woman and child in Canada, something over $60 a year is spent on education. At the same time, our per capita expenditure on liquor and tobacco is $90 and on the purchase and maintenance of cars, $120. . . . We cannot defend such priorities. . . . Russian sputniks in the sky, and the persistent hard core of unemployed, made up of people without skills to survive in the labour market, are sharp reminders that we have fallen behind in the development of our human resources.

The reason for the concern about the costs of education was no mystery: too much of the financial burden had been left at the municipal level, and as the costs of an expanded system mounted, the burden had become intolerable for property taxpayers.

The Conservatives had been elected in 1943 on a twenty-two point platform, one plank of which was that the province would pick up 50 per cent of education costs. By 1964 that promise had not been fulfilled. I argued that the province should pay more, but so should the federal government, which, after all, levied seventy-five cents of every tax dollar.

Although provincial grants for elementary grades, in both the public and the Roman Catholic separate school systems, had been equal since before Confederation, practically all industrial and commercial taxes went to the public schools. As a result, the revenue available per pupil in the separate schools was distinctly less than that in the public schools.

Mitch Hepburn's Liberal government in the 1930s tried to deal with the inequity by stipulating that industrial and commercial taxes be distributed according to the religion of the shareholders. But this plan was unworkable because shareholders change frequently, and it was dropped after a couple of years.

During the hearings of the Hope Commission (1946-50), appointed by the Drew government to review the educational structure, representations regarding the inequity were repeatedly made, but they did not receive a sympathetic response. In fact, the majority of the commission was so critical of the very existence of the separate schools that Roman Catholics were fearful the system might be cut back to grade six, as part of a proposed restructuring of the schools into elementary (grades one to six), intermediate (grades seven to nine) and secondary (grades ten to thirteen). This antipathy aroused such religious feelings that Premier Frost, once George Drew was out of the provincial picture, stated that "the Government in no way considers itself bound to the Report in whole or in part." In writing to a supporter, the new premier objected to stirring up of religious animosities; he felt the report had "no relation to reality."[2]

Throughout the 1950s, the issue simmered on the political back-burners, but it was during this period that the CCF, and then the NDP, played a leadership role in working toward an eventual solution in the so-called foundation program for school financing. Stripped of the religious antagonisms that bedevilled the issue, the basic question was whether children were entitled to equality of educational opportunity, wherever they lived, and whichever school system they attended. It wasn't simply a matter of separate school students suffering from lower per capita expenditures because of being denied corporation and commercial taxes; the same was true for rural and small town public school boards, which had limited, or no, corporate assessment base.

Franklin Walker, the leading historian on Catholic education in Ontario, has observed that, as early as 1954, CCF policy statements had supported "something very close to the [foundation] scheme."[3] With the emergence of the New Democratic Party in 1961, detailed proposals for a foundation plan for education financing were worked out. The basic elements were:

(1) Equalized assessment throughout the province, to establish a uniform basis of comparison among school boards.

(2) A formula to determine how much spending would ensure adequate standards, for all pupils in each school board.

(3) A basic mill rate, which all boards would be expected to levy. Since assessment would be equalized, the mill rate would mean equality of financial sacrifice for ratepayers across Ontario.

(4) Provincial grants, to bridge the gap, if the basic mill rate was not enough to ensure adequate standards.

(5) Mill rates higher than the basic rate, at a board's discretion, to provide higher standards than those guaranteed by the province.

These proposals would lay a foundation for adequate education without imposing an unequal sacrifice on ratepayers in less wealthy communities.

The Liberals found the issue difficult. Until late 1962 they advocated a 100 per cent provincial takeover of school costs, to relieve local taxpayers. But that would cost the province another $300 million and remove the last vestiges of local autonomy. Faced with mounting criticism within the party, the Liberals discarded that policy, and backed a foundation program. While I welcomed the support, I wondered publicly what the Liberal policy would be next month.

With both the NDP and Liberals in support of a foundation program, the only opposition the government now faced was within the Conservative party. On 1 February 1963, Premier Robarts announced its adoption. There was debate over differences in the specific details of each party's proposal, but there was agreement on the essentials. The foundation plan solved the problem: public schools in rural areas and small towns, and separate schools everywhere, would receive higher provincial grants, to bring their revenues up to the level deemed necessary for adequate and equitable education for each child.

The solution was accepted by all, with practically no protest, and over several years the grants to separate schools were phased upwards, to remove the discrepancy between the two systems. However, as separate school grants rose, militant Protestant supporters of the public system renewed their protest. I recall a delegation of Protestant clergymen in my office at Queen's Park in the late 1960s vigorously protesting what they saw as discrimination against the public system. They conceded that higher separate school grants were inevitable under the foundation program, but they were unappeased. The undercurrents of religious antagonism between the two school systems were to break out again years later.

In the mid-1960s post-secondary education took centre stage. There had been a phenomenal expansion during the previous decade. The established universities of Toronto, Queen's, McMaster, Western Ontario and Ottawa had been joined by York, Carleton, Windsor, Wilfrid Laurier, Waterloo, Trent,

Laurentian and Lakehead. But I warned that more post-secondary facilities were needed:

> The first wave of postwar babies will hit the university level in 1965. If even the same percentage of our grade thirteen graduates — and it should be higher — seek entrance to our universities, there simply will not be places for them. . . . The wave of wartime babies has been moving through our school system for more than ten years now. . . and yet the Robarts government is failing to take the necessary action.

My warning was based on a report by a committee of university presidents, who studied the situation and predicted that by 1965 there would be a shortage of six thousand spaces, and this would gradually increase to a shortage of up to thirty thousand places by 1970. They recommended establishing new liberal arts colleges — Scarborough and Erindale, affiliated with the University of Toronto, the newly chartered Brock University in the Niagara peninsula, and an arts faculty at the Ontario Agricultural College in Guelph.

One of Ontario's leading education researchers, R.W.B. Jackson, told the Canadian Education Association meeting in Quebec City in 1963 that admission requirements were so high that up to 40 per cent of those accepted in his time, including himself, would now be refused. He predicted that social pressure would force the universities to open their doors wider. This was an accurate foreshadowing of the government's promise that no child with the necessary ability would be excluded from post-secondary education. The costs, however, would be staggering, both for capital expansion and operating expenses, and the Tories had slowed down the expansion program.

The NDP called on the federal government to assume more of the capital costs, just as it had in developing technical and vocational schools. "The logic of the present situation is simple: if the Robarts government is not going to press the federal government to extend its . . . capital grants . . . then the public can rightly assume that the government feels it can meet the financial load from our provincial resources. If that is possible, then the initiative for more vigorous action rests solely with Queen's Park — and there should be public evidence of such action without delay.''

When the first students began to pour out of the three-year vocational stream in secondary schools in 1966, the government suddenly realized it had done virtually nothing to provide post-secondary education for the great majority of students who would not be going on to university.

"The result," I noted, "was an unseemly scramble to establish our system of colleges of applied arts and technology. . . . They emerged in such a relatively unplanned fashion that the full consequences are as yet inestimable, both in terms of cost and the unnecessary duplication of vocational facilities, which had just been built into our secondary school system." The Minister of Education, William Davis himself, had to accept responsibility for the lack of planning. "It cannot be blamed on his predecessors. It is a product of his day, and his direction — or lack thereof."

A debate began that went to the roots of educational philosophy. Probably worried about overcrowding in the universities, early in 1966, Davis had expressed his personal opinion that for five years community college credits should not be accepted by universities. That seemed to me to ensure that even the new education system would solidify the class structure of our society. I tried to put to rest the mythology that North American society has no class structure. The collegiate system in Quebec and Ontario traditionally had been designed to meet the needs of the professions, and the 94 per cent of students who did not go on to university got little or no useful education to suit their needs or aptitudes. Studies showed that children from families with income under $3,000 a year in the 1950s rarely got higher education, while those from families with $7,000 or more got every opportunity, even if they were below average in ability.

The new system might perpetuate the class structure, by

denying full education to all young people of ability, regardless of the economic or social status of their families. While 43 per cent of the Canadian labour force had grade eight education or less, from now on education would become the prerequisite to getting a job.

"Increasingly in the future," I emphasized, "the undereducated will be unemployed; the unemployed will be the poor; the poor will be the dropouts; the drop-outs will be undereducated and unemployed — and so the vicious circle goes round and round."

Children from so-called culturally disadvantaged homes were marked as drop-outs from their first day at school:

> If they survive to grade nine, the odds are overwhelming that they will be slotted for one of the streams, leading at best to the labour force after four years.
>
> And now developments indicate, as the Minister's "personal opinion" foreshadowed, that young people will be caught beyond escape at the post-secondary level: even if they overcome all the initial disadvantages and develop later, they will find themselves in a community college, technically oriented, with no parallel or transfer courses so they could readily transfer to university.
>
> While we have blithely believed otherwise, our education system has bolstered a class structure. To the extent that it does, we have fallen short of the goal of any genuinely democratic society — that educational opportunities will be open to all on the basis of ability and interest, not the economic or social background from which they have come.

This wide-ranging attack on the nature of Ontario education led me to demand that the boards of governors of universities become more than the enclave of the social elite or wealthy benefactors. They should include representatives of staff and students, as well as community groups such as labour.

In February 1967 I sponsored a resolution in the Legislature to replace the boards' traditional corporate structure with a community of scholars. Among other things, my resolution called for an inquiry into the functioning of existing boards of governors and urged their replacement by a broader group. I called on the boards to open their meetings to press and public, and on the government to pass legislation preventing governors from using their position for personal or corporate gain. These changes, I added, should come from within the university, "consistent with the autonomy and academic freedom which must be safeguarded in a democratic society."

Walter Pitman became the education critic after his election to the Legislature in 1967. He brought prestige and authority to the role, as he was the first MPP to be concurrently president of the Ontario Education Association, the umbrella body representing all groups in education.

When Colleges and Universities became a separate department, I found myself education critic again. In 1970 I noted two significant changes in the field of education. First was the critical public attitude toward education. "Education used to be a panacea. Today it is rapidly becoming another of the gods that have failed. . . . The result is a dangerous crisis of confidence, concerning one of the most important services which governments provide."

The second change concerned the minister, William Davis himself. "During the Sixties, the Minister became Mr. Education in Ontario. . . . Certainly he has presided over the destinies of education during a period when it has been transformed almost beyond recognition from the system which existed only a short decade and a half ago. . . But the far-reaching changes have been as much the product of irresistible pressures, too long ignored, as they have been of the Minister's planning and initiative. Too often fundamental changes have been belated, tragically unplanned and badly coordinated. . . . His role has been that of a technocrat trying to cope with mounting pressures, rather than a grand architect who was in control of the situation, anticipating needs soon enough that they could be rationally met." I documented this in the development of the three streams in secondary schools, the expansion of the universities and the belated scramble to set up the community colleges. But there was another telling example, and that was the way the government moved to county school boards, which I termed little short of calculated deception. During the election campaign in 1967, there was never a whisper on the hustings of the government's plan. Then, within a month after the election, Premier Robarts had dropped the bombshell, announcing plans to have county school boards in place less than a year later, by January 1969. Not only had the government withheld knowledge of its plans for county school boards from the public; it hadn't even informed a departmental committee that was planning for a gradual changeover. I described the situation as follows:

> The result was a political storm which rocked the Tory party establishment to its very foundations. In the process there has been created an atmosphere of public fear and hostility that has seriously jeopardized any move to larger administrative units in the broader municipal field through regional government. . . .
>
> Any lesser man would have been destroyed by the political consequences of his actions. The Minister has survived, but in surviving he has created a mood of quiet indignation that will be fully revealed at the next election.

It was strong language, but proved to be prophetic. The public mistrust of the imposition of larger units of administration in regional governments as well as school boards didn't fade, and was a major factor in reducing the Tories to a minority government in 1975.

The 1970 estimates committee provided an opportunity to assess the minister's role during the 1960s. "The Minister has always been the educational technocrat," I said. "More and more he is becoming the skillful educational politician, but less and less is he playing an effective role as Minister of Education. . . The approach is pragmatism run rampant." That approach was justifiable, I suggested, "as long as these tactics are part of an overall strategy that, in turn, is shaped by an educational philosophy.'' But the government had no philosophy. ''What it parades as a philosophy is little more than a rationalization of what it has already done, rather than any guide to what it should be doing.''

Events soon revealed the public concern with educational matters. Davis became the focal point of protest, and what should have been an easy win, at the leadership convention to replace Robarts, became instead a forty-four vote squeaker over Allan Lawrence. Education had given Bill Davis a chance at the top job, but the backlash over what he had done earlier nearly snatched the prize from him.

Most of the old political problems in education lingered through the 1970s. The province's share of education costs, which had risen to over 60 per cent in the 1960s, slipped to below 50 per cent. Grants per university student dropped to the lowest of any province, as the 1980s began.

It was extension of provincial funding beyond grade ten in the separate school system that opened the 1970s in heated controversy, simmered through the decade, and exploded with Davis's dramatic reversal of government policy in 1984, playing a role in ending the forty-two-year Tory dynasty.

My views were heavily conditioned by my schoolig and teaching in the separate (Protestant) system in Quebec. There, I had benefited from government policies that had scrupulously maintained equality in grants between the Catholic and Protestant schools. In contrast, Ontario had frozen separate school grants at the elementary level following Confederation, extended them to grades nine and ten in the 1890s, but ended them there throughout the twentieth century. Catholic children either had to switch to public schools after grade ten, or pay to attend privately funded Catholic high schools. The Hall-Dennis report on Ontario education, released in 1968, emphasized how disruptive this was, and stressed the need for a continuum in education from kindergarten to grade thirteen. Added to this, was the inequity of Catholic parents having to pay taxes to underwrite a complete high school system, but having to pay a second time if they exercised their constitutional right to send their children to separate high schools.

In the public mind, this was viewed as the separate school issue, but within the NDP, at both the party and caucus levels, the goal was the structuring and financing of an education system which would provide equality of educational opportunity. A caucus committee had been set up as early as 1965, and it had wrestled with the problem over a four-year period. Following the 1967 election, the committee was chaired by Walter Pitman, and included Pat Lawlor, Elie Martel, Jim Renwick and Jack Stokes. I attended some of its meetings, and kept in close contact with its work.

Paralleling the caucus committee work, there were intensive studies within the party. At the fourth biennial provincial convention on 15-17 November 1968, the provincial executive was instructed to appoint a committee to make a thorough study of the subject. The committee was chaired by C.D. McNiven, a professor at York University, and included George Cadbury, John Harney, Walter Pitman, Murray Kernighan, Jim Norton and Mel Swart. With this committee, too, I kept in close touch. The overlap in personnel between the caucus and party committee resulted in a coordinated effort.

On 13 May 1969 McNiven reported to the executive on behalf of his committee. The submission was entitled "Equality of Educational Opportunity," and opened with a restatement of the ultimate objective, namely, "an educational system which places emphasis upon the needs and interests of the individual child and which will make equality of educational opportunity available to every young person in Ontario." Despite sharp differences in approach between those favouring sectarian as opposed to confessional schooling, agreement was reached on the issue of extending the separate school system as necessary for achieving the ultimate objective of equal educational opportunity. However, the agreement was based on the supposition that the two systems would ultimate integrate, and the committee consensus collapsed over interpretation of what integration meant. The conflicting interpretations were set forth in the appendices to the committee report.

All these documents came to be known, within the party,

as the McNiven Report. It was widely circulated, and became the basis of an intensification of the ongoing debate. Faced with the unresolved differences which, ostensibly, were matters of interpretation but in fact dealt with fundamentals, the caucus committee renewed its efforts at research and study.

In a report which was presented to caucus in August 1969 it was noted that the work had been divided among James Renwick, who produced a paper on the constitutional and legislative background; Patrick Lawlor on philosophic and ideological considerations; me on the financial implications; Elie Martel on concepts of sharing; and Walter Pitman on educational imperatives.

Out of the caucus report emerged the concept of sharing between the two systems, whenever they were in a position of surplus or shortage of facilities. Sharing would avoid unnecessary new capital outlay when idle school capacity was available in the same community, and it became a major element in the party's new policy formulation. In fact, the concept of sharing resolved the differences which had emerged in the interpretation of "integration" in the McNiven Report.

In September I took the precaution of reviewing the situation with the provincial executive in order to assure myself that the caucus proposal for sharing between the two systems was acceptable to the party. Having received that assurance, public announcement of the caucus decision was made at a press conference on 16 October. In attendance were not only Walter Pitman and I from caucus, but the two top officers of the party, provincial president Gordon Vichert and provincial secretary John Harney. Because of their presence, it was widely (and not inaccurately) perceived that separate school extension had become NDP policy, although its formal adoption could not be made until the provincial council met in December. Not surprisingly, with the extensive collaboration of caucus and party officers and members, the new policy received strong majority support at council, and has been reaffirmed by each succeeding convention.

The concept of sharing became a basic component of the policy of separate school extension when it was finally accepted by Premier Davis in June 1984. But in the subsequent implementation of the policy, another distinction became the subject of controversy, that of sharing (where the two systems would have classes in the same building) or transfer of facilities (where idle facilities would be sold, or rented, to the system in need).

Thus, the NDP became the first party to advocate extension of funding to all years in the separate school system. In May 1968 Liberal leader Robert Nixon had said that "we cannot at this time afford to continue the development of the separate school system beyond grade ten," and Walter Pitman recalls that, following the NDP caucus announcement, there was great stir among Liberal MPPs. Faced with a threat to their traditional hold on the Catholic vote, they moved quickly to catch up. On 4 November 1969 the twenty-seven-member Liberal caucus issued a statement in favour of separate school extension.

The Tories delayed until Davis's vigorous statement of opposition on the eve of the 1971 election. The old fears throughout Ontario were such that the Tories benefited politically. The NDP vote held, but the more optimistic hopes for significant electoral progress were not fulfilled. The Liberal vote slipped below the 30 per cent mark for the first time in the postwar years.

The separate school issue appeared to lie dormant for the next thirteen years. The foundation program, begun by Robarts in 1964, had, by the late 1970s, practically eliminated the discrepancies between public and separate school grants and the Davis government had quietly begun to raise the grants to grades nine and ten in separate high schools as well; they had reached a level of 90 per cent of public high school grants. In view of this, Davis's sudden switch in 1984 was a logical evolution. He argued that extension of separate school funding followed from the foundation program twenty years earlier, and that, for him, the move was "a matter of conscience." Clearly, however, demographics played a role as well. The Catholic population, especially with immigration, had grown significantly, and would continue to increase. The future interests of the Tory party required some effort to counter the traditional anti-Catholic bias associated with it.

In any case, the policy reversal, made on 12 June 1984, was acclaimed by all parties, although the standing ovation from the Tory benches became harder to understand as time passed, and the strong opposition of many members became clear. The way the Tories handled the matter later was an unmitigated disaster. The switch had been made without consulting those who had to implement and live with the change. Undoubtedly, the decision was based on extensive surveying by Decima Research, the Tories' chosen pollster. Support for extended funding had been found to be as high as about 70 per cent of the population. Six months later, a Decima poll for the Ontario Secondary School Teachers Federation, which strongly opposed the extension, found support still at 61 per cent.

If the government had handled the issue expeditiously and introduced legislation quickly, it would easily have passed with the support of all three parties. But the Tories dithered. A full year after Davis's announcement, with the Miller government and the forty-two-year Tory hegemony about to fall, Larry Grossman, then education minister, admitted that they had gone through eleven — or was it twelve? — drafts of a bill, without finding one that was acceptable. When the Liberals took over with NDP support, they introduced a bill within two weeks.

While the Tories procrastinated, opposition grew on a host of points, which were never satisfactorily clarified. Moreover, during the 1985 election campaign, Anglican Archbishop Lewis Garnsworthy gave focus to that opposition with the highly inflammatory charge that Davis's new policy had been introduced by decree, in precisely the way that Hitler operated in Nazi Germany. That aroused old Catholic-Protestant antagonism, and guaranteed the stormiest possible future for the issue.

In my view, the separate school issue played a major role in the wholesale desertion of Tory supporters in that election, and the subsequent removal of the party from office. It was perhaps not so much the issue itself, but the revelation that the Tories had lost their capacity to manage affairs capably. They had long been viewed as the most able to govern; the way the funding extension was handled put the end to that.

Bill 30, An Act to Amend the Education Act, was finally passed in July 1986, but the scars remain, and the debate continues.

The matter was challenged in the Ontario Supreme Court, and in late February 1986 the Court of Appeal ruled that, first, full funding of separate schools is constitutional, and, second, that grants for grade eleven, the first year to be phased in, could be provided by cabinet decree without further legislation. The latter was a direct refutation of Archbishop Garnsworthy's outburst about Hitlerian decrees.

The court's reasoning on the constitutionality question was that separate schools were rooted in the province's history, and had been a right, reaffirmed by the Confederation agreement in 1867, for over one hundred and forty years. To abrogate that right, in favour of only one publicly funded system, would have been a sacrifice of history to ideology. However, the court split three to two, with the minority dissent asserting that the right to separate school funding was restricted to elementary education at the time of Confederation. I found this, particularly when it was shared by Chief Justice Howland, to be a gross misreading of history. To argue that any funding of secondary grades in separate schools, including grades nine and ten since 1896, had been unconstitutional, was bad history and worse politics. But the divided court kept the issue alive and ensured further appeals.

In June 1987 the Supreme Court of Canada responded to those appeals and, in a unanimous judgment, confirmed the views that I had advanced from the outset on the issue of separate school extension. "The basic compact of Confederation with respect to education," the judgment declared, "was that rights and privileges acquired by law at the time of Confederation would be preserved and provincial legislatures could bestow additional rights and privileges in response to changing conditions. . . Roman Catholic separate school supporters had at Confederation a right, or privilege, by law, to have their children receive an appropriate education which would include instruction at the secondary level. . . . An adequate level of funding was required for this right to be meaningful."

The Supreme Court therefore asserted that Bill 30, financing separate school extension, "was a valid exercise of provincial power to return rights constitutionally guaranteed to separate schools by s. 93(1) of the Constitutional Act, 1867." The Supreme Court went further, and dismissed a new threat which had been raised by opponents of Bill 30. It declared that none of these constitutional rights and privileges can be "prejudicially affected" by the Charter of Rights and Freedoms.

This would appear to have resolved the basics of this thorny issue, dare one hope, for ever. But feelings run so deep that there will likely be reverberations for years to come. Certainly, the reaction of many, including politicians, clergymen and teachers, in the final crescendo of public controversy, has not represented the finest hour in Ontario politics.

You'd need to be an optimist for an NDPer to espouse the cause of agriculture for over thirty years. This was a CBC artist's depiction of my optimism at an inter-party debate on the Loeb Report.

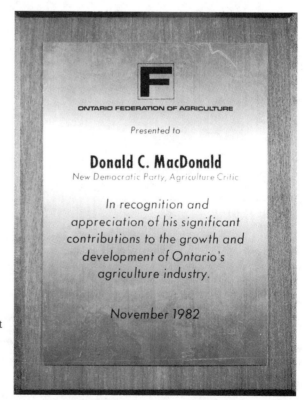

ONTARIO FEDERATION OF AGRICULTURE

Presented to

Donald C. MacDonald
New Democratic Party, Agriculture Critic

In recognition and appreciation of his significant contributions to the growth and development of Ontario's agriculture industry.

November 1982

If there wasn't a great harvest of Farmers' votes, at least there was appreciation of my efforts by the Federation of Agriculture — which I shall always treasure.

17
Agriculture

"The asphalt farmer from York South." Those who regularly, and with gusto, hurled this epithet across the House, didn't realize that I had grown up on a farm, that the traditional problems of agriculture were my introduction to economics, and that the lasting value of hard work close to the soil was part of my being. Even if we'd had a rural-based member of caucus, I would joyously have taken on the agriculture portfolio.

Down through the years, I'm sure I've visited as many farms, and made it to as many farm meetings, as any of the successive agriculture ministers. Gradually, farm leaders accepted me as one of the family. Hanging on the wall in my office is one of my most prized mementoes, a plaque from the Ontario Federation of Agriculture, "In appreciation of significant contributions to the growth and development of agriculture." Not a mention of asphalt.

My support for the cause of agriculture sprang directly from my political philosophy. The right of association may have been recognized since Magna Carta, but workers who tried to exercise the right over the next six hundred and fifty years were guilty of conspiracy. Although unions were legalized in the 1870s, farmers weren't given legislative authority to band together to market their own produce until 1937 — and they had to fight for many more years to make that theoretical right meaningful in the real world.

I'd been told that a party sympathetic to organized labour could make no inroads with farmers, that the two interests are unalterably opposed. While it is true that democratic socialist parties in Europe have traditionally grown out of alliances with organized labour, the CCF was more broadly based, and also had roots in farm movements. Saskatchewan's political history is the most obvious example, but it should be remembered that a coalition of the United Farmers of Ontario and the Independent Labour Party actually formed a government in Ontario in 1919.

Despite that, by the 1950s, it was still considered an impertinent challenge to the conventional wisdom to campaign with the conviction that workers and farmers had common interests. Luckily, I was no stranger to either impertinence or challenge. My beliefs have strengthened as the years have moved on, as farmers face the same problems as their parents and grandparents, and as the years of neglect by business-oriented governments reap a fearful harvest.

In the early 1940s, with food needed for wartime survival, orderly marketing and pricing meant a fair deal for farmers. But after the war free enterprise gradually took over again, and by the mid 1950s, farmers were back in a depression. While the economy in general prospered, middlemen reaped profits. During 1951-54, for example, Canadians spent $417 million more on home-grown food, but the farmers who produced it got $87 million less. None of this depressed Premier Frost, who in his 1954 budget speech dismissed the drop in farm income as "a mere ripple on the broad stream of Ontario's economic prosperity."

The unstated, though indisputable, objective of federal agricultural policy was to cut farm production to where it would not greatly exceed domestic need, thus removing embarrassing political and economic problems of surpluses (despite a world where two-thirds of the people go to bed hungry every night). "The chief result of the Diefenbaker farm legislation," I said, "will be to perpetuate the depressed income into which agriculture has fallen."

I travelled the concession roads in the 1950s, arguing wherever I could get an audience, that our economy was dominated by industry, commerce and finance — basically unsympathetic to farmers. The farmer was pinched between monopoly traders and processors, who pushed down prices paid farmers, and the great manufacturing corporations that maintained high prices for farm implements, building materials and fertilizers. And in a free enterprise economy, those who have no control over the prices of what they sell or what they buy get fleeced both ways.

The mechanization of farming was a revolution that changed for ever the way farmers plowed, sowed, reaped and shipped their crops, and housed, fed, milked and marketed their livestock. It also meant — and this was to have monstrous repercussions — that farmers needed credit, as they had never had before.

As I drove the back concessions I was struck by something else. Homes and living conditions hadn't improved, despite the vast changes in farm operations. The 1951 census showed that, while 18 per cent of all Ontario had no inside piped water, the figure rose to 54 per cent for rural homes, and 59 per cent for farm homes. While 22 per cent of Ontario homes lacked inside toilets, 62 per cent of rural homes, and 70 per cent of farms had no such convenience.

Things didn't improve much in the next decade. In 1961, I met a young minister in a village near the St. Lawrence Seaway — that spectacular application of modern engineering — whose home was the only one in his parish with indoor plumbing; not a single farm parishioner bordering that immense triumph of technology had an indoor toilet.

The root of the problem was inadequate farm income. After the war the federal government talked of continuing the minimum pricing policy to underpin farm incomes, but the pressure to maintain a "free market" won out. As the farmers shrank in numbers, and as their income shrank in dollars, they obviously needed political allies, so that, in the short run, they could pressure governments for a better deal and, in the long run, could help elect a government more sympathetic to their concerns. A government, I suggested, to greatly differing reactions, like the one I wanted to lead.

While I took the message along the back roads, some farmers began to fight, at least, for more control over marketing what they produced. The hog producers were in the forefront, and I became deeply involved in their battle.

Under the hog marketing plan, set up in 1945, farmers could negotiate a minimum price with the packers, and unresolved disputes went to arbitration. This worked for six years, but never sat well with the few big packers who dominated the industry, and whose philosophy was summed up by J.S. McLean, head of Canada Packers: "We pay the farmers as little as we can. We charge the consumer as much as the market will bear. That's business." In 1951 packers boycotted the arbitration board, and the Tory government accepted this defiance of its own law. More, it actively supported the big packers.

Faced with marketing their own products, the hog farmers set up a series of regional yards, where hogs were delivered for sale to the highest bidder, thus undercutting the control the big packers had exercised through direct delivery from farms to their plants, and giving small packers access to a competitive hog market beyond the control of the big packers.

The Tories said farmers had the right to work out their own marketing plan. Hog producers took them at their word and asked that no vote be taken on what sort of plan that should be until they'd had a year's experience with the new system of regional yards. Suddenly the government, pressured by its rural caucus members, who in turn had caved in to the big packers' lobbying, announced that a vote would be held in March (later delayed to July), when only fourteen of the producing counties had been able to set up assembly yards.

The marketing legislation said that a majority of eligible voters, rather than of those voting, would be required to keep the new legislation in effect. This was plainly undemocratic, I argued, because packers could defeat the scheme simply by pressuring enough farmers to stay home. I introduced a private member's bill in the Legislature to change the requirements to a majority of those voting.

The agriculture minister, William Goodfellow, stepped up his efforts. He no longer said farmers had the right to set up their own plan, but that changes had to be made to the so-called Dutch Clock system, that would have let big packers know when small packers were buying a shipment of hogs, and at what price. This was the kind of knowledge that had allowed the big companies to make a mockery in the past of the so-called free market by fixing prices behind the scenes, and I strongly condemned the suggestion. "Government policy now," I stated, "is that the producer must accept the kind of marketing plan which the processor demands. . . . It now becomes clear that the packers' lobby at Queen's Park is more influential than the whole of organized agriculture."

The result was a stand-off between the hog producers and the government. In May 1958 the government called representatives of the Hog Producers' Cooperative and the Marketing Board to Queen's Park for private meetings that went on for three days, with Mr. Goodfellow in continuous attendance, and Premier Frost popping in frequently to add his weight. In effect, the government backed the big packers in demanding the Dutch Clock system.

However, the hog farmers stood firm, and the government retaliated by calling a vote for 25 July, forcing the farmers into a campaign at a time of year when they worked twelve to fifteen hours a day. Despite the obstacles, the hog producers reaffirmed their support for the new marketing plan by a 68 per cent majority of those who voted. They even exceeded the undemocratic provisions of the legislation by getting more than 50 per cent of those eligible to vote.

The problems were not restricted to the hog producers. Other farm groups sought to exercise the bargaining power granted to them by legislation, only to find both the government and processors running interference. In 1958 the tobacco board was faced with a virtual boycott of its plan by the dominant companies, despite a two-to-one endorsement by the growers. The fruit farmers of the Niagara peninsula were faced with Del Monte, the giant American canning company, buying local plants and shutting them down, so that most of the crop rotted on the tree. Whenever marketing legislation was challenged by powerful corporations, the Frost government proved to be a fair weather friend of the farmer. It stonewalled and played off one farm organization against another, in the old divide-and-rule strategy.

The situation was complicated by the uncertain position of the Liberal party. John Wintermeyer told a legislative committee that marketing plans might conflict seriously with "normal business practices." That, of course, is exactly what an effective plan was designed to do, I argued, because so-called normal business practices gave the farmer no control at all.

When campaigning for the Liberal leadership, Wintermeyer expressed concern about the "compulsory" aspects of farm marketing — equivalent, I pointed out, to making income tax voluntary. Farm marketing could only work if all farmers went along with the will of the majority; otherwise a minority could frustrate the plan that most farmers had voted for. Pressure from the farm community eventually forced the new Liberal leader to retreat to the position that his party wanted whatever the farmers wanted — a safe, but rather meaningless posture in the face of the ongoing struggle between producers and processors.

While the Liberals ran for cover, the Tories had just begun to fight. They had no trouble choosing between the wishes of farmers and the demands of processing companies, whose philosophy they shared, and whose financial support they enjoyed at election time. They brought in Bill 86, giving the government-appointed Ontario Farm Products Marketing Board the power to dictate how commodity marketing boards could spend their money. In effect, the government could force a marketing board to reduce what it spent on education and information work, could prevent it from giving grants to any other organization, and could even put it under trusteeship at any time.

"They have powers," I said of the Tories, referring to a labour leader prominent in those days, "that would make Jimmy Hoffa look like a piker."

Despite our best efforts, the Tory majority rammed through

Bill 86 in the spring of 1960. Then, at a press conference in October, the minister disbanded committees that were studying alternative methods of hog marketing, saying the directors of the hog marketing board, who were elected by the farmers, had "repeatedly broken faith with the government," and might be replaced by a board appointed by the government.

To their everlasting credit, the hog producers stood firm, displaying a solidarity and determination unprecedented in Ontario farm history. Charlie MacInnis, their indefatigable leader, called an emergency meeting, and three hundred and fifty farmers crowded into the Seaway Hotel in Toronto on 3 January 1961. Agriculture Minister Goodfellow and an assistant deputy minister responsible for marketing, Everett Biggs, were there to hear the farmers vigorously and unanimously support the present sales method and denounce the government's efforts, as one delegate put it, to "open the door once again to discrimination, not only by the packers against the producers, but by the big packers against the small and medium-sized processors."

I introduced Private Member's Bill 97 to rescind these restrictions on producer-controlled marketing. It was enthusiastically supported at the hog farmers' annual convention in March 1961. These were exciting days for me, after the many months of slugging it out with Frost, Goodfellow and the Tories. "I'm no CCFer, but there's only one man working for Ontario farmers in the Ontario Legislature, and that's Donald MacDonald," Harry Baker, a former president of the Dufferin Hog Producers Association, told the delegates. Irwin McCoy, a Hastings hog farmer, put it this way: "Normally, I vote P.C., but the time has come for a change. The government's been in too long." The *Rural Cooperator*, leading farm paper of the day, on 28 March 1961 gave full coverage under the caption, "Hogmen Back Bill 97."

Such open support was heartwarming, particularly since the hog farmers' organization was a member of the Ontario Federation of Agriculture, which until then had such close ties with the Tory government that it even refrained from meeting with opposition parties to discuss its annual brief to the cabinet. The hog farmers' struggle changed that; the OFA realized that opposition parties had a vital role to play, particularly when the governing party was so clearly against the producers and for the big processing companies.

Early in 1961 the struggle took a new twist. Speaking in Woodstock on 4 February, Everett Biggs said that "the misunderstanding between hog producers and the Ontario government springs, not from the hog sales methods, but from the hog producers' attitude towards the responsibility of the marketing plan." Hitherto government spokesmen, including the minister, had contended that the sales method was the source of the trouble, but now the assistant deputy minister had switched the emphasis to the "producers' attitude."

"I think we are getting closer to the real trouble," I observed. "The government has never been able to make a case against the hog producers for acting illegally. Rather, the government just doesn't like the producers' attitude. . . . In short, behind a facade of disagreement with the hog producers over the sales method, the government is, in fact, engaged in a political vendetta against the leaders."[1]

The government remained unrepentant, in spite of massive farm opposition to the arbitrary and restrictive powers. The minister of agriculture professed to be a good friend of the hog producers, but in the next breath he continued his vendetta against them. Speaking at the Legislature on 27 March he stated, "Bill 86 would never have been necessary if it had not been for the hog producers running rampant across the province."

However, when the government introduced a new Milk Industry Act, the minister smuggled the restrictive power into it. "He is determined," I pointed out, "that the big stick which the government had shaped in Bill 86 must be maintained, even in the milk industry, where the producers haven't been 'running rampant'."[2]

There was a final chapter in the saga of the hog producers. Faced with the government-backed campaign of the big packers, the farmers realized that they would have to move into the processing end of the industry themselves, to prevent the corporations from re-establishing monopoly control. They set up a cooperative, the Farmers' Allied Meat Enterprise (FAME), and started raising money for the head office in Toronto and a network of packing plants across the province. The government was hostile. Premier Frost was scornful — the hog producers, he said, shouldn't be getting into something that was none of their business. But the enterprise was warmly supported by prominent farm leaders. During the next five years, some thirteen thousand farmers raised $1.3 million in share capital and $896,400 in debentures. (I still have two $100 shares in my files at home. They are now worthless in dollars, but invaluable to me as symbols of a dream that was denied.)

The forces of free enterprise won out in the end. The farmers tried to raise $1.5 million, as a first mortgage on a packing plant in Burlington, early in 1955. Since the cooperative's value had been appraised at $4.5 million, the farmers couldn't understand why financial interests refused the investment. I was convinced the government and the packers used their influence in the business world to deny the cooperative's appeal. I called on the government to underwrite FAME's credit — just as the Tory government of Nova Scotia was doing in very similar circumstances, and just as the Ontario government itself was doing for other kinds of enterprise that were denied credit.

In January 1965 the *Rural Cooperator* again gave my statement full coverage, in a review of the whole FAME situation, with the headline, "Eleventh Hour Effort to Save Co-op Plant." But it was to no avail. The packers, backed by the government, were determined to keep the hog producers out of the processing business. After all, as Premier Frost had said, the processing of their own produce was none of their business!

The government attack on producer-controlled marketing was not restricted to hogs. Today, agriculture ministers support marketing boards' right to exercise supply management powers, but at that time they fought for the so-called free market. So the restrictive powers of the government's infamous Bill 86 were brought to bear. When the tobacco board decided to cut production, and seven freelance growers defied the board's ruling, without discussion the government took away the board's negotiating and arbitrating powers, at the request of the Ontario Farm Products Marketing Board (OFPMB).

"It is the right of farmers through their own local board members, to run their own affairs, and not to be subjected to day-to-day intervention of the government," I argued at the time. "Farm marketing is a classic example of the growing tendency of government to meddle unduly in local affairs, when those affairs might better be run by the farmers themselves."

The government's ultimate power, under Bill 86, was to dismiss a local marketing board, and in 1966, Agriculture Minister William Stewart used this against the bean growers' board, after accusing it of not obtaining as high a price as possible for the produce. He refused the board's request for an increase in the marketing levy to finance new processing facilities. The farmers voted on the matter, but were up against an active campaign by the bean dealers, as well as the government's opposition. The increased levy was defeated on a split vote, but the bean board announced an expansion of its facilities in London.

The stage was set for the final confrontation. The government wouldn't tolerate such defiance. Two days after an OFA meeting, when the top farm leadership was out of the country at an international conference, the government moved. Its excuse was that the bean growers had violated an agreement to separate the bean company from the marketing board. Its tactics were reminiscent of a Latin American coup. The bean board directors were called to a meeting in a London hotel, where they were told that they had been dismissed. While the bean board directors were lured from their offices, representatives of the OFPMB moved in and seized their books. The government had prevailed — temporarily. But in a subsequent election, the growers defiantly re-elected all the directors of the bean board.

Among the many consequences of this draconian action, the position of the OFPMB had been compromised beyond repair. Never again could it be regarded as an independent, quasi-judicial body. It had been clearly revealed as nothing more than a political arm of the government, obediently responding to the dictates of the minister of agriculture.

By this time, all the marketing boards, with the backing of the Federation of Agriculture, were ranged in opposition to the government's determination to destroy producer-controlled marketing. But, understandably, the actions of the powerful Tory government had created a crisis in marketing, throughout the farm community. I had warned as far back as 1963 that if these conditions continued, marketing plans in Ontario would be doomed. Now, three years later, a corn plan has been turned down; the onion plan had been voted out because it had failed by a fraction of 1 per cent to achieve the necessary two-thirds majority; and efforts to establish an egg board had foundered.

"We are fast approaching the day," I declared, "when farmers will not establish any new plans, and will ditch the ones they have because the feeling is growing that if governments want to run marketing plans from behind the scenes, by day-to-day intervention when it serves their political purposes, then they might as well take over the whole job of marketing themselves. Either we have producer-controlled marketing plans, operated within the powers delegated by the Farm Products Marketing Act — powers that can be altered if they are abused — or we might as well have out-and-out state marketing."[3]

Developments were heading for a climactic showdown. For farmers, the situation was going from bad to worse. From the peak year of 1951 the trend in net incomes had been steadily down, as the costs of production outstripped commodity price increases. Agriculture had achieved phenomenal increases in efficiency, but for farmers that was a mixed blessing: if they increased their production to bolster their income, surpluses resulted, and their per unit returns dropped

below the cost of production. The government's repudiation
of its earlier commitment to producer-controlled marketing
had weakened, if not denied, farmers the capacity for self-help.

For me, there had been ten years experience as agricultural
critic. During that time I had attended not only the annual
conventions of the farm organizations and the major commodity groups, but countless rural meetings convened by farm
groups, as well as by the party. In organizing the farm committees for the New Democratic Party, I had visited farm
leaders on their home turf, all across the province, and had
been rewarded by nearly fifty of them becoming members of
the committee, which shaped the agricultural policies of the
new party.

As for the government, it was in trouble, but so far the trouble had proven manageable. It played a skillful divide-and-
rule game, playing off one farm organization against the other.
Each commodity group had its problems, but there was little
united effort. The rural community remained conservative in
outlook and Conservative in politics. Farm problems had no
impact on the general population; they were always overshadowed by broader provincial issues in a general election.
The Robarts government had been swept back into office, with
another big majority in 1963.

But the pressures were building. There were limits to how
long the farmers could survive the bankruptcy of government
policies, and in 1966 those limits were reached. Massive protest erupted. Not surprisingly, unified action was inspired by
the persistent problem of inadequate income.

Dairy farmers believed they had been promised $4 per hun-
dred pounds for industrial milk, including a seventy-five-cent
federal subsidy. Overnight, more than half of the subsidy
disappeared as the dairies cut ten cents from the price they
paid the farmers, eliminated the fifteen-cent premium they
paid for bulk shipments, and increased transportation costs
by fifteen cents. Led by the militant Ontario Farmers' Union,
the dairy farmers' protest in southwestern Ontario drew support from OFA affiliates such as the vegetable producers who
were getting two cents for lettuce, which sold for twenty-six

cents a head.

Agriculture Minister Stewart inflamed matters by conceding in the House that the $4 demand was valid, then arguing that it was Ottawa's responsibility, and that, if the farmers got $4, the OFU would next be asking for $5. This insensitivity led the farmers to take to the highways in tractor demonstrations, first near where they lived, then en masse to Queen's Park. The scene was unforgettable, as the mechanical monsters lumbered slowly up University Avenue, like tanks on the Western Front, and lined up in front of the legislative building in an awesome array. At first, the minister refused to come out to speak to the twelve hundred farmers. The farmers stormed into the building to get him. Stewart finally responded to the pleas of the rural Tory MPPs, after being assured that he would be listened to courteously — and after having three burly plainclothes policemen lined up to protect him.

Despite the protest, Stewart and the federal minister, J.J. Greene, continued to pass the buck back and forth. Stewart provoked laughter on every concession road with his claim that "I'm just a simple country boy. I don't know how to play politics." Clearly something had to be done to repair the government's image. The Tories called a conference for six months down the road, and used that to try to deflect the questions.

Preparing for debate on the spending estimates of the agriculture ministry, I travelled seven hundred miles one weekend — from Huron County to Middlesex, Perth, Oxford, Simcoe, Brant, Norfolk and Hamilton-Wentworth. As an example of what I heard, I told Stewart of a farmer from Holland who marketed wheat soon after he arrived in Canada at $2.25 a bushel, while his wife paid ten cents for a loaf of bread. Now, he was getting $1.50 a bushel for wheat, and his wife was paying twenty cents a loaf. This was the farmer's plight in a nutshell. Stewart remained unmoved.

However, at the October meeting, in Vineland, both general farm organizations backed an Incentive Income Program, the idea being that farmers would be guaranteed a fair income and, if necessary, the government would use subsidies to keep the price of staples, such as bread and milk, within the reach of the average family.

Faced with this united front, the minister appointed a Special Incomes Committee, to be chaired by Deputy Minister Everett Biggs. The prospects weren't promising, as Biggs said publicly that consumer subsidies would be "an administrative nightmare," indicating clearly that the committee was not sympathetic to the proposal. In August 1967 agricultural economists working for the committee confirmed, in an interim report, a shocking situation: that only 20 per cent of farmers were receiving adequate income, 40 per cent might be helped enough by subsidies, and the other 40 per cent might have farms that could not survive.

While the committee laboured on, a provincial election took place in October 1967. I reaffirmed our party's support for working out an income policy, but warned that the Tories had no intention of doing so, and could not be taken at their word. A large number of voters agreed. The NDP, which had seven MPPs before the election, returned twenty and increased its popular vote from 16 to 26 per cent. Our support was significantly increased in rural Ontario.

The minister's Farm Income Committee reported in January 1969. Its message was clear:

> Since World War II, confused by wartime policies and misled by the immediate postwar prosperity of agriculture, the farmer has placed his reliance on a series of temporary expedients, as a substitute for long-term planning and comprehensive programmes. The result is an income crisis of major proportions. . . . Unless immediate steps are taken to tackle this crucial issue, the entire agricultural industry faces a violent upheaval that will bring little or no benefit to society, but would disrupt and destroy the social and economic structure of Ontario. The warning signals have been flying for some time.

The tone of the report suggested action, but the result was, once more, disappointing. Farmers had been betrayed again by Tory and Liberal governments. During the postwar years, they had gone through a weary succession of solutions to the income problem, but all required economic planning, and none was accepted or implemented with conviction by federal or provincial governments. As I saw it — and still do — farmers had to seek salvation from a party that was not business-oriented, particularly since they now made up no more than 5 per cent of the population, and a government need not fear their votes so much.

The Farm Income Committee report had pointed out that an excessive number of dealerships was the method used by manufacturers of farm machinery to keep prices high, and suggested that the government should intervene to set up a central wholesale agency, distributing all farm machinery to dealers. They could then handle any make of machine. The NDP advocated such a move, but it acknowledged that free enterprise was a facade to hide monopoly operations, so federal and provincial governments would not move.

Another major contributor to farm costs was the long-standing inequity in farm assessment and taxation. This escalated, with the sharp rise in property values in the early 1970s. It stemmed from the fact that the farm is both the farmer's home and the tool of his trade. While he paid increasing property taxes on his house, as did other homeowners, the farmer faced the same rate on all the land for crops and grazing.

The NDP at its first full policy convention in 1962, called for farmers to be relieved of property taxes except on their homes and other buildings. When nothing had been done by 1971, leaders of both major farm organizations supported a campaign to withhold education taxes (which make up at least half of local property taxes) until taxes were reformed.

The government announced a 25 per cent rebate on farm taxes — a measure of relief, but clearly not tax reform, and obviously politically motivated in a provincial election year. *The Grower*, the publication of the Fruit and Vegetable Growers Association, called this "payola . . . an attempt to stifle the critics by gagging the mouth of a farmer with a few dollars.'' I argued that, if the government was acknowledging that taxes were too high, let them replace farm taxes with larger grants to municipalities, rather than going to all the bureaucratic expense of collecting excessive taxes, then repaying them, in the form of a pre-election refund.

The government, now headed by William Davis, handled the problem over the next decade by gradually increasing the 25 per cent rebate to 50 per cent, then finally removing education taxes from farm lands altogether, and compensating municipalities for lost revenue with larger grants. As Premier Frost used to say, "In the fullness of time. . ."

Over the years, the crisis of confidence in marketing boards, created by the controversy of the early days, gradually faded, and now Ontario has twenty-five boards, more than any other province, although most of them are merely product promotion agencies; only a half dozen exercise pricing and supply management powers. As an example of the kind of model producer-controlled marketing operation that emerged from all the efforts, we have the Ontario Milk Marketing Board. It has democratic participation: county milk committees meet every fall at Geneva Park on Lake Couchiching for consultation on expected problems, and I was a guest for years at those meetings. It has a complicated formula for milk pricing that reflects the farmers costs of production, but that also takes into account consumer spending.

The problem with milk marketing, however, is that there is no control over the price at the retail level. The dairies make a practice of piggy-backing an increase for themselves onto every approved increase to the farmer, so three cents a litre more to the producer, for example, usually means six or seven cents more a litre when milk is bought at the corner store. The NDP has supported the milk board's fight for government review of milk prices beyond the farm gate, but so far to no avail.

While most of the problems in agriculture were long-standing, a new issue emerged in the 1970s, and played a crucial role in the 1975 election campaign. This was the loss of highly productive farm land in rapidly developing southern Ontario, to make room for housing subdivisions, shopping malls, industrial parks and highways.

From 1966 to 1971, statistics showed that foodlands had disappeared at the rate of twenty-six acres an hour — a startling figure that Stephen Lewis used dramatically, and to good effect, when the election came in 1975. I had pounded away at the issue across Ontario in the early 1970s. It provoked an immediate response from urban audiences. Even as far away as Kenora, in northwestern Ontario, people reacted with anger to the fact that half of the precious fruitlands of the Niagara peninsula had already been lost to production.

During the election, the new agriculture minister, William Newman, tried to blunt the effectiveness of Stephen's campaign by saying that there were millions of acres of agricultural land awaiting development in northern Ontario — a laughable argument that ignored prohibitive weather conditions and the billions of dollars needed to develop such acres to where they could replace the best land in the south. The Ontario Institute of Agrologists called on the government to designate and protect the best foodlands from development, granting exceptions only for high priority projects, and only when poorer farm land was not available.

Reduced, on election day, to the first minority government since 1943, with the NDP as official opposition, the Tories were still unwilling to intervene so massively in the marketplace. They found allies within the farm community, who argued that it was their inalienable right — whatever the consequences for the industry in the future — to sell their land to developers for the best price they could get.

The Tories finally proclaimed guidelines to protect prime land, which had no force in law and were often breached when political pressure was applied, either at the local level or at Queen's Park. For me, the issue took on new life with evidence of what could be done by a government willing to tackle the problem. The NDP government in British Columbia had legislated to protect agricultural land and to stabilize farm incomes. Unfortunately, they did so in that order, and for a time real estate agents and developers joined forces with those farmers who violently objected to being denied the right to sell their land for a million or so. But once the government introduced legislation assuring farmers of a stabilized income, the protest dwindled. Indeed, the B.C. Federation of Agriculture became a strong supporter of the NDP legislation to halt the erosion of precious foodlands, and their spokesmen accepted an invitation from the Ontario Federation of Agriculture to tour Ontario, to counter the government's contention that the NDP policies in British Columbia were having disastrous consequences.

I was personally caught in this interprovincial warfare. On 5 June 1975 I had celebrated my twentieth anniversary as an MPP. There had been warm words from all sides of the House, and in the evening my riding association had sponsored a testimonial, where a few hundred friends and colleagues had heard Stephen Lewis, the featured speaker, declare that, if I had been on the *Titanic*, it never would have sunk — an example of his colourful hyperbole. Ironically, the next day I was expelled from the Legislature — the first and only time in my experience!

The circumstances were part of the ongoing battle over farm income stabilization. The minister of agriculture, William Stewart, in his last session before retirement, had repeatedly stated that farm stabilization in British Columbia was bankrupting the province. I had a letter from David Stupich, the B.C. agriculture minister, indicating that the drain on the public treasury for farm income security was only $20 million. I produced this letter in the Legislature, and in what I felt were carefully chosen words, to avoid breach of House rules, stated that, if the minister continued to repeat that the B.C. government was being bankrupted, it "would be tantamount to a lie."

The use of the word lie, under any circumstances, no matter how qualified, is a definite "no-no" in the clubbish atmosphere of the Ontario Legislature. The Speaker demanded that I withdraw. Under the circumstances, with the B.C. agriculture minister's letter as documentation, I felt that withdrawal was impossible. So I was expelled for the day.

When the media tackled Stewart in the "scrum" following

question period, he backed off, saying that his information was merely rumour (emanating, no doubt, from the opposition in British Columbia). He made no attempt to dispute the evidence that farm security in British Columbia represented a drain on general revenues of no more than the manageable sum of $20 million.

The whole episode however, was merely a skirmish in a battle which the government could no longer avoid. In 1976 a farm income stabilization bill was introduced. It fell so far short of what the OFA had been demanding that both the Liberals and the NDP opposition, in a minority government situation, defeated the bill. Since it was a major piece of the government legislation, defeat was tantamount to loss of confidence of the Legislature, traditionally requiring prorogation and an election. However, the government introduced a confidence motion the next sitting day. The Liberals supported it, and the government regained its right to continue in office.

Later that year, the government introduced a revised farm income stabilization bill which, in some respects, was even worse. The OFA presented briefs to all MPPs, proposing a number of amendments, which I introduced, but they were defeated by the combined Liberal and Conservative vote. The old parties' concern was that, if farm prices were stabilized at a level assuring coverage of the costs of production, and a fair return for farm labour and investment, the inevitable result would be over production and the need for marketing boards to exercise the highly controversial supply management powers, which were deemed to be a questionable restriction on free market operations.

"Thank God the farmers are still free enterprisers," proclaimed the Liberal agriculture critic, Jack Riddell.[4] (Ironically, within five years, supply management was under such attack that the minister of agriculture was convening meetings to bolster support for it.)

"There's a fundamental difference between the New Democratic approach to farm income security, and that of the Liberals in Ottawa and the Tories at Queen's Park," I stated. "The Tories and the Liberals are in favour of so-called farm income stabilization . . . not in terms of the reality of

today, but in terms of some average of years in the past —
stabilizing farm prices at a level where farmers are on the verge
of bankruptcy. It's really just saving them from bankruptcy."

The inadequate farm income stabilization legislation became
law, and set the stage for the next massive farm revolt to rock
rural Ontario. The traditional cost-price squeeze, which
farmers had lived with both before and after the war, had
tightened to the point of strangulation for a growing number
of farmers. The new element was skyrocketing interest rates.

Credit had long been a farm problem. In the 1920s the banks
considered farmers such a questionable risk that they refused
to make farm loans. This led the Farmer-Labour government
of E.C. Drury to establish the provincial savings offices, to
accumulate capital for farm loans. But the mechanization of
agriculture led to larger family farms, all of which, in turn,
required long-term credit for capital investment, and short-
term for seasonal operations. Gradually banks recognized
farmers as lucrative borrowing prospects, and agricultural
indebtedness grew to billions. As interest rates soared to over
20 per cent, at the peak of the 1980s crisis, the farmers' interest
outlay actually exceeded net incomes. Ontario had traditionally
insisted that responsibility for long-term farm credit rested with
the federal government. When Ottawa's response was inadequate, most provinces provided supplementary programs, but
not Ontario.

This was the situation when high interest rates struck. The
consequences were devastating. Farmers who had begun operations in recent years, and were heavily in debt, faced impossible interest burdens. The OFA approached the government
repeatedly with briefs outlining short-term and long-term solutions. It backed up its appeal with a province-wide task force,
in which it gathered documentation of what was happening
on the farm. Concerned Farm Women entered the fray, an
organizational phenomenon not seen since the days of protest during, and following, the First World War. This time
the farmers didn't take to the roads on tractors, as they had
in the sixties, but their protest built until it began to draw
headlines even in the urban press — proof that the crisis was

reaching critical proportions.

In fact, the farm mood was expressed in moves of unprecedented challenge. Various county organizations within the OFA passed resolutions, calling for the resignation of Lorne Henderson, the minister of agriculture, whose well-developed capacity for back-concession politicking was inadequate to deal with the mounting crisis. On a number of occasions the OFA provincial council debated these resolutions, but tabled them, shying away from such a frontal attack upon the government.

The situation reached a climax when some twelve hundred farm men and women left their work in the fields during peak season and converged on the Constellation Hotel in Toronto for a showdown. They had demanded the presence of the minister of agriculture and the provincial treasurer, Frank Miller, but that day their political harvest was richer. Although uninvited, Premier William Davis turned up.

The premier led off in his folksy fashion, concluding with a plea that the farmers should present specific proposals. It was an incredible request, because the OFA had done so, not once but twice, in the previous three months, and had received no government reply. The premier left the meeting, saying that he had to get back to the Legislature for question period. It was as well that he did leave, for the militant mood of the audience was captured by a Grey county farmer who spoke next. He declared that farmers were tired of being treated like mushrooms — "kept in the dark on a diet of horse shit." The retort was greeted with thunderous applause. When Frank Miller spoke, he promised the farmers that he would provide help in his budget, scheduled for later that month. He delivered on his promise — the beginning of another succession of piecemeal grants, a band-aid solution to a basic problem, from which agriculture has never escaped.

The best that can be said for this latest farm crisis is that its proportions have captured the concern of all society. "Food glut is good for mankind, but bad news for our farmers," declared David Crane, Toronto *Star* columnist on 14 June 1986. In prospect is "the probable erosion of the wealth and livelihood of many who now farm," added John Grant, chief economist of Wood Gundy. That's a calm understatement of a situation far more painful for those experiencing it.

Looking back over thirty years, there is one obvious question: was all the effort on behalf of the farmers worth it?

Personally, the answer is an emphatic yes. I felt at home with farm issues, even when the response was cool, if not hostile, among farmers as well as the government. In fact, I became involved with so many phases of farming and rural life (only the highlights of which have been dealt with here) that, in recording these memoirs, it has been difficult to avoid slipping into an overall history of postwar Ontario agriculture.

Politically, however, the answer is mixed. Certainly, there was no rich harvest of support from farmers in general, though when the NDP vote jumped 60 per cent in the 1967 election a significant increase in rural ridings contributed to that breakthrough.

Why did the emergence of farmers in the vanguard of progressive politics, after the First World War, not carry through into the CCF/NDP? Basically, the answer lies in the fact that, although farmers were engaged in vigorous protest against wartime and long-term injustices, the protest had no ideological base, other than a greater commitment to cooperative action. Most of the membership of the movements which underpinned the Progressive Party and the United Farmers of Ontario, led by men like Harry Nixon and Farquhar Oliver, drifted back into the old political folds. A hard core, headed by the indomitable Agnes Macphail, pursued the logic of their protest into the democratic socialist movement.

Meanwhile, farmers' thinking was heavily conditioned by the conviction that they had been burned by their venture into politics, and henceforth, organizationally they should remain strictly non-partisan. The political potential of the farmer-labour coalition was lost in the growing farm concern over the radicalism of socialists and trade unionists. The alliance of the old parties with the corporate world kept the rural community persuaded that organized labour was the farmer's enemy, responsible for many of his problems, instead of a potential ally against the exploitation of the dominant political-business interests.

Shortly after becoming CCF leader in 1953, I was sought out for frequent chats by W.C. Good, a pioneer in the cooperative and UFO movements, and a Progressive MP, who had worked closely with J.S. Woodsworth and the Ginger Group in the House of Commons.[5] His son, Robert Good, was active in the CCF/NDP and played an important role in launching the New Democratic Party, as chairman of its first farm committee. Linkages like those, with the antecedents of the CCF, were strengthened by periodic visits with E.C. Drury, retired on his farm at Plum Hill, outside Orillia. A venerable octogenarian, he was being gently pushed and assisted in writing his memoirs[6] by radio newsman, Peter McGarvey, then at CFOR in Barrie.

Quite apart from this gradual retreat from the vanguard of progressive politics, rural thought is essentially conservative. Farmers are given to protest, but not to radicalism. Their rugged individualism is shaped by a constant struggle with nature and the seasons. They are genuine private enterprisers, readily captivated by the rhetoric of free enterprise, even while being victimized by it. Ideologically, they are schizophrenic: while preaching free enterprise they strive for a planned and producer-controlled economy which will alleviate, if not remove, the basic inequality from which they suffer in a business-dominated economy. Farm conventions are often a baffling contradiction — on the one hand criticizing government intervention, on the other hand calling for government action and assistance.

For all these reasons, despite the NDP espousal of their cause, there was no significant switch in farm votes at the grass-roots level. That was balanced, however, by a growing acknowledgment by the farm leaders of the NDP commitment. In the 1977 election, for example, among the growing number of farm candidates were Gordon Hill and Walter Miller, at the time leading figures in the Federation of Agriculture and the National Farm Union. Prestigious though their candidacies were, neither man won; but even in the lower fortunes of the 1981 election, the NDP was commended by the farm leadership, if not by the rank and file.

"NDP Leader Michael Cassidy stole the show from his Liberal and Tory opponents . . . in an appearance before one hundred directors of the Ontario Federation of Agriculture," the Kitchener-Waterloo *Record* reported on 19 February 1981, during the 1981 campaign. In one of his columns, the *Record*'s agricultural columnist, Jim Romahn, summed up the situation in a frank fashion:

> The NDP performance in the legislature has been the best of the three major parties, ranging across a broad front of issues, from the inquiry on discounts and allowances, to Ontario Hydro and rural tax reform. . . . The NDP has tended to bring a refreshingly urban view to long-standing and complex rural issues, but the same strength has been a weakness . . . some farmers are suspicious of urban and urbane Ontarians. There is also an unfortunate tendency in Ontario to think stereotypes and labels so that the NDP continues to suffer because it is labelled socialist, pinko, communist, pro-labour, academic, etc. The NDP will not become a major force in rural Ontario, no matter how appealing and logical their platform.[7]

For all these reasons, the NDP's political harvest in the farm community has never been a bumper crop.

18
Energy

During a celebration at Ontario Place on 3 September 1985, marking the twenty-fifth anniversary of the Ontario Energy Board, one oldtimer singled out another. Robert Macaulay, chairman of the board, and a former minister of energy resources when it was first set up, told the hundred people present that I also had been around from the beginning, as a vigorous opposition critic.

The political antagonism of yesteryear was submerged in the cordial atmosphere that day. But my mind jumped back to my very first weeks as provincial CCF leader in January 1954, when I toured the fifteen ridings in northern Ontario. The political topic at that time was the exciting prospect of natural gas being piped in from western Canada. Two American corporations, which had been scrambling for the profitable pipeline rights, had just combined, with the approval in Ottawa of federal trade minister C.D. Howe, to create Trans-Canada Pipe Lines Limited.

A 1951 Stanford University study estimated that the cost of natural gas to Ontario consumers would be fifty to fifty-five cents per thousand cubic feet. But only twenty-one cents of that represented the construction and operation costs, while the rest was long-term financial costs, including bond interest, taxes and returns on equity capital. What that meant seemed clear to me: if the pipeline development were handled as a public utility, bonds could be issued at 2.77 per cent interest (the going federal rate), thus reducing long-term financial charges and cutting the consumer price of natural gas by thirty-five to forty per cent.

It seemed to me that Trans-Canada Pipe Lines was little more than a front for American investment banks. The whole deal had been worked out under the auspices of a federal cabinet minister, apparently with the blessing of the Frost cabinet. It just went to show how far the government would go, in sacrificing the future welfare of the people of Ontario to powerful financial interests.

The pipeline was only half the picture. Controversy also raged around the distribution system within the province. Reliable rumours had said the provincial government was going to develop a public commission to oversee distribution, and the policy would be gas at cost, just as the Hydro system was supposed to deliver electricity at cost. But Tory Treasurer Dana Porter ruled out the suggestion of mixing a publicly owned distribution system with a privately owned trans-Canada pipeline. He called it a "half-baked type of business." It was a policy, in my opinion, that would result in the price of natural gas to Ontario domestic and industrial consumers being twice as expensive as it needed to be. The advantage of cheaper power would be frittered away.

This was particularly tragic for northern Ontario, where natural gas offered the prospect of more economic development than it had ever known. Combined with its comparable resources, efficient power meant the north could share more equitably in Ontario's industrial expansion. There was an even more negative result of private distribution. The pipeline would enter Ontario near Kenora, then go by way of the Lakehead to Sudbury, south to Toronto and east to Montreal. Local distribution from this main line would cream the market, while communities such as Timmins, Kirkland Lake, Cochrane, North Bay, Sault Ste Marie and Parry Sound would only be serviced if a vast distribution system were developed.

"If handled as a public utility, the profits from the lines built first in the more heavily populated and industrialized areas would become available for extending the distribution system, with little or no delay, into the more lightly populated and less industrialized areas," I pointed out in Kirkland Lake. "Handled privately, these profits will be drained off, so that the distribution system will not be extended as quickly and the very communities which need natural gas will get it last, if ever. Thus, their economic disadvantage will become even greater.''

The Frost government had deliberately wiped out the potential competitive advantage that natural gas offered, because of its doctrinaire belief that it would be "unfair" competition for coal and oil. Instead, they opted for private distribution, with its higher capitalization costs, profits and taxes, which raised the price to that of coal and oil. The economics were deplorable, the politics unconscionable.

Just how bad the economics were became increasingly clear as the years unfolded. Trans-Canada Pipe Lines was controlled by American oil and investments interests, with a few Canadian directors fronting for them. Having sold the government a false bill of goods to get the franchise (namely, that they would build an all-Canadian line completely as a private enterprise) it wasn't long until TCPL was back on the government doorstep pleading financial inability and asking for a subsidy by way of a government guarantee of their bonds.

The government agreed, in return for enough common shares to give it a voice in the company. Trans-Canada accepted the proposition. But the Gulf Oil Company of Texas, which was to supply Trans-Canada with one-third of its gas in Alberta, vetoed the whole proposition when it heard that the Canadian government would have a say in the direction of the company. The government gave in. "This provoked one of the most shameful episodes in Canadian history," I told a regional CCF conference in Kirkland Lake. "Seldom have these private interests been revealed more clearly for what they are — a law unto themselves. This is a situation more humiliating than any government should be willing to tolerate. . . . The Canadian people are going to be shamefully exploited for the privilege of using our own resources."

It was not too late to do something. TCPL's franchise was to run out at the end of April 1955, and we in the CCF called upon the federal government not to renew the franchise but to "heed the cry rising from its own back benches that this historic development should be carried out as a public enterprise." Of course, C.D. Howe did not heed the rising cry. But he soon learned that, although the controlling American interests refused to tolerate government intervention in the direction of "their" company, they were not inhibited in asking for more government assistance.

Trans-Canada now wanted to break its contract to build an all-Canadian line. It would build the eastern and western links, but skip the northern Ontario section, because it was too difficult to build and, besides, it wouldn't immediately be profitable. To their everlasting shame, the Liberal government at Ottawa bowed to this proposition. They now proposed to spend Canadian taxpayers' money, through a crown corporation, building the unprofitable section of the line, thereby guaranteeing the profits to the American interests on the rest of the line! And the Ontario government was going to join forces in bailing out Trans-Canada. Here indeed — to borrow Dana Porter's inimitable phraseology, was a "half-baked sort of business."

I felt that Trans-Canada's refusal to build the northern Ontario link really let the cat out of the bag. It was very clear that the main objective of the American controlling interests was not to build a pipeline to serve Canada, but to get Canada's natural resources into the American market. Their proposal was to build the line from Alberta east to Manitoba, then pipe the gas across the border at Emerson, and sell it to the Tennessee Gas Transmission Company. Tennessee would then distribute the gas through the midwest and eastern states and, most of all, get it into the lucrative New York market. "These American interests," I pointed out, "are going to be so kind as to buy the gas at the Manitoba border for about twenty-four cents per thousand cubic feet and sell our own resource back to us at the Niagara border for about fifty-nine cents. In the Bible, we're told of a man who sold his birthright for a mess of pottage. I don't know what we've sold our birthright of natural gas for. Only the future will tell. But of this we can be certain: we've sold it. It's going, going. . . and tomorrow, if we don't wake up, it will be gone."

Events proved my comment to be prophetic.

The cost of natural gas was gradually becoming a matter of concern to consumers, if not to their governments. Consumers Gas Company, the Metro Toronto distributor, submitted a list of reduced rates to the Ontario Fuel Board, to meet the promise of a drop in prices when natural gas replaced manufactured gas. But even the reduced rates didn't represent a significant lowering of fuel costs, which were contributing to the high cost of living.

Basically, the high gas prices were the product of provincial government policies, working hand-in-glove with private companies to maintain profits, by keeping gas prices at levels that would not be competitive with coal and oil.

At that time, American natural gas cost 53.17 cents per thousand cubic feet at the Toronto city limits, including 16.40 cents for gas at the wellhead and transmission to the American border at Emerson, 22.05 cents to Tennessee Gas Transmission, 3 cents to customs and 11.72 cents to the Niagara Commission Company. Distribution and administration costs were another 12 cents, for a total of 65 cents. But Consumers' had been charging $1.60 (even their reduced price was only $1.28), and the difference went to capital write-offs and profits. "A study of these costs suggests that a publicly owned system would be able to reduce retail prices to one dollar per thousand cubic feet," I told the High Park CCF Club in 1955. There would still be enough left for interest and amortization payments.

Moreover, Niagara Gas Transmission, which brought the gas eighty miles from Queenston to Toronto, got half as much as the American company for bringing it twelve hundred miles. Niagara had risked no capital of its own, and would be able to repay its $7.5 million bank loans in under three years.

When a memorial was planned to Robert Saunders, former chairman of Hydro, a newspaper pointed out that the statue of Hydro founder Adam Beck "ironically stands unlighted in darkness" on University Avenue in Toronto. That was not ironic, I commented, but highly appropriate. "For the principle of public ownership in utilities, of power at cost, for which he lived and died, has long since been buried by the Tory administration. Sir Adam's statue should not only be kept in darkness, a wreath should be hung on it in perpetuity, or at least until we have another man of his stature and vision who, by restoring the principles for which Sir Adam stood, could give us the biggest single remedy for high gas bills.''

A report by J. Glassco for Clarkson, Gordon in late 1955 confirmed the basic conclusions of all the previous studies of the Trans-Canada pipeline by concluding, ''It also appears that an all government-owned pipeline would be economically feasible even though no sales were made to the United States.'' I suggested that it ''may be taken for granted that the representative of a firm with the standing of Clarkson, Gordon would not have reaffirmed this point, if there was any doubt with regard to it.''

Premier Frost indicated that the government might reconsider its position, and, in fact, it was in the process of a complete reversal of policy regarding the desirability of the Trans-Canada pipeline. They had agreed to pool resources with Ottawa in a public corporation to build the vital northern Ontario link, and they were openly favouring public ownership of the whole line. This fired the CCF's campaign for an Ontario-controlled distribution system — especially in February 1956, when the government moved to establish a commission along the lines of Hydro, to handle water. Why move for public ownership in water distribution, yet stick to private ownership for gas distribution? While the CCF supported Ontario's sharing in the public construction of the northern Ontario link, we were critical of the growing contradictions in policy.

Was it necessary, I asked in a CBC provincial affairs broadcast on 27 February, for the Ontario government to join forces with the Liberals in Ottawa to ''bail out the American interests controlling Trans-Canada Pipe Lines Limited and, in effect, guarantee their profits from the very first year of operation. . . to get the line through northern Ontario? Government spokesmen said yes. Quite frankly, I'm not convinced it was.''

Trade Minister C.D. Howe represented a northern Ontario seat, so when Trans-Canada violated their agreement to build the northern Ontario link, the federal Liberals had no alternative but to complete it themselves. "What the federal government wanted," I stated, "was to share, and thereby escape, some of the political consequences of their capitulation by trying to draw the Ontario Conservatives into it. And they have succeeded."

Howe then agreed to give Trans-Canada first option to buy the northern Ontario link — at the original cost of construction minus the amount that they paid for using it during the intervening years. That's having your cake and eating it too! And that's what Trans-Canada paid for the line — after it had proven to be profitable, and its value had appreciated by tens of millions of dollars.

I wondered aloud at the time why Premier Frost, normally a very tough bargainer with Ottawa, had given in so easily on this issue. Three years later he revealed that Ontario never advanced any of the authorized $35 million, and that it had been freed of its obligation to do so. Sober second thoughts.

That the deal had been accepted in the first place, however, led me to call it "another chapter in the old story of what makes the Conservative Party tick. . . . The Frost Government, first and foremost, is a businessman's government. In its scale of values, business profits, even American business profits, have rated higher than human need, even Canadian human needs. For the old parties, public enterprise is not something they believe in — even when the circumstances point to its superiority. Rather, it's an economic method of bailing out private operators, when they welch on their contract. It's a way of using the public purse to underwrite private profits."

The political fallout from this sorry tale of the federal government's surrender to U.S. corporate interests mounted in 1956. A debate in the House of Commons led to unprecedented scenes. The Speaker had to resign, his credibility destroyed. The usually mild-mannered M.J. Coldwell advanced to the Speaker's dais, shaking his fist. C.D. Howe held firm, and drove the legislation through by invoking closure. This episode, more than anything else, laid the groundwork for the fall of the Liberals in 1957. And the CCF's Douglas Fisher

used Howe's record on the pipeline, with its sellout of northern Ontario interests, so skillfully that he felled the political
giant in Port Arthur riding. Since I had been instrumental in
persuading Fisher to enter politics, I regarded his victory not
only as something of a personal triumph, but just retribution.

Another remarkable feature of the pipeline debate was that
George Drew, the federal Conservative leader, finally came
out flat-footedly in urging government construction of the
whole line. "This belated switch," I told the Thorold CCF
Club on 6 June 1956, "was a futile gesture that served no purpose, other than to reveal the doubletalk that has characterized
Tory pipeline policy. There is only one practical alternative
to the disastrous pipeline policy of the Liberal government.
That is public ownership. . . . Yet, as leader of the Opposition, [George Drew] refused to advance this practical alternative until the eleventh hour. For that reason, much of the
tragedy in the House of Commons during these past weeks
stems from the failure of the Official Opposition to play the
role of a real opposition — that is, to advance practical alternatives to the policy of the government."

The reason for this, I argued, was that Drew agreed with
the Liberals that the project should be handled by private
operators. "George Drew's belated conversion represents a
fumbling effort to capitalize on Liberal bungling, rather than
real conviction that public ownership is the answer to the
pipeline problem." That the Tory "conversion" was an exercise in political expediency was confirmed the next year, when
they were in power and made no effort to change the pipeline
deal that they had called "infamous."

Gas obtained at five cents a thousand cubic feet at the
wellhead in Alberta, would now cost the householder in the
Oshawa-Toronto-Welland area $2.50, a 5000 per cent markup.
I hammered away at this across the province. In Port Arthur
I pointed out that, with the taxpayers subsidizing the least profitable portion of the line, the company's stock "became a
bonanza from the time it came on the market:"

Now there is added the spectacle of the officials of the
company holding an option to buy 50,000 shares at $8.

Since the stock hit the market at $10 and is now reported at $25 or more, it simply means that these gentlemen have netted a cool $1 million apiece. Here, even before the gas reaches us in eastern Ontario, is dramatic fulfillment of the warning the CCF has made for years: the public is going to pay the shot for this line, and the private interests in control are going to walk off with the profits.

The shameful yielding to the demands of the pipeline promoters was not over. They returned for yet another dip in the public trough. Despite the hundreds of millions in the reserves of the American corporations controlling Trans-Canada, they pleaded more financial difficulties in building the easiest portion of the line across the prairies. And they got an $80 million loan from C.D. Howe.

The fallout in Ontario was slowly building to a climactic series of events. Although the Frost government had become an ardent, if belated, advocate of public development of the Trans-Canada line, it remained loyal to the private promoters of the provincial distribution system, for reasons that soon became evident: top Tories, both in the party and in the cabinet, were personally involved.

The Tories, with the Liberals tagging along, defeated a CCF amendment to the 1957 throne speech that called for a fully integrated, publicly owned distribution system. They did so in spite of the fact that Northern Ontario Natural Gas Company (NONG), the emerging distribution agency for communities from the Manitoba border to Barrie, was as completely under American control as was Trans-Canada Pipe Lines. The president, R.K. Farris, was the Canadian front man; the general manager and all four directors were American utility or investment banking figures. They, and their collaborators within the Conservative party, made personal profits to match those of the Trans-Canada promoters. The resulting political crisis dominated Ontario politics in the late 1950s and blew three cabinet ministers out of office.

In southern Ontario, unlike the north, either manufactured gas or natural gas from local wells or the United States had been available for some years. Here, too, the issue of private versus public distribution became a lively debate. In keeping with its doctrinaire stand for private development, the Frost government's policies were driving existing utilities out of the field and making it difficult, if not impossible, to finance municipally owned gas distribution systems.

"Under the guise of a credit shortage, the government's adamant stand is protecting the vested interests of existing fuel companies in the field and, in effect, depriving the Ontario consumer of the possibility of securing power at cost from natural gas," I told the Sarnia CCF Club on 19 June 1958.

This was not a new Tory policy, since Dana Porter had said in 1954 that it would be unfair for the province to enter the gas distribution field because it would be competing with private distributors of coal and oil. It became clear, however, that through its power to withhold credit, the Frost government was determined to impose this same policy on the municipalities.

When several western Ontario councils objected, they were told that municipalities wanting their own gas distribution systems could set them up — but without any financial assistance from the province. "This is just about the equivalent of saying to a man that he is free to eat, but you are going to see that he gets no food," I said.

Mr. Frost argued that the shortage of capital was a convincing reason for staying out of the gas business — but Ottawa and Ontario had been willing to use public funds to bail out the Trans-Canada Pipe Lines when they welched on their commitment. "The answer," I concluded, "is that the Frost government is seeking primarily to protect the vested interests of political friends, who are likely contributing to the Tory election funds in return for the protection."

I gained support from prominent municipal Liberals throughout the province such as Vince Barrie, mayor of St. Thomas and Dr. Robert Hay of the Kingston public utility, who could get no backing from their caucus. I pointed out that, in addition, the Ontario Association of Mayors and Reeves, the Ontario Municipal Association, and the Ontario Federation of Labour were all arguing for public ownership.

"In short, the battle, which the CCF was fighting alone in the House, against Liberals as well as Tories, has growing support across the province."

When a CCF amendment in the 1959 throne speech called on the government to take the lead in building a province-wide gas distribution system, an interesting series of events followed. Liberal leader John Wintermeyer bowed out of the debate altogether because his caucus was so badly split on the issue. Premier Frost contended, in his hour-long defence of his policies that the problem was a lack of enthusiasm among municipalities. I answered that this arose from defeatism "engendered by the government's stubborn refusal to give a lead," and I was supported by the Tory Toronto *Telegram* which editorialized: "Leadership comes from the top down, not from the bottom up. The municipalities are the creatures of the province."

A second important issue connected with the gas pipeline was storage. Lambton County, in southwestern Ontario, has an extraordinary asset: natural caverns with the capacity for one hundred billion cubic feet of gas, from which oil and gas have been removed. There is virtually no leakage, and these natural basins present an unparalleled opportunity to buy cheaper gas at off-peak prices from Trans-Canada, and store it until it is fed into the distribution system at peak period and prices. Of this hundred billion cubic feet capacity, only forty-two billion was leased and used by Union Gas, the long-established distributor in southwestern Ontario. I argued that an integrated, publicly owned system, covering all of southern Ontario, would make lower prices possible by using all the storage capacity.

Premier Frost had said there was no reason, even under the present set-up, why the storage space could not be more widely used. In fact, Consumers Gas was storing some of its off-peak purchases there under a contract with Union Gas. But this was a small amount, and the Lambton Gas Storage Association had estimated no more than 50 per cent of the space would be in use in twenty years, that is, by 1978.

"What is going to be the alternative?" I asked, during the

1959 Estimates debate in the Legislature. "The alternative is this: any time Trans-Canada Pipe Lines Limited finds itself with more gas than it can use (sell) at any one time, they have a contract with Tennessee Gas Company across the line and . . . this contract permits them, on any one day, to shoot across the border into Pennsylvania, 200,000 mcf of gas, which will be stored over there, and it will be the Americans who reap the benefits of the lower price."

The government procrastinated, and two years later the storage problems were still unresolved. Byron Young, an indefatigable spokesman for the Lambton Gas Storage Association, invited me to tour the area, and get a first-hand account from local farmers on the whole question. The tour, on 29 April 1961, ended with my speaking at a public meeting in the Moore Centre Hall, near the town of Brigden.

First, I said that contracts should be renegotiated with farmers who owned the resource, since many had been signed before the value was known; other farmers had sold the rights to slick corporate lawyers for a song. Secondly, Imperial Oil, which had applied for rights to storage areas over 52 per cent of the hundred billion cubic feet, did not distribute gas, and was thus a middleman. "In view of the fact that the storage charge passed on to the consumer is eight times what the companies pay for rental of storage . . . it is obvious that this company is in a position to reap very great profits at the expense of both the consumer and the farmer."

An Imperial Oil official said 90 per cent of the landowners in the area agreed to lease storage rights. This may be true, I said, but Imperial Oil should not be proud of it. Farmers had told me personally that, when they objected to the piddling prices being offered, company officials said, with varying degrees of bluntness, that they might as well sign, because Imperial Oil was going to get the area designated, and they would be obliged to become part of the pool.

I raised more questions. Since Imperial Oil was not a distributor, to whom was it going to sell the gas? Shouldn't we see these contracts, before granting storage rights? Or was Imperial going to sit on the gas, to lessen competition for its oil?

The third, and most important, subsidiary development to natural gas was the belated and ineffective regulation of private corporations given monopoly franchises.

The natural gas industry in Ontario started in the late 1880s with discoveries in Welland and Essex counties. Much of the production was sold to the United States. During the Second World War, gas supplies came under federal control, but reverted to provincial jurisdiction after 1946. C.D. Howe, the federal minister, said the Ontario Energy Board could regulate prices charged by the distributors. But this was absurd, because the Fuel Board would have to accept unquestioningly whatever Trans-Canada charged the distributors, and it was not under provincial control.

The refusal of either the federal or provincial government to exercise normal regulatory power, indicated the extent to which those powerful interests had both the old parties in their pockets.

A second absurdity was that large industrial consumers, such as the International Nickel Company, could buy directly from Trans-Canada, rather than through a distributor, and thus weren't under either federal or provincial jurisdiction. "The Fuel Board has unwittingly become the instrument, not of government policy (which it should be), but of the companies in the field, who were given pretty complete freedom to do as they pleased," I concluded during legislative debates.[1]

Public safety was another area of inadequate regulation by the Fuel Board. Acceptable safety codes were finally formulated by 1959 — but there had been explosions at Palermo, near Oakville, and Ottawa (in the Odeon Theatre, which two hours later would have been crowded with hundreds of children). An inspection by the Fuel Board in the Burlington area found that 92 of 233 valves examined were not approved. And about twenty valve boxes had to be corrected, after one-third of those between Port Hope and Brockville were inspected.

"In keeping with the government policy of tolerating unbridled free enterprise in this field, the Fuel Board made no inspection at all when the pipelines were laid in the ground, even though it was fixed with the responsibility of regulating and controlling pipeline installation," I told the Toronto and District CCF Council in 1959. "Driven to action by a stinging coroner's report, following the death of a mother and infant son, this is what the Board inspections now reveal."

In the Legislature, the government's position was nothing short of incredible. The responsible minister, J.W. Spooner, acknowledged that the board's explanation was that it didn't have to inspect the faulty valves. "This government was guilty of nothing short of criminal neglect," I concluded.

Pricing and profit limitations were a final area of inadequate regulation by the Fuel Board. The public was supposed to be protected by limiting utility profits to 7 per cent, but there was interminable argument over the appropriate base for the calculation.

In the wake of the federal storms over gas pipelines, the Diefenbaker government had appointed a royal commission on energy. It was sharply critical of the profiteering which had taken place, and recommended that profits be calculated, not on physical assets, but on equity capital. In other words, borrowed capital would be excluded.

In the case of Trans-Canada, 80 per cent of its capital was either borrowed or resulted from what I described as gouging of the public treasury. Only 20 per cent of its capital came from the American controlling interests. "The people in the gas field today," I argued, "are operating on the basis that they can make a profit that is almost as outrageous as that of the East India Company two hundred years ago in India, and they do it on other people's money."

In addition, the companies were inflating their capitalization figures to justify higher rates, and the Fuel Board was obliging. Union Gas bought Dominion Gas for $15 million, and immediately wrote it up in the books to $25 million. Consumers Gas had its capitalization structure reviewed by an American firm and wrote it up by $39 million. The situation was intolerable, and while defending it publicly, the government was moving to change it. In the 1959 session of the Legislature, a bill was introduced to set up the Department of Energy Resources. Its minister was to work closely with the board — an implied confession of inadequate past policies and administration.

The door was opened to change in May 1959, when Robert Macaulay, the minister with more energy, imagination and ideas than anyone else in cabinet, became minister of energy resources. For the first time, all energy issues were brought under the direction of one ministry. And changes resulted. In September, the Ontario Energy Board replaced the Fuel Board. On 1 January 1960, the Ontario government's submission to the National Energy Board, on applications for natural gas export licences, contained two items that caught my eye.

First, Mr. Macaulay contended that it was better to store cheap surplus gas to benefit Canadian consumers eventually, rather than export it for the ultimate benefit of American consumers. Those words had a familiar ring! Secondly, the Ontario submission confirmed that Canadians were being fleeced, and by how much. Consumers Gas users were paying $7.24 for 3,000 cubic feet of gas, compared with residents of St. Lawrence County in New York State who paid only $4.71. Moreover, that county was being served by a subsidiary of Consumers Gas. Again, that had a familiar ring.

The government had been stealing my lines. Opposition efforts, often frustrating, always prolonged, sometimes did have an influence on policy.

These, even if rarely conceded, are the rewards of public life. In the 1960s political preoccupation with natural gas gradually subsided, but was quickly taken over by Hydro's generation and pricing of electric power. For me, Hydro affairs were not a new concern. Even before my first election to the Legislature, I suggested on a CBC program in February 1955 that while attention was focused on spending for highways and public works, we should look more closely at Ontario's most important crown corporation, the Hydro-Electric Power Commission. That began thirty years of what I meant to be constructive criticism of Ontario Hydro, even though it was not always seen that way.

While John Wintermeyer accepted the Tory claim that we were getting power at cost, and went on merely to criticize Hydro's excessive spending on publicity, I pointed out that the problem was that we were *not* getting power at cost. "We are now getting hydro at cost plus — all down the line," I said, dismissing Liberal criticism of Hydro publicity as "typical of the kind of superficial criticism, the kind of sham battle, carried on by Liberals and Conservatives, because they have no real differences. The amount of money, excessive or otherwise, spent on publicity by Hydro represents chicken feed by comparison with the millions of dollars drained off every year to bolster private business — all in violation of the principle of power at cost."

I gave many examples of unnecessary costs being passed on to the people in Hydro rates: private construction companies building for Hydro; transmission hardware bought, not directly, but through middlemen; power sold to industry below cost, so other consumers had to pay more; and cost-plus prices for electrical appliances (whereas the original Hydro shop was conceived as a competitive retail outlet for appliances, it had become merely a show window). Hydro had also turned over its work on frequency standards to Canadian Comstock Limited without tender, on a cost-plus-graded-fee basis, and, in addition, supplied Comstock with much of its equipment and one-third of its personnel, at an outlay of millions of dollars.

"This much is certain," I concluded. "The Hydro Commission is administered at the top by men who see nothing wrong in operating public enterprise for the benefit of private business. Indeed, under a previous Liberal administration, the Hydro chairman was even permitted to draw a retainer as a counselling engineer for outside interests. After a generation of Liberal and Tory administration, the basic principle of power at cost is dead and buried. And with full government blessing."

Hydro provided rich material for opposition critics. For instance, in 1958-59 it procrastinated in negotiations with an Indian band near Sarnia for properties it needed. As a result, a hastily incorporated development company bought a large block of land for $2,000 an acre, and then sold a small portion to Hydro at $7,000 an acre. A royal commission on the matter merely produced a "whitewash" report.

In addition, to these issues, I was frustrated from the beginning in trying to find out what was going on within the commission. The stone wall blocked out the public, and even the government, because Hydro traditionally operated at arm's length. Originally, this was a defence against takeover by private power interests. But it became such a problem that eventually Robert Macaulay, while a minister without portfolio, was appointed vice-chairman of Hydro, to try to bring the utility under more effective legislative control. (This ultimately failed because neither the government nor Hydro was committed, and the next Hydro vice-chairman was William Davis, who was not inclined to rock the boat.)

During the 1960s, Hydro's borrowing for its expansion program grew to $500 million a year, and in the 1970s, high costs, including nuclear plant construction, doubled, trebled, then quadrupled Hydro's annual capital requirements. Rates began to rise, and the government and public no longer quietly accepted the arm's length relationship. They wanted answers, and that led to a succession of public reviews of one kind or another.

A task force in 1972-73 recommended that Hydro's proposed bulk power rate for the coming year no longer be automatically implemented, but instead be referred for review to the Ontario Energy Board. This has been done since 1974.

Then, because Hydro's long-term expansion plans involved many new stations and tens of billions of dollars, a royal commission, under Professor Arthur Porter, was set up to look at Ontario's electric power needs throughout the 1980s.

When Hydro's proposed rate increase for 1976 was a towering 30 per cent, a political storm of major proportions led the energy minister, Darcy McKeough, to set up a select committee to review the increase. (I always believed he did so because he himself found the proposed increase too high.) Since the government was now in a minority, it could no longer pick committee chairmen only from the ranks of Tory back-benchers. I became the chairman of the select committee.

As well as these inquiries, Hydro faced a long series of environmental hearings into the impact of proposed transmission line routes. These were often drawn out with references to the courts, and have frustrated Hydro's plan to bring power from the nuclear plants in the Bruce peninsula to the provincial network.

After decades with no, or limited, outside scrutiny, Hydro has now faced so many reviews that it has extensive facilities (and staff) to deal with public hearings. Whether this has led to greater accountability is still a matter of controversy.

Chairing the select committee, that lasted throughout the 1975-81 minority government period, was the most satisfying single experience of all my legislative years. I had sat on many committees, but until then had no real idea of the considerable influence wielded by the chairman. The first step was to hire staff. Conservative Frank Drea, Jim Foulds of the NDP and a rookie Liberal MPP named David Peterson made up a steering committee that interviewed, then hired, lawyer Alan Schwartz, former counsel for the Association of Consumers in hearings before the Energy Board, and Jim Fisher, an economist with the Canada Consulting Group. I called them "the gold dust twins," and they were superb at all the preparatory work in finding a balance of witnesses, and analysing the millions of words of testimony — jobs that members simply didn't have time for.

The committee began with narrow terms of reference — reviewing the proposed rate increase for 1976. But it had only ten weeks to do the job, and it had to strike a balance between the fight against inflation and the short-term "financial integrity" of Hydro and the province.

In our interim report, tabled on 12 December 1975, the committee concluded that Hydro's plans to expand the system required close scrutiny, since the proposed $30 billion cost of new plants and transmission lines would be the most significant factor in future hydro rates. We asked for more time to study all the components of Hydro's costs. We concluded that a "responsible" reduction of the proposed new rate was justified, and recommended an interim rate increase of only 22 per cent. The government accepted the recommendation.

Our final report — "A New Public Policy Direction for Ontario Hydro" — was tabled on 16 June 1976. Of its thirty-nine recommendations, only one of any consequence was rejected by the government. Significantly, the government agreed that the committee should be reappointed to review what action was taken, and should be allowed to assess Hydro's commitment to nuclear energy.

The government was committed to providing two-thirds of Ontario's electrical energy from nuclear generation. The forecast $28 billion cost to build these plants was horrendous, far exceeding either Hydro's or the province's debt. Hydro asked for $2 billion capital borrowing for 1977 alone. This led Darcy McKeough, now back as provincial treasurer, to limit Hydro's capital spending to $1.5 million for each of the next three years.

Meanwhile, our select committee concluded that the planned expansion was unnecessary, and recommended that Hydro reduce its target for new generating capacity over the next ten years. Hydro warned that demand for power would continue to grow at 7 per cent a year, while Darcy McKeough said he had figured "on the back of an envelope" (in reality, analysis by ministry staff) that it would be no more than 5.4 per cent. He proved to be right, and Hydro wrong.

Despite the generators built or planned at Pickering and Bruce, Hydro argued that it needed a huge plant at Darlington, east of Oshawa, because it predicted a shortfall of 4,000 megawatts of reserve power it wanted in case of an emergency. Committee staff analysed these data and found that, with action which Hydro could take, it had a surplus, not a deficit, reserve capacity.

Nobody challenged our analysis. Nevertheless, in July 1977, the government authorized Hydro to proceed with Darlington, whose planned capacity was 3,500 Mw — twice the size of the whole complex at Niagara. Hydro said the huge plant would be needed to prevent brown-outs, or even black-outs, in the mid-1980s. Not only have there been no shortages, but

Darlington's construction has been extended, and its first unit is not now scheduled to come on stream until 1989.

Given the committee's solid case that Darlington was premature, if not unnecessary, why did the government authorize it? Some years after McKeough had left provincial politics and become head of Union Gas, I wanted to satisfy myself on this point. I asked him, at a breakfast meeting at the King Edward Hotel, why a cabinet including both himself and James Taylor, an energy minister who lost that post because of open differences with Hydro, would have approved Darlington. McKeough said he had no recollection of the issue ever coming before cabinet. "Who, then, would have authorized it?" I asked. "I presume, the premier," was the quiet reply.

So that was it. Premier Davis was not simply an ardent advocate of nuclear power, he was a crusader. In speeches from Kapuskasing to Texas, he could be counted on for a favourable mention of two things: his home town of Brampton and nuclear power.

The re-established committee got under way again in 1978, with virtually unlimited terms of reference, in keeping with its new name — the Select Committee on Hydro Affairs. Before we could get back to studying power supply and demand, a political hot potato was tossed in our laps. The Liberals had learned of excessive costs in building heavy water plants as part of the growing Bruce nuclear complex. Premier Davis referred the issue to the select committee, and we launched a lengthy investigation.

Atomic Energy of Canada Limited (AECL) firmly asserted that there was no foreseeable need for Ontario-produced heavy water, and the New Democrats on the committee supported the staff's recommendation that construction of the final plant be stopped. Tories and Liberals, however, wanted work stopped on half the plant, with the other half completed. Their majority prevailed in committee, but Hydro, on its own, ultimately cancelled the facility. That saved $60 million, but much more could have been saved.

In April 1979 the North American nuclear industry was

shaken by the near meltdown of a generator at Three Mile Island, in Pennsylvania. The repercussions were felt around the world, but nowhere more so than in Ontario, whose commitment to nuclear energy was a major item in the committee's terms of reference.

We held intense hearings over the next year, into the safety of nuclear plants and the related problems of disposal of radioactive wastes from the mining, milling and refining of uranium. This was the most challenging phase of the committee's work because, while it was easy to get testimony from proponents or critics of nuclear power, it was difficult to find authoritative neutral testimony. Our investigations covered nuclear plants, the mines at Elliot Lake, refining at Port Hope, and the hitherto highly secret operations of AECL which had the lead responsibility for safe disposal of nuclear wastes.

Our final report in June 1980 concluded that nuclear generation with Canada's Candu system was "acceptably safe." The NDP members dissented, contending that the report failed "to identify the elements of safety, supply dependence and economic considerations, which inter-relate in the judgment of acceptable safety." The Conservatives dissented from a recommendation for a study of the likelihood of a catastrophic accident in a Candu reactor. They said it would only conclude that such an accident "is possible but highly improbable."

In the dialogue of the deaf that characterized the nuclear debate, our report satisfied proponents of nuclear energy but left critics unconvinced.

Despite these important distractions, the basic work of the committee was to analyse Ontario's future electric power needs, and how they could best be met. The growing evidence of a costly, oversized system led to a "Special Report on the Need for Electrical Capacity," tabled in the Legislature in December 1979. It concluded that Hydro should plan for growth in demand of 2 to 3 per cent a year, until the year 2000. As a result, the committee said, the Darlington plant would not be needed before 1996, and the government should "inform Hydro that no additional contracts for the construction of the Darlington generating station [should] be awarded until the government has reported to the Legislative Assembly its policy for the construction of additional generating capacity.''

The Conservatives dissented from this startling recommendation, on the grounds that it would be more prudent to consider a range of growth of from to 2 to 4 per cent. In fact, during the economic recession of the early 1980s the growth in electricity demand dropped below 2 per cent, and in 1982 there was an actual decrease in demand. In the mid-1980s, Hydro's own forecast was 2.7 per cent average annual growth to the year 2000. The committee had been dead on.

In the winter of 1980-81, listening to weeks of authoritative testimony on all the factors involved, the committee was nearing a decision on Hydro's expansion. As far back as 1976, we had recommended that alternative means of meeting power demands, such as conservation and load management, be exploited to the full, before building new generation capacity. Our staff believed, and I agreed, that Darlington should, at least, be deferred — something that would have been highly defensible at that early stage in construction.

However, the committee never got a chance to report. Its work abruptly came to an end. In February 1981 Premier Davis called an election and won a majority government on 19 March. Despite widespread calls for reappointment of the committee — from opposition parties, editorials, even from Hydro — the Tories felt otherwise. Legislative scrutiny of Hydro collapsed until 1985, when an Energy Committee was set up by the Peterson government, to fulfill a commitment in the accord with the NDP that brought the Liberals to power.

Unrestrained, the Davis government forged ahead with Darlington, even calling for speeding construction during the 1981 campaign. A year later, under spending restraints imposed by Treasurer Larry Grossman, the Darlington schedule finally slowed, with completion dates for the four units set in 1988-92.

Far from suffering power shortages in the 1980s, Hydro was plagued with growing surpluses. From 1983 to 1992, twelve more nuclear units are gradually coming on line, four each at Pickering, Bruce and Darlington. This has forced cancellation, deferment or mothballing of thousands of megawatts of generating capacity. Hydro conceded it would not need any significant increase in capacity until the late 1990s, which emphasizes again the question of developing alternative energy sources, rather than building costly generating facilities.

Electric power represents only 16 per cent of Ontario's energy requirements, while 75 to 80 per cent are met by imported power. That raises the question of an overall energy policy. In the summer of 1979, Energy Minister Robert Welch released the first and only statement of energy policy in forty-two years of Tory government. The major objective of the report, *Energy Security for the Eighties*, was to reduce Ontario's 80 per cent reliance on out-of-province energy sources. This meant moving away from oil, which fueled 50 per cent of the province's consumption. The report recommended hydraulic generation of electricity on small sites, development of lignite reserves at Onakawana, near James Bay, increasing such non-conventional renewable energy sources as wind, solar and biomass from the proposed 2 per cent to 5 per cent of our total energy demand by 1995, and more diversified generation by Hydro, with no more nuclear commitments.

Within three years, this energy policy was in a shambles. The drop in demand, and Hydro's accompanying surplus of power, led to the abandoning of all the recommendations. In fact, far from diversifying its mix, Hydro was headed for fully 70 per cent nuclear-generated electricity by the 1990s.

I once quipped that Hydro was like China: often beaten in battle but always victorious eventually, by simply absorbing its enemies. Like those before him, Robert Welch was absorbed. He began by challenging the basic thrust of Hydro's policies, and ended as one of its leading apologists.

Meanwhile, my personal situation changed radically, when I resigned my seat in the Legislature, but I carried on scrutinizing Hydro through an internal NDP task force on Hydro affairs.

During 1982-83 I reviewed all aspects of Hydro's operations, updated information gathered by the select committee, and produced eight reports. The task force concluded with two seminars, to isolate areas for further research and to discuss a draft report. In June 1984, *Harnessing Hydro* was produced. It stated the energy goals of the New Democratic Party — greater efficiency in overall energy consumption, greater emphasis on the developing and marketing of renewable energy sources, and a restatement of Ontario Hydro's mandate with assurance of greater public accountability of the corporation — and made specific proposals for their achievement.

Freed of legislative responsibilities, I spoke across the province, and Hydro was a regular topic. There was a succession of articles and editorials in the media dealing with the theme that Hydro was out of control, was spending too much, and was relying too much on nuclear energy.

In February 1983 I visited the Tennessee Valley Authority (TVA), whose electric power complex was almost identical in size to Hydro's. But, in contrast to Hydro, TVA had responded sensitively to the phenomenal drop in power consumption in the 1980s: it deferred, and then cancelled, eight of its seventeen nuclear units, writing off $2 billion already spent, in order to save the $8 billion it would cost to complete the plants. Hydro, meanwhile, forged ahead to complete twelve more nuclear units, in addition to the eight already in operation.

I stressed the major difference in the approach of the two utilities in a news release on 13 February 1983: "TVA is profoundly convinced that conservation is the cheapest, the most effective, and environmentally the most benign 'source' of new energy. . . . Everybody, from the Board of Directors, down through the organization, regards conservation as an integral part of the system. It is the growing focus of TVA's planning and resources. . . . In TVA's view, it makes solid economic sense to invest in conservation rather than new plants." TVA calculated that the cost of all its programs to conserve energy came out to $300 for every kilowatt saved. "Compare that," I pointed out, "with Darlington's ultimate cost of $3,400 per kilowatt." Hydro's conservation program was "more of an advertising slogan than a commitment," I concluded.

American utilities were so successful at developing new conservation techniques that General Public Utilities (GPU), which had suffered the Three Mile Island disaster, dropped a planned purchase of 1,000 Mw of power from Ontario Hydro (by way of a transmission cable under Lake Erie), in favour of spending the money on a more efficient use of its existing power supply. For the power consumer, GPU offered an irresistible deal: at no cost, it would retrofit residential, industrial or commercial buildings to make them energy-efficient. The savings were shared with the servicing company on a five-to-seven year contract, but after that the owner enjoyed all the savings.

It costs less to save a kilowatt of existing power, than to build the generating capacity to produce a new kilowatt. That's a guiding principle of modern energy utilities that has yet to be accepted by Ontario Hydro.

In a speech to District 4 of the Ontario Municipal Electrical Association and the Association of Municipal Electrical Utilities (the elected and appointed officials and professional managers of utilities in the Golden Horseshoe, from Burlington through Metro Toronto to Scugog), I dealt with Hydro's overbuilding. "It isn't simply the cost of building these new generating facilities. There is also the cost involved in growing nuclear-generated surpluses, which are forcing existing stations into standby, or mothballing, or cancellation, or even demolition . . . sometimes when their life span is far from exhausted."

I went over the record of the past few years. Wesleyville, cancelled after costing $300 million, now the most expensive warehouse in Ontario; Lennox, mothballed; Hearn's eight units, all mothballed; the J. Clark Keith plant in Windsor mothballed and rumoured for demolition, after tens of millions were spent on renovations; one of two units at Atikokan cancelled; a unit at Thunder Bay mothballed; and Nanticoke, Hydro's most modern coal-fired plant that cost nearly $1 billion, operating at only 40 per cent capacity in 1983, and dropping to 20 per cent in the 1990s. "What is the cost," I asked, "of all of this sometimes premature shelving of billions in assets, simply to make room for new nuclear generation that costs billions in new money? Nobody has done this calculation. It cries out for investigation and public scrutiny in the fashion that was possible during the days of the select committee."

Concluding that the government had "neither the will nor the capacity to alter Hydro's course," I hoped aloud that the municipal power utilities which my audience represented would play a greater role in the future. But Hydro's domination of the industry is so effective that none of the grass-roots sympathy my speech elicited had any influence at the top. Hydro simply absorbed the municipal utility people.

Beyond this chronological review of Hydro affairs, I have three reflections. First, on the value of the select committee to Hydro, to the politicians and public, and to private corporations: Hydro officials had never been subjected to legislative scrutiny, and their initial reaction was one of discomfort and apprehension. But toward the end they admitted that public debate was necessary for sound public policy decisions, and they joined the widespread plea for the committee's reappointment. The committee hearings brought major elements of the nuclear industry and its operations into the public domain. While they didn't dispel all the concerns, they at least replaced suspicions and ignorance with an assessment of the basic facts, and public discussion became somewhat more rational.

Equally significant was the change that took place with large corporations, such as Lummus of Canada Limited, which was involved in the heavy water controversy. They objected to government "interference," and feared their reputation would be tarnished. The hostile attitude faded and, by the end, company officials admitted privately, if not publicly, that the process had been useful.

The hearings revealed a fundamental weakness in Hydro's management structure. The forecasting, planning and construction phases of the vast corporation's work were not adequately coordinated, so that, on occasion, construction proceeded at premium costs to meet deadlines, while forecasts showed the new facility would not be needed for some time, if ever. Many improvements in Hydro's operations were made as a result, often voluntarily, before the committee recommended them.

The second area of reflection concerns Hydro's basic policy direction. It has not adjusted to the changing circumstances, maintaining its fixation of building more generating capacity, instead of focusing on the least costly way to assure adequate power. (Announcements in 1987-88 suggested that some changes are under consideration.)

The committee recommended, back in 1976, that conservation should be vigorously pursued, but Hydro persists in its outmoded approach. Given its great over-capacity, Hydro simply can't afford conservation. Its challenge is to sell as much electricity as possible from its surplus, and thereby meet the carrying charges on a debt which, until recently, was larger than that of the provincial government. As a result, Hydro's "conservation" advertising is really designed to convince consumers to switch to electricity.

Amory Lovins, a world expert on energy who is familiar with the Ontario situation, pointed out to the legislative energy committee in 1985 that a utility can make money by selling less electricity, as long as it is cheaper to save electricity than to make it. Every time Hydro builds a new plant at today's costs, its average price for power goes up. In contrast, once installed, efficiency measures initially cost much less than new capacity, and have zero operating costs.

Ontario needs legislation, as in the United States, that assures small producers of electricity that they will be paid a price for their power approximating what it would cost the utility to build new capacity. This could lead to many small new generating plants, lessen Hydro's needs for new capacity, help decentralize the system and save on transmission line costs.

A final area of reflection: the need for more effective accountability of Hydro, both in reality and in the public perception. The problem was set forth succinctly in the NDP taskforce report:

Despite the fact that electricity represents only sixteen percent of Ontario energy consumption, Hydro has dominated energy policy. Decisions are made in private by the corporation, with little involvement from the public or even from the government. Reviews of Hydro decisions by the Ontario Energy Board, the government, the Legislature, royal commissions and select committees have essentially been of an advisory nature. In the final analysis, Hydro shapes policy in keeping with its corporate needs.

Although Hydro argues that every major decision requires the government's prior approval, in reality, the Ministry of Energy has never developed the capacity to be in control, and the cabinet has never had the will to alter Hydro's course. The persistent criticism that Hydro is too much of a law unto itself must be directed at the government, for Hydro has co-opted governments and energy ministers as effectively as it has co-opted local utilities. This was put most colourfully by James Taylor, after he lost his battle with Hydro in 1977, and was replaced as energy minister. He said he had "walked the corridors of power only to be mugged in the back alleys of bureaucracy."

I firmly believe there is an answer to the question of whether the government or Hydro is in control. We need a comprehensive statement of government energy policy. a clear indication of Hydro's role in it, and the capacity within either the government or outside agencies, such as the Energy Board, to subject Hydro's decisions to independent judgment. Until this is done, the public image of an institution of which Ontarians have been justly proud will continue to be unnecessarily tarnished by criticism and controversy.

An MPP's visit to underground at a Sudbury mine. I am in the front row, third from the right.

The Hydro Select Committee observing the "pond" of radio-active mine tailings which, in the early years, contaminated the water courses in the Elliot Lake area.

A breakfast meeting of MPPs, sponsored by the Forest Industries Association in 1979, to discuss the state of the industry. I am centre front.

19
Resources and the North

Politically, northern Ontario is much more like western Canada than the rest of Ontario. It is the province's remaining frontier. The pioneering spirit prevails. Long before southern Ontario achieved its current multicultural mix, the North had many people from different races and nationalities, people who, as newcomers, weren't so imbued with Ontario traditions.

These circumstances created a free spirit, which was all the greater because of a persistent sense of alienation from the south, particularly Toronto. The North is a hinterland, whose economic development is often under the control of corporations directed from Bay Street or a foreign country. Too often, the interests of northern communities and their people have been neglected, not only by the absentee owners, but also by government policies that do not insist on a fair share of the wealth remaining in the North.

Not surprisingly, therefore, the North has always been fertile ground for the CCF/NDP. In fact, when the CCF was almost swept into minority government status in 1943 all but one of the seats north of the French River were in its ranks. And while the fortunes of the party have ebbed and flowed over the past forty years, the North has always remained one of its power bases.

As a native of western Canada, whose roots had been strengthened by CCF organizational work in northern Ontario and the western provinces, my interest in the problems of the North has always prevailed.

There is a quality to life in the North that is captivating. For me a visit was always an inspiration. The warmth of its people was an open invitation to return. It is easy to forget the range and magnitude of its problems — yes, even its isolation — in the face of the lingering romance of a frontier. Disappointment and failure are overshadowed by the excitement of new prospects.

For centuries, northern Ontario stood as a barrier — a vast wilderness of lakes and trees and rocks stretching for a thousand miles, from Manitoba to the Quebec border, separating the West from eastern Canada. Early explorers found this barrier so formidable that they often avoided it by travelling south through the United States, or north through Hudson Bay. When the foundations of Canada were laid at Confederation, we sought to knit the nation by ribbons of steel — the railways, whose construction through the rocky terrain of northern Ontario presented a challenge, exceeded only by the massive barrier of the Rockies.

In this century, however, northern Ontario has become the link binding this country, rather than a vast wilderness dividing it. The expanse of trees and rocks has proven to be a vast treasure house of minerals. New mines and boom towns spring up: years ago it was Sudbury, Kirkland Lake and Cobalt, Steep Rock and Red Lake; later it was Terrace Bay, Marathon and Manitouwadge; then Elliot Lake and Texas Gulf; today, Hemlo. The airplane has brought the hinterland within reach. The Trans-Canada transformed bush roads into a modern highway. The availability of natural gas and hydroelectric power means potential development of secondary industries based on natural resources, raising the prospect of holding the young people, rather than forcing them to leave for the south and west.

In 1957 MPPs from all parties were exposed to the lure of the North, by touring some of its expanse. For those from the south, it was an eye-opener — both the vastness of the land and the excitement of new settlements that sprang into existence overnight. Members of the forestry staff in Cochrane challenged us with the query: Where is the geographic centre of Ontario? The answer left us momentarily speechless: it lies a hundred or more miles northwest of Kapuskasing!

Most memorable was the story of Elliot Lake. For centuries it had been known only to the trapper and the prospector who passed by; or to the fisherman who flew in and departed. Then uranium was discovered by Franc Joubin. Touring MPPs found in 1957 a population of fifteen thousand, with the prospect of a city of twenty-five thousand, all springing into being before their eyes. It was an indescribable picture of construction companies laying sewers, mapping out streets, and building houses, hotels and shopping centres. Three townsites were rising from the rocks and sand. Belying the appearance of confusion was modern planning of the whole development: gasoline stations alloted by auction; land within three hundred feet of the lake reserved for public parkland. The schools closed in June with seven hundred pupils and eighteen teachers. They opened in September with a thousand pupils and twenty-seven teachers. A little building on the main street proclaimed itself as "Elliot Lake Laundry," and beneath the sign, in equally bold lettering, "Established Since 1956."

That's how things happened in the North. It was a learning experience for established southerners.

While the potential benefits of the North leapt out at the southern visitor, less obvious was how that potential would be frustrated by government policies, and promises that were solemnly repeated election after election but remained unfulfilled for decades. I vividly recall one example, concerning roads, from a fifteen-day personal tour in September 1957, immediately following the MPPs' visit.

Hornepayne was a railway town, with no road link to the provincial highway network. The truly remarkable fact was that the community of seventeen hundred had more than five hundred registered vehicles. In spite of three dead-end roads that led nowhere, there was a higher percentage of cars per capita than elsewhere in Ontario. Residents of Hornepayne had to put their automobiles on railroad flat cars for transportation to Longlac, to gain access to the provincial highway system.

How did the three dead-ends occur? Thereby hangs an illustrative tale. As far back as 1927 a first start was made on a road destined to connect with White River to the south. No more than a few miles were completed, and for thirty years the people of Hornepayne had the questionable pleasure of driving out to this dead-end in the bush.

A second start was made during the Depression, in 1932 — this time heading north to Hearst. The road was completed for only eleven miles; the outer half was used by forest rangers to reach a watch tower, while the first five miles provided a second dead-end in the bush.

In 1957 the people of Hornepayne were being tantalized with a third project, linking the community to Highway 11, some thirty miles west of Hearst. In four years, the Department of Highways completed only nine miles. The excuse offered for 1956 was that wet weather had interfered, so that only four miles had been built. But in 1957, with one of the best construction seasons, only one mile had been completed. An explicit promise to build the road connection had been made by Premier Frost, while speaking in Geraldton back in 1954.

"The government is merely toying with the project," I commented. "So much so that the road dominates, to the exclusion of every other issue, the political thinking of the community. . . . To make matters worse, it is obvious that an exorbitant amount of money is being spent to build these few miles each year. This is not a serious road project; it has all the earmarks of being a local pork barrel," in a riding that has been consistently held by the CCF.

"Politicians have often been accused of leading the voters up the garden path, but a new variation has been added," I suggested to a local audience. "At Hornepayne, the Frost government has led them out into the muskeg, and left them bogged down there."

Because the economy of the North is resource-based, it has all the excitement of discovery and development, so often followed by a slow death, as the resource is depleted. With mining, there is a certain inevitability about that process, because the resource is not renewable. But that need not be the case with forestry because, with government policies that insist on intelligent harvesting, the resource would be available in perpetuity. From the outset I was obsessed with the folly of the destructive handling of our forest resources.

Repeatedly, since the turn of the century, the ruthless exploitation of the forest industry had been studied by provincial governments, but never more so than in the years just before my entry into Ontario politics. In 1947, a royal commission headed by General Howard Kennedy warned of what was happening. Kennedy stated that his recommendations might come as "a shock to those who are well-satisfied with forestry matters as they are," but added, "I believe that such people need a shock."

He stressed that the timber resources of Ontario were within a generation of complete destruction. He condemned single-purpose cutting, and urged that operators be compelled to exchange pulpwood for sawlogs, railway ties, mining timbers and poles. Because it was more convenient, saw logs were often put through the chipper by the pulpwood companies. "The lack of cooperative effort is unsound and costly," the report asserted.

Kennedy's observations regarding regeneration were equally scathing. He pointed out that there were between two and a half and five million acres of crown land which had been stripped of forest cover by the timber barons of yesteryear; it now lay as an economic wasteland, with the responsibility for reforestation reverting to the crown. Faced with this situation, the minister of lands and forests attempted to impress by declaring that twenty- four million trees were being planted per year. However, fifteen million of those were provided for private planting, leaving only nine million for crown lands. I pointed out that at one hundred trees per acre, the minimum two and a half million acres awaiting reforestation would require 250 million trees. At the pace of the government's program, it would take nearly thirty years to complete the job.

Despite Kennedy's solemn warnings, the response was no more than token gestures of conservation and regeneration, by either the government or the big corporations. Our forest resources were, I contended, being slaughtered into extinction. The CCF accepted the Kennedy report's proposed forest policy. It recommended that the crown reclaim all the timber limits leased to private companies; publicly owned operating companies be set up in the twelve principal forest areas of the province; and these operating companies be responsible for all cutting and directing of raw material to existing and new forest industries, in accordance with their needs. Existing mills would be assured of timber supplies, without excluding the special needs of new companies. In this way, expansion of the forest industry would not be restricted by the monopoly holdings of timber licensees. The result would be an effective forest management policy, assuring the government and the people of Ontario of scientific cutting, and adequate regeneration and reforestation.

In 1954, another study revealed how little progress had been made in the seven years since the Kennedy report. The government tabled a White Paper on Forest Policy — a white paper which, I asserted, should have been edged in black. "It is estimated that the present stands of white and red pine will last for seventeen years at even the present small cut," the white paper stated. "It will have taken less than a century to deplete the once-great pineries of the Ottawa-Huron region in Ontario to the vanishing point. . . . Unless remedial measures are taken, the saw-milling industry in Ontario will dwindle to insignificant proportions within the next couple of decades."

The white paper emphasized that the same forces were at work destroying our pulp resources — too rapid a removal of virgin stands, and a lack of regeneration on an adequate scale:

> It should be pointed out that, on a sustained yield basis, the allowable depletion is declining, for the valuable softwood species, which are being utilized far in excess of their proportion in the forest. Three-quarters of all pulpwood cut in Ontario is spruce, while this species forms much less than fifty percent of the total allowable cut. . . .
>
> From the above analysis and having regard for the valuable softwood species it is apparent that we can only provide for the present requirements and normal expansion for a period of twenty years. After that period,

industry will become increasingly dependent on currently immature stands and regrowth on cut-over areas.

Forest policy had been a major concern during the first eighteen months of my leadership. When I was elected, the stage
was set for carrying the battle from the hustings into the
Legislature. And with good reason, if, according to independent assessment, within seventeen years our lumber industry
would be nearly gone and within twenty years our pulpwood
industry would exhaust our present stands.

Throughout these years the government was fumbling its
way toward a forest management program. In 1953, with
amendments to the Crown Timber Act, all timber licensees
were absolved of any obligation for regeneration on lands
previously cut over; this became the crown's responsibility.
Henceforth, in theory, each company was obligated to assure
regeneration on the area of its annual cut. But the government was unable to lay down standards, so the policy was
inoperative.

In 1958, the minister contended, "We now have the basic
plan. . . . We are in the process of getting ready to sign yearly
agreements [with each company] on what shall or shall not
be done in a given area. We have agreed on a principle of one
year contracts, and the companies have agreed to go along
with us."

However, it took another four years before the basic plan
was implemented, and its inadequacies became obvious. All
licence holders with fewer than fifty square miles still were
not obliged to regenerate their timber. The government
accepted this, thereby adding to the wasteland. For licence
holders with more than fifty square miles, an annual agreement was required. But two years after the government
announced this new policy, agreements had been signed with
only two of the more than two hundred companies in this
category.

"In short," I stated to the annual meeting of the southern
Ontario section of the Institute of Foresters, "our reforestation program is so inadequate that we are not catching up on

the backlog created by past failure to implement modern forest management programs. And to make matters worse, we are still not implementing such programs, so that we are adding to the proportions of our problems every year. . . . The heritage of future generations is being destroyed through neglect and failure.''[1]

Despite the "new" program, requiring private companies to accept responsibility for regeneration, their record was deplorable. My colleague, Ted Freeman, member for Fort William, asked how many trees were grown and planted by the companies. The answer made a mockery of the government's contention that it had finally developed an effective forest management program. Four of the major companies — Great Lakes Paper, Marathon, Abitibi Ontario and Minnesota — had planted absolutely none. Spruce Falls Power and Paper had planted 1,022,000, and Kimberley-Clark, 1,182,000. Thus, the total on reforestation by private industry was just over two million.

"There are no government policies to protect the forest heritage of the North," I asserted in 1964. "Until the people of the North demand that the government quit pretending, and take meaningful action, your heritage will continue to be depleted. With mining, this is inevitable, but with renewable forest resources, it is tragic."

Mining is the other resource base of the northern Ontario economy, and it too was in a period of decline. There had been a steady growth, until production reached the billion dollar mark, but then decline set in. Uranium was the real problem, because the boom prospects of the 1950s had faded. There were fillips, such as the discovery of the Texas Gulf ore body in the Timmins area, but a growing malaise throughout the industry had lowered production to $900 million. The government was sufficiently concerned that, in 1964, it set up a select committee to investigate what might be done to revive the industry.

Part of the problem lay with the leaders of the mining companies. Just as the timber barons had been willing to destroy the basis of their industry through failure to assure regeneration of their renewable resource, mining magnates were increasingly using the wealth they had taken out of northern Ontario to diversify their portfolios, while neglecting exploration. Recent years had witnessed a rash of efforts by mining companies to take over other industries. Consolidated Denison bought a cement company; and then, of all things, a bakery. The Rio Tinto group bought Atlas Steel. The Dorado Uranium Mining Company assigned its contract to somebody else, and then moved down to the Bahamas, where it bought out a gambling establishment.

The trend continued, to a point where voices within the industry began to sound the alarm. Early in 1967, speaking to the Institute of Mining and Metallurgy, Duncan R. Derry, a Toronto mining consultant and former vice president of Rio Tinto, warned that the industry was relying on a backlog of mineral deposits found prior to 1930. An average of only four and a half new ore bodies justifying production were being found each year. "I am afraid that we will wake up one morning and find that suddenly there are no new ore bodies to bring into production," Mr. Derry warned.

The problem didn't end there. It extended from exploration to development. All across northern Ontario there were proven ore bodies. Often they had been found by prospectors who didn't have the capital for development, so they were ready victims for being bought out by an operating mining corporation, which then sat on the new find until it suited the economies of their particular operations to start production. The result was that mining communities often degenerated into ghost towns, while deposits sat idly by. The classic case in 1967 was Geraldton, which faced increasing economic difficulty because of the closing of the gold mines, while two proven ore bodies just north of the town remained undeveloped; or the nickel deposits at Shebandowan, west of Thunder Bay, which had been acquired by Inco, and held in reserve.

"The New Democratic Party does not believe that a mining corporation has a right to sit on proven ore bodies," I reminded my colleagues on the provincial council. "Nor has a timber licensee the right to sit on great timber limits, when other companies are willing and anxious to enter into production.''

Faced with the same situation in 1965, the Province of Quebec established the Societé Québécoise d'Exploration Minière (or Soquem, as it was popularly known). In its first year it concluded eleven partnership agreements with companies, involving capital from France, Germany, Japan, the United States and Canada. In addition, Soquem had initiated twenty-six individual exploration ventures on its own. The president of Soquem admitted that there was some hostility to their operations. ''They don't like us, because we are playing in their field. But we feel ours is a more systematic and economical means of carrying out explorations. . . . We are not in competition with private enterprise; we complement the private sector. Companies came to us. We did not need to go looking for partners.''

In its first annual report, Soquem indicated that the crown corporation was seriously considering an extension of its activities from exploration into actual development, because more money could be available for exploration from the profits of producing properties. ''In general terms, this is precisely the kind of proposal which the New Democratic Party is advocating for Ontario,'' I stated, in commenting on the select committee's investigations as to how the mining industry could be revived. ''Where private companies are doing a job, they need have no fear that either the company or its workers will find their status altered one iota. The aim is to supplement the efforts of private enterprise so that Ontario's vast mineral resources can be more fully developed.''

There was another aspect of the mining industry that was a source of public irritation and political controversy. Traditionally, the industry had been the political favourite at Queen's Park, enjoying tax benefits not granted to any other sector. In 1965, for example, when mining production was hovering in the range of a billion dollars, the total mining taxes collected by the provincial government were $14.8 million. This mining revenue — technically a mines profit tax — covered two things: first, the rental paid by the mining corporation for use of the resource legally owned by the people, the equivalent of stumpage dues in the forest industry; and secondly, the equivalent of municipal taxes, from which the industry was exempted. From the revenue the government gave a grant in lieu of taxes to the municipality.

The inequity of this extraordinary procedure was dramatically revealed in 1965. Of the $14.8 million levied in mines profit taxes, only $5.8 million went to municipalities, and the people of Ontario were short-changed by netting only $9 million in "rental" for the exploitation of their resources. At the same time, Inco's profit after taxes had been running in excess of $100 million for years.

"In reality, it is little more than a licence to carry on business," I hammered away on the hustings. "Meanwhile, at the municipal level, other businesses and the homeowner have to pick up the tab for underwriting municipal services. It's an incredible situation, when you stop to think about it: the little man paying a good proportion of the big corporation's municipal taxes!"[2]

The inequity of the tax structure became a major political concern in the 1960s, leading to the federal Carter Commission, and the provincial Smith Committee. The Carter Commission was devastating in its comments on the mining industry. Mining corporations had enjoyed a complete write-off of all prospecting, exploration and development costs as a deductible item in calculating corporation tax. They also had generous depreciation allowances on machinery, equipment and buildings. New mines enjoyed a corporation tax holiday for the first three years of operation. Furthermore, they could defer claiming depreciation and pre-production costs for these years, so that further write-offs were available as soon as the three-year tax holiday was over. Due to this, many mining corporation were, in effect, tax-free for up to ten years.

The Carter Commission recommended a complete elimination of depletion allowances and the three-year holiday on corporation taxes, because they "appear to us to be not only more generous than is necessary to compensate for any risk factor but are, in addition, inappropriate and inefficient incentives."[3]

However, the Carter Commission provided a balance for the companies with a second recommendation: to permit an accelerated write-off of all costs, including the cost of acquiring properties, depreciable assets and development cost. "The operator of a mine or oil well would therefore pay little until he has recovered all his costs. After that point, there is no reason why his income should not be taxed to the full," Carter stated.

The mining industry mounted a lobby that nullified the Carter recommendations. They were assisted in the process by their partners in the media. On 6 May 1967, the Sudbury *Star* dismissed the NDP's espousal of the Carter recommendations as "typical socialist hogwash." And the inequities continued.

The New Democratic Party consolidated its years of work on resource issues as the 1967 general election approached. I proclaimed at Kenora, on 29 March 1967 that our program for a development breakthrough in northern Ontario, "will harness the mighty potential of our northern hinterland, the skills and ingenuity of its people, and the industrial possibilities of its communities." Moreover, this was not advanced simply as an election gimmick, but as an integral component of proposals for regional economic development throughout the province. All Ontario, not just the North, was being deprived of the benefits and the wealth which the North could give us.

The key to this development was an efficient network of modern services; the infrastructure to attract secondary industries; good communications by telephone, road, air, and air services; cheap and reliable power, both hydroelectric and natural gas; well-organized and accessible government services; a well-trained and mobile labour force, backed by schools, colleges and retraining centres; adequate health services, more doctors and dentists, public health units, ambulances and anti-pollution measures. "Northern Ontario cannot expect to attract and keep a growing population," I stated, "unless the amenities of life are more fully available: specialized education, sports arenas, cultural and recreational centres, libraries, and so on."

These services would be underpinned with economic development: positive government initiatives through Soquem and the Ontario Development Corporation for new industry, both basic and secondary; up-to-date policies for forest management and regeneration, with licence holders firmly committed to implementation; action to protect water resources from pollution at Red Lake, Dryden, the Lakehead, Elliot Lake and Espanola; reform of provincial-municipal revenues, with realistic resource taxes, to make certain that mining and forest corporations contributed fairly from the wealth they extracted. The NDP also made specific proposals for an air transport company (subsequently realized through Air Ontario), and an overall policy on radio and television, now available in TV Ontario's service to the North.

Political efforts are not always rewarded, but in this instance, they were. This program had a significant impact during the general election. NDP northern representation quadrupled, when Elie Martel, Don Jackson and Bill Ferrier were elected from the northeast, and Jack Stokes from the northwest.

In his final years in office, Premier Robarts moved to bolster the government's position in the North. There were repeated hints of policy changes, suggesting government largesse to come. At a luncheon for northern delegates at a provincial-municipal conference held at the Ontario Science Centre in 1970, the premier made five specific promises: government responsibilities for transportation and mineral resource policy would be centralized in one department; the chief engineer of mines, from the safety branch, would be physically located in the North; northern regional districts in the Department of Highways would be established; the minister of mines, Allan Lawrence, would set up a network of deskmen to report on conditions in each part of the province; and a Northern Ontario Development Corporation would be set up to strengthen the economy of the North.

"Promises of government action aren't all that they're made out to be," I warned in North Bay on 2 May 1970, for the Northern Ontario Development Corporation was charged with the same job that the Ontario Development Corporation had been doing — with unsatisfactory results for the North:

> One is tempted to ask whether these twenty-five new Northern Affairs officers [the Minister's deskmen] will be able to serve the people of the North as well as their information will undoubtedly serve the politicians of the South.
>
> It is clear that no one, least of all the Bay Street lawyer to be ordained as Minister of the North, is going to tackle the most urgent problem of ensuring that this region has a balanced economy, an economy that has important secondary manufacturing enterprises as well as resource exploitation. It is clear, in fact, that despite all the window dressing, and all the administrative shuffling, in the final analysis nothing very much is going to happen to the economy or to the people of the North under a Conservative regime.

It was a warning that did not go unheeded by the electorate in the 1971 election. The NDP added to its northern representation with Jim Foulds from Port Arthur and Floyd Laughren from Nickel Belt.

Developments through the 1970s and into the 1980s are worthy of a volume in themselves. When I left the leadership in 1970, Stephen Lewis picked up on northern matters with great impact. He played a major role in arousing the conscience of the province about the mercury pollution of the water courses of northwestern Ontario by the Reed Paper Company in Dryden, destroying the livelihood of tourist operators and the peoples of the Grassy Narrows and Whitedog Indian bands.

An even greater political storm developed over the government's grant of a licence to Reed Paper, for cutting rights over nineteen thousand square miles of the last sizeable timber limit in the province. So great was the protest that the government appointed a royal commission to investigate the broad range of northern problems. For its first years, Mr. Justice Patrick Hart headed the commission, then dropped out, to be succeeded by J.E.G. Fahlgren. The commission lingered on, at a cost of $12 million, and reported only after the change of government in 1985. By that time, history had swept by it.

In 1981 the Conservatives fought the election on the basis of the so-called Brampton Charter, involving the grandiose commitment "to replacing at least two trees for every one harvested, and to regenerate every acre harvested." It was an extravagant claim, designed to overshadow the abysmal failure to assure regeneration, during all their years in office. It was evident from the outset that it was an idle boast.

So much so, that the NDP caucus launched a comprehensive and detailed study of all important aspects of the forest industry, again a combination of extensive field work and solid research back-up.[3] It revealed that the situation had gone from bad to worse. According to official figures for 1981-82:

— cutting was taking place at a rate of sixty-four acres per hour;
— regeneration was taking place at a rate of twenty-seven acres per hour;
— forest lands were being written off at a rate of thirty-seven acres per hour.

Even more disturbing was the official contention that of the 562,000 acres cut over, 181,000 acres, or 32.21 per cent, were not available for regeneration because of site constraints — that is, too rocky and/or too wet; access constraints — that is, winter cuts which are inaccessible in spring or summer; or utilization constraints — that is, areas with residual stands of trees, which precluded the use of silvicultural equipment. In other words, not only is the economic wasteland of former forest cover being relentlessly expanded, but the government now contends that much of it is unrenewable. Moreover, during the past decade, the percentage of the annual cut deemed to be unavailable for regeneration has risen from 6.54 per cent in 1973-74 to over 30 per cent.

Meanwhile, the government has been wrestling with its umpteenth effort over the decades to develop, and have signed, binding forest management agreements. When the Tories left office in 1985, only twenty-six of the 539 operating licensees had signed agreements, covering 44 per cent of the timber limits.

The nub of the problem is that Ontario's forest resources are effectively controlled by the corporations exploiting them, not by the government, and there is a basic conflict between the business objectives of these companies and the public interest of protecting a renewable resource. Kennedy recognized this in his 1947 royal commission report when he contended that Ontario forests must be emancipated from the control of the mill executives, and detailed a procedure for its achievement.[5]

But it never happened, and as the Conservatives left office in 1985, the extent to which those corporations were still in control was dramatically revealed. Between 30 May and 12 June the cabinet granted forty-seven cutting licences to 2,337 square kilometres of crown timber. In addition, four management agreements were signed with two giant pulp and paper companies, covering a total of 32,116 square kilometres of boreal forest.

As Rosemary Speirs commented in her Toronto *Star* column from Queen's Park on 22 June 1985:

> Shockingly, two of the forest management agreements are with Great Lakes Forest Products (which had taken over Reed Paper), the company which had for nearly six years been dragging its heels on compensating the Grassy Narrows and Whitedog Indian Bands for the mercury pollution from the company's Dryden mill.

It would be difficult to conceive of a sorrier tale of government and corporate failure than the relentless destruction of Ontario forest resources. One new commitment after another has been made down through the years, only to be broken, and then unashamedly replaced by another.

The reason is simple: nothing fundamental has changed. Forest policy at Queen's Park, for practical purposes, has been made by the licence holders of the timber limits. Periodically, for election purposes, the government has promised tougher enforcement, but invariably those promises are nullified during the implementation process. Meanwhile, a precious renewable resource, basic to the economy of the North, dwindles. The present generation suffers; future generations will suffer even more. From his grave, General Kennedy must be taunting, "I told you so."

Part Three
Reflections

20

Four Tory Premiers

George Drew

My political activities spanned the regimes of the four Tory premiers, who maintained such a formidable dominance of Ontario politics for more than forty-two years. With three of them — Frost, Robarts and Davis — it was something of a personal relationship, because we were contemporaries. But with George Drew I had no relationship; in fact, I met the man only once, fleetingly, when he visited Queen's Park after his retirement, and Frost brought all the party leaders together for a picture.

A review of these associations with the first ministers provides a vehicle for other aspects of Ontario's postwar politics. I begin with Drew, because my first awareness of Ontario politics was in the early years of his ascendancy. As far back as 1937, I was at home on the farm near Ormstown, Quebec, occupied with Queen's extramural studies, when the Ontario general election was taking place. It was the first campaign with extensive radio coverage, and as I listened to broadcasts from eastern Ontario stations, Drew's controversial role was a highlight of the contest between Conservative leader Earl Rowe and Premier Mitch Hepburn. Drew started out as campaign manager for the Tories, but resigned that post and ran as an independent, because he disagreed with Rowe's opposition to Hepburn's ruthless efforts to destroy the emerging autoworkers union in Oshawa.

Six years later, Simone and I were on a bicycle trip during a naval furlough — a belated honeymoon — which coincided with the 1943 election. During a stay at a hotel in Prescott, we got a first hand view of the reaction of the local burghers on election night — delight with the Drew Tories winning thirty-eight seats, but puzzlement, if not consternation, with the little-known socialist party, the CCF, breathing down their necks, with thirty-four seats.

Of course, I followed events of the disastrous provincial election in 1945, albeit from a detached position in the armed services and behind-the-scenes activities with the CCF national office and caucus. Thus, even before getting into full-time party work in 1946, I felt very much a part of the Drew era. Not only did it inaugurate the Tory hegemony, bringing into public life men (but virtually no women) with whom I was subsequently associated, but it established the pattern of the next generation of Ontario politics.

In contrast with the chaos and the drift, which character-ized the latter years of the Hepburn-Conant-Nixon regime, Drew presented economic and social policies, all encapsuled in his twenty-two point program during the 1943 election, which offered some vision for the postwar years. Among other things, these policies illustrated the pragmatic approach of the Tory years, such as the socialization of the Toronto stockyards, to assure farmers of a fairer price for their produce.

It was Drew's idiosyncrasies which are too often forgotten. They were reflective of old prejudices and tactics which thankfully, have faded, if not disappeared. He was never a strong party man; he consorted with the Liberals as much as he worked with his own team, particularly in the early years. Not only did he break with his leader in the 1937 campaign, but there were recurring efforts to establish a coalition with the Liberals.

Some of the motivation arose from a conviction, shared with Hepburn, that the federal Liberal government was not pur-suing the war with adequate vigour. That concern resulted in an unprecedented motion in 1940, introduced by Hepburn and seconded by Drew, sharply criticizing the war effort. The motion had sensational consequences: Prime Minister Macken-zie King seized upon it to call a snap election, which returned his government. Nevertheless, the federal Liberal party was so outraged by the betrayal by one of its provincial sections that, for years, it hamstrung the provincial party, financially and organizationally. Ultimately, the provincial Liberals escaped from the federal domination only by setting up a separate party, but not until the late 1970s.

Drew's obsession with coalition was much more deep-seated. He had a close working ally in George McCullough, then publisher of the *Globe and Mail*, who promoted throughout the 1930s his so-called Leadership League, which sought to bring both old parties together. Drew shared McCullough's views, even though they represented a radical departure from traditional party politics and the peacetime operation of the British parliamentary system, of which he normally was a fierce champion.

Kelso Roberts, long-time Tory cabinet minister, has provided another interesting glimpse of the close working relationship of the two old party leaders. In 1942, when the Conservative party was pulling itself together after the devastation wrought on it by Hepburn, and a conference had been held in Port Hope to work out new policies and strategy, Roberts records, "He [Drew] called a meeting of his members of the Legislature and defeated Conservative candidates in the previous election at the Military Institute, University Avenue, Toronto. We were discussing problems when an unexpected guest, in the person of Hon. Mitchell Hepburn, was escorted into the caucus by George Drew. We then got some off-the-record views of Mitch on the federal Liberal leader and some other topics."[1]

Rather strange, to put it mildly, particularly since it took place at a time when Tory strength was building, and when Hepburn was losing his grip and about to give way to Arthur Conant.

Drew and Hepburn were political soul-mates for another reason: they shared rabidly anti-communist and anti-labour views; for them, industrial unionism was just a cover for communist infiltration into Ontario. In his memoirs, Kelso Roberts quotes Hepburn as saying on one occasion, "We know what these agitators are up to. We were advised only a few hours ago that they are working their way into labour camps, the pulp mills and our mines. Well, that has got to stop and we are going to stop it. If necessary we will raise an army to do so!"[2] That, of course, is precisely what he did. The Hepburn Hussars were recruited to crush the CIO efforts to establish industrial unionism in Oshawa — all with Drew's public support.

Another persistent theme in Drew politics was his anti-Catholic and anti-French Canada views. When he was appointed organizer for the provincial party in 1936, one of his first tasks was to run a by-election campaign in East Hastings. The dominant issue was Hepburn's legislation to give Catholic schools a fairer share of corporate education taxes. "The whole Conservative campaign was fought on viciously anti-Catholic lines . . . rumours — unauthorized, of course, by the Tories — flew among the doughty farmers of Hastings, claiming that Casa Loma in Toronto was being prepared as a papal residence and that the crowns on highway signs would be replaced by romanish crosses. . . In fact, he [Drew] was said to be responsible for one of the strongest electoral appeals to racial prejudice in modern Canadian history."[3]

Moreover, the anti-French and anti-Catholic theme continued into his premiership, the most outrageous manifestation of it being in his opposition to family allowances. At one time, in the mid-1940s, the Queen's Park grapevine buzzed, as Drew's remarks to a gathering at the Albany Club got a wider circulation. Drew had said, in effect, that he did not favour legislation which would encourage even more "little French Canadian bastards."

The single most important political event in Drew's career was the so-called Gestapo Affair, and his role in the subsequent Lebel Royal Commission investigation. A bit of background: given Hepburn's pathological antipathy to communism and his conviction that unions were the vehicle for communist infiltration, it is not surprising that in the latter years of his regime he set up a special branch in the OPP to investigate communist activities. The branch was closed down in the spring of 1943 — on the instructions of the new premier, Harry Nixon, so it is believed — but it was re-opened in November, three months after Drew took office.

During the 1945 election campaign, OPP Constable Rowe reported through Agnes Macphail, his MPP, to Ted Jolliffe, the CCF leader, on the activities of Osborne Dempster, who ran the special branch. Under the code name D.208 he worked out of an office on the second floor of an old garage at 18 Surrey Place, within the shadow of the legislative buildings. Reports were made to the attorney general on CCF members of the Legislature, on other CCF officials, on union meetings, even on prominent Canadians who had nothing to do with the CCF or unions, such as B.K. Sandwell, editor of *Saturday Night* and Principal R.C. Wallace, of Queen's University. From tracking communists, the special branch had developed into general espionage. Its reports found their way to Gladstone Murray, W.A. Anderson and B.A. Trestrail, self-appointed political hatchet-men, who were engaged in virulent anti-CCF and anti-union campaigns.

On 24 May 1945, less than two weeks before the 4 June provincial vote, CCF leader E.B.Jolliffe gave a broadcast, written by Lister Sinclair (then, as now, a well-known broadcaster), in which he presented the whole situation in dramatic fashion. The key charge was:

Colonel Drew is maintaining in Ontario, at this very minute, a secret political police, a paid government spy organization, a Gestapo to try to keep himself in power.

Of course, Drew angrily denied Jolliffe's accusations, appointed a royal commission of inquiry, and publicly undertook to resign his seat if the commission should find him guilty.

The Lebel inquiry took place with dispatch, after the election, and reported within a few months. In his testimony, Drew not only denied all knowledge of the operations of the special branch, and of the reports of agent D.208, but he professed to have only fleeting social acquaintance with men such as Gladstone Murray. While Lebel's report confirmed the substance of many of Jolliffe's specific charges, it completed cleared Drew and gave the attorney general a mild slap on the wrist.

The scene now shifts ahead forty years. In the preparation of his memoirs, David Lewis, with the assistance of his research director, Dr. Alan Whitehorn (now associate professor in the department of political and economic science at the Royal Military College in Kingston), revealed more of the story from the Drew Papers in the Public Archives of Canada. Only restricted access was available to those papers, but researchers could draw specific files, in connection with other research projects. Knowing precisely what they wanted, they drew files, such as those on Gladstone Murray, and got a fuller picture of the operations of the special branch, indicating how the reports of D.208 had gone to the attorney general, some of them to the premier, and all of them to the anti-CCF propagandists. Furthermore, there were letters indicating Drew and Murray had been on a first-name basis for years.

David Lewis concluded, "We found that Premier Drew and Gladstone Murray did not disclose all the information to the Lebel Commission; indeed, they deliberately prevaricated throughout. The head of the government of Ontario had given false witness under testimony. . . . The perpetrator of Ontario's Watergate got away with it."[4]

When the Lewis memoirs were published in 1981, with this explosive chapter, tongue in cheek I asked Attorney General Roy McMurtry, whether, in view of the revelations on the Gestapo Affair, he would care to correct the record. Not surprisingly, the Tory response was that all sides of the story had not been told, implying that Lewis's revelations were coloured by partisan bias. It is true, of course, that the full story is not available. Nor will it be for some years. After Lewis's revelations, Drew's son Edward (who has authority over his father's papers), placed total restrictions on their availability. As a result, Professor J.L. Granatstein, who had undertaken the Drew biography for the Ontario Historical Studies Series, has had to forsake the project. As the *Globe and Mail* lamented in a lead editorial, it is regrettable that the official papers of so important a personage should be denied to the public until 1998, or beyond.

However, what David Lewis did reveal cannot be disputed: it is based on documents in the Drew Papers to which he got access, and it proves beyond a shadow of doubt that Drew did lie in his submission to the Lebel Commission; that he did give false testimony under oath, and therefore, that he committed perjury. The Tory grip on Ontario was consolidated in a campaign highlighted by this kind of conduct. It wasn't the finest hour of their forty-two-year rule.

I have a final recollection of George Drew, more first-hand in nature. After securing the federal Tory leadership, Drew fought a by-election in the Ottawa-area riding of Carleton. I was on staff at the CCF national office, and played a small part in the campaign. The CCF candidate was the redoubtable Eugene Forsey. Following the filing of papers on nomination day, the tradition in Carleton County was to hold a so-called "contradictory" meeting with all the candidates, at a centrally located hall in the village of Richmond. The audience packed the accommodation, as loyal supporters in this traditionally Tory riding flocked out to launch their new leader's campaign.

Tradition called for the candidates to speak first, followed by an eminent supporter. The Liberals had not nominated, so it was a straight Tory/CCF contest. John Bracken was Drew's back-up, and the CCF had brought in Bill Temple, newly elected MPP, who had defeated George Drew in High Park. Appropriately, Drew was seated on the extreme right of the platform, and Bill Temple on the left. Other platform guests were Don Morrow, provincial MPP for Carleton; Lorne Ingle, CCF federal secretary who was Forsey's campaign manager; and Drew's wife, Fiorenza. By the toss of a coin, the CCF was to speak first.

I was outside, milling around with crowds, which followed the proceedings by peering through the door and windows. But Lorne Ingle, a long-time CCF/NDP colleague, provided a blow-by-blow description from inside. Forsey spoke first. The crowd was angry and annoyed at the very idea of an upstart CCF running. In vain, Eugene attempted to ingratiate himself with the Tory crowd by some friendly remarks about one of his heroes, former Tory leader Arthur Meighen. He started to tell a story about Meighen and his dog. Somehow the idea spread through the audience that he was likening Meighen to a dog, and angry heckling developed. The more

Eugene tried to explain his story, with voice rising to a higher and higher pitch, the angrier the crowd became.

When Bill Temple rose to speak, in keeping with his life-long prohibition crusade, he castigated Drew for being a "tool of the liquor interests." Those interests, Temple contended, had been trying for a long time to get a man they could manipulate in the seat of power, and had been frustrated by teetotalling figures like R.B. Bennett, Mackenzie King and Robert Manion. Now they were on the verge of success with Drew.

Throughout it all, Drew became more red-faced and explosive. For understandable reasons, the very presence of Temple nearly drove him wild. When his turn to speak came, he was shaking with anger. He launched into a diatribe about Bill Temple being a carpetbagger, who had no business coming down from Toronto to tell the solid citizens of Carleton how they should vote. At each of two or three such attacks, Temple stood up in his place, smiled and bowed. This infuriated Drew further. In resuming his seat following one of these attacks, Bill Temple said: "I'm honoured."

Drew thought he had said: "I'm honest." He turned, and waving an accusing finger, shouted, "Honest? Why, there isn't an honest bone in your body!!" This was too much even for Temple. He stood up and moved towards Drew who, at this point, had his fists drawn. Don Morrow stepped in between them. Lorne Ingle grabbed Temple by the arm, and headed for the back door on the stage, while John Bracken took hold of Drew. The meeting came to a sudden and inglorious end. Bracken never had an opportunity to speak. Some of those involved were afraid that a donnybrook would develop, but the situation cooled and there were no casualties. I can vouch for that from my mingling with the dispersing crowd.

I do not pretend to have presented a balanced view of Drew, but these are documented accounts of certain aspects of his policies, and particularly of his political practices, which have tended to become lost in the public image of the man that now prevails. They can be placed in a more balanced perspective when the Drew Papers are unlocked for future research.

Leslie Miscampbell Frost

There were many Leslie Frosts. One, the most familiar to the public, was the grandfather figure, usually viewed from afar, but seen in closer proximity only at meetings or on television, rarely attacking his political opponents, but rather chatting about local history and the merits of the province of Ontario in general, and his government in particular.

Another was the charmer, who subjected visiting delegations, individually and collectively, to a process of political seduction that became legendary. I can recall countless occasions when delegations would visit the opposition party leaders after seeing the premier, and it was as though they were just coming out of a trance. They had gone to see him, loaded for bear, with complaints and demands. Invariably, they were greeted with warm hand-shakes, softened with the friendly arm-around-the-shoulder confidentiality, and out-talked from start to finish. They emerged in a soft glow of promises and commitments, which gradually melted away as they returned to the real world. Their reactions ranged from "it was a pleasant meeting," to "we were conned." I dubbed him the Great Tranquilizer.

Then there was the real Leslie Frost, the patriarch who dominated the political scene, who could ruthlessly discipline an errant cabinet minister, and who ran a one-man government and legislative show. I was both the victim and the beneficiary of the many facets of the personality of this master politician.

Frost had enjoyed an extended political honeymoon in the four years between the 1951 and 1955 elections. The CCF had been reduced to two members; the Liberals were a demoralized, leaderless and ineffective official opposition; all of the domineering qualities of the premier were unchecked. Frost came to believe that the opposition was as malleable and submissive as his own backbenchers and cabinet. When, after 1955, I insisted on presenting a tough opposition, even though it had to be very much of a "one-man-band," he didn't like it. That wasn't the way things were done in the Ontario Legislature.

On the other hand, he could be ingratiating. Operating on the unfounded rumour that I had once been a Conservative, he periodically reminded me that "the light is always in the window," to lead the wandering sheep back into the fold. In spite of our political differences, which produced some raucous exchanges, there was a civility in our personal relationship that sometimes went to surprising lengths. For example, we shared an interest in local history. Shortly after my entry into the Legislature, I sent over, for his perusal, a copy of my M.A. thesis on Richard Cartwright. Cartwright was a United Empire Loyalist who came to Canada in 1778 and settled in Kingston. In partnership with Robert Hamilton, whose son George founded the city of that name, he became a well-known merchant throughout the inland waterway. He was often irked by his shiftless brother-in-law, the husband of Laura Secord. He brought out from Scotland, as tutor for his children, a young Scot named John Strachan, who became an influential figure in the church and political circles of the colony; and as a member of Upper Canada's first legislative council, he opposed many of John Graves Simcoe's rather fanciful notions about building Britain anew in the wilds of North America.

For Frost, this was captivating. In his inimitable way, he instructed me to have it published. I pursued the idea but no publisher responded. A year later I discovered that he had appropriated $5,000 and directed the provincial archivist to publish a volume of *Three History Theses* on early Ontario, one of them being mine. Furthermore, a copy was placed in every school and university library. So twenty years after I had written my thesis, it was published and given province-wide circulation by the very person with whom I was engaged in vigorous political battles!

Frost's capacity for warm personal relationships extended into the most unexpected quarters. One day I saw him walking down the hallway past the legislative assembly doors, arm over shoulder, in confidential discussion with a certain well-known figure. Could it possibly be? Yes, it was Joe Salsberg, the long-time Communist member of the Legislature, who had been defeated in the previous election. The average Ontarian would never have believed it: a Tory premier in genial embrace, and friendly discussion, with a communist.

The fact is, however, that Joe Salsberg, and his communist running mate, A.A. McLeod (who had been defeated in 1951) were two of the ablest parliamentarians of the times. When they left the Communist party, they were accepted in Toronto society. Joe Salsberg, to this day, is a respected member of the Jewish community, and Alex McLeod became an elder statesman around Queen's Park, first surviving financially by securing government contracts for a printing firm; later becoming editor of the government publication, *Human Rights*, and eventually becoming a member of the staff of the Education Department. He was a wise counsellor for many who sought his advice, and most unbelievable of all, he was a periodic speech writer for two Tory premiers, Leslie Frost and John Robarts.

Frost's dominance in the Legislature became legendary. It was as though there were two sets of rules — one for him, and one for the rest of the House. If he wished to intervene, he simply rose and took over. This was accepted by his own members, including those in the cabinet, and was tolerated by the Speaker. Periodically, there were protests from opposition members, but even they lived with his breach of parliamentary procedures, partly because they were powerless to stop it, and partly out of gratitude that what they had to say was worthy of attention from the premier.

Yet there were exceptions. On one occasion when A.W. (Wally) Downer, an Anglican priest who was a well-known figure around Queen's Park and the Royal York Hotel for his poker games, was the Speaker, Frost rose to take over. For whatever reason, Mr. Speaker was not in a mood that day to permit this breach of procedure, and he quietly, but firmly, asserted that a certain other member had the floor, and requested that the honourable member for Victoria take his seat. He had to repeat the instruction, to the astonished disbelief of all present. Gradually it dawned on Frost that he was being denied the floor, and he wilted back into his chair.

On another occasion — the only one of its kind that I ever witnessed — a cabinet minister wouldn't permit the premier to take over. That minister was Dr. Matthew (Matt) Dymond. A feisty Scot, the most eloquent speaker in the cabinet, he was well launched into the presentation of the estimates of the Department of Reform Institutions, his first portfolio, when something he said caught Frost's attention. In his usual way, he simply rose to preempt the floor. Instead of giving way, as ministers invariably did when the Great Man intervened, Matt Dymond rather imperiously waved the premier down, and forged ahead with his own remarks. Frost quickly realized that to persist would create an embarrassing situation, so again, he quietly slumped into his seat.

Perhaps the best example of Frost's view of the rules was unwittingly provided by the premier himself. One day I came to the House well prepared to argue an issue. My desk was piled with volumes of Hansard, parliamentary rule books and other documentation. The ammunition was clearly visible, but Frost forestalled any debate by saying that he had a story for me. On one occasion, he said, a certain circuit judge was holding court in Killaloe, a small town in Renfrew County. A young lawyer arrived, laden with legal tomes, obviously prepared for a long and detailed exposition of the law. But the judge intervened, saying to the eager counsel, "You've researched all the law, but there's one thing you've forgotten: It isn't the law in Killaloe!" For some time the Law of Killaloe was part of the folklore of the Ontario Legislature. Whenever Frost arbitrarily took over, there were jeers from the opposition that he was invoking the Law of Killaloe.

What puzzled me most about Frost was his willingness to mislead the public by skirting the whole truth, or by simply not acknowledging the truth, even when it had become known. As has been noted, not once, but three times, he told the House that Mines Minister Kelly's resignation had nothing to do with NONG stock promotion. As with Drew's prevarication on the whole Gestapo Affair, he got away with it. There was an aura of untouchability about Tory leaders in those days, which resulted in the public giving them the benefit of the doubt.

In 1959 Frost campaigned for the re-election of the two cabinet ministers, whose resignations he had demanded because they continued to hold NONG stock, after he had ordered its disposition. He described them as "honourable men," guilty of nothing more than an "indiscretion." It was he who had caused the embarrassment they had suffered, yet he chastised opposition spokesmen for pursuing the issue, and adding to the anguish of them and their families. Interestingly, in this instance, the electorate did not respond favourably; both were defeated.

Of course, every misdemeanour, no matter how great and of what nature, was automatically wiped out if the party was returned in the next election. The highest jury in the land had spoken. For a lawyer — indeed, for a man of unquestioned personal integrity — it was a strange posture. He had a double moral standard: virtually anything that advanced the party interests was acceptable, particularly if it could be done without public scrutiny.

Ultimately, Frost's political astuteness was nowhere greater than in his sense, as the decade of the 1950s closed, that it was time for him to go. An added incentive came with the death in 1960 of A.D. McKenzie, the key figure on his political team — indeed, the man who had been the party's organizational genius for twenty-five years.

McKenzie had been a working colleague of George Drew when Drew was on Guelph city council, latterly as mayor. He had masterminded the Drew leadership campaign in 1938 to a first ballot victory, in spite of Drew's break with the party and its leader in the election campaign the previous year. When Drew switched to federal politics, McKenzie played the kingmaker role, by switching his allegiance to Leslie Frost. Throughout the Frost years, McKenzie, as president of the Progressive Conservative Association, with his formidable network of contacts, remained the second most powerful political figure in the province. Now he was gone, and Frost was very much alone.

Personal factors also played a part. Frost's war wounds were plaguing him increasingly; the stoop in his walk became more pronounced. Most important of all, the growing complexity of government made his one-man style of operation less and less feasible. The growing urbanization of the province rendered his view of public affairs "from the barber's chair in Lindsay" increasingly out of date.

So he left politics. The inevitable range of corporate directorships came his way, among them one of the major banks. I remember meeting him in the hall at Queen's Park a few years later. Two of his comments remain as fresh as yesterday.

Speaking of the business world, "You have no idea," he said, "how ignorant these boys are about how governments operate." I could just see the Old Fox sitting at the end of a board-room table, listening to his fellow directors berating Queen's Park, and advising a frontal attack. "Hold it a moment," Les would caution, "that's not the way to go about it." And his advice would likely be worth the thousands a year he was drawing.

His second comment was even more significant. "You know, Donald," he said, "when I come in here, I don't feel at home. Things have so changed . . . ." He got out of politics because he felt that a new world, which he didn't quite understand, was overtaking him. For a man who had literally ruled Queen's Park for twelve years, it was a little sad.

John Parmenter Robarts

In October 1961 John Parmenter Robarts succeeded Leslie Frost as leader of the Progressive Conservative party. Four years earlier, Farquhar Oliver had relinquished the leadership of the Liberal party for the second time (and would do so a third time in the 1960s), and John Wintermeyer took over. With these two developments, I suddenly realized that I was dean of the leaders in the Ontario Legislature. With only six years seniority, I was the oldest of the pack! Such is the mortality rate in politics.

Robarts had been an MPP for ten years, and for more than half that time I had shared membership in the House with him. Relations with him were on a more personal basis than those I had with the other three premiers.

In 1955, the year I entered the Legislature, Robarts was chairman of a select committee on toll roads and highway finance. I was a member of that committee. Its deliberations went on for the better part of two years, with hearings not only at Queen's Park, but in many areas of Ontario, as well as in American states which had resorted to toll roads.

Select committees provided a rare opportunity for building relationships. The day-to-day routine of the House permits of little more than normal business. Because my home was in Toronto, I did not have the same opportunity as many of the out-of-towners had to socialize with other members in off-hours. But on a select committee there were countless hours, while travelling, or sitting around hotels, to get to know other members of the committee on a personal basis. That was my privilege with John Robarts, during my first years in the House.

I recall, for example, one occasion when we boarded the train in Fort Frances sometime after midnight. Six of us crowded into the leather-seated smoker at the end of the car on that inimitable "push-and-pull." Two or three came with bottled libations. Matters of high state — and others not so high — were thrashed through frankly, and vigorously. When we arrived in Atikokan, after four o'clock in the morning, I felt I knew John Robarts much better, and I venture that he felt he knew me better.

In addition, Robarts and I were both "graduates" of the navy and, I always felt, shared the particular bond of veterans. Not that it reduced one iota our political and ideological differences, but it did create a relationship, which permitted a more civilized working out of the inevitable partisan differences.

Robarts was sharply different from both his predecessor and his successor in that he was not, first and foremost, a politician. He was the quintessential management man. He much preferred governing to politicking. That resulted — not always, but generally — in a lower temper in consideration of issues. He viewed his role as that of chairman of the board of the biggest business in the province, the people's business. If there was a problem, he set up a royal commission, or a task force, to study it. If the study confirmed the existence of the problem he tackled it; if not, he lived with the status quo. No change for change's sake but, given the nature of his times, a recognition that change was inevitable, and likely to be faster and greater than ever before. In the process, Robarts stretched conservative ideology to limits which his predecessors would never have contemplated, or tolerated.

In many of the basic elements of Ontario life, significant, even drastic, changes were made. Education was moved to township, and then to county, boards. Regional government reshaped 110-year-old municipal relationships. The process of law reform was launched. In the whole structure of government and its decision-making, the Robarts years saw far-reaching changes made or, at least, initiated.

While Robarts was a solid Tory — no one ever had any reason to believe otherwise — his pragmatic, relatively low-key approach shattered the mould of old Ontario, moving the province from "the personal, rural-dominated, government of Leslie Frost to the professionally administered, urban-dominated regime of William Davis."[5] Others might not have been able to institute such changes, and retain power. Robarts escaped most of the backlash, though his successors suffered it. He escaped because, as many observers have commented, he was often underestimated; his low-profile, no-nonsense, approach did not provoke opposition. For a government whose ideology emphasized non-intervention, he lulled the public into acceptance of the most massive range of intervention by any government in Ontario history.

Robarts's style of government, stripped of much of the usual politicking, had many unusual ramifications. He never courted the press; on the contrary, "the Press Gallery . . . was a grudgingly tolerated nuisance," according to Jonathan Manthorpe, whose opinion was based on his years of experience as a reporter and columnist at Queen's Park.[6] As a result, a more critical style of reporting emerged in "the shift from Frost, who had charmed the press, to Robarts, whose evident distaste for journalists turned many from admirers of the Conservative government to adversaries."[7] As premier, he virtually refused to give TV interviews, contending that editing could misrepresent his position — a puzzling attitude, when, of course, editing is always possible with any medium. "I've been quoted out of context" is a familiar complaint of politicians.

Organization was another victim of Robarts's style. Although he had revealed an interest in, and capacity for, planning and organizing his own campaigns, from university days through municipal politics to provincial elections and his leadership challenge, once he became involved in government his interest in party and organization affairs dropped sharply. This responsibility was left to Ernie Jackson, who had succeeded to the long-term role of A.D. McKenzie.

Jackson, however, proved to be no McKenzie. After the first flush of enthusiasm, stemming from the successful leadership race and the 1963 general election, he failed to give organization the detailed attention it required, a neglect from which the party began to suffer. So much so, that Allan Eagleson, a former Tory MPP and well-known agent for sports figures, ran for the presidency of the provincial association, primarily on the claim that the party organization was badly in need of a shake-up.

Taken in conjunction with Robarts's soured press relations, this deterioration contributed to the drop in Tory support in 1967. The NDP was the beneficiary, with a jump in popular vote from 16 to 26 per cent and a caucus increase from seven to twenty.

On issues, too, there were exceptions to the normal ease with which Robarts introduced change. The most outstanding was the political storm aroused in 1964 by Bill 99, the so-called police state bill. Toward the end of Robarts's premiership, the government suffered from its handling of medicare. His uncharacteristically violent reaction to the federal Liberals' imposition of health insurance, which, he argued, would result in a gross distortion of provincial priorities, became an issue on which the NDP feasted — to the point of winning the Middlesex South by-election, right in Robarts's London backyard.

The premier's interest in the management perspective of

politics fitted the times, with all the problems arising from
a period of unprecedented growth. The province achieved its
first billion dollar budget on the eve of his taking office; by
the mid-1960s it had passed the two billion mark, and has increased more than a billion dollars each year since. In addition, government was becoming infinitely more complex.
There had been a day when issues usually fitted neatly into
the vertical departmentalization, but that day was fast passing.
Too often, important issues overlapped the normal jurisdiction of two, three or four departments.

As a result, ad hoc cabinet committees were set up, bringing the involved departments (now called ministries) together.
That procedure didn't prove satisfactory. I recall a speech in
the mid-1960s by Professor R.R. Krueger of the University
of Waterloo at a Toronto conference called by Economics and
Development Minister Stanley Randall. The account was
highly amusing, but devastatingly critical of ministerial rivalry,
overlapping jurisdiction, and conflicting or postponed
decision-making.

Robarts wrestled with these problems of growth, and finally,
in typical chairman-of-the-board style, appointed the Committee on Government Productivity (COGP) under the chairmanship of his fellow Londoner, John B. Cronyn of Labatts,
with members from business and the civil service. The results
were changes in cabinet committees and establishment of
policy areas which, according to Premier Davis, his successor
as premier, represented "the most comprehensive restructuring of government in this country."[8]

For the latter half of Robarts's tenure, the most outstanding
feature was his gradual emergence as a national statesman.
This stemmed initially from the working relationship, which
he developed with a succession of Quebec premiers from the
Liberals' Jean Lesage to the Union Nationale's Daniel Johnson
and Jean-Jacques Bertrand. Robarts's strong sympathy for
French-Canadian needs and aspirations is one of the
fascinating aspects of his very complex personality. How did
this son of a banker, reared in a community, usually suspicious
if not hostile, toward French Canadians, become instinctively
such a francophile? The always latent, and sometimes blatant,

anti-French attitude of Drew was never evident with Robarts. I suspect it had roots in his passionate espousal of Canadian unity which depends on bridging the two solitudes of Canadian nationhood.

In any case, I personally witnessed the event which was perceived as the launching pad for Robarts's role on the national scene. The Quebec legislative press gallery had invited their counterparts from Queen's Park, along with the party leaders, for a fraternal visit. Robarts's biographer, A.K. McDougall tells the story well:

> Robarts gave the keynote speech on Saturday, 16 June [1963] at a formal dinner thrown by the Quebec government for the visiting Ontarians. It was a carefully prepared, landmark expression of goodwill from the premier and people of Ontario to the government and people of Quebec. Robarts described Confederation as a "partnership in fact, in spirit and in purpose," and, using words loaded with soothing connotations for Quebec nationalists, talked about Ontario and Quebec as contemporary manifestations of the "two nations" that had made Canada great. More practically, he mentioned how the bonds of union between the provinces included a shared common need for greater fiscal resources, currently controlled by Ottawa.
>
> Robarts's act of interprovincial statesmanship surprised and pleased Lesage and members of the Quebec press corps. The Ontario premier seemed to have an unusual willingness to work with Quebec and to understand the type of Confederation Quebec desired.[9]

This speech, in its original draft, was one of those written by Alex McLeod, the former Communist member of the Ontario Legislature. It is certain that much of the spirit of Robarts's appeal on this occasion came from McLeod, but it was a theme for which Robarts had great sympathy, and one that he readily espoused.

The Royal Commission on Bilingualism and Biculturalism (B&B) was meeting during this period. When its first report came out in 1966, within a matter of hours Robarts accepted its basic recommendations in a statement before the Legislature, and set up task forces to work out the details of their implementation.

Having grown up, gone to school, and taught in Quebec, I have always thought of myself as a Quebecker. My sympathies were strongly in line with those of Robarts. I seized every occasion, in throne and budget debates, or in consideration of the Estimates of the premier's office, to lead the way in advocating future efforts at building stronger relations with Quebec. This was needed, partly because the B&B Commission report had solemnly warned how French-English tension was threatening the future of the nation, and partly because the opposition to Robarts's leadership on this issue was coming primarily from the ranks of his own party, adherents of the Drew brand of Toryism.

I recall one occasion when, as Robarts was voicing his familiar position, members on his side of the House were audibly mumbling their dissent. On another occasion, in my hearing, Fred Cass, a prominent figure in the party, expressed criticism of Frost's naming Highway 401 the Macdonald-Cartier Freeway: "Too much attention been given the French Canadians," he observed.

To his credit, Robarts forged ahead, and suffered no political consequences. The francophobes were mostly Tories who had nowhere else to go. The rest of the story is a familiar one. Robarts, with the active support of Premier Daniel Johnson, took the lead in calling the Confederation of Tomorrow Conference. Many of his colleagues and close advisers were nervous about the project, but it came off well, and helped to break the impasse which had developed in federal-provincial affairs at the federal level.

As an opposition leader, I attended that conference as an observer. It was a memorable event, held on the fifty-fourth floor of the spanking new Toronto-Dominion bank building. The magnificent vista inspired a vision of Canada that engendered the right mood among provincial leaders. Robarts, along with Premier Johnson, presided with the air of solid statesmanship that he had acquired. The fears of the powers-that-be in Ottawa that such a conference was doomed to disintegrate in the all-too-familiar squabbling did not materialize. There was a measure of common purpose, which forced the federal government to move again on federal-provincial matters.

However, in subtle ways, the Robarts era was coming to an end as the 1960s closed. A working relationship with Quebec became less feasible with the more nationalist stance of the first Bourassa government, and the emergence of the separatist Parti Québécois. Under Trudeau's prime minister-ship, the initiative in federal-provincial affairs swung back to Ottawa. At Queen's Park, as Robarts's biographer has put it, "Life in the Legislature was becoming less of a ritual or game, more of a war, with knives bared and safety catches released, and basic issues raised about the role of government and the rights of the individual."[10]

Equally important, at the pinnacle of his power John Robarts "was starting down the long road of physical decline." He was eating and drinking too well. There were too many long nights with cabinet buddies at Toronto jazz clubs. The job was losing its challenge. His marriage was breaking up.

After he left politics, Robarts had a new lease on life. He married again, and free of the discipline imposed by public office, he and his new wife cut quite a social swath. There was the inevitable range of corporate directorships for a retired Tory premier and opportunities for significant public contribu-tions: a royal commission to review the structure and divi-sion of powers within Metropolitan Toronto, and co-chairing with Jean-Luc Pepin an inquiry into the basic problems in achieving Canadian unity.

The lust for life, privately and publicly, had taken its toll. Having attended board meetings in New York, and while en route to another in Texas, he was struck down with massive strokes. The result was physically and psychologically devastating. When it became clear that complete rehabilita-tion was not possible, Robarts took his own life before dawn on the morning of 18 October 1982.

As the news swept through Queen's Park, political friend

and foe were stunned by the enormity of the tragedy. His first wife had died under distressing circumstances. His son had committed suicide while wrestling with a drug problem. Physically disabled, the bloom had come off his second marriage. For a man who had lived to the full, there were no more satisfactions.

Hundreds filled St. Paul's Anglican Church in Toronto to overflowing for the funeral services. The contrast of a career which took him to the heights of first minister and national statesman, yet beset with such private disaster, left everyone awed by the mystery of life. The full drama of his political achievements and personal tragedy will one day be captured for one of the most important chapters in Ontario's history.

William Grenville Davis

I attended the Tory convention in Toronto, in February 1971, which chose William Grenville Davis as leader. My role was that of a CBC/TV panelist providing colour commentary between the votes, which were to be held from early afternoon through to the evening. But the party attempted to use the American-style voting machines, and they broke down. Confusion and indecision reigned behind the scenes for hours. Ultimately it was decided to repeat the first vote in the evening, using hastily-printed ballots. Not until the fourth ballot, in the small hours of the next morning, was Davis declared the winner.

From high atop Maple Leaf Gardens, the CBC panelists found they had an eternity of time to fill. One of my long-time CCF/NDP colleagues, Gordon Brigden, rubbed salt in the open wounds of the Tories by wiring them an offer of NDP assistance. At our provincial convention a few months before, we had conducted leadership votes among eighteen hundred delegates in about twenty minutes, and actually delayed the announcement of the first result in order not to forgo too much of prime TV time.

But that little by-play was nothing compared to the excitement generated in the convention, when the voting did get under way. Each succeeding result narrowed the Davis margin, until the final squeaker by only forty-four votes. Allan Lawrence had emerged as the challenger, in a masterly campaign organized by those who subsequently became known as the leaders of the Big Blue Machine. In the hour or so before the final vote, despite the exhaustion of the campaign and the prolonged convention, the delegates maintained a frenzy of political hoopla greater than anything I had ever seen.

For me, the event was memorable for another reason. Over the following two or three years I periodically met Tories who had been voting delegates. All were strangers, but they expressed appreciation for my comments during the convention. This mystified me. Finally one of them provided a clue: a fellow panelist had been Frank McGee, a former Tory MP, who was a Davis supporter. So much so, in fact, that he wore his Davis button on camera and in his commentary tended, so I felt, to be openly pro-Davis. That afforded me the opportunity to balance the picture with what apparently sounded like an anti-Davis interpretation of developments. When the final vote was recorded, close to 50 per cent of the delegates did not support Davis. These were the people who appreciated my commentary.

The closeness of the victory appeared to unsettle Davis, and his performance in the early months of his premiership was lacklustre. He and his leading supporters, people like Clare Westcott and Hugh Macaulay, had difficulty forgetting and forgiving the tactics of the Lawrence campaigners. And yet the Lawrence campaign leaders had proven to be superb organizers and tacticians, whom the party could ill afford to alienate. With an election in the offing, building the new team was the top priority. Davis focused on that rather than on the Legislature.

As is well known, the new team was built — the Big Blue Machine. And it was well oiled. The party's new bagman, William Kelly (now a senator), perfected fund-raising techniques, to milk the business world on the basis of the dollar value of their contracts with the government. Over $5 million was raised, three times the amount spent in Robarts's last election. Those resources, combined with announcements on important policy issues (such as stopping the Spadina expressway through the heart of Toronto, and denying extension of separate school funding) altered the Davis image of indecision, and produced a convincing election victory.

It will be noted that this account, so far, contains no indication of any personal relationship with Davis. The fact is that none existed. Davis is a very private person. It is my impression that even his closest associates never established the kind of camaraderie that existed in Robarts's inner circle. He had entered the Legislature in 1959, as successor to Tom Kennedy, who had been interim premier between Drew and Frost, and had become an institution around Queen's Park. I felt that Davis had some sympathy for my position in face of the Tory onslaught in those early years; certainly he never participated in it. We shared a common interest in retarded children's education, a subject which I raised because an experimental class had been launched with federal funding in my riding. Spokesmen for retarded children and their parents in Davis's area had exacted a pledge of support from him before his election, and he fulfilled it early in his tenure as education minister, by financing the integration of retarded children's classes into the regular school system.

From my first year in the Legislature, I had devoted a great deal of debating time to educational matters, and that continued throughout the 1960s. On more than one occasion Davis privately expressed appreciation of the role which I had played in the field of education. There was an unspoken understanding, but always at arm's length.

Shortly after becoming leader in 1971, Davis attended the federal-provincial conference in Victoria. He was the "new boy" among the provincial leaders, many of whom were old war-horses at this stage. The conference atmosphere was soured by the red-neck reaction of some of the western premiers. I always felt that if Robarts had been there, he would have, with gravelly-voiced intervention, countered the anti-Quebec sentiments. In a subsequent legislative debate, I stated that I felt Robarts's absence was felt more than Davis's presence at Victoria. It was a cutting observation, not premeditated; it simply emerged in the course of extemporaneous remarks. But I learned afterwards, from those who were close to Davis, that the observation hurt.

In short, while I think a mutual respect grew with the years — he had a habit of ribbing me about my "intellectual" activities as a part-time university lecturer — it took some time for it to develop into the modified kind of personal relationship that I had had with Robarts, and even Frost. Part of the reason was that I became a private member at about the same time that he became premier, and therefore the closer working relationship, which existed among leaders, was never possible.

In striking contrast to the relative stability enjoyed by his predecessors, Davis experienced a period of growing unrest. Skyrocketing energy prices, and the phenomenon of growing unemployment in conjunction with inflation, presented the kind of insoluble problems which Ontario normally escaped. The far-reaching changes initiated in the Robarts regime — changes such as regional government — had a delayed negative reaction. The difficulties were compounded by a perceived insensitivity on the part of the government. It was increasingly felt that Davis was unduly cut off, not only from the public, but even from members of his own caucus. By 1975 there was a backlash, and the government suffered the consequences, being reduced to minority status.

Two years later, Davis misjudged the situation, and called a snap election on the flimsy issue of a difference of 2 per cent on rent control levels, in the hope of regaining a majority. It was my impression that the longer the campaign went on, the more Davis feared that he had "blown" the prospect, and nobody was more relieved than he on election night, when the government retained at least its minority position. From that point, I was convinced that he would live with minority government, and in fact, he did so in a masterly fashion. He actually grew to enjoy the challenge of survival by manipulating House strategy. It was during this period that he built his reputation as a consummate politician, and regained a majority in the 1981 election, after a full four-year term. That reputation persisted, in spite of recurrent political setbacks, until the end of his premiership when polls placed him at the dizzying height of 56 per cent public approval.

This achievement was made, however, at the price of sacrificing principle to political expediency. The government's resistance to the acceptance of official bilingualism, in spite of pleas from all parties at the federal level, including his own, was a classic example. And the government simply stonewalled on a wide range of domestic issues, from freedom of information to comprehensive rent control and adequate environmental protection. In fact, the last two years or so of the Davis regime were a period of drift, with a growing backlog of neglected issues. These became the substance of the NDP-Liberal Accord, which formed the initial program of the Peterson government.

Davis himself recognized the inequity resulting from this inaction, and nowhere more so than on the extension of separate school funding. Having staked a position of impassioned opposition in 1971, and reaped a harvest of electoral support, he reversed it thirteen years later as "a matter of conscience." I suspect it was also a matter of demographics: the Catholic proportion of the Ontario population had grown to be the largest single denomination. With an unerring political instinct, he recognized that the long-term interests of the Conservative party dictated that it had to shed the remnants of anti-Catholicism with which it had been traditionally associated.

There is another aspect of this episode that played a major role in ending the Tory regime. It is widely believed that Davis's announcement of 12 June 1984 was a unilateral decision, taken without consultation with his cabinet colleagues. Davis categorically denies this.[11] The timing was a unilateral decision — as is the prerogative of the first minister — but the substance of the decision, he asserts, had been the subject of cabinet discussion many times. In those cabinet discussions there was only one open opponent — Norman Sterling, who held to his position as the single opposing vote against the subsequent legislation. And when Davis made his announcement to the House, it was greeted by a standing ovation from the Tory members.

In any case, once the announcement had been made, the issue was so mismanaged during the final year of Davis's tenure, and even more so in the Miller administration, that it left all parties, and the people of Ontario, faced with a revival of old religious prejudices that developed into a veritable political minefield, in which the Tory party was the major casualty.

Davis left politics, it has always been my view, because he was wearying of the burden of office and the party had run out of ideas. Indeed, the BILD (Board of Industrial Leadership and Development) program on which he had regained a majority in 1981, was an unashamed repackaging of old programs, dressed up with new slogans. With the party's massive resources, and Davis's personal stature, it was successful, but primarily (as is often not recognized), because of the drop in NDP fortunes. By "sleepwalking the electorate to the polls" (to borrow Stephen Lewis's graphic description of the Davis technique), backed by a multi-million dollar campaign, the party won more seats, with essentially the same popular vote. Three years later, the party appeared to be in a strong position, organizationally and financially. The rot had set in, but was not apparent. So Davis resigned, and the floodgates were opened to political change, such as he could never have foreseen.

If Davis had stayed, there is little doubt that the Tories would have won again in 1985, perhaps reduced to a minority government. But there was a legacy of unresolved issues. When the party lost the towering stature of his leadership, and the perception of a management capacity that went with it, and made the disastrous choice of Frank Miller, who took the party out of the mainstream of progressive conservative politics, one of the longest political regimes in Canadian history came to an end.

Davis remains one of the most baffling, and therefore intriguing figures, in modern Ontario politics. He's a very easy person to underestimate. On so many occasions an opposition member would deal substantively with an issue in an all-out attack on the premier, only to have him reply in a rambling, politicking, obfuscating evasion. The result was sheer frustration and wonderment at how he succeeded. But he did succeed, more often than not.

On 8 December 1984 a dinner was held for Bill Davis at the Royal Canadian Yacht Club in Toronto. One of those roasting the premier was Clare Westcott, a long-time aide. He was disarmingly frank about his boss on many occasions, but never more so than on this one. He opened his comments with the assertion that to understand Davis you had to understand his management style, which no one did. He continued:

Helen Radcliffe Anderson [Davis's long-time secretary] pretends to understand it, because she doesn't want to hurt his feelings by asking him what the hell he's up to. Edward Elsley Stewart [Davis's deputy] doesn't understand it — and doesn't care — because he's going to do it his own way anyway. John Howard Tory [Davis's principal secretary] doesn't understand it, which is rather odd, for his job is to go around and explain to everybody how wonderful it is. I, on the other hand, understand it fully, for his management style is like Einstein's theory. It's easy to understand — it's just hard to believe.

It's a combination of small town native intelligence — a ouija board — a never ever do today what can be put off for three years — all rationalized in statements that hang together with his own specially personalized repertoire of clichés. A vocabulary that includes meaningful and decisive words like — "with great respect"; "if I may be permitted to say"; "if in a real sense I can say" — and the classic, used to confirm that he knows where he is — "in this jurisdiction."

This is not a bad habit, or a contrived scheme to baffle the media. It's a long-standing and honoured conservative tradition — brought down from one leader to another. In Mr. Frost's day it was "let me tell you this"; "human betterment"; and "in the fullness of time." John Robarts's style differed from that of Premier Frost and Davis, both in what he said and in the decibel level. Mr. Robarts was much more decisive. One could hear things like — "Where the hell is Ernie [Jackson]?"; "Is it raining in Grand Bend?"; and, "Who's got the ice?"

Let's face it, our Premier has had something going for him for twenty-five years that helped move him step by step to the very top. In Latin it's knows as *bonna fortuna*. In English it's called good luck. He has made procrastination a vital and important instrument in the running of a government. He has literally turned it into a science. Taking quick action is considered sinful. When he's asked "Do you have trouble making up your mind?", his answer is, "Well, yes and no." Does he have trouble deciding on a course of action? Not a bit — he doesn't decide. He just waits for another day — or another year. . ..

He has devised numerous ways to remove problems of the day from his shoulders — he phones in sick, or an even better one: "The fog in Brampton is so thick that you can't see to drive." However, through it all he has remained the same — neither his character nor his soul tarnished by the rigours or cynicism of politics. Imagine — leading a government for fourteen tough years and still being a true optimist. Someone who can smile and not really worry about what happens. As long as it happens to somebody else.

That may not be the definitive assessment of Bill Davis, but there are many insights buried in the needling humour. A memorable personal experience provides others: I was finalizing plans with John Tory, who had agreed to be a guest of my class on government and politics of Ontario at Atkinson College. We were standing within earshot of Davis, when I was startled by his query, "When am I going to be invited to your class?" I assured him that it would be soon; and it was, for an extraordinary evening. Atkinson students are part-time, more mature, coming from any and every sector of the work world. They relished the opportunity to question a first minister, and on this occasion, they did so incisively. For two hours, they asked questions, personal and political. There was no circumlocution, no obfuscation no bafflegab — the answers were frank and straightforward. Members of the Legislature would have listened in disbelief.

21

Legislative Reform

Changes in the government and politics of Ontario over the past thirty years have been great, but nowhere more so than in the Legislature. For the first hundred years after Confederation, Ontario's Parliament operated along essentially the same lines. In the 1960s change began to overtake the venerable institution. The pace quickened in the seventies and in the eighties, when technological change became the order of the day — almost every day.

To grasp the significance of these changes, one need only go back to the situation in 1955, when I first entered the Legislature. Sessions rarely ran more than ten to twelve weeks, neatly tucked into the period between ploughing in the fall and seeding in the spring. Urbanization had passed the 50 per cent mark as far back as the first decade of the century, but the Legislature continued to reflect a rural society.

My suspicion was that Leslie Frost checked the calendar for the date of Easter, counted back ten weeks or so, then called the MPPs into Queen's Park in late January or early February. As Easter approached, MPPs knew that the business would be crammed into longer sittings (the 10:30 p.m. adjournment hour didn't come until later), sometimes running well beyond midnight. It was the Procrustean bed approach: anything that extended beyond Easter was simply chopped off.

Government business was given virtually exclusive consideration. Questions before the Order of the Day, now the glamour portion of legislative proceedings, were not permitted. Often written questions stood for weeks on the order paper, and died unanswered when the House prorogued. Private members' bills and resolutions were squeezed into the late hours, in the final days of the session. Often, too, games were played to euchre members out of any consideration of the legislation standing in their name.

I recall one occasion when Premier Frost seized the opportunity to call a private member's bill, introduced by Art Reaume, a Liberal MPP for Windsor, when he happened to be away for a dental appointment. Art was a colourful, rather volatile character, and when he returned to learn that his bill had not only been called, but struck off the order paper, he raised a memorable storm. But to no avail. Frost ran the show. Private members were not deemed to be major players. They had to be on their toes not to be out-foxed.

Working conditions for members were ludicrously inadequate. They had neither offices, nor any staff. Each caucus was allocated a room, where members milled around en masse. If they needed a secretary, one was summoned from a stenographer pool maintained by the Speaker. Members could often be seen sitting in their Legislature seats in the morning, when the House was not in session, catching up on their correspondence.

Legislative membership was regarded as part-time, for which an indemnity was paid, to cover the loss while away from their regular jobs. In my first year in the Legislature the remuneration was raised from $3,900 to $5,400, two-thirds of which was "pay," and the remaining one-third a tax-free expense allowance. It was all available at the end of the session but, upon request, advances would be made.

Though I entered the House as a party leader, it was six months before I was able to get a full-time secretary, rather than drawing on the Speaker's pool. My two colleagues, Tommy Thomas from Oshawa and Reg Gisborn from Hamilton, and our shared secretary, each occupied a corner of the room. But we were relatively well off: we had desks and telephones. The Liberals and Tories were herded into one large room, without individual facilities.

John Robarts started the process of bringing the Legislature into the twentieth century. Working conditions were improved.

By the end of his premiership, each member had an individual office and shared a secretary with a colleague. Most important for those of us in opposition, Robarts was the first premier to acknowledge that we had an important role to play. Gradually, resources were provided, to establish some balance with the well-equipped and staffed cabinet offices.

The traditional attitude toward the opposition had been that, when governments changed — in a paraphrase of the biblical injunction — they did unto others as the others had done unto them. For the Leslie Frost generation, memories of what happened when Mitch Hepburn stormed into office in 1934 never died. To his credit, John Robarts broke this tit-for-tat cycle. Robarts admitted privately that he was not interested in this kind of approach. Government business was big business; the opposition had a vital role to play in parliamentary government, and therefore it was entitled to resources to perform that role. Slowly, the opposition parties were given more resources to counter the government's advantages. A case can be made that they haven't achieved a balance yet, and may never do so. But progress began in the sixties.

As that period now falls into some historical perspective, it is interesting to recall how it unfolded. Very early, it became obvious that, if the opposition party leaders were treated as no more than private members, they would be seriously outclassed by the premier, who had a sizeable complement. In fact, for years the appropriation for the premier's office was greater than all the money made available for the opposition parties. Therefore the demand was made, and gradually conceded, that there should be a special allocation for "the leader's complex" in each opposition party.

Research was soon isolated as another great need. In shaping policies, the government had the assistance of hundreds of departmental officials and thousands of civil servants. The opposition was supposed to respond without research assistance, beyond what they could scrounge from voluntary sources. Therefore the opposition appropriation was raised, to include a research component.

Changes in the government's operations hastened changes

in the Legislature. As the business load grew in size and complexity, governments tended to be overwhelmed. Robarts appointed the Committee on Government Productivity (COGP), to streamline the structure and decision-making process. When the first six of COGP's ten reports had been delivered, and were being implemented, some of us in the Legislature protested even more strongly. The Legislature had been specifically excluded from the terms of reference of the COGP. All very well, we argued, for the government to seek streamlined operations, but to the extent that it succeeded, the executive would dominate the Legislature even more. Was it not time to do something about streamlining the creaky operations of the legislative forum, which was also being overwhelmed with the growing business load?

In 1972 Premier Davis responded with the appointment of the Commission on the Legislature, familiarly known as the Camp Commission. Through to 1975, five reports were produced — four on the Legislature, and one on election finances. The government appointed a select committee, chaired by former Speaker Donald Morrow, to review the Camp Commission recommendations, and the floodgates of change were opened.

The details of those changes are readily available in the commission and select committee reports. But in the progress towards legislative reform, the stated objectives are worth noting. In its overall review of the functions of the Legislature, the commission's major objective was to provide private members with a more meaningful role. Investigations revealed that members had become victims of the "caseload" syndrome — responding to the myriad problems their electors faced in coping with the government policies and bureaucracy. Essentially, the members had become social workers, to the detriment of their responsibilities as legislators.

To correct this trend, a wide range of changes was recommended, and implemented. Each member was given not only an office at Queen's Park, with a full-time legislative assistant, but also a constituency office, staffed with another assistant, who could more readily and effectively cope with constituents' problems at the ground level. The members' remuneration was increased, and pensions made more generous, in order to attract a higher calibre of candidates. The rules were changed for legislative and committee work, to provide the private members with more opportunity for input.

Equally important, the commission insisted that the Legislature should be rescued from its complete dependence on the premier's office and government services for its every need. In effect, the Legislature was established as a separate ministry, headed by the Speaker, and assisted by his two deputies, the clerk of the legislature and the director of administration. Legislative funding was placed with the Board of Internal Economy, which became a separate treasury or management board for the operation of the Legislature and those agencies which are servants of the Legislature, rather than the government, namely the provincial auditor, the ombudsman, the election finances commissioner, the chief election officer and the freedom of information commissioner.

"The Commission is intent," Camp and his associates stressed, "on a similar independence [to that at Westminster] for the Speaker and the Clerk in Ontario, and on emphasizing the privacy of their functions as officials of the Assembly." They drove their point home by recommending that in the Table of Precedence in Ontario, the Speaker shall rank fourth, next to the lieutenant-governor, the first minister and the chief justice of the Supreme Court.

It is significant that, in seeking these changes, the Camp Commission directly confronted the government, in its traditional reluctance to entertain change. They pointed out in their second report that "the Office of the Speaker, and consequently the administration of the Legislature itself, had not grown and developed along lines consistent with modern parliamentary democracy." They sharpened their point by noting that four studies had been done in the previous five years, dealing with the office of the Speaker, but none of the recommendations had been adopted. The commission commented acidly, "We can only assume that the government, for its own reasons, declined to act on the recommendations of these reports, or, perhaps more likely, there was a failure to attach priority to implementing them." At one stage, when the government was procrastinating, the commission delayed its next report so as to pressure cabinet out of its lethargy and/or opposition.

Having broken through the official intransigence, the commission stressed that, henceforth, the responsibility for on-going reform to cope with changing conditions and needs rested with the members themselves. Flowing from the commission reports, the machinery was established, within the legislative framework, for doing that, and the members have accepted the challenge.

Today, the financing of the Legislature, in the full range of its activities, rests with the Board of Internal Economy, chaired by the Speaker, with representation from the opposition parties, as well as the government. Its appropriations are accepted by the provincial treasurer, and included in the budget. Responsibility for rule changes was placed with the Procedural Affairs Committee, subject to approval by the Legislature. Changes in working conditions were placed with the Members' Services Committee, subject to approval of the Board of Internal Economy, if an expenditure was involved. The whole of the legislature building (with an increasing overflow to the neighbouring Whitney Block) was placed under the jurisdiction of the Speaker.

These changes were hastened, in part, by the fact that the Camp Commission proposals coincided with minority government (1975-81), and although they tended to slow with the return of majority government (1981-85), the new pattern proved irreversible. Moreover, with the return to a new minority government in 1985, the pace of reform accelerated once again — of which, more later.

In this twenty-five-year period, the Ontario Legislature escaped from being an appendage to the premier's office, beholden to the government for its every need, and emerged as an independent institution, freer to fulfill its role in parliamentary government. This achievement was the prerequisite for the major objective of reform, namely, providing a more meaningful role for the private members, and rescuing the Legislature from total domination by the executive branch of government.

One of the obstacles to achieving this objective was, ironically, Roderick Lewis, the clerk of the Legislature from 1953 to 1986. Though nominally a servant of the Legislature, he was appointed by the Tory government and maintained in his position by them. Particularly when the chips were down, he operated as a servant of the government.

The Lewis family held the position of clerk for sixty years. Lewis's father, Major Alex Lewis, was appointed in 1926. Lewis became assistant to his father in the 1940s, and when the father retired, at age seventy-nine in 1953, Lewis succeeded to the position. There is no doubt that Rod Lewis knew the rules, but there was always a lingering suspicion, especially among opposition members, that his knowledge was selectively used to meet the needs of the government, whenever the circumstances required.

My first and most vivid recollection of his efforts was as clerk of the Committee on Elections and Privileges, when I was put through the wringer for having accused government members of voting for a bill in which they had a private interest — the Scarborough oversized watermain episode.[1] He pursued his task with all the zeal of a high clergyman determined to rid the church of a heretic.

If the premier, or some other government spokesman, was flaying the opposition, playfully or otherwise, Lewis would beam from his seat at the table. But if an opposition spokesman was giving the government a hard time, he would scowl, and even motion to the Chair to cut off debate.

A classic example of this quarter-backing of government strategy took place in 1975, when the Legislature was called into emergency session to pass back-to-work legislation during the TTC strike. News accounts had indicated that the government expected to pass the bill in one day, despite the rules, which stipulated that all three readings could not take place in the same day without unanimous consent. Vernon Singer, then the Liberal member for Downsview, encountered Lewis in the legislative dining room, and asked how the government expected to proceed within one day, when unanimous consent might not be given. Lewis smilingly assured Singer that the situation was in hand. As events unfolded, we found out how. Once the bill was introduced, the opposition leaders requested adjournment, so that their caucuses could study the bill. The government concurred. When the House resumed an hour or so later, it was discovered that the clerk had a second order paper available, which normally would be for the next day. In this cute fashion, the rules were circumvented, and the clerk was an accomplice in the government strategy.

Lewis felt that, in fact, he was running the House. Speakers might come and Speakers might go, but he would go on forever — or so he thought. He viewed them all as protégés, whose tenuous grasp of the rules had to be bolstered by his superior knowledge. Often during sittings Lewis could be seen turning to instruct the Speaker on what should be done, even without being requested. He perceived himself as master, not as servant, and frequently attempted to act as such. Above all else, Lewis was an arch-traditionalist. His instinctive reaction was to maintain the status quo. Instead of assisting the Legislature to live and grow with the times, he presided over the demise of traditional rights and procedures, such as the right of the opposition to amend a motion with a want-of-confidence motion, before voting Supply. When I entered the Legislature, this honoured tradition of Parliament had disappeared completely. It was revived in the 1960s.

The most significant changes during Lewis's dominance over legislative procedures was when John White, the member for London South, was appointed government whip. He had been denied a cabinet post because of the concentration of cabinet ministers from his area of the province and he took up his new post with zeal. Having an innovative turn of mind, he streamlined the committee structure and pushed for a fuller recognition of the backbencher's office needs.

Again, after Lewis suffered a heart attack toward the end of the 1967 session, and sittings grew to 173 days and 81 nights in 1969, further changes had to be made, to accommodate the increasing load. Events, rather than any initiative from the clerk, forced these changes in the standing orders.

It was only when a review of the legislative procedures was

delegated to an independent body, the Camp Commission, that the long-neglected needs were recognized. The shackling control of the clerk was broken. The brake on the wheel of progress was removed.

Nevertheless, Lewis remained in his central position, and attempted to retain his dominance. In the Camp Commission's efforts to establish the independence of the Legislature, Lewis submitted that the clerk's role should be elevated to the status of a deputy minister. This was granted, at a salary in the range of $60,000, which grew to more than $90,000 by the time of his retirement.

When the post of director of administration was created to handle the wide range of administrative details associated with the Legislature (beyond the actual proceedings of the House itself), and Robert Fleming, who had been secretary of the Camp Commission, was appointed, Lewis sought to have the post made subservient to his own. Speaker Allan Reuter vetoed the effort, by directing that the clerk and the director of administration should report directly to him. But to the end of his career Lewis sought to retain the clerk's role as the first deputy, even though the increasing burdens of his responsibilities were being alleviated by assistant clerks, particularly by the first clerk assistant, John Holtby.

Holtby was reform-minded. He shared the growing feeling that parliaments had to adapt to the changing times. While highly respectful of the traditions of Parliament, he felt that those traditions should not be used to block experimentation with new and more effective procedures. In short, he was no soul-mate for Lewis. Increasingly, members sought his advice on rules, and this threatening role led to a deteriorating relationship with the clerk and ultimately Holtby's departure to become chief of staff for the special committee on Reform of the House of Commons. As his departure became imminent, there was one amusing occasion, when the Ontario delegates to a Commonwealth Parliamentary Association conference, on the Isle of Man, learned that Lewis had been inquiring of the association president whether there were openings anywhere, to which Holtby might be directed.

With Holtby's departure, the post of first clerk assistant

remained vacant through to the end of Lewis's career. His recommendations for replacements were turned down by the Board of Internal Economy as he drifted toward retirement, all the while proclaiming in press interviews that he hoped to "fulfill his obligations for quite a while longer."[2]

Lewis's influence was not restricted to the Legislature. His 1953 appointment was as chief election officer, as well as clerk, and in this role he was no less frustrating in his failure to uphold the existing statutes, or press for desirable changes. The kind of loose administration, which was seen at its worst in Frost's days, prevailed in the running of elections. When violations of the Elections Act were drawn to Lewis's attention, he refused to take any initiative to uphold the act, which he was responsible for administering. Those who protested were told to launch civil action — at their own expense, of course.

In the 1967 provincial election, a retired deputy attorney general, Bill Common, assumed the responsibilities of the chief election officer, because Lewis had suffered a heart attack. The irregular accounts of returning officers so offended him that charges were laid, and convictions secured, against a number of these loyal Tory appointees. One of them happened to be the returning officer in my own riding. As the election loomed, I had asked Lewis why the "permanent" returning officer had not been appointed in York South, so as to give time for the necessary preparatory work. In an unguarded moment, Lewis confided that he was having a problem: the local Tory riding association was so divided on the question that they had not been able to submit a name. As a result, the actual appointment was not made until after the writs were issued. The appointee was a lifelong and faithful supporter of the party, who had to scramble to keep on top of the job. He followed the "normal" practices, and was charged with irregularities and convicted — an experience which shattered him.

When the Commission on Election Contributions and Expenses (now renamed Election Finances Commission), was first set up in 1975, the government strengthened Lewis's position by including the chief election officer among the membership. However, the Commission was well balanced, with two appointees by each party, so as to safeguard against partisanship.

In yet another way, the government extended the influence of the chief election officer by his appointment to the Redistribution Commission, following the decennial censuses of 1961 and 1971. Hitherto, redistribution had always been conducted by a legislative committee, with a majority of government members in control. The door was open to gerrymandering, to meet the wishes of sitting Tories. The redistribution following the 1951 census was under way when I first entered the Legislature, so I had first-hand experience with the traditional system. The wheeling and dealing behind the scenes often culminated in favourable boundary shifts for government members.

The 1960s saw redistribution assigned to an independent commission, headed by a judge, plus a second member from the academic community, but with the third member being the chief election officer. Lewis was the most influential member of the trio, because he had all the detailed information and intimate knowledge of past experience. The government assisted by providing loopholes in the terms of reference of the commission, which permitted serious violation of the basic principle of representation by population.

The prize example was granting the redistribution commission the right to depart from the established population quota for ridings when, and if, they saw fit. Strangely, they always saw fit in a number of ridings known to be Tory "pocket boroughs." These were left with populations far below the norm. By significant coincidence, this loophole was not exploited by the Redistribution Commission of the 1980s, when Lewis was not a member. While he fully expected to be appointed again, even though Warren Bailie had taken over as chief election officer, he was not, and for the first time redistribution reflected a genuine attempt to implement the basic principle of "rep by pop."

In all his wide-ranging efforts, Lewis was a faithful servant of the government. The pity is that, as an agent of the government, while nominally a servant of the Legislature, he accommodated the interests of an administration, which had to be blasted out of its reluctance to entertain change. As late as January 1986, he gave an interview to the Canadian Press, indicating that he had no plans for retirement.[3] But with a new government, his days were numbered; the Liberals had regarded him as "a Tory family retainer," and after a decent lapse of time, Premier Peterson announced Lewis's retirement in July 1986, followed a few weeks later by the usual testimonial dinner. Presumably, that was the end of Lewis's career as clerk, but what followed was an unprecedented spectacle.

"Certain undertakings were given to me which, unfortunately, I accepted orally and did not have . . . put in writing," Lewis declared in a letter to the three House leaders. He accused the premier, Treasurer Bob Nixon and Cabinet Secretary Robert Carman of failing to live up to the commitment. The settlement which Lewis sought was a pension at the deputy minister's level of $60,000, supplemented by a lifetime annual $31,500 to match his pre-retirement income of $91,500, ostensibly to enable him to write books on the Legislature, plus an office, a secretary and a chauffeured limousine service. In the background was the top legal firm of McCarthy and McCarthy, retained to take the matter to court, if Lewis's interpretation of the full commitment was not met.

Lewis held out in his office while his successor, Claude L. DesRosiers, cooled his heels across the hall, arguing all the while that the clerk is appointed by cabinet order-in-council, and the job can be rescinded only by death, voluntary resignation or resolution of the Legislature.

The public outrage knew no bounds. "A golden handshake has turned into a golden fleecing of the taxpayers," editorialized the Windsor *Star*. "Roderick Lewis . . . has taken the province to the cleaners," declared the Toronto *Star*. The cartoonists were merciless. Only after days of such pummelling did Lewis agree to a settlement with no further threat of court action — a settlement that was widely characterized as a "a platinum handshake."

A settlement was finally arrived at without court action: a government annuity for $174,243 to bring his pension up to the $60,000 level; while the supplementary annual income of $31,500 was denied, the retirement package of $275,499 included attendance gratuities (unused sick leave) of $45,000 and vacation pay to $50,000. While an office and secretarial service were granted, the personally-chauffeured limousine was denied, but it subsequently emerged that Lewis had access to the government limo service, at a cost of over $8,000 for the fiscal year of 1986-87. Moreover, the Legislature underwrote the type-setting and printing costs of his first book, *The House Was My Home,* to the extent of $17,000. It was a pretty thin volume, most of which was a reprinting of information already readily available to MPPs and the public in other publications. As I commented in a review for the Toronto *Star,* "Seldom if ever, has the public treasury paid so much for so little."

In all my years around Queen's Park, Rod Lewis was the one, and virtually the only, person whom I could not bear. For reasons which, ironically, he finally confirmed, he is inescapably a major exception in my otherwise fond recollection of the Legislature.

Meanwhile, change continues at such a pace that it is difficult to recognize the institution. The chamber itself has been renovated. While maintaining the integrity of the original architecture, TV cameras have now been set within the walls. Modern lighting facilitates television coverage, which is beamed by satellite to all corners of the province. The equipment is "state-of-the-art." Now every Ontarian can "attend" and view the proceedings of the House and its committees — a development which has the potential of drastically changing Ontario politics.

Members are now masters in their own house. The Legislature has achieved a measure of independence of the executive branch of government, inconceivable a generation ago. Through the Board of Internal Economy there is control over the financing and administration of all the activities, ranging from income and pensions to Hansard, security and the library. The board's membership is made up of the Speaker, as chairman, three cabinet ministers, and a representative of each of the three parties in the House. The governing party still has a majority, and cabinet influence is evident on matters such as incomes and pensions, but there is considerable autonomy on everything else.

The Committee on the Legislature has been given the responsibilities of the former Procedural Affairs and Members' Services committees, and it is now free to recommend changes, both in working conditions and procedures. The Liberal/NDP Accord called for an opening up of the process at Queen's Park, particularly in the committees, to provide for more meaningful participation by the private members. A greater role has been given to opposition members: through statements prior to question period; the right to respond to ministerial statements; the cross-questioning of speakers during debates; and limits on leaders' questions to ensure more backbench participation.

Offices are now computerized, so that data banks can be built, and information exchanged efficiently. Every part of the building can tune into the House or committee meetings. There is now a research capacity, not only for caucuses as a whole but for individual members. The shackles of outmoded traditions have been loosened. Mechanisms are now in place for the institution to evolve with changing times and needs. The Ontario Legislature didn't start to move into the twentieth century until the 1960s, but it has now broken into the lead among Canadian parliaments, provincial as well as federal.

22

The NDP and Organized Labour

No aspect of the New Democratic Party's role in Canadian politics is more frequently raised — usually in negative terms — than its relationship with the trade union movement. In my varying capacities in the CCF and the NDP it has been my privilege to work with organized labour in pursuit of our common political objectives. Thus, another area for reflections.

Labour's political role, and the NDP relationship with it, can best be understood in the context of the development of political parties in Canada. The Liberal and Conservative parties, as we know them today, emerged after Confederation. As the franchise was extended to men during the last century, and to women in this century, the old parties have had to make broader appeals, in order to get elected. But that does not alter the basic fact that, as parties, they have been rooted in the business world, and therefore responsive to the demands of the business world, even though those demands have often been granted at the sacrifice of the interests of other groups in society and the economy.

Not surprisingly, labour was part of every effort to build an alternative to the business-oriented parties. In the 1890s, the Knights of Labor were in a loose association of forces with the Patrons of Industry which came within striking distance of emerging as the largest single party in the 1893 election.[1] In 1919 the Independent Labour Party provided the margin of seats, in coalition with the United Farmers of Ontario, to form the majority government of E.C. Drury. When the Great Depression struck, remnants of those earlier third parties and protest movements gathered in Regina in 1933 for the first convention of the Co-operative Commonwealth Federation (CCF).

Labour was represented at this new beginning notably by Aaron Mosher, a titan of the labour movement, who headed a Canadian union of railroad and other transport workers. It is important to note, however, that at that time organized labour in all Canada numbered few more than one-quarter of a million members. Unlike Britain, it was unrealistic to conceive of a party exclusively based in labour. Some unions, representative of the old trades, such as the printers, carpenters or ironworkers, had been in existence for more than one hundred years.

Organized labour, as we know it today, with its expansion into industry, is a product of the depression, wartime and postwar years. From the outset, the development of industrial unionism had close association with politics, through the CCF and, later, the NDP. Indeed, many of the organizers of industrial unions were party activists, who perceived their day-to-day role to be on the economic front. Men like Eamon Park of the Steelworkers, or Fred Dowling of the Packinghouse workers, were members of the Co-operative Commonwealth Youth Movement (CCYM) in the early years of the party. Others like Charlie Millard, who was involved in the defence of the automobile workers in Oshawa against Hepburn's Hussars, were socialists before they were trade unionists. They became trade unionists precisely because they were socialists.

While there was opposition to partisan political activity, often spelled out in the constitution of many of the older unions in the Trades and Labour Congress (TLC), the same was generally not true of the industrial unions in the Canadian Congress of Labour (CCL). As early as 1942 the CCL adopted a resolution at its national convention designating the CCF as its political arm. At every subsequent convention it has reaffirmed its support for the party.

To the extent that there was any organic association between the political party and the local unions in the early years, it was in the pattern of the British Labour party, through affiliation at a nominal membership fee of five cents per member per month, which was shared between the federal party and the provincial section where the local union was located.

The first affiliates of the CCF were the mineworkers of Cape Breton. It is not surprising, therefore, that in the yeasty atmosphere of trade union and political development during the early 1940s, one of the leading crusaders for trade union affiliation with the Ontario CCF was Clarie Gillis, a mineworker from Glace Bay, who was elected to the House of Commons in 1940. Some progress was made in the affiliation drive, but nothing spectacular.

In the postwar years a new approach emerged, that of the Political Action Committees (PAC), under the leadership of Murray Cotterill, a steelworker who played a prominent role in the political activities of the Ontario Federation of Labour. I always regarded the PAC approach as being something of a reversion to the old American Samuel Gompers's tradition, in which labour supported its friends and opposed its enemies, while avoiding partisan association with any party. The Canadian version was that, with each election, or with each of its annual cap-in-hand sessions, labour would present its demands to each party, on the assumption that the party which reacted most sympathetically would get labour's organized support.

The PAC committees knew in advance that neither of the old parties was sympathetic to their basic demands and that the CCF was the only party which would respond positively, while not necessarily accepting every labour demand. So, having gone through this charade, labour ended up officially supporting the CCF in an ostensibly arm's length manner. Cotterill's hedging approach was accurately reflected in his comment, as late as 1957, that endorsation did not "tie the Federation to the coattails of that party. Any support must be conditional and temporary; support must be earned."[2]

For a time the new approach seemed to work effectively. In 1948 the CCF was swept back as the official opposition, with twenty-one MPPs, including leading trade unionists. Some of them, such as Eamon Park and Lloyd Fell, were nominally Catholic, and won in West Toronto, which had traditionally been solidly Tory. Their election represented nothing short of a quiet revolution, an overnight change from Tory WASP to working-class Catholic. However, the CCF electoral fortunes, both federally in 1949, and provincially in 1951, clearly indicated that something more was needed. In fact, the CCF was almost wiped out in Ontario, when its provincial legislative representation was cut back from twenty-one to two.

There were others in the trade union movement who gradually became the day-to-day leaders, striving for more effective political action. Prominent among them were Henry Weisbach, a Sudeten-German immigrant and lifelong social democrat, and Morden Lazarus, a former CCF provincial secretary, who had been active in the councils of the party from its earliest days.

This search for a new political approach was part and parcel of the movement to unite the house of labour in Canada. It culminated in the founding convention of the Canadian Labour Congress (CLC) in 1956, and its resolution calling for a new political party encompassing the CCF and other progressive minded persons, at its next convention in 1958. "What is certain," Azoulay concludes, "is that the New Party idea was an [Ontario] CCF initiative, and that it began to receive serious attention with the CLC merger announcement in 1955."[3]

The three-year build-up to the founding convention of the New Democratic Party in 1961 led to the development of closer relationships between the unions and the party, in planning and campaigning. However, once the NDP had been launched, organized labour, at the national level, tended to take an independent position, arguing that it had to deal with parties and governments of every political stripe, and therefore the responsibility for political action was left to local unions, with leadership from regional labour councils and the provincial federations.

This was an improvement over CCF days, but there was a growing recognition that something more was needed. Useful as it was for labour to pass resolutions calling for support of the NDP, it was not enough.

Those sharing the widespread anti-trade union sentiment

among the public were readily convinced that the NDP was a patsy for labour. Furthermore, unless the passage of a resolution was followed by intense educational and organizational work among the rank and file, it didn't result in support in elections, even from some trade unionists.

The necessary work has continued throughout the years, with particular emphasis on the so-called Parallel Campaign in the unions, with a strong lead from the top in the CLC, especially during Dennis McDermott's tenure as president. This process of developing a greater political consciousness in a North American continent without the European tradition of working-class solidarity is greatly misunderstood, not only among the public in general, but also among many trade unionists. The proposition that great blocs of workers are, or can be, corralled by union leaders into voting for the NDP is a myth believed by no one, even though the old parties and their supporters assiduously propagate it for their own purposes.

In speaking with trade unionists, I have often resorted to the reminder that, in Great Britain, where the Labour party was an outgrowth of the trade union movement, there have never been more than 60 per cent of local unions affiliated to the party; if every trade unionist and his or her spouse had always been voting Labour, the party would never have been out of power for the past fifty years. In a free, democratic society, it is simply impossible — I would add, undesirable — that blocs of the population can be delivered one hundred per cent to any party. It is a long-term educational job to persuade working people that, in their own interests, they should vote for their party, the party which they shared in founding in Canada. Some of them will not have changed their minds, and forsaken their family party commitment, before they die. So be it: everyone has a right to be wrong!

There are a number of other features in the relationship between labour and the political party of their choice, which admit of misunderstanding or misrepresentation. For obvious reasons, trade unionists (other than some left-wing elements in their ranks) have never sought to build a strictly labour party. Organized labour is a relatively small segment of the overall population, and the trade union movement lives and works in a hostile climate in North America; these two factors require a broader base for a political party.

As noted earlier, when the CCF was founded in 1933, organized labour's numbers were obviously too small to form the basis of a national party. Even when organized labour had grown to millions, and the house of labour was united in 1956, its leadership still had no illusions as to its viability as the exclusive base for a national party. The CLC leadership resisted efforts on the part of some to choose Labour Party as its name.

Doug Hamilton, secretary treasurer of the Ontario Federation of labour, told the *CCF News* in September 1959 that "we must organize a political party that can speak and act for working people. While we in organized labour have taken the lead in this regard, it is not our intention to control or dominate this party."

Labour does not control or dominate the New Democratic Party. Influence it, yes. Have an acknowledged role within its structure and operations, yes. Labour is constitutionally given a place within the councils of the party, both at the federal level, with ten positions in a council of well over one hundred, and at the provincial level, with one representative for every local (or group of locals) with an aggregate membership of five hundred, in a council of nearly three hundred. But labour's views are subject to a democratic vote which requires a convincing presentation of its case — yes, even to some NDPers who are no more sympathetic to unions than the general public.

And why shouldn't unions have such a role within a political party? With their families, they represent literally millions of people. Their needs and interests have a legitimate place on the political agenda. In fact, if the political agendas of trade unionists were examined in the resolutions passed at their conventions, no more than one-third of them, perhaps fewer, reflect narrow self- interest, that is, strictly trade union matters. The vast majority deal with a wide range of issues, from health services to pensions and housing, to issues in international affairs, such as nuclear disarmament and aid to Third World development, all of which are of concern to the whole population.

When old parties are reminded of the influence of "organized business" within their councils, there is often a tendency, if not an assertion, to equate it with the influence of "organized labour" within the NDP. I submit that the analogy is not accurate — that the influence is qualitatively, and quantitatively, different. Organized business represents relatively few in society, and its demands are primarily related to the balance sheet of profit and loss. To the extent that it ranges beyond direct self-interest, business seeks to cut back on services to people, which would increase demands on it to meet a fair share of the cost. Moreover the political demands of business are not arrived at publicly, and are backed by financial resources, which are not made available through any form of democratic vote worthy of the name.

By contrast, organized labour represents millions of men, women, and children in every school, church or organization in society. Some of their demands are designed to protect their own family income and welfare, but most of them are of wider application, and would benefit society in general. Those demands are decided in open convention, and reported by the media. Moreover, they are backed by financial resources, admittedly in much smaller amounts, which are made available through democratic approval of the membership.

Notwithstanding the validity of this contrast, it must be conceded that society regards business more favourably than it does labour. The misdemeanours of the business world are forgotten, if not forgiven, while those of labour become grist for an on-going, anti-labour campaign.

It would be idle to pretend that the relatively greater advantages of business over labour in this political influence do not present problems for the NDP. But there are developments in modern society which will have a long-term favourable impact.

First is the increasing exercise of the basic right of association on the economic front, as reflected in collective bargaining. An ever-increasing number of social and economic groups, from blue and white collar workers to professionals and para-professionals, is engaged in collective bargaining. Indeed, there are fewer and fewer groups in society which do not claim such a right. Those groups are the growing edge of the trade union movement, and even those which won't formally become part of the trade union movement will, in my view, be increasingly sympathetic to a party which is solidly committed to the basic right of collective bargaining.

Secondly, women are becoming a significant force in politics. Their influence derives partly from their 50 per cent participation rate in the labour force — doubled in the past generation or so; their growing numbers in the trade union movement and in the most embattled sectors of labour-management; and partly from the fact that the movement has succeeded in persuading the public at large of the legitimacy of women's rights. The NDP has been an acknowledged leader on women's issues. Already, this is having political influence: in the 1980s the gender gap has narrowed, so that today women vote for the NDP in almost as great a percentage as men. Indeed, the latest polls indicate that older women (because of the pension issue) and working women below forty (because of issues like pay equity and day care) are actually outvoting men in the same age category.

There is a third, even more influential development. In the past, trade unions fought their economic battles in isolation. They pursued their broader social goals very much on their own. Government restraint programs and economic recessions have now forced the unions to seek allies. Today on the economic, and even on the social and political fronts, labour is more often than not working in coalition with churches, anti-poverty groups, teachers, social workers, the peace movement, nuclear disarmament advocates, and on and on. In this unity, there is greater strength, for each and every member of the coalition.

Ultimately, this will have a political impact. Too often in the past, the NDP too has operated in isolation. It espoused causes on behalf of groups, but did not get the support of significant numbers of those groups. There was not enough linkage and interaction with them. Here, networking has emerged, sometimes by the party alone, often in coordination with labour, churches, the peace movement and others.

There is another development, of inestimable political significance. It was assumed that the inclusion of the right of association in the Charter of Rights and Freedoms would protect the concomitant rights of workers, and thereby enhance the prospects of disadvantaged Canadians. However, in April 1987 the Supreme Court ruled, in three separate judgments, that the Charter does not guarantee the right of workers to bargain collectively or to strike.

Professor Allan Hutchinson, of the Osgoode Hall Law School has assessed the resulting situation:

> By announcing that the modern rights to bargain collectively and to strike are not fundamental rights and freedoms, as Mr. Justice Gerald LeDain put it in the majority report, the Supreme Court has sent out a strong message that the interest of workers don't deserve special protection. . . . By refusing to interpret freedom of association to include striking and bargaining, the Supreme Court has rendered the provision's protection meaningless. Workers are now free to form and join unions, but can be kept from doing the thing that really makes such actions worthwhile in the first place.[4]

In short, we have reverted to the pre-Charter days: the means for realizing the workers' right of association are subject to acts of Parliament and the legislatures. Professor Hutchinson's conclusion is inescapable: "The most positive message of the Supreme Court is that unions will have to return to the political arena and take their case to the people of Canada, not their judicial proconsuls." When they do, they may have the support of a growing proportion of the electorate who are exercising those rights. In the same month as the Supreme Court judgment, a Gallup poll revealed that 67 per cent of Canadians favour the right to strike (although the figure drops by one-half for workers in essential services).

The Supreme Court judgment has ensured that the political struggle will continue. The fundamental right of association, first proclaimed in Magna Carta in 1215, was considered a conspiracy, if exercised on the economic front, until trade unions were legalized in the 1870s. Today the workers' capacity to render that right effective must still be fought for. The social democratic movement has been, and will remain, a part of that struggle.

All of these factors in modern society will have a political impact, sooner or later. In this continuing struggle, the assets and liabilities of NDP identification with unions will come into a more favourable balance. In any case, these are problems, which the New Democratic Party and, I venture to predict, the trade union movement, are willing to live with, because both have a commitment which is solid and long-standing.

Despite its image of self-interest, the trade union movement has consistently been one of the progressive forces in Canadian society, in part because of its association with a political party of social democratic persuasion. This has been true, not only for domestic policies, but in its attitude on world affairs, where the Canadian union stance has often been in striking contrast to its American brothers and sisters, on issues such as Vietnam in days past, or Nicaragua today.

As for the party, no democratic socialist party has ever been built without sinking its roots in the economic organizations of the people. It is the social democratic alternative to being rooted in the business world. With all its problems, it is the reason for the NDP's existence, and the justification for its future.

23

The NDP in Ontario Politics

During the course of these reminiscences, I have reflected on individual aspects of Ontario politics. Now is the time to focus on the role and the future of the New Democratic Party.

In the politics of the last thirty years, one thing stands out: the importance of the opposition in the parliamentary process. In political science circles it is sometimes argued that a government is as good as its opposition. If so, Ontario has had better government because of the opposition of the CCF/NDP.

In each of the six major issues considered earlier, the CCF/NDP led in pressuring for changes, which were of growing public concern, so much so that, ultimately, the government accepted and implemented them. This proved to be true to a greater extent than I realized at the time, for in the heat of the day-to-day battle, it was impossible to know what influence one was having.

When I have been asked how I maintained my enthusiasm throughout so many years, the answer has been simple: the issues were of vital concern, and therefore hastening their implementation by the government, even if belatedly and partially, was satisfying. In addition, there was the bonus of building a new party, more fully committed to the interests of working people.

What has been the impact of these efforts on the fortunes of the party? It is more appropriate for others to judge that. But I want to dismiss any impression that the NDP is destined forever to an opposition role. The future of the NDP in Ontario can best be seen in the perspective of the province's history.

Ontario politics have tended to be dominated by one party for long periods. For the first forty years after Confederation, it was the Liberals, in this century the Conservatives, with their ascendancy broken only by the Farmer-Labour government of 1919-23, and the Hepburn era of 1934-43.

The collapse of the Tory dynasty in 1985 and the inauguration of the Liberal administration, through the Accord with the New Democratic Party, prompts speculation as to whether Ontario politics have experienced another historic watershed. The Liberal sweep in the 1987 election, and all the difficulties experienced by the Tory party, suggest that the answer may be yes. However, a long period of one-party dominance is unlikely, for a variety of reasons which I shall explore, not the least of which is that Ontario politics, in contrast to their extraordinary stability in the past, have become more volatile. But no matter what government is in power, the dominant characteristic of cautious conservatism is likely to persist.

That characteristic first emerged with the British colony of Upper Canada, established by the Constitutional Act of 1791. The scattered settlements along the St. Lawrence and lower Great Lakes were cradled in pervasive anti-revolutionary sentiments — an aversion, on the one hand, to the American Revolution, firmly implanted in Upper Canada by the United Empire Loyalists, and, on the other hand, to the French Revolution, enunciated philosophically by Edmund Burke, and reflected in the policies of John Graves Simcoe, the colony's first governor.

But embedded in the conservatism of the United Empire Loyalists were progressive, even radical, elements. They brought to Canada the practice of freehold land, rather than the seigneurial tenure of the French colony; English law, instead of the Napoleonic Code; and a strong commitment to representative legislative institutions. As J.J. Talman has stated, "The Loyalists were Tories, but they were not prepared to surrender the political privileges they had gained before the revolution."[1] This progressive leaven became an enduring element in the Ontario political culture.

Thus, as the conservatism of the Family Compact congealed into High Toryism, it provoked the reform movement, ultimately the Rebellion of 1837, and a succession of developments which democratized the basic conservatism, leading to the establishment of responsible government in 1848, by the Baldwin-LaFontaine administration — an achievement which paved the way for the evolution from colony to nation, and empire to commonwealth.

Events of this era of Canada West, from 1841 to 1867, firmly consolidated another characteristic of Ontario's conservatism — the rejection of extremes, whether of the right or left. The radicalism of the Clear Grits or the High Toryism of the Family Compact gave way to more moderate views. Indeed, the amalgam of conservatism and reform was acknowledged as far back as 1854, when John A. Macdonald chose the inspired name of Liberal-Conservative Party, a name which persisted into the twentieth century. "Progressive conservative" was the dominant philosophy of Ontario politics long before that nomenclature was adopted by the party, at John Bracken's insistence, when he became federal leader in 1942.

Notwithstanding its name, when the Reform/Liberal party held office for forty years after Confederation, the progressive conservative character of Ontario politics continued with Sir Oliver Mowat. However, his administration, solidly rural-based, became insensitive to the changes needed in an increasingly urbanized and industrialized society. By 1905 the Conservatives of Sir James Whitney were perceived as more progressive than the Liberals. So much so, that they are regarded as being the pioneers of the Conservatives who held office for sixty-seven of the next eighty years.[2]

Throughout this century, the Ontario electorate has continued to eschew extremism of either the right or left. The Conservatives gave way to the UFO in 1919, because they had become too conservative to cope with the ferment of the war years. The UFO gave way to the Conservatives in 1923 because they were perceived to be too radical (and disunited) to govern well. The Conservatives gave way to the Hepburn Liberals in 1934, because they were not progressive enough in their response to the problems of the depression. The Hepburn Liberals, from a progressive image at the outset, swung to a right-wing, anti-labour stance, which drove two ministers (David Croll and Arthur Roebuck) out of the cabinet; ultimately, for a spate of reasons they were repudiated by the electorate in 1943. The Conservatives, from George Drew through to Bill Davis, maintained what was perceived by the electorate to be an acceptable balance of progressive and conservative elements. The right-wing swing of Frank Miller in 1985 destroyed that balance, and brought an end to the forty-two-year Tory hegemony. Thus it is seen that, with remarkable consistency, the Ontario electorate has responded to centrist politics, rejecting governments which were perceived to be excessively radical or unresponsively conservative.

The obvious question arises: where and how, does a democratic socialist party fit into a political culture so consistent that governments have been turned out in only seven of the thirty-four elections since Confederation? The answer lies in the progressive element in the conservatism which has broken to the surface in every generation during the last one hundred years or so. It is interesting to review the persistent efforts to establish an alternative to the two old parties, striving for a stronger commitment to the change which has accelerated during the twentieth century.

The dominant group in the financing and policy-shaping of both the Conservatives and Liberals has traditionally been the business interests. As other groups — first, the farmers, then unskilled and industrial workers, and later elements of the middle class — felt that their needs were not being adequately met, new political groupings arose to voice their neglected concerns. They emerged in the 1880s with the Patrons of Industry, a farm protest movement, and with the Knights of Labour, North America's first working class movement. There was considerable common ground in the political platforms of these two groups, though no organic unity, and in the general election of 1893, with the swing of only 3 per cent in a few ridings, they would have elected the largest single group.[3]

But, as happened regularly to third parties which represented a protest but sought no fundamental change, once they had popularized an issue, it was taken over by one or another of the established parties, and they faded into history. A generation later, with ferment among farmers and labour arising from conditions of the First World War, the United Farmers of Ontario and the Independent Labour Party won a majority of the seats and formed the Farmer-Labour government of E.C. Drury. After one term in office, that wave of protest subsided.

With the depression of the 1930s, the remnants of third parties, which littered the Canadian political scene, coalesced in the launching of the Co-operative Commonwealth Federation. Unlike its predecessors, however, it was not just a protest movement but a party of avowedly democratic socialist philosophy. As another generation passed, amid the wartime search for a brave new world, the CCF stormed from nowhere, in 1943, to within four seats of George Drew's minority Conservatives.

Once again, in the 1950s, left-wing third party fortunes began to fade, and democratic socialists responded by regrouping, in 1961, in the New Democratic Party. In the succeeding generation, the Ontario NDP regained major party status in 1967, missed the official opposition by only one seat in 1971, won the official opposition in 1975, missed it again by one seat in 1977, and regained it in 1987.

Throughout this roller-coaster scenario, the NDP has established the support of a solid base of one-quarter of the electorate: not enough to win government when the Tory dynasty collapsed, but sufficient to play a critical role, as an agent for change, through the Accord with the Liberals.

It is in this historical context that I view the forty years of Ontario politics, which are the span of these memoirs.

Ever since the emergence of the CCF in 1943, Ontario has had a three-party system, with one party dominating the centre of the political spectrum, and the other two, to the right (the Liberals) and to the left (the CCF/NDP). When the Tories under Frank Miller forsook the centre in 1985, the Liberals, with the advantage of official opposition and a well-executed campaign, moved into it.

The Accord, which the Liberals signed with the NDP before

assuming office, saved David Peterson "from floundering indecision he'd displayed in the past", as Rosemary Speirs put it in *Out of the Blue*. Once the Liberals escaped the commitment of the Accord, which imposed upon them a left-of-centre posture with which much of their traditional constituency is uncomfortable, they gradually reverted to Ontario's more cautious conservatism. Indeed, within a few months of assuming office in 1985, despite the Accord, the Peterson government gave evidence of "making haste slowly." The *Hamilton Spectator*, on 5 October 1985, captioned a Queen's Park dispatch: "The progressive conservative Liberals," noting that, while Peterson claimed major achievements, the Davis style lived on. Beyond style, the substance of Liberal policies has become more conservative, particularly after achieving majority government.

It is interesting that Agnes Macphail, that redoubtable pioneer of the Progressive movement and the first woman member of the House of Commons, assessed the situation accurately fifty years ago. Farquhar Oliver had been her protégé in the Progressive movement in Grey County, but he drifted back into the Liberal party, while she pursued the logic of the earlier protest, as a CCF member of the Legislature. On one occasion during legislative debates, when Oliver had rationalized his return to the Liberal party, she replied simply, "There isn't room for two conservative parties in Ontario."

Believing that to be the case, I feel there is a place for the NDP in Ontario politics. It is now solidly rooted. The demands of society, in our fast-moving world, require a party of the democratic left. It is the natural champion of Ontarians who seek fairness in the distribution of our collective wealth. It is the party most firmly committed to the progressive element of Ontario's conservatism. In a rapidly changing society and economy, that will be important in meeting the needs of the majority of Ontarians.

The reality is that, today, Ontario alone among the provinces has a highly competitive three-party system. In other provinces, especially in western Canada, the old two-party system has been reshaped into a new two-party system of the democratic right and the democratic left. In any given election in Ontario, it is not impossible for any one of the parties to win.

While Ontario has eschewed ideological extremism, the forces working for a rationalization of the party system will, sooner or later, provide the electorate with a clearer choice between the progressive and conservative elements of its political culture. Political scientists, notably John Wilson, of the University of Waterloo, have contended that Ontario has a three-party system in transition. Maybe so, but as I have so often quipped, "It is taking an unconscionable length of time to transit."

Given the basic conservatism of Ontario politics, to build on the one-quarter of the electorate which the New Democratic Party has consolidated, the party cannot indulge in the rhetoric of socialist dogma. To suggest such does not mean that the commitment to democratic socialist principles has, or need be, lessened. As it has evolved in the twentieth century, democratic socialism is as much a fulfillment of democracy as of the economic and socialist principles enunciated by its theorists. A greater fulfillment of democracy involves the implementation of socialist principles. In fact, the two are inseparable: democracy without socialism will remain unfulfilled; socialism without democracy can degenerate into as oppressive and destructive an assault on human rights as any right-wing dictatorship.

When the New Democratic Party was founded in 1961, a great debate ensued over what name should be adopted. Some favoured an explicit identification with traditional socialism, but the majority, with an intuitive appreciation of the nature of Canadian politics, opted for *new democratic*. In recent years there have been periodic suggestions that the name should be changed; that the adjective "new" has become inappropriate with the passage of time. It has always been my belief that the name should not be changed, partly because NDP has become established in the lexicon of Canadian politics, but more important, because it is an expression of the true nature of socialism for the Canadian, and notably, the Ontario, electorate. Socialism is not only the fulfillment of democracy, but as such it dovetails with Ontario's non-ideological predisposition to moderate, balanced pragmatism.

Here again, the perspective of history is instructive. As it is understood today, democracy is a product of the extension of the franchise, to men in the nineteenth century, and to women in the twentieth century. Hitherto, parliaments had been representative of only the elite in society, and in turn, reflected only their perception of national needs. The great majority of the population were the mute, inarticulate masses, who were born, struggled for survival throughout life, were conscripted to fight foreign wars, and died. Only with the extension of the franchise did the needs of the population as a whole gain a place on the political agenda.

As Bruce Hodgins has pointed out,[4] the Ontario Fathers of Confederation were resourceful men of their age, but they were not democrats. George Brown wrote in the *Globe* that "democratic theories" were inadequate "to the wants of a mixed society," and that the broader the suffrage, "the more we add to the dangerous element." Like all the Fathers, John A. Macdonald "rejected both the word democracy and many of those attributes essential to it. He rejected political equality, favoured privileges for the propertied classes and the well-off, and seemed more concerned about protecting the rights of the minority than providing for majority rule." This is the heritage out of which the Ontario political culture has evolved.

Not surprisingly, early demands focused on the right of association, to express and advance the collective needs of the majority through voluntary organizations such as trade unions, and the need to assure family income through full employment, or in its absence, a social security network to cope with adversity, whether from unemployment, ill health or disability. "A democracy," Frank Underhill once contended, "is simply a society in which all interest groups have an equal chance to present their claim from the gains of civilization and to get them adjusted."[5]

Democratic socialist parties emerged to champion the needs of the neglected majority, and thereby rescue Parliament from being the handmaiden of the privileged minority. Policies ranging from health insurance to old age pensions were first dismissed as socialist, and opposed by established parties, until their acceptance became necessary to retain political power from a widely enfranchised population.

This process of the acceptance of socialist policies by the established parties presented the CCF/NDP with a perplexing problem. In the North American atmosphere, socialism has been — and still is — a dirty word. The persistent coupling of democratic socialism with communism has compounded the problem. As a defensive tactic, I never wore the socialist label on my sleeve. Its use resulted in closed minds, rather than opening them to consideration of new policies to meet acknowledged needs. Yet, if asked, I unhesitatingly asserted that I was a socialist. To do otherwise created a no-win situation. Instead, the more effective approach was to address the acknowledged problem and present the socialist solution, without labelling it.

The best example of this whole process was one which I used on the hustings. When I first emphasized, in 1953, the need for public hospital insurance, as had been introduced in Saskatchewan, Premier Frost dismissed it as a denial of the right of the individual to spend his money as he saw fit, and therefore, destructive of the moral fibre of the Ontario people. Two years later, hospital insurance became a major issue on the federal-provincial agenda, and, as I have related earlier,[6] the provincial Tories and the federal Liberals euchred themselves into its implementation. Overnight, hospital insurance became the proudest achievement of the Tory party. This practice of stealing socialist policies has gone on down through the years, so much so that today right-wingers, such as the National Citizens Coalition, are critical of all parties as being socialistic.

This implementation of socialist policies has resulted in continuous democratization — the extension of basic rights and privileges to many members of society who had hitherto been denied them. This democratization process has been spearheaded by two major movements in the twentieth century.

The first is the trade union movement, whose political role

was more fully reviewed in the last chapter. The right of association, first enunciated in the Magna Carta, had been denied to workers; until the 1870s their collective efforts were legally deemed to be a conspiracy. In organic association, the CCF/NDP and the trade union movement fought for an extension of these rights — a fight which is on-going, for yesterday's victories can be wiped out with a stroke of the legislative pen.

The second — potentially, the most influential of all — is the women's movement. From the early days of the suffragettes to the feminist crusaders of the 1980s, it has been a relentless struggle to extend rights won by men down through the centuries to the other half of the population — whether in politics, the church, or the workplace. Socialist parties have been identified with that struggle, because the goals of the women's movement are an integral part of the socialist program.

Much has been accomplished, but even more remains to be achieved. Notwithstanding the social security network whose advocacy socialists pioneered, the policies implemented by the old parties continue to benefit disproportionately the more privileged; the rich have become richer, and the poor more numerous. Equal rights for women are still a distant goal. The socialist drive for the fulfillment of democracy is never-ending, particularly in a political culture like Ontario's with its strong strain of conservatism.

For all these reasons, I am convinced that, in the ebb and flow of politics, the New Democratic Party will have a continuing role in Ontario politics. One day, it will be the government. I was persuaded of that when I entered the Legislature in 1955. I am no less so today. For the NDP is the most committed champion of the enduring progressive element in the Ontario political culture.

How will it be achieved? In 1973, I wrote:

Socialism is not a doctrinaire stereotype which can be brought down from the mount, or out of the ivory tower, and imposed upon any given society. Rather, it is a set of principles whose application must be adapted in each and every jurisdiction. The process of adaptation must grow out of the lives and struggles of its people and their organizations. It must be indigenous, becoming part of, and evolving out of, the mainstream of their politics and economy.

In short, if socialism is presented in such a manner as to offend, even challenge the political culture of Ontario, it will certainly be regarded by the electorate as alien. But if it is presented as an evolutionary growth from the mainstream of Ontario political and economic history, then it may be accepted more quickly in this age of rapid change than we dare to believe possible at the moment.[7]

Socialism is the wave of the future, precisely because it is the fulfillment of democracy. The old parties will continue to steal NDP policies, but they cannot steal the basic commitment which is the soul of the party.

Epilogue

On 1 May 1986 I was appointed chairman of the Election Finances Commission, one of the agencies reporting, through the Speaker, to the Legislature, rather than to the government. This commission was first established in 1975, to assist local constituency officials in the regulation of contributions and expenditures for political activities between, as well as during, elections. The original legislation was updated in July 1986 by the Election Finances Act, which sets limits on expenditures, as well as on contributions, for election campaigns. With the extension of public accountability for income and expenses of leadership candidates, Ontario now has the most comprehensive system of control and public accountability of the financing of political activities to be found in any jurisdiction.

Shortly after assuming this responsibility, I was visited by an Oxford University professor, who was travelling the North American continent to study election laws and financing. After we had reviewed the scope of Ontario's new legislation, he shook his head and commented, "By comparison with your set-up, we're back in the dark ages."

The fact is that, despite remaining deficiencies in our legislation, all Ontarians can be proud of the achievement which it represents. There has been a growing concern about the excessive amounts of money being spent on elections, and through the cooperative effort of all parties, that undesirable trend has been checked. The financing of politics has been democratized, by the exclusion of large contributions, and by the encouragement of wider financial participation, through tax credits.

My new responsibilities represent a radical change. After forty years of partisan politics, overnight my role has become that of a non-partisan servant of the Legislature. Any assertion of this status invariably provokes derisive laughter from former legislative colleagues, political friend and foe alike. My response has been that I make no pretence of being non-partisan; rather, I am now multi-partisan. And when that doesn't quieten the derision, I add that my biases are neither greater, nor less, than those of many of our judges appointed from political ranks. Whenever I have lunch at the Queen's Park dining room, I make a practice of joining the Liberals, Conservatives and New Democrats in turn. It's not only a pleasant way of keeping in contact, but a symbol of my responsibility to work with all parties.

Inevitably, my new position was viewed by some as a patronage appointment, in the wake of the Liberal/NDP Accord. The fact is, however, that the appointment was made by order-in-council, after prior approval of all three party leaders, in keeping with the new approach envisaged in the Accord. The new approach was formalized by the Legislature on 10 July 1986. It establishes that the choice of an officer of the Legislature will now be made by the Board of Internal Economy after an open process of advertising, interviewing and committee consensus. Once the recommendation has been approved by the Legislature, appointment by order-in-council is a formality.

For me, the non-partisan restrictions are not wholly new. As a journalist in my early years, and as a commentator at political conventions of all parties, I have never felt unduly hampered by the need for reasoned and fair observations. In fact, with political science students at Atkinson College over the past seventeen years, I have always frankly acknowledged my bias at the first class, but with this caveat: no one is without bias, and those who suggest otherwise are kidding themselves and the public. I would sooner have an acknowledged bias than the posture of an intellectual eunuch, particularly when the circumstances, as in politics or a university seminar, permit of a greater understanding, if not acceptance, of differing views.

In any case, for the first time in over forty years, I did not attend the NDP conventions, provincially in Hamilton (1986), or federally in Montreal (1987). For me, that is being out of politics — with a vengeance. But the restrictions are tolerable, for the compensations are great: it would be difficult to conceive of work, such as that at the Election Finances Commission, which is outside of partisan politics and yet so close to the whole political process. For one so incorrigibly a political animal, I find that satisfying. If nothing else, it proves that there can be life after electoral politics.

Meanwhile, I have no difficulty filling time beyond office hours — university teaching, continuing membership on the board of York Community Services and the Churchill Society for the Advancement of Parliamentary Democracy, book reviewing, gardening, fishing, more holidaying than usual — along with research and reflections for these memoirs. They all help to wind down to a normal work day.

Notes

Unless otherwise indicated, all references are to my papers which have been deposited with the Archives at Queen's University, Kingston. They now comprise over 200 linear feet of letters, memoranda, documents et al, but those most extensively used were the hundreds of press releases which are catalogued in chronological order. I did not keep a diary, but the releases provide a running account of both my travels and public statements — major ingredients of any political diary.

Preface

1. Persons who were high profile in their day sometimes recede deeply into history. Graham White, formerly assistant clerk at the Ontario Legislature and now with the Political Science department at the University of Toronto, has discovered another Ontario politician who has done some writing. Charles Clarke (1826-1909) was MPP for Wellington Centre (1871-91), Legislative Speaker (1880-86), and Clerk of the Legislative Assembly (1892-1907) — obviously a person of considerable note during the Mowat era. In the year before his death, he responded to the pressure of friends and wrote *Sixty Years in Upper Canada* (Briggs, 1908), which captures some of the highlights of Ontario politics, particularly in the records of the Legislature. Despite its title, it deals primarily with the post-Confederation period, and includes "autobiographical recollections." Clarke's son, Dr. Charles Kirk Clarke, was

a pioneer in Canadian psychiatry; his life work was com-
memorated in the Clarke Institute of Psychiatry.

Chapter 1

1. A copy of my Father's "History of the MacDonald
   Family" is included with my papers.
2. Years later, when clearing our old files, Dorothy Seiveright
   returned many of my letters. These, too, have been
   deposited with my papers.
3. Now with my papers at the Queen's Archives.

Chapter 2

1. Apart from the Regina Manifesto, which set out the policies
   and objectives of the CCF, the broader case of democratic
   socialist thinking in Canada was detailed in *Social Planning
   for Canada.* In 1942 *Make This Your Canada,* co-authored
   by David Lewis and Frank Scott, provided a more popular
   account of the CCF's challenge to wartime Canadians.

Chapter 3

1. David Lewis, *The Good Fight: Political Memoirs,
   1909-1958* (Toronto: Macmillan of Canada, 1981), p. 321.

Chapter 4

1. The riding of York South was first won by Joe Noseworthy
   in the 1942 federal by-election, which ended the political
   career of Arthur Meighen. It was the home riding of three
   CCF/NDP Ontario provincial leaders — Ted Jolliffe,
   myself and Bob Rae (the fourth provincial leader, Michael
   Cassidy, represented the riding of Ottawa Centre). While
   the boundaries were not coterminous, it was also the seat
   held by David Lewis in the House of Commons.

Chapter 5

1. *Globe and Mail*, 12 March 1954.
2. Ontario, *Legislative Debates*, 9 February 1956, pp. 122-64.
3. Ibid., 10 February 1956, p. 168.
4. Ibid., 13 February 1956, pp. 185-87.
5. Ibid., 6 March 1956, p. 815.
6. CCF Coordinating Council, 16 December 1958.
7. For fuller details on these issues, see chapters 14 to 19.

Chapter 6

1. A. Kelso Roberts, "Thirty Years of Ontario Political Actions," p. 93. A mimeographed private edition of this autobiography is available in the Legislative Library.
2. Ibid., p. 94 et seq.
3. Ontario, *Legislative Debates*, 12 March 1958, pp. 745-47.
4. *Globe and Mail*, 5 July 1958.
5. *Legislative Debates*, 18 March 1959, pp. 1324-46.
6. Roberts, "Thirty Years," pp. 101-102.
7. Toronto *Star,* 23 January 1960.
8. *Legislative Debates*, 11 April 1959, p. 2583.

Chapter 7

1. Quoted in a CBC provincial affairs broadcast, 28 April 1958.
2. Riverdale CCF Riding Association, Toronto, 28 May 1958.
3. Sault Ste Marie, 29 May 1959.
4. Welland, 3 June 1959
5. Ontario, *Legislative Debates*, 25 March 1958, p. 1279 ff.
6. Alan Phillips, "Corruption," *Maclean's,* 10 May 1962.

Chapter 8

1. Stanley Knowles, *The New Party* (Toronto: McClelland and Stewart, 1961), pp. 19-20.
2. This meeting of Lewis and Bryden with labour leaders, including Jodoin, does not seem to have been recorded elsewhere. But the most detailed and authoritative account of the developments of the New Party in Ontario, running to over 140 typed pages, is to be found in the unpublished M.A thesis at York University by Dan Azoulay, "The Politics of Pragmatism: The Founding of the Ontario New Democratic Party, 1958-61." There's a minor error in it — the apparent confusion of myself with Donald Mac-Donald (no middle initial), a top officer, ultimately president, of the CLC. This was a frequent source of confusion when we were both working out of the national capital. He had earlier been leader of the CCF in Nova Scotia; I had originally hailed from British Columbia; we both ended up in Ottawa, he as secretary-treasurer of the CCF and I as national treasurer and organizer of the CCF. The similarity in entitled positions was too much, and we were constantly reading each other's mail. Moreover, later the confusion became even greater when Donald S. Macdonald, MP for Toronto Rosedale, entered politics.
3. Azoulay, "The Politics of Pragmatism, pp. 88-91.
4. Ibid., p. 128.

Chapter 9

1. See chapters 14-19.
2. Norman Jaspan, *The Thief in the White Collar* (Philadelphia: Lippincott, 1960).
3. New Party club, Ajax, 1 May 1961.
4. Roberts, "Thirty Years of Political Action," pp. 80-81.
5. A.K. McDougall, *Robarts: His Life and Government* (Toronto: University of Toronto Press, 1986), p. 115.
6. Ontario, *Legislative Debates*, 23 March 1964, p. 1851 et seq.
7. Press statement, 11 January 1964.
8. Niagara Falls, 26 April 1965.

Chapter 10

1. For fuller detail, see chapters 14-19.

Chapter 11

1. For a fuller account of these major issues, see chapters 14-19.
2. Ontario, *Legislative Debates*, 28 March 1968, p. 1195 ff.
3. Terry Morley, my executive assistant, 1969-70, wrote his MA thesis at Queen's University on the Renwick challenge. He subsequently completed a Ph.D. thesis which, abridged, was published as *Secular Socialist — The CCF/NDP in Ontario: A Biography* (Montreal and Toronto: McGill-Queen's University Press, 1984).
4. Harold Greer, Kitchener-Waterloo *Record*, 7 October 1970.
5. Quoted in a report to the NDP Provincial Council, held at Carleton University, 13 June 1970
6. Jonathan Manthorpe, *The Power and the Tories* (Toronto: Macmillan of Canada, 1974), p. 78.
7. Canadian Press dispatch, Orillia *Packet and Times*, 6 July 1970.

Chapter 12

1. *New Democrat*, October, 1973; Caplan to *New Democrat,* 9 November 1973.
2. Hamilton *Spectator*, 27 July 1982.
3. For agriculture, see chapter 17; for energy, chapter 18.

Chapter 13

1. Rosemary Speirs, *Out of the Blue* (Toronto: Macmillan of Canada, 1986), pp. 179-80.
2. Personal communication, Eugene Forsey to MacDonald, 22 March 1985.

Chapter 14

1. Ontario, *Legislative Debates*, 23 January 1964, pp. 184-88.
2. Ibid., 23 February 1968, p. 191.
3. Address to the Winter Conference of the Canadian Institute of Public Affairs, Toronto, January 1965.
4. Ontario's role in the constitutional negotiations has been set out by Senator Nathan Nurgitz and Hugh Segal in *No Small Measure — The Progressive Conservatives and the Constitution* (Ottawa: Deneau Publishers, 1983).

Chapter 15

1. Malcolm G. Taylor, *Health Insurance and Canadian Public Policy* (Toronto: Oxford, 1956). Chapter 3 gives the full story of negotiations leading to Ontario Hospital Insurance.
2. CBC provincial affairs broadcast, 30 May 1958.
3. Toronto *Star*, 14 December 1959.
4. Weekend Institute of the Packinghouse Workers, held at the Workers Educational Association School, Port Hope, 20 September 1958.
5. Ontario, *Legislative Debates*, 7 February 1966, pp. 257-60.

Chapter 16

1. Ontario, *Legislative Debates*, 28 March 1957, p. 1761 ff.
2. Franklin Walker, *Catholic Education and Politics in Ontario*, Vol. III (Toronto: Catholic Education Foundation of Ontario, 1987), chapters 3 and 4, notably p. 80.
3. Ibid. , p. 117.

Chapter 17

1. Farm meeting sponsored by the Halton New Party Committee, Milton, 17 February 1961.
2. Annual meeting of the Culross Township Federation of Agriculture, Teeswater, 10 April 1961.
3. Grey South NDP Riding Association, Markdale, 6 June 1963.

4. Ontario, *Legislative Debates*, 23 November 1976, pp. 4979-5001.
5. During this period W.C. Good published his autobiography, *Farmer Citizen* (Toronto: Ryerson Press, 1958).
6. E.C. Drury, *Farmer Premier* (Toronto: McClelland and Stewart, 1966).
7. Kitchener-Waterloo *Record*, 4 March 1981.

Chapter 18

1. Ontario, *Legislative Debates*, 23 March 1959, p. 1491.

Chapter 19

1. Hart House, University of Toronto, 26 January 1964.
2. Weekend tour of the ridings of Algoma West, Algoma-Manitoulin, Sudbury and Nickel Belt, 18-20 March 1966.
3. Queen's Printer, Ottawa: (Carter) *Royal Commission on Taxation*, 1966, Vol. 4, p.333.
4. Report of the NDP caucus Task Force on Forestry, December 1983.
5. This was also the conclusion of Floyd Laughren, NDP natural resources critic, speaking to the Southern Ontario section of the Canadian Association of Foresters, 7 November, 1984.

Chapter 20

1. Roberts, *Thirty Years of Ontario Political Action*, p. 115.
2. Ibid. p. 7.
3. Manthorpe, *The Power and the Tories*, p. 25.
4. Lewis, *The Good Fight,* pp. 276, 287.
5. McDougall, *Robarts*, p. xi.
6. Manthorpe, *The Power and the Tories*, p. 70.

7. Fred Fletcher, in *Government and Politics of Ontario,* 3rd ed., (Toronto: Nelson of Canada, 1985), p. 196.
8. James G. Simeon, in *Government and Politics of Ontario,* 2nd ed. (Toronto: Van Nostrand Reinhold, 1980), p. 102.
9. McDougall, *Robarts,* p. 100.
10. Ibid., p. 183.
11. Luncheon conversation, 1 April 1987.

Chapter 21

1. See chapter 6.
2. Canadian Press dispatch, Oshawa *Times*, 27 January 1986.
3. Ibid.

Chapter 22

1. S.E.D. Short, "Social Change and Political Crisis in Rural Ontario, The Patrons of Industry: 1889-1896," in *Oliver Mowat's Ontario,* ed. by Donald Swainson, (Toronto: Macmillan of Canada, 1972), pp. 211 ff.
2. Azoulay, "The Politics of Pragmatism," p. 20.
3. Ibid., p. 16.
4. *Globe and Mail*, 16 April 1987.

Chapter 23

1. J.J. Talman, "The United Empire Loyalists," in *Profiles of a Province*, Ontario Historical Society, Toronto, 1967, p. 5.
2. For a fuller account, see Charles W. Humphries "The Sources of Ontario 'Progressive' Conservatism, 1900-1904," in the Canadian Historical Association Annual Report, 1967.
3. S.E.D. Short, "The Patrons of Industry, 1889-1896," in *Oliver Mowat's Ontario*, ed. by Donald Swainson (Toronto: Macmillan of Canada, 1972), pp. 211-235.
4. Bruce Hodgins, "Democracy and the Ontario Fathers of Confederation," in *Profiles of a Province,* pp. 83-91.

5. Frank Underhill, "The Canadian Party System in Transition," in *In Search of Canadian Liberalism*, (Toronto: Macmillan of Canada, 1960), p. 193

6. See chapter 15, on Health.

7. Quoted from a review for the *New Democrat* of Gerald Caplan's *The Dilemma of Canadian Socialism: The CCF in Ontario,* Sept./Oct., 1973.

Index